# National Identities in Soviet Historiography

Under Stalin's totalitarian leadership of the USSR, Soviet national identities with historical narratives were constructed. These constructions envisaged how nationalities should see their imaginary common past, and millions of people defined themselves according to them. This book explains how and by whom these national histories were constructed and focuses on the crucial episode in the construction of national identities of Ukraine, Azerbaijan, and Kazakhstan from 1936 and 1945.

A unique comparative study of three different case studies, this book reveals different aims and methods of nation construction, despite the existence of one-party rule and a single overarching official ideology. The study is based on work in the often overlooked archives in Ukraine, Azerbaijan, and Kazakhstan. By looking at different examples within the Soviet context, the author contributes to and often challenges current scholarship on Soviet nationality policies and Stalinist nation-building projects. He also brings a new viewpoint to the debate on whether the Soviet period was a project of developmentalist modernization or merely a renewed 'Russian empire'. The book concludes that the local agents in the countries concerned had a sincere belief in socialism – especially as a project of modernism and development – and, at the same time, were strongly attached to their national identities. Finally, the Soviet understanding of external threat and international relations influenced the content of the new national narratives.

Claiming that local communist party officials and historians played a leading role in the construction of national narratives, this book will be of interest to historians and political scientists interested in the history of the Soviet Union and contemporary Eastern Europe, the Caucasus, and Central Asia.

**Harun Yilmaz** holds an MSc and PhD from the University of Oxford, UK. He was a postdoctorate research fellow at Harvard Ukrainian Research Institute, USA (2012) and a tutor at the University of Oxford. Currently he is a British Academy postdoctoral Research Fellow at Queen Mary University of London, UK. His area of interest and published research covers modern history of and contemporary politics in Russia, Ukraine, Caucasus, and Central Asia.

# Central Asia Research Forum

Series Editor: Shirin Akiner
*School of Oriental and African Studies, University of London*

**Sustainable Development in Central Asia**
*Edited by Shirin Akiner, Sander Tideman and John Hay*

**Qaidu and the Rise of the Independent Mongol State in Central Asia**
*Michal Biran*

**Tajikistan**
*Edited by Mohammad-Reza Djalili, Frederic Gare and Shirin Akiner*

**Uzbekistan on the Threshold of the Twenty-first Century**
Tradition and survival
*Islam Karimov*

**Tradition and Society in Turkmenistan**
Gender, oral culture and song
*Carole Blackwell*

**Life of Alimqul**
A native chronicle of nineteenth century Central Asia
*Edited and translated by Timur Beisembiev*

**Central Asia**
Aspects of transition
*Edited by Tom Everett-Heath*

**The Heart of Asia**
A history of Russian Turkestan and the Central Asian Khanates from the earliest times
*Frances Henry Skrine and Edward Denison Ross*

**The Caspian**
Politics, energy and security
*Edited by Shirin Akiner and Anne Aldis*

**Islam and Colonialism**
Western perspectives on Soviet Asia
*Will Myer*

**Azeri Women in Transition**
Women in Soviet and post-Soviet Azerbaijan
*Farideh Heyat*

**The Post-Soviet Decline of Central Asia**
Sustainable development and comprehensive capital
*Eric Sievers*

**Prospects for Pastoralism in Kazakhstan and Turkmenistan**
From state farms to private flocks
*Edited by Carol Kerven*

**Muslim Reformist Political Thought**
Revivalists, modernists and free will
*Sarfraz Khan*

**Economic Development in Kazakhstan**
The role of large enterprises and foreign investment
*Anne E. Peck*

**Energy, Wealth and Governance in the Caucasus and Central Asia**
Lessons not learned
*Edited by Richard Auty and Indra de Soysa*

**The Politics of Knowledge in Central Asia**
Science between Marx and the market
*Sarah Amsler*

**The Economics and Politics of Oil in the Caspian Basin**
The redistribution of oil revenues in Azerbaijan and Central Asia
*Edited by Boris Najman, Richard Pomfret and Gaël Raballand*

**The Political Economy of Reform in Central Asia**
Uzbekistan under authoritarianism
*Martin C. Spechler*

**Turkmenistan's Foreign Policy**
Positive neutrality and the consolidation of the Turkmen Regime
*Luca Anceschi*

**Religion and Security in South and Central Asia**
*Edited by K. Warikoo*

**Conflict and Peace in Eurasia**
*Edited by Debidatta Aurobinda Mahapatra*

**Social and Cultural Change in Central Asia**
The Soviet legacy
*Edited by Sevket Akyildiz and Richard Carlson*

**Leadership and Authority in Central Asia**
The Ismaili community in Tajikistan
*Otambek N. Mastibekov*

**National Identities in Soviet Historiography**
The rise of nations under Stalin
*Harun Yilmaz*

# National Identities in Soviet Historiography
The rise of nations under Stalin

Harun Yilmaz

Routledge
Taylor & Francis Group
LONDON AND NEW YORK

First published 2015
by Routledge
2 Park Square, Milton Park, Abingdon, Oxon OX14 4RN

and by Routledge
711 Third Avenue, New York, NY 10017

First issued in paperback 2017

*Routledge is an imprint of the Taylor & Francis Group, an informa business*

© 2015 Harun Yilmaz

The right of Harun Yilmaz to be identified as author of this work has been asserted by him in accordance with sections 77 and 78 of the Copyright, Designs and Patents Act 1988.

All rights reserved. No part of this book may be reprinted or reproduced or utilized in any form or by any electronic, mechanical, or other means, now known or hereafter invented, including photocopying and recording, or in any information storage or retrieval system, without permission in writing from the publishers.

*Trademark notice*: Product or corporate names may be trademarks or registered trademarks, and are used only for identification and explanation without intent to infringe.

*British Library Cataloguing in Publication Data*
A catalogue record for this book is available from the British Library

*Library of Congress Cataloging in Publication Data*
Yilmaz, Harun.
National identities in Soviet historiography : the rise of nations under Stalin / Harun Yilmaz.
  pages cm. – (Central Asia research forum)
  Includes bibliographical references and index.
  1. Historiography–Soviet Union–History. 2. Historiography–Political aspects–Soviet Union. 3. Nationalism–Soviet Union–Historiography. 4. Nationalism and communism–Azerbaijan. 5. Nationalism and communism–Kazakhstan. 6. Nationalism and communism–Ukraine. 7. Azerbaijan–Historiography. 8. Kazakhstan–Historiography. 9. Ukraine–Historiography. 10. Soviet Union–Politics and government–1936-1953. I. Title.
DK38.Y35 2015
947.0072–dc23                                                2014033675

ISBN 13: 978-1-138-09842-8 (pbk)
ISBN 13: 978-0-415-84258-7 (hbk)

Typeset in Times New Roman
by Wearset Ltd, Boldon, Tyne and Wear

# Contents

| | | |
|---|---|---|
| | *Acknowledgements* | viii |
| | *Note on the narrative and transliteration* | x |
| | Introduction | 1 |
| 1 | The construction of Azerbaijani identity under the shadow of Iran and Turkey | 19 |
| 2 | The miraculous return of Babak to Azerbaijan | 38 |
| 3 | Pure Slavic blood for Ukraine | 49 |
| 4 | The adventurous lives of Bohdan Khmel'nyts'kyi | 68 |
| 5 | The rise of red batyrs in the Kazakh steppe | 87 |
| | Introduction to the war period | 109 |
| 6 | Soviet and Iranian Azerbaijan at war | 114 |
| 7 | Kazakh batyrs marching in Stalingrad | 135 |
| 8 | Bohdan Khmel'nyts'kyi fighting against the Germans | 149 |
| | Epilogue | 169 |
| | *Bibliography* | 176 |
| | *Index* | 219 |

# Acknowledgements

I am very thankful to Prof. Robert Service and Prof. Edmund Herzig for their continuous academic guidance while I wrote my doctoral thesis at the University of Oxford which constitutes the starting point of this book. I am grateful to Prof. Geoffrey Hosking and Dr Catherine Andreyev, who examined my thesis and provided thoughtful and critical comments. They have been extremely patient and generous in supporting my academic endeavour after the graduation. I am also grateful to Prof. Jane Caplan, Prof. Robert Gildea, and Prof. David Priestland for their comments and critiques at the earlier stages of my work. I should also express my gratitude to Prof. Bruce Grant of New York University for reading Azerbaijani and Kazakh sections of my work and sharing his comments and suggestions and also for his wide range of support after the writing up of my work. I am also grateful to Dr Shirin Akiner of SOAS for her endless support during and after my doctoral research and to Prof. Margaret MacMillan, the Warden of St Antony's College, for the Warden's Doctoral Bursary and for the Warden's pre-Doctoral Bursary; to the directors and members of the Russian and Eurasian Studies Centre at St Antony's College for providing the Geoffrey and Fay Elliott Bursaries; and to the Royal Historical Society for their travel grant.

Above all I owe gratitude to Dr Lubomyr Hajda at the Harvard Ukrainian Research Institute, whose support at different stages has been crucial for me to finish this work. This book would have been impossible without the Jaroslaw and Nadia Mihaychuk Postdoctoral Research Fellowship by the Ukrainian Research Institute at Harvard University. I would like to thank the selection committee for giving me this precious opportunity. The fellowship enabled me to exchange opinions with the leading Ukrainian, Canadian, and American scholars and discussing various topics in Ukrainian history and literature. I owe a special debt of gratitude to Dr Lubomyr Hajda and Prof. Serhii Plokhy at the Harvard Ukrainian Research Institute (HURI) for reading my draft chapters on Ukraine and sharing their knowledge and commenting on my work. Their critiques and comments gave me precious clues to develop this work further. Thanks to the fellowship, I also had the unique opportunity to have access to archival sources and published manuscripts in the libraries of the HURI and Harvard University; this enabled me to improve my manuscript substantially. I am also grateful to the Ukrainian Summer Institute at Harvard. Their generous scholarship enabled me to enjoy academic sources and Ukrainian language classes at Harvard at an earlier stage.

I would like to thank Prof. Jenny White and Prof. Houchang Chehabi of Boston University, who gave their time to read the first chapter and helped me to improve it. I have presented pieces of my work and received valuable comments at the Annual National Conventions of the American Association for the Advancement of Slavic Studies (the Association for Slavic, East European and Eurasian Studies) in 2008, 2009, and 2010, and at the Annual Conferences of Central Eurasian Studies in 2007, and 2009. I owe an academic debt to the comments that I have received in these conventions. I am especially thankful to the valuable comments and suggestions that I have received from Professors Adrienne Edgar of the University of California, Mark Beissinger of Princeton University and Shoshana Keller of Hamilton College. I should also express my gratitude to Prof. Peter Golden for sharing his knowledge on batyrs and nomads; to Dr Alexander Dmitriev for his important suggestions and comments on the Russian and Ukrainian intellectual history; to Mrs Gul'zhan Jäger, Mrs Gul'mira Zhezbaeva, and Dr Gul'mira Orynbayeva for sharing their suggestions on Kazakh history; to Prof. Yuri Shapoval for his support during my stay in Kyïv, and to Prof. Stanislav Kul'chyts'kyi and Dr Olesya Khromeychuk for sharing their knowledge of Ukrainian history; to Mrs Tamara Nary for her support during my scholarships and fellowships at Harvard Ukrainian Research Institute; to Ms Paulina Dominick for her translations of Polish and Iranian texts; and to Dr Adam Berry for his translations of Iranian texts; to Ms Aliya Sadenova and Ms Aygul Adilkhanova for their support and friendship during my stay in Almaty Kazakhstan, and to Dr Elmir Qasimov for his support and friendship in Baku, Azerbaijan.

I would like to thank archivists and librarians of nine archives and seven libraries in Baku (Azerbaijan), Almaty (Kazakhstan), and Kyïv (Ukraine) for their help in finding necessary archival documents and printed materials. It would be impossible to find some of these materials without the assistance of archivists in this particular part of the world. The professionalism of those archivists deserves great applause. I am also thankful to Mr Richard Ramage, the librarian of the Russian and Eurasian Centre at St Antony's College, for his constant support and understanding.

Finally, my greatest and broadest debt is to the apple of my eye, Nilufar. She has always been more than patient and supportive. This book could not have been completed without her moral and intellectual companionship. I would like to dedicate this work to Nilufar, to my hayat yoldaşım.

# Note on the narrative and transliteration

For Russian and Ukrainian words, I have used a simplified version of the ALA-LC transliteration system. However, I have used the Ukrainian letters ï and i because both derive from the Latin script. I have removed accents from Polish words. Turkish and contemporary Azerbaijani languages are written in alphabets based on Latin script. Kazakh still uses Cyrillic script with additional signs for Kazakh voices. For the Kazakh voices, I have used a simplified version of transliteration. The unfamiliar sounds in the Turkish and Azerbaijani alphabet for the Western reader and the simplified Kazakh transliteration are listed below.

The contemporary Azerbaijani alphabet and the Turkish alphabet are the same, with three exceptions (ə, x, q), and very similar to the one used in Azerbaijan in 1929–39, with six exceptions (ɔ, ь, z, ө, ү, j).

The archives in the former Soviet republics are cited and numbered by collection (*fond*, or *f.*), inventory (*opis'*, or *op.*), file (*delo* or *d.*), and page (*list* or *l.* or

| Kazakh (Cyrillic) | Transliteration (Pronunciation) | Azerbaijani (Cyrillic) | Modern Turkish | Modern Azerbaijani (Latin) | Transliteration (Pronunciation) |
|---|---|---|---|---|---|
| - | - | Чч | C-c | C-c | c (j as in just) |
| Ч-ч | ch (ch) | Ч-ч | Ç-ç | Ç-ç | Ç-ç (ch) |
| Ә-ә | Ә-ә (ä) | Ә-ә | - | Ә-ә | Ә-ә (ä) |
|  |  | К-к | G-g | G-g | G-g |
| Ғ-ғ | Ğ-ğ (gh, guttural g) | Ғ-ғ | Ğ-ğ | Ğ-ğ | Ğ-ğ (gh, guttural g) |
| һ-һ | H-h | һ-һ | H-h | H-h | H-h |
| Ы-ы | y (i in nation) | Ы-ы | I-ı | I-ı | I-ı (i as in nation) |
| Х-х | Kh (kh) | Х-х | – | Х-х | X-x (kh) |
| Ж-ж | Zh | Ж-ж | J-j | J-j | Zh |
| Ө-ө | Ö-ö (same as German) | Ө-ө | Ö-ö | Ö-ö | Ö-ö (same as German) |
| Қ-қ | K-k (Q-q) | Г-г | - | Q-q | Q-q |
| Ш-ш | Sh (sh) | Ш-ш | Ş-ş | Ş-ş | Ş-ş (sh) |
| Ү-ү | Ü-ü (same as German) | Ү-ү | Ü-ü | Ü-ü | Ü-ü (same as German) |
| – | – | J-j* | Y-y | Y-y | Y-y (y as in year) |
| Ұ-ұ | U | – | – | – | – |
| I-i | I | – | – | – | – |
| Ң-ң | Ng | – | – | – | – |

Note
* The letter J-j in Azerbaijani Cyrillic Alphabet replaced Й-й in 1959.

*Note on the narrative and transliteration* xi

in plural *ll.*) numbers. Although there are also Azerbaijani, Kazakh, and Ukrainian equivalents of this terminology, Russian is used in the bibliography of this book for simplicity. When an archival document is cited, only these numbers are used and they are divided by a dash (–) in this order, unless it is marked otherwise. Runs of pages in archival documents are divided by a slash (/). Numerical citation of an archival document is followed by the date of the document.

All dates are given in the form of 'day-month-year', unless they indicate an archival document. In the latter case, they are in the form of 'month-day-year'. This is done to avoid any confusion between the page number and the numerical part of the date of a document. Unfortunately, it is not always possible to identify the exact date of archival documents. When the day or the month is missing, the available or estimated information is recorded after the numerical citation of the document in parentheses.

Ukrainian personal and geographical names pose another challenge. Archival sources and printed materials are both in Russian and Ukrainian and some names occur both in Russian and Ukrainian forms. The archival materials usually record persons with their surnames, without mentioning first and middle names. However, printed materials included this information and the initials sometimes change according the Russian or Ukrainian version of the name. In order to easily trace one person in all records and citations, I have used the Ukrainian form of surnames. This book uses the Ukrainian spelling of Ukrainian personal names, including those originally appearing in the Russian spelling in Russian documents. Similarly, all the Ukrainian place names are rendered in their Ukrainian form.

In the Azerbaijani case, personal names and toponyms may have Azerbaijani and Iranian versions. The literature is dominated by the latter. That is why, in order to provide familiarity, in most cases I have chosen the Iranian version.

# Introduction

Stalin was a dictator of a totalitarian state. He used state terror more effectively than any other modern ruler. His faith in Marxism and his political goals literally destroyed millions of lives. In the Soviet Union and abroad, millions of people detested him. When he died in 1953, he left a monstrous system of surveillance, terror, arbitrariness, and deficits. Yet, he was worshipped by millions. When the Red Army reached Berlin in May 1945, military victory was utilized to validate his rule on a popular basis. After the Second World War, he personally symbolized the military destruction of Nazi expansionism and confirmed the USSR as a great power. But his popularity was not only based on military victory. Alongside his brutal system, his achievements made millions love and revere him earlier in the 1930s and emerged as a realist problem-solver after the theorizing windbags of the 1920s. Stalin was a modernizing dictator who changed both his own country and the world. He wanted to turn the Soviet Union into an industrial colossus that would catch and surpass leading capitalist countries. This goal was accompanied by increasing Soviet military power to an unchallengeable level. All these aims were facades of an even higher goal, building an alternative or Soviet modernity, though an illiberal one.

The Stalinist state not only built railroads, canals, factories, and steel mills but it also constructed national identities with historical narratives. Millions defined themselves according to these constructed identities. The construction of national identities was an important phase in developing Soviet modernity. These constructions envisaged how nationalities should see their imaginary common (national) past. The central feature of this study is to understand how national histories were written under Stalin in Ukraine, Azerbaijan, and Kazakhstan, and what the political and ideological reasons were behind the way they were written. Earlier analyses demonstrated how Russocentrist historiography, which was developed after 1936, changed the narrative of the historical relations between Russians and non-Russians towards a construction of mythical friendship. In the current work, the comparison of the three non-Russian cases with different historical components and geographies liberates us from this well-studied dichotomy and shows that Soviet nation-building and construction of national narratives were beyond this. Furthermore, this work examines each example of nation-building in the context of international relations, and points to the impact of parallel nation-building policies or relevant historiographical theories in neighbouring countries.

Why do we need to know Soviet nation-building policies in these countries? By investigating the Soviet past, the book helps us to understand contemporary issues of national identity construction in these countries. The Soviet economic system failed in competing with the capitalist market economy. Despite this failure, Soviet modernization and nation-building policies were more persistent and successful than its economic system. By and large, countries in Central Asia, the Caucasus, and to an extent Ukraine, still function according to Soviet codes. The construction of national histories in the 1930s and 1940s has a continuing impact, even after the independence of these countries as separate nation-states. It is true that, these histories were rewritten and values attached to them have been altered after 1991. However, numerous elements, which were incorporated into national histories in those years, continue to decorate contemporary national narratives, or at least constitute subjects of discussion. There is a long list of pre-Soviet symbols venerated in a highly Soviet tradition of propaganda, thus the Soviet attempt at nation-building forms a key part of post-Soviet national identities. Also, understanding these continuities and discontinuities gives us an idea about the changing political and ideological priorities of the new elites.

The controversy over how to interpret and understand the Soviet period (1917–91) has presented particular problems for historians and politicians in the newly independent republics (Lindner 1999; Popson 2001; Rodgers 2007), including Russia (Slater 1998; Smith 2002; Adler 2005; Kirschenbaum 2006; Kaplan 2009; Kolonitskii 2009; Ro'i 2009; Uldricks 2009; Todorova and Gille 2010). Since their independence in 1991, the political elites of the former Soviet republics have embarked on rewriting their Soviet past, with responses ranging from a complete rejection of the Soviet past as colonial and repressive to various degrees of affirmation and incorporation, depending on the political agendas of the particular actors. Though Vladimir Putin called the collapse of the USSR the 'greatest geopolitical catastrophe' (BBC News 2005) of the twentieth century, not everyone in the territories of the former Soviet Union shares this nostalgic sentiment. For instance, in the Baltic States, anti-communism became a kind of foundation myth (Brüggemann and Kasekamp 2008). The Ukrainian–Russian conflict that began in 2014 is decorated by Soviet and anti-Soviet symbols and values. While some of the protesters were eager to pull down Lenin statues, others were ready to gather around the same statues to form human shields and use the familiar hammer and sickle for their struggle. This demonstrates that the division over the interpretation of the Soviet past among the ex-Soviet territories is still a popular issue. In Central Asia and the Caucasus the interpretation of the Soviet past is also not clear cut.

One reason for this obscurity is the complicated nature of the Soviet rule (Kandiyoti 2002) and an ongoing debate over defining the Soviet period as a colonial period (Michaels 2003; Northrop 2004; Hirsch 2005), or mobilization by the state for modernization and nation-building (Slezkine 2000; Kotkin 2001; Kamp 2006; Khalid 2006), or even as a region within the neo-traditionalism of the Soviet rule (Jowitt 1993, 121–158; Martin 2000; Kandiyoti 2006). In any case, the three republics experienced the critical wave of modernity such as high levels of literacy, secularization, urbanization, industrialization and homogenization of cultures and identities under Soviet rule. This long and penetrating experience had an enormous and lasting impact on the form and content of national identities and histories in these republics. Studying Soviet nation-building efforts and detecting continuities and discontinuities in national narratives reveal the strength of the Soviet modernization project and gives us a better understanding of these countries.

Moreover, there is a trans-regional aspect of this focus. Historically speaking, the Caucasus and Central Asia were part of a cultural world that is now called the Middle East and had already been defined as the 'Soviet Middle East' (Nove 1967). The nation-building policies in the Soviet Caucasus and Central Asia went simultaneously with two different examples in the greater Middle East: Kemalist Turkey, and the Iran of the Pahlavis. Now we are experiencing a period when the nation-building policies and even state borders of the twentieth century in the region are challenged. Thorough understanding of Soviet nation-building policy helps us to understand better the difference of Central Asian and Caucasian republics from the rest of the greater Middle East or Western Asia today and make more accurate predictions.

## Pervasiveness of nation-building

Stalin was not an unusual example of his time in constructing national identities. The same practice has repeated itself in different countries and at different decades of the last two centuries. Since the nineteenth century, European historians, archaeologists, ethnographers, and anthropologists have been busy in constructing national identities. The past of certain geographies became national histories; patchworks of dialects were homogenized into standard languages of literature; regional folk tales, peasant costumes, festive plays and dances were collected to be rebranded as national. Emulating the German example, the intellectuals of Hungarian and Slavic populations of Eastern Europe joined the marathon of nation-building. The same waves floated down the Balkan Peninsula from today's Romania to Greece in the south and soon to follow was the mass uprooting of large segments of populations from their homes and daily lives. From the Caucasus in the early 1860s to the Balkans on the eve of the Great War, Europe was remapped around forced resettlements, population exchanges, or ethno-religious cleansing. These forced migrations increased the ethno-linguistic homogeneity and established fertile grounds for further nation-building policies. These ideas and practices were not confined to the European continent. The national independence movements in the Balkans and the Turkic ideologues of the Russian Empire, led by the Crimean and Kazan Tatars, influenced the Ottoman Turks. The émigré intellectuals from the decaying Ottoman Turkey and Qajar Iran closely observed the dawn of the national era in Europe. At the turn of the century, the elites of both states found themselves discussing their national identity. This frenzy of nation-building continued in full swing well into the twentieth century.

In the first decades of the twentieth century, authoritarian 'gardener states' populated Europe, actively seeking the transformation of their subjects, and the Soviet Union was just one of them. The First World War changed the European and Middle Eastern political maps for ever. Austro-Hungarian, Russian, Ottoman, and Iranian imperial systems and identities collapsed, both the core territories and peripheries with particularities reorganized as nation-states. From Finland to Iran, an impressive array of new states launched vigorous campaigns to homogenize identities and cultures. The Bolshevik state did not stand far from the non-socialist counterparts that aimed to shape their societies to construct national identities and histories. Both sides of the ideological borderline considered the modern state to be the responsible body for the spiritual, social, and physical well-being of its subjects. They were eager to remould society and individuals. The same tools and knowledge to tame the unpredictable forces of nature could be also applicable to human nature and society. There was a continuous attempt to sculpt a 'new man'. In the Soviet Union, this was aimed at through the abolition of the market and private property, elimination of social classes, and establishing a one-party dictatorship, accompanied by intensive indoctrination and education campaigns. If nationalists forcibly removed 'ethnic weeds' the Bolsheviks terminated 'social weeds'. These states mobilized millions towards an ideal future (Scott 1998; Weiner 2003).

These gardener states were also after harmonious societies and homogeneous nations, which were not limited to contemporary values and definitions. It also expanded well into the past. All national identities have been grand narratives of the past. Although identities differed in content, they all aimed primordial and sometimes racial definitions of nation. These romantic narratives aimed to answer multiple questions such as where do we come from? Who were our ancestors? What is the border of our historical fatherland? Who are our leading figures that we, as the whole nation, should venerate? Who are our historical enemies? When was the golden age of our nation and our re-birth in the modern era? These histories were important to constitute a scholarly proof that the subject nation was a homogenous population with its own historical process. Writing large-scale national histories was a culmination of a series of research and examination of massive sources in different periods. It also begged for close collaboration with other disciplines including paleontology, archaeology, ethnography, and linguistics. In Eastern Europe, this culmination came to the surface in the nineteenth century. František Palacký wrote *History of Bohemia* for the Czechs, Sergei Solov'ev and Michał Bobrzyński wrote Russian and Polish national histories. Mykhailo Hrushevs'kyi, a historian born and educated in the Russian Empire but holding a chair in history at L'viv University in the Austro-Hungarian Empire initiated his life-long project, the construction of the Ukrainian national history in 1894 (Sysyn 1999; Kohut 1999).

The national narratives constructed under Stalin were no exception. They were also constructed in order to define the milestones of nations' past histories.

Nationalities policy under Stalin turned millions of peasants and nomads living within the Soviet borders into Russians, Ukrainians, Azerbaijanis, Kazakhs, and other nationalities. The narrative that was constructed under Stalin continued to guide further research and development in the following decades. Consequently, a strong narrative backed by a scrupulous literature appeared. When young historians developed alternative routes to the past in the 1960s and 1970s, the historians of the Stalinist era became ardent defenders of their own constructions against any alternative or unofficial interpretations of the past.

## The Soviet Union: a special case

How Stalinist national history construction differed from other gardener states was rooted in the totalitarian nature of the Soviet system. In Marxist–Leninist theory, the intelligentsia, the obscurely defined class that historians were part of, was a dependent amalgam on the dominant class in a given economic system. Thus, in capitalism, the intelligentsia had no other choice but to develop culture according to the needs of the owners of capital and bend to the patronage of the bourgeoisie. In the Soviet system, the theory asserted that the intelligentsia was emancipated because there were no oppressing-exploiting classes that would create limitations. The dictatorship of the proletariat was ready to provide facilities for the development and distribution of culture for free. Of course, in practice, things did not work as such. The lives of historians and their works became vulnerable to control by state or Communist Party apparatus, and in some cases by Stalin, in a way that other states or politicians that endeavoured nation-building never achieved. None of the nation-builders in other countries had the absolute monopoly on defining and propagating one definition of national identity and terminating alternatives. The Stalinist system did not accept any parallel narratives to the officially approved ones to be voiced. The names, figures, values, movements, events, or physical objects that were not incorporated into the official narrative were 'weeded out' by state terror. Books that contained alternative narratives were banned and burned to the last single copy, the publications that merely cited banned works also vanished from the shelves. Historians, writers, poets, and others who had the potential to reproduce an alternative past were exiled and killed. In order to clear 'undesired' events and figures from popular (and unofficial) narratives of the past, the Soviet regime exterminated even blind folk bards wandering from one village to another in Ukraine (Shostakovich 1995, 214–215). Stalinist nation-building tried to remove any building material that would be used to construct an alternative national narrative. Perhaps the endurance of these national narratives after the Soviet Union can be explained by this thoroughly 'sanitized' environment.

Stalin saw history as an ideal propaganda tool for the consolidation of the cult of personality and repeatedly changed his political priorities based on the tensions in international relations. Stalin personally intervened numerous times to show Russian historians the 'right' way of interpreting the selected past events or figures in the Russian national narrative. The famous examples of these interventions in Russian history were on the evangelization of the Kyïvan Rus' (Kievan Rus'), Ivan the Terrible, the Napoleonic Wars and his Russian campaign, General Kutuzov, and the Crimean War (Burdei 1991, 159–204; Dubrovskii 2005, 137–169). Aleksei Tolstoi (1882–1945), a Russian writer and a distant relative of the famous Tolstoy, wrote a theatre play, *Peter I*, in the 1930s in compliance with the demands of Stalin. He summarized his situation in 1937 to a close friend, which was similar to the position of historians:

> You see, while I wrote it, 'the father of nations' [Stalin] reviewed the history of Russia. Peter the Great became the 'proletarian tsar' without my knowledge and the prototype of our Joseph [Stalin]! I rewrote it in accordance with the discoveries of the Party, and now I am preparing the third one, and I hope this will be the last version, because the second version could not satisfy our Joseph. I can see in front of me all those Ivan the Terribles, Rasputins, and others rehabilitated and became Marxists and glorified.
> (Dubrovskii 2005, 147)

Next to the totalitarian system and practices of the Soviet Union, Marxist ideology or at least the Stalinist interpretation and application of this ideology in the USSR also made a difference in the construction of all national narratives, including the Russian one. The importance of Marxist–Leninist ideology in the Soviet Union has always been acknowledged, but it has nevertheless been underrated. One reason for this is that many treatments of the Soviet Union isolate the Russian ingredient and consider developments in other republics as background noise. Moreover, they see the Soviet Union as merely the second colonial empire ruled by Russians, replacing the tsarist regime. Some emphasize that the Bolsheviks indeed started as an essentially internationalists–Marxists, but they postulate a steady dilution of this internationalism under Stalin. Stalin's formula of 'socialism in a single country' is understood as the beginning of the end to internationalist Marxism. The re-emergence of Russian national identity and culture after 1936 is also taken as a cardinal moment for the Bolshevik leaders to turn their back on internationalist Marxism. Still more crucial in other accounts were the partial restoration of the Russian Church and the Russian nationalist propaganda during the Second World War. The famous speech of Stalin at the Kremlin right after the war in 1945 praising the Russian nation as the key part of the Union only confirms this treatment. The Cold War rhetoric and the publications of various émigré writers also only strengthened this. Such treatments of the Soviet Union seriously downgrade the internationalist–Marxist ideology. In fact, the official ideology in the first communist state had always a paramount place in making decisions. Even pragmatic and hasty solutions had to be justified by ideological tenets.

In the first fifteen years of Soviet rule, the revolutionary fervour sought after the Marxist purification of history writing. National and imperial narratives of the past were outdated. M. N. Pokrovskii (1868–1932) was a Russian historian who was prominent well before the Russian Revolution owing to his Marxist interpretation of Russian history. In the 1920s, he became the chief historian of the Bolshevik regime when the new socialist order that was about to be built asked for a new and Marxist history. With the typical enthusiasm of a world revolutionary, Lenin suggested that Pokrovskii's works should not be confined to the borders of the Soviet Union. They had to be translated to the major European languages and published for the Western readers.

Pokrovskii and his followers aimed to reconstruct previous national and imperial narratives according to the Marxist scheme, in which classes (and the conflicts between them) were the main agents of all narratives. Pokrovskii minimized the role of institutional structures such as the state that could be depicted as the focal point of the nation. In Marxist terms, the state was the suppressing apparatus held by the owners of the means of production. It did not have a separate 'spirit' or 'reason' to exist, it was a device that guaranteed the economic exploitation and did not deserve particular attention in history writing. Pokrovskiian history also de-emphasized historical personages, their ideologies, and their national identities.[1] Who was Julius Caesar without his slaves and greedy legionnaires? What could the Russian tsars achieve without the army of toiling serfs and the coffers of merchant capitalists? Was there a reason to glorify such military aggressions where the real beneficiaries of these 'victories at battlefields' were rulers and exploiters? Instead he emphasized 'folk leaders', those who had led uprisings against their contemporary political structures (Pokrovskii 1933a, 44, 66–68). These figures, backed by popular support, were considered to be examples of the real 'national' identity. Pokrovskiian history writing focused on the relations of production and classes. It developed a historical literature in the emergence of merchant capitalism and its impact on the political system of Russia, the rise of the working class, class struggles, the analogies of the German peasant wars in Russian history, and the regional aspects of the industrialization in Russia. While looking for an analogy of the Jacquerie in France, the Hussite War in Bohemia, and the Peasant War in sixteenth-century Germany, Pokrovskii identified four popular revolutions in territories of the Russian Empire: the Khmel'nyts'kyi Uprising (1648–54) in Ukraine, the Time of Troubles in Russia (1604–13), the Uprising of Stenka Razin (1670–1), and the Pugachev rebellion (1773–5) (Yaresh 1957, 241–259; Eissenstat 1969, 604–618; also see Tomsinskii 1925, 1927, 1932, 1934a, 1934b; Pokrovskii 1933a; Schlesinger 1950a, 298–301, 1952, 156; Black 1962; Shteppa 1962, 28–35; Sokolov 1966, 5–71, 66; Szporluk 1970, 1–46; Enteen 1978). As the study groups at the first congress of Marxist historians in 1928–29 argued, the important part of history commenced with the French Revolution, and for Russian history with the 1861 reforms (Trudy Pervoi 1930a, 1930b). Additionally, Pokrovskii was not focused on non-Russian histories and he left this area to be addressed by burgeoning Marxist historians of the non-Russian republics. Pokrovskii dispelled all kinds of national and imperial narratives, including the Russian one. He described Russian rule over non-Russian peoples (Poles, Jews, Ukrainians, Caucasians, Siberians etc.) as a ruthless force of oppression, plundering and mass killings. He categorically refused to acknowledge any progressive aspect to this relation (Trudy Pervoi 1930a, especially pp. 426–522; Pokrovskii 1933b, 225, 235, 244; Tillett 1969, 26–30. Also see Bochkarov, Ioannisani et al. 1931; Pokrovskii 1970, 108–116; Neretina 1990, 32–35. On the reasons behind the lack of interest of Pokrovskii: Plokhy 2005b, 346; Masanov 2007a, 13–15). Finally, Pokrovskii was also against the classical teaching of history. Classical history classes asked pupils to memorize the names and deeds of princes, kings, and emperors, who were nothing more than representatives of exploiting classes.

## New histories emerging

From 1934, the priorities and concepts of the Pokrovskiian era were gradually removed from the discipline of history.[2] New historical narratives were closer to romantic national narratives than internationalist–Marxist class struggles. The ideal form of these new histories can be summarized in five points. First, great leaders and great events were incorporated into the history. The historical figure had an extraordinary life and personality. He could once again influence the course of history. He had an independent consciousness and the power to lead the masses. Second, instead of class conflict and building communism, another purpose became the teleological reason of history: 'building a centralized state structure'. The state had a historical and progressive mission. Interest in revolutionary events and revolutionary movements slightly yielded to interest in diplomatic relations and wars. The description and selection of the 'other' as a nation also came to the fore because international or inter-state relations also became an elementary part of history. Third, economic history ceded its primary position to political history. Statist (etatist) or dynastic periodization replaced materialist periodization. The linear trajectory of history followed the formation of consecutive states from antiquity until the 1936 constitution of Stalin. Fourth, the difference between the pre-revolutionary period and the Soviet period was blurred.[3] Fifth, the 'lesser evil' became the paradigm for interpreting the historical relations between Russians and the non-Russian nationalities of the Soviet Union. It was true that these nationalities had suffered from the colonial rule of tsarism. However, their incorporation into the Russian Empire was a better choice with historical importance, as compared to alternatives (Tillett 1969, 40–49). Yet the official ideology continued to limit these tendencies and none of these points were fully established in the new narratives.

At the same time the importance of ethnogenesis returned from a decade of hibernation. In national narratives the positing of a collective ancestor or common ethnic roots is an attempt to provide a genesis for all members of the nation. Emphasizing common ethnic roots, first, consolidates the ties among the imagined community – the nation (Anderson 2006). It creates a sense of loyalty and belonging for everyone. When a particular past of an ethnicity becomes a national history, the nation does not only share a contemporary culture but also a common past, with its glories and sufferings. In this way, nationalism usually glorifies ancient traditions shared by the common ancestors of the members of that nation.[4] According to Hroch, this common past or common memory is one of the irreplaceable ties. Furthermore, if nationalism is a metaphoric kinship, then common ethnic roots transform this metaphor into a tangible object. Eriksen stresses that, consequently, the nation becomes a very large family – a union of brothers and sisters – or a living individual – a tree, a friend, a mother, and a creature with a soul – by virtue of its constructed ethnic past (Eriksen 2002, 107). Finally, ethnogenesis and the first spatial location of the nation's ancestors are important for assigning the borders of an ancient homeland. In the 1930s, archaeology was already a study of finding the ancient roots of nations in the debris of prehistoric pottery and human skeletons, providing national histories with the necessary evidence to demarcate the ancient fatherland (Diaz-Andreu and Champion 1996. P. J. Geary names this archaeology as ethnoarchaeology; see Geary 2002, 34–35). Aryan theory and the Nordic–Aryan superiority thesis that challenged other national identities raised the question of ethnogenesis in all national histories.

However, the writing of Soviet prehistory in those years was under the influence of Nikolai Marr, a well-trained orientalist and linguist, especially in Armenian and Georgian philology. According to Marr, ethnogenesis was not a priority in historical research, because modern languages and peoples themselves were of mixed ancestry and had emerged from close interrelations among various populations deep in the past. History was an endless process of intermixing between contiguous ethnic groups. Thus, one had to study universal stages of cultural evolution rather than particular lines of development of cultures. 'Homelands' or 'proto-peoples' and their 'proto-languages', concepts that were very popular among the nation-builders, were rejected and seen as the products of fascist pseudo-science. Everyone was autochthonous in a spatial sense and at the same time did not bear a single ethnic root. This autochthonous development was claimed to be of primary importance, and it took place locally and continuously. According to this perspective, migrations played a lesser role or were completely rejected (Kushner 1927; Marr 1933, 236).[5] Every contemporary nation turned into another one as a result of socio-economic transformation, not as a consequence of the migration or diffusion of ethnicities.[6] According to Marr, the reason for linguistic and cultural change was not external mass immigrations but revolutionary shifts that resulted from qualitatively different conditions of material life.[7]

Although sociological arguments continued to shape the interpretations of archaeologists, Marrist arguments lost their initial impact on Soviet studies of prehistory and archaeology after 1936 (Matorin 1932; Efimenko 1934; Auerbakh, Gammerman *et al.* 1935; *Kratkii otchet o rabote Akademii* 1936; Rykov 1936; Efimenko 1938. Also see the following special collections of articles for interpretation of prehistory in this period: Marr 1934; Deborin 1936). Socio-economic periodization remained the primary task of archaeology, the role of migration was acknowledged and the search for the ethnic roots of nations was added to the task of prehistoric studies.[8] Ethnos began to be considered as durable and static in time, and a link between archaeological cultures and contemporary ethnic groups gradually became established (O vreditel'stve 1937;

10  *Introduction*

Artamonov 1939a). In the following decades, prehistory and explanations of the ethnogenesis of different nations contained a mixture of Marrist concepts and archaeological cultures in prehistory gradually identified with ethnicities. Consequently, in the Soviet Union, nations were increasingly constructed on the basis of ethnic identities and nations were understood as ethnicities. (For the Russian case see Derzhavin 1944, 5–6; for all-Union policies see Shnirelman 1995, 130; 1996b; Slezkine 1994). Historians, archaeologists or ethnographers had to demonstrate that the contemporary inhabitants of each republic were descendants of the autochthonous people of those lands (Formozov 1993). This was an all-Union policy that had an impact on every republic to varying degrees. Although the Bolsheviks considered national identity a stage in history, a function of capitalism and the modern era (Suny 1993; Zaslavsky 1993; Tishkov 1997), these national identities were gradually described as primordial entities (Martin 2000). Archaeological cultures became evidence of the autochthonous evolution of nations. In other words, these cultures were attached to a specific ethnos (Shnirelman 1995, 130–133). The aim was to legitimize the Soviet state by historically legitimizing each Soviet republic separately. It was encouraged to conduct research in ancient history and archaeology in order to reveal the ethnogenesis of Soviet nations in the antiquity and in prehistory (Avdiev *et al.* 1940). It only remains to remind ourselves that, in the age of nationalism, the Soviet Union was neither the first nor the last example (Kohl and Fawcett 1995; Diaz-Andreu and Champion 1996; Kohl 1998; Geary 2002, 34–35; Kohl *et al.* 2007).

## Drivers towards national histories

The new type of history that was written after 1936 was a consequence of interconnected issues.[9] In the mid-1930s, the Stalinist state declared that the Soviet Union was a socialist country in economic terms. The first three five-year plans increased the levels of industrialization and urbanization. Yet national identities were stronger than a decade before and there was not a sign of a merger. It became clear that it would take much more time before national identities would be displayed in the museum of antiquities. The ideological reply to this reality was the Stalinist concept of 'socialist nations', which would disappear only as a consequence of a global socialist economy. These socialist nations or the titular identities of each republic were supposed to have ethnic roots that historians and archaeologists could find in the past (Motyl 1992; Suny 1995; Lieven 1995; Szporluk 1997; Baberowski 1998; Hoffmann 2000; Michaels 2000; Northrop 2000; Slezkine 2000).

By the late 1930s, when Stalinism claimed that socialist principles established in economy and classes had disappeared, the theoretical consequence had to be the withering away of the state (Engels 1972, 232; 1987, 254, 268). Instead of class-based quotas, polls and identity cards, the national identity became dominant (Slezkine 1994, 442). However, the state remained and was even consolidated. At this stage, national identities and their histories provided ever more legitimacy for the system. Each nationhood and nationality was codified and institutionalized (Brubaker 1994, 49–52). The codification and institutionalization of the nations in the Soviet Union encompassed a broad area, including their cultures, languages, symbols, and histories.

The content and direction of the new national histories bring us to the external factor. In the 1930s, actual fascist war danger against the USSR and the long tradition in Bolshevik ideology and politics of fear of subversion and sabotage of socialist state by capitalist countries coincided. The international situation deteriorated sharply, which was meant to be a nightmare of fighting on two fronts against Germany and Japan. Stalin and other Bolshevik leaders did not doubt the reality and immediacy of the fascist war threat against the Soviet Union. In spite of the industrialization of the USSR in 1929–33, Germany remained industrially and technically more advanced than the Soviet Union. The Soviet military developments soon proved inadequate in the face of German rearmament. The massive investment in military industry was the sign of a dramatic shift in the perception of the international threats (Harrison 1985, 250; Simonov 1996, 81–124; Harrison and Davies 1997). The complex relationship between war and revolution, which had demonstrated itself in 1905 and 1917, was something Stalin was acutely aware of. The state-terror operations of 1937–8 targeted those social or national groups which the authorities regarded as the basis for forming a 'Fifth Column' in the event of a possible war (Benvenuti 1995; Khlevnyuk 1995). Parallel to the rearmament and terror, there were also cardinal consequences of the imminent war threat on nationalities policy. Russian national identity and culture was promoted to glue the Soviet patchwork of multi-ethnic structure together (Brandenberger 2002). The Soviet government forcibly migrated 'unreliable' nationalities from the border regions (Martin 1998). Their unreliability came from two sources. The state having hostile relations with the USSR was also the historical homeland of this nation. This was the case with the Germans. Alternatively, the historical homeland of deportees (such as the Kurds, Turks, Koreans and the Poles) was right beyond the borders of the Soviet Union. The overall aim was to secure Soviet borderlands in case of a war (Martin 1998; Khlevniuk 2000). As can be seen in the chapters on Azerbaijan and Ukraine, this external threat influenced the content of the new national histories.

## The rise of national histories under Stalin

The reconstruction of the past is not a phenomenon of the modern states and societies and it can be found in traditional forms. For instance, in Central Asia, the traditional reconstructions of the age of Tamerlane were very popular centuries after the medieval ruler died (Sela 2011). Other than Tamerlane's popular histories, there were two major types of traditional reconstructions in Central Asia. One of them was dynastic. These histories were produced at the courts of local rulers. The second one was sacred histories including hagiographies of pre-Islamic prophets, Muslim saints, and mystics. The picture was no different in Ukraine. The Cossack aristocracy wrote traditional reconstructions of the heroic past of the Cossacks to emphasize their subordination to the Muscovite Tsar in the eighteenth century (Plokhy 1992).

The construction initiated after 1937 was formative in the national identities of the three republics for the fact that Azerbaijan, Kazakhstan, and Ukraine lacked a modern historical narrative that could have been developed in the nineteenth century. Compared to Kazakh and Azerbaijani national identities, Ukrainian national identity had a pre-Soviet construction. When the Soviet rule was established in Ukraine in 1920, Hrushevs'kyi was halfway through writing his national history. Nevertheless, the national identity in Ukraine is far from a unifying formula for the country (Himka 2006). The Kazakh and Azerbaijani narratives did not even exist yet. Some Jadid activists[10] were concerned with writing a history in modern forms but nothing came out before the First World War (Khalid 1999). In fact these nationalities-to-be were not odd examples. The construction of Russian national identity still had some way to go before the Bolsheviks came to power. The construction continued until and under Stalin (Hosking 1997, 2002; Brudny 1998; Lieven 2003; Brandenberger 2002; Szporluk 2006). The Soviet national history constructions after 1937 arrived in these pristine lands with multiple tools. In the 1920s and 1930s, the academic intellectual life was institutionalized and organized. The Soviet regime established pedagogical institutes, publishing houses, universities, and local branches of the Academy of Sciences of the USSR in each republic early in the 1920s. In the following decades, the number of local archaeologists, historians, ethnographers, and linguists who energetically contributed to the colossal effort of building a national narrative rapidly increased. At the same time, the Soviet effort to increase literary rates and the creation of infrastructure for primary and secondary education in native tongues and in Russian disseminated modern national narratives at the grassroots level.

The historians who wrote the national narratives were part of a society in flux. In the 1920s and 1930s, millions of peasants became workers, and workers who upgraded their skills became foremen, managers, and party or state officials. These were *vydvizhentsi*, or the ones who move upwards in the career ladder. They were the leading figures of the time, and their image was polished by their everyday appearance in the press. They were typically young, of peasant or working-class origin, politically militant, impatient to get the job done. Most of them had peasant origins and their early life until the Soviet period was like that of so many others at that time – early experience with work, deprivation, hopelessness, and lack of proper education. Thousands of peasants and workers and young communists were sent to higher education to become the technicians, experts, and intellectuals of the new order. After their graduation, some of them became propaganda chiefs in the party organization, or the historians, ethnographers, linguists, and archaeologists of the scholarly world. The graduates of the Institute of Red Professors or the Communist Academy, which was founded to bring up Soviet experts in humanitarian disciplines, filled the ranks. They were taught that the true history was the one written according to Marxism, and Pokrovskii was the best available example in Marxist history writing. In the first decade of Soviet rule, the old specialists, historians who were trained before the revolution and did not switch to the Pokrovskiian–Marxist narrative, were prosecuted. The prosecutions, exiles, and show trials against historians intensified from 1928 to 1933. Libraries were scanned to find and terminate volumes that were not in line with the new narrative. Pokrovskii, his followers and students rewrote Russian history and the histories of some other nations in the Soviet Union.

In the mid-1930s, when the Marxist history writing was partially abandoned, the exiled, outcast or denounced ones returned to the stage. In 1933, old specialists such as Tarle, Picheta, and Bakhrushin, who were not party members and had been exiled, jailed or unemployed, were invited back to fill the ranks and assist with their historical knowledge in building a new narrative.[11] Old specialists seemed to fit better with the writing of this new narrative. This time, a wave of denunciation was launched against the ones who were close to Pokrovskii. Numerous historians who wrote in the line of Pokrovskii and developed their career in the 1920s were executed during the Great Terror of 1936–8. After consecutive prosecutions, exiles, and executions, there were two opposing groups of historians, who were all terrorized by the same totalitarian system: old specialists and former followers of Pokrovskii started to live an uneasy life and share the same institutions (Dubrovskii 2005, 110–136).[12]

In less than a decade, historians were terrorized twice. Following the removal of Pokrovskii's historiography, a gap appeared both in the minds of historians and in Soviet historical narrative. The ones educated according to the Marxist principles and who considered themselves as the Marxist historians were suddenly accused of 'vulgarizing' Marxism. If the Pokrovskiian history was not Marxist–Leninist, then what was the alternative? In his letter to Stalin, Radek, who was one of the voices of the new Soviet patriotism in the 1930s (Radek 1936) and involved in writing a new history after 1934, reveals the mood of historians in 1936. Historians were like a flock of sheep in shock discovering that their shepherd (Pokrovskii) had disappeared. They did not want to make another 'mistake'. '[Marxist–Pokrovskiian historians] were afraid of a defeat.' Nobody knew the correct reading of the past. The situation at the historical front was 'vague'. 'Nobody developed Leninist principles and elaborated or used them in bigger historical works.' The history writing of Pokrvoskii was not liquidated yet because there was not an alternative reading of history.[13] This gap in reading the past could have serious ideological implications for the Soviet regime. That is why the problem of writing a new history was discussed at the highest level in Moscow among Stalin and others in the Politburo on 5 March 1934.[14] One week later, A. I. Stetskii, the head of the section of culture and propaganda of Leninism of the Central Committee of the CPSU (Communist Party of the Soviet Union) conveyed Stalin's opinions on this gradual turn and gave the first signals to the historians.[15] In the following weeks, the Politburo initiated the project of writing a new textbook, and the Central Committee accepted a resolution 'on the education of civil history in the schools of the USSR' which organized the writing of new textbooks and re-established history faculties at universities.[16] Again in March 1934, when Stalin met with historians at the meeting of the Politburo, he demanded more historical facts, events, figures, concrete explanations,

14  *Introduction*

names, and traditional periodizations (ancient, medieval) instead of obscure titles of the epoch of feudalism or capitalism (Dubrovskii 2005, 191). When the first plans of textbooks appeared in 1934 and 1935, Stalin reviewed them scrupulously.[17] Nevertheless, initial attempts at writing a new history failed because historians were scared. The Pokrovskiian interpretation had to have the volume turned down, but how far they would go? Kirov summarized this situation:

> [P]eople are scared ... we understood the situation.... and we came to their [historians'] help and said: take our old history textbooks until Kliuchevskii, collect all, order [textbooks] from France, there are good ones there, order from Germany and take a look at all of them, and based on what had been written, compose in a way that it would fit to our conditions to our Soviet education.
>
> (Dubrovskii 2005, 231–232)

Instead of using his messengers, Stalin, along with Zhdanov and Kirov, wrote a short manual for historians later in the same year (Zhdanov 2004, 147–148). They wanted historians to shed light on the heroic and patriotic past of both Russian and non-Russian nations. While building this nationalist discourse they had to correct the mistakes of Pokrosvskiian historiography, which did not value enough the glorious past and traditions of Soviet nations (Pankratova 1942, 36). They also wanted a history that would blend the past of Russian and non-Russian nations. No one had to be left out. The emphasis had to move from class to nation but at the same time two Marxist dicta, 'the Russian tsarism's annexationist-colonialist role inside the country ("tsarism – the prison of nations") and its counter-revolutionary role in Europe (international gendarme)' had to be retained. In conclusion the trio wanted 'such a history textbook of the USSR that first the history of Russians should not be separated from the histories of other nations, second, the history of the Soviet nations should not be separated from the European and world history'.[18]

These directives and Stalin's direct intervention did not solve the problem. In his letter addressing Stalin in 1936, Radek puts it well:

> You gave the principal instructions. It needs time so that people could digest it and applied [in their works]. This [process] can be accelerated, if we had known concrete and detailed answers to all questions appeared after the collapse of the school of Pokrovskii.

According to Radek, in order to find Marxist answers, someone had to sit and read all the works of Pokrovskii and his students, especially in the last five years, and the discussions within the Pokrovskiian school. However, Radek could not see any historian who could accomplish such a task. In Radek's words, 'our comrades' (i.e. the admonished Pokrovskiian–Marxist historians) were left without guidelines. Those 'comrades' now occupied a weaker position in front of the 'bourgeois scholars who sit in the Academy [of Sciences] and outperform us by possessing much more [historical] knowledge'. Stalin and Zhdanov agreed with the conclusions of Radek.[19] As Radek described, the gap that appeared after the removal of Pokrovskiian school was slowly filled by the old specialists. In the following years, the nationalization of the past parallel to the internationalist official ideology remained a confusing experience for everyone. Where did the nationalism end and proletarian internationalism begin? Soviet readers continued to ask questions on 'ethnicity', 'national identity', 'proletarian internationalism', and 'Soviet patriotism' (Otvety 1940; Kammari 1940).

In January 1936, Stalin organized a committee headed by Zhdanov to solve this ambiguity and to finalize the attempts at writing a new history textbook. The committee included prominent Bolsheviks with different nationalities.[20] Stalin frequently used his closest comrades-in-arms as outlets for his ideas in the sphere of ideology as well as others. One of these essential figures was A. A. Zhdanov, whom Stalin called 'the supervisor of the ideology' (Mar'iamov 1992, 11).[21] Zhdanov chaired the committee on behalf of Stalin to construct a usable past. At the same time multiple teams of historians wrote different drafts and competed for the prize of elementary textbook. The draft co-authored by A. V. Shestakov and a brigade of historians won the competition. When the project moved towards the end, Stalin wrote comments on the whole text of Shestakov's manuscript and made dramatic changes in the narrative.[22] Yet, the textbook of Shestakov was a basic text for elementary schools. When the jury members chose Shestakov's textbook for the third and fourth grades (1937), they were still displeased with various shortcomings and could not find any book projects for the first prize. Among other issues, the jury argued that textbooks under review were not merely the history of the Russian [velikorusskyi] nation any more. Yet other nations, which were enslaved by the tsarist monarchy and liberated by the great socialist revolution, still did not become the primary subjects of the written histories (K izucheniiu 1937, 37). After Shestakov's history, another history textbook, this time for secondary education, was prepared under the editorial of Anna Pankratova, a leading Russian Marxist historian. This volume was also somewhere in between the proletarian–internationalist and national romantic narrative, taking elements from each (Pankratova 1940). Although this history dragged the narrative from the Pokrovskiian line, it still could not satisfy everyone. According to the critiques, the role of individual rulers was not emphasized enough. The 'progressive acts' of Ivan the Terrible and Boris Godunov, such as their struggle for the centralization of the Russian state and fight against the boyars (Russian feudal landlords) had to be explained. Russian colonial and expansionist policies had to be watered down by showing an even greater colonial power: Britain. The heroic episodes of the Russian Army at the battlefields against Turkey and Iran had to be shown (Lebedev et al. 1941). Probably E. Tarle, another prominent old-school Russian historian, was closer to the nationalist end in his narrative of the Crimean War (Tarle 1941a).

The re-emergence of national themes and narratives started with the Russians. Publications referred to the Russian nation as 'great' and defined it as 'the first among equals'. Russian national identity was rehabilitated (Dubrovskii 2005, 60–72). Stalin redefined the concept of state and ideologically justified its existence

(Dubrovskii 2005, 72–82). The historical figures such as Peter the Great, Minin and Pozharskii, Kutuzov, and Suvorov reappeared in historical narratives (Dubrovskii 2005, 82–88). At the same time, this was a hand-picked list next to the 'revolutionary traditions' of the Russian nation. The progressive names of the modern era and repressive measures and colonial policies of the imperial period were also added to the picture. The best aspects of this constructed past, such as 'progress', 'high culture', 'patriotism', and 'revolutionary traditions' reached their zenith in the Soviet era. It was neither a Pokrovskiian narrative, blind to everything but class conflicts, nor a purely nationalist fantasy (Leont'ev and Mikhaikov 1938; Volin 1938a, 1938b).

The question is how far this turn to nationalistic discourse influenced the non-Russian republics. Previous scholarship on Soviet historiography was both limited in terms of access to archives in the Soviet Union and restricted to Moscow and Leningrad. Before the 'archival revolution' in the 1990s, scholars could glean from their research that a Russocentric narrative of Soviet historians falsified historical relations between Russians and non-Russians and could address non-Russian nations and their histories only to the extent of indicating this falsification. These researchers could comment authoritatively on the published histories, but they were not able to discuss the process of writing official histories behind the scenes (Karpovich 1943; Schlesinger 1950a, 1950b, 1950c, 1951a, 1951b; Powell 1951; Mazour and Bateman 1952; Tillett 1961, 1969). Lowell Tillet demonstrated how Russocentrist historiography changed the narrative of the historical relations between Russians and non-Russians. However, as he mentions in his fundamental work, he used merely secondary materials in Russian, available in the Library of Congress. That is why he and others could comment authoritatively on the published histories but could not depict the process and details of writing non-Russian national histories and the reasons behind particular decisions (Tillett 1969, viii–ix). Parallel to Tillet's work, broader studies on Soviet historiography have been produced by Cyrill Black, Anatole Mazour, Nancy Heer, and Konstantin Shteppa. These studies focused on the Soviet historiography of the Communist Party, the Russian Empire, or broad issues such as collectivization and the Great Terror, accompanied by particular attention to developments at the institutes in Moscow or Leningrad. Similar to Tillet, these authors also covered non-Russian nations and their histories, only to indicate how Soviet historians falsified the relations between these nations and the Russian Empire (Black 1962; Keep 1964; Mazour 1971 (in this seminal volume there is a long list of studies as footnotes that have been done on Azerbaijan, Ukraine and Georgia. However, these sources are predominantly from Moscow and not from the member republics; see pp. 102–104); Heer 1973).[23] In recent years, Yuri Slezkine and Victor Shnirelman have examined the issue of ethnogenesis. Their research explains how strategies of writing national history shifted in the 1930s, from the universalizing linguistic thesis of Nikolai Marr to an increasingly primordial ethno-centric formulation (Shnirelman 1995, 1996a, 1996b; Slezkine 1994). While these works are very helpful in exploring the increasing importance of ethnogenesis in Soviet national historiography, the issue has remained isolated from the broader project of Soviet construction of national histories. Since the Soviet archives became available, it has been much better understood that Russian national identity with its history and culture was promoted, and the Soviet policy on history writing was altered well before the Second World War. Historical figures who had been previously condemned as feudal exploiters were now praised as state-builders and heroic leaders (Dubrovsky 1998; Brandenberger 2002; Yekelchyk 2004). Recently, Ukrainian–Canadian and Ukrainian–American historians have published their meticulous works, in English, on the Ukrainian case (Yekelchyk 2004; Plokhy 2005a, 2006). There are also works in Russian, which cover the Soviet historiography, on the developments both in Moscow and Leningrad and in the republics. However, these works, until 1991, could not cover the whole story for political reasons. After 1991, there has been a tendency to present the picture as a struggle for writing national histories despite the Russian rule, which was disguised behind the Soviet mask (see for example, on the history of Soviet historiography, at all-Union level, Ocherki istorii istoricheskoi nauki 1966; Illeritskii and Kudriavtsev 1971; Alekseeva and Zheltova 1977; Ocherki istorii istoricheskoi nauki 1985, v; Burdei 1991. In Azerbaijan, Kazakhstan and Ukraine: Sumbatzade 1987; Dakhshleiger 1969; Rozvytok nauky v Ukraïns'kii 1957; Lenins'ka teoretychna spadshchyna 1969; Rozvytok istorychnoï nauky 1973; Santsevich and Komarenko 1986. After 1991: Kozybaev 1992; Balashov and Iurchenkov 1994; Afanasieva 1996; Alekseeva *et al.* 1997; Formozov 2004).

The above-mentioned English literature on the Soviet historiography puts emphasis on the re-emergence of Russian culture and history after 1936. It is true that Russian national history came back with its heroes and battlefields, and an all-Union history was constructed around the Russian Soviet national history. This is an accurate conclusion for the construction of Russian national narrative, as well as for the unifying narrative for the whole Soviet Union. The rehabilitation of Russian culture and the formulation of an all-Union history around a Russian narrative, supported by Moscow after 1934–6, should be considered only the first half of the story. This manuscript on the rise of national histories under Stalin aims to reveal the other half of the story – that is, the construction of national histories from the perspective of the union-republics.

## Notes

1 For example, Ivan the Terrible did not play a significant role in the organization of *oprichniki* (special police forces for mass repressions), because the struggle was not between individual men but between classes. He was the speaker of the exploiters of merchant capitalism, far from being an autocratic ruler feared by all his subordinates. This was also valid for the Peter the Great. See Pokrovskii 1933a, 44, 66–68.
2 A special collection of essays was printed to underline the change: Grekov 1939; Grekov 1940.
3 The periodization was according to the 'state principle'. The changes in the state structure, in state policy and legislation were put to the forefront, whereas the history of peoples or classes was downgraded to a secondary position. See: Ob itogakh diskusii 1951. This distinct change of the policy of writing history at an all-Union level is examined in other works. See Shteppa 1962, 187; Brandenberger 2002, 28–62.

18  *Introduction*

4 For the construction of a link between the ancient and modern 'rediscovery of the past' by intellectuals and historians, see Deletant and Hanak 1988.
5 For example, according to Bykovskii, Eastern Slavic tribes were Cimmerians (Bykovskii 1931); Marr claimed that Eastern Slavic Language was a descendant of Scythian and Sarmatian languages (Marr 1933). According to another Marrist, the descendants of Cimmerians were Scythians, the descendants of Scythians were Sarmatians and the descendants of the latter were Goths (Ravdonikas 1932).
6 Historians who defended theories of migration of peoples were accused of being racists and ideologists of imperialists (Ravdonikas 1931).
7 For example, it was the discovery and expansion of metallurgy that forced Japhetic languages to turn into Indo-European ones. For the theories of Marr, see Alpatov 1991; Slezkine 1996, 843; Shnirelman 1995. Härke claims that this immobilization covered only the Slavs. Other migrations were accepted (Härke 1998, 23).
8 N. P. Tret'iakov attempted to identify early Eastern Slavic archaeological monuments with the Slavic tribes mentioned by Nestor's Chronicle: Tret'iakov 1939; Artamonov 1939b, 1940.
9 Shteppa points to the following reasons for the change of the history writing: one-man rule (Stalin) demanded historical justification; the subjection of economy to political purposes required a reappraisal of base–superstructure relations in history; the victory of fascists in Germany raised an alternative nationalist narrative (Shteppa 1962, 131–132). Brandenberger counts three reasons for this change: state-building, legitimacy for the regime, and the need for a popular mobilization. Marxist tenets were too complicated for these tasks and a simple popular discourse was created (his Brandenberger 2002, 61). Erickson in his article counts the reasons as the emphasis on the construction of 'socialism in one country', and the threat posed to the Soviet security by the rise of fascism in Germany and Italy (Erickson 1960, 205).
10 An indigenous movement of reform and modernization among the Muslim peoples of Russia in the beginning of the twentieth century.
11 The employment of 'old specialist' Bernadskii as a member of the committee of historians to write a history textbook can be seen as one of the first such steps. GARF 2306–70–1886–30, April 2, 1933.
12 Report on the Academy of Sciences to the Politbiuro of the Central Committee CPSU, AP RF 3/33/142/7–10 (Winter 1936); The resolution of the Politbiuro of the Central Committee CPSU approving the return of E. V. Tarle to the Academy of Sciences: RGASPI 17/163/1191/163–166, April 25, 1938.
13 RGASPI 17–163–1097–35/37, February 2, 1936.
14 RGASPI 17–163–1013–4, March 5, 1934.
15 Arkhiv RAN 350–1-906–1/34, March 13, 1934.
16 The meeting of the Politburo: GRASPI 17–163–1017–60, March 29, 1934. The resolution of the Central Committee: RGASPI 17–163–1023–92, 96/98, May 15, 1934.
17 RGASPI 558–11–1076–102, 103, 132, 165/167, July 7, 1934; RGASPI 558–11–1076–9/22, July 7, 1935.
18 With the amendments of Stalin: RGASPI 558–1-3156–2/4, August 8, 1934. The degree of the Politburo Central Committee CPSU: RGSPI 17–163–1035–190, August 25, 1934. Published in *Pravda*, January 27, 1936.
19 RGASPI 17–163–1097–35/37, February 2, 1936.
20 RGASPI 558–1-3156–8, January 21–26, 1936; Published in *Pravda*, January 27, 1936.
21 There were also A. S. Shcherbakov, L. Z. Mekhlis, S. Kirov, and G. Malenkov (Dubrovskii 2005, 95–108).
22 Stalin's detailed amendments and comments in July 1937 can be seen in RGASPI 558–3-374; RGASPI 558–3-375; RGASPI 558–11–1584; RGASPI 558–11–1585.
23 Also a recent publication on the post-Stalin Soviet historiography; see Markwick 2001.

# 1 The construction of Azerbaijani identity under the shadow of Iran and Turkey

Until 1937, Soviet publications and official documents referred to the titular nation of the Azerbaijan Soviet Socialist Republic as *Tiurk* (Turkic) in Russian and *Türk* (Turkish and Turkic, as there are no separate words for these two concepts in Turkic tongues) in the local Turkic language. But as if a magic wand had touched the country in 1937, everyone began to define the titular nation as Azerbaijani. The current literature says that the term 'Turkic' (Russian: *Tiurskii*; Azerbaijani: *Türk*) was replaced by 'Azerbaijani' in the Stalinist years. However, when this change happened is not always clear. Some authors refer to the period from 1927 to 1931, when the first wave of purges occurred among the local modernist groups that joined the Bolsheviks following the 1917 Revolution, and claim that 'Stalinist policies' or 'Soviet repression of Muslim peoples' was responsible for this change (Wimbush 1979; Swietochowski 1994, 122). Others saw this change in identity definition as an effort to cut off the Turks of Turkey from their kin in the Soviet Union, and suggested that the Azerbaijani identity was artificially created as a result of the 'divide and rule' policy that was applied to all the Turkic nations in the Union (Altstadt 1992, 124; Leeuw 2000; Grenoble 2003, 124; Swietochowski 1993, 191–192; for a broader literature on the 'divide and rule' policy of the Soviet regime on Turkic peoples including Turkic Central Asia see Hayit 1963; Conquest 1970; Pipes 1997; Connor 1984, 1992; Carrere d'Encausse 1992; Simon 1991; Benningsen and Lemercier-Quelquejay 1961, 1967; Allworth 1990; Blank 1994; Hirsch 2000; Carrere d'Encausse 1989; Roy 2000). This approach implies that changing the definition of national identity was a calculated act on the part of Moscow and that the new policy was imposed upon Azerbaijan, and dutifully executed by Mir Jafar Bagirov, the first secretary of the CPA (Communist Party of Azerbaijan) and Stalin's henchman in Baku. Certainly, the new policy aimed to further differentiate Turkic identities in Anatolia and Azerbaijan. However, this argument alone does not explain why this change happened seventeen years after the Bolsheviks assumed power in Baku. The Great Terror, a state act which claimed the lives of millions in 1937 and 1938, was probably decisive in the timing of the change but it was not the cause of such an ideological and political transformation. This chapter explains the most crucial decision of the nation-building and history-writing in Soviet Azerbaijan. It is argued here that, contrary to the claims above, it was the international and domestic political developments between 1920 and 1937 that left the Bolsheviks without a choice but to alter the Turkic definition to the Azerbaijani one.

## A summary of the 1870–1920 period

At the end of the nineteenth century, national identities in the region were in flux and were not popular concepts. Yet, prior to Bolshevik rule, rival ideologies defined in different ways the Turkic-speaking majority which populated both historical Azerbaijan to the south of the Aras River and the Russian-ruled Baku and Elizavetpol *guberniias* in the north. The Russian colonial power had an ethno-linguistic definition in mind: 'Azerbaijani Tatars were erroneously called Persians. They were Shi'ite by denomination and imitated Persians in many ways, but their language is Turkic-Tatar' (Russian: *Tiurko-tatarskii*) (Baku 1891, 2a: 771). The official records of the Russian Empire and various published sources from the pre-1917 period also called them 'Tatar' or 'Caucasian Tatars', 'Azerbaijani Tatars' and even 'Persian Tatars' in order to differentiate them from the other 'Tatars' of the empire and the Persian speakers of Iran (Veidenbaum 1888; Svod 1893; Kovalevskii 1914, i). This was a result of a broader usage of Tatar in the Russian language as a generic name for all Turkic speakers. For the local people religious or regional identity came first and there was still a long way to go to transform peasants into a nation. For the Azerbaijani identity this was an age of ambiguities and discussions (Swietochowski 1994; Swietochowski 1995, 17–61). Mirza Fatali Akhundov (1812–78), a publicist, writer and intellectual in Tbilisi, who is claimed by both Azerbaijanis and Iranians as a nation-builder, defined his kinsmen as *Turki* but at the same time considered Iran as his fatherland (Swietochowski 1995, 28). When the first signs of modern national identity construction surfaced, the different definitions and tendencies also became clear cut. For example, Həsən bəy Zərdabi (or Hasan bey Zardabi, 1837–1907), a science teacher and graduate of the Moscow University, and his newspaper *Əkinçi* (Akinchi, 1875–7) raised the issue of Turkic identity, which was still an idea of a minority. Following him, a new generation promoted a Turkic identity. Əli bəy Hüseyzadə (or Ali bey Huseynzade, 1864–1940) and his publication *Həyat*, for instance, defined Azerbaijanis as Turks. Three consecutive events – the 1905 Russian Revolution and the following ethno-religious clashes with Armenians; the Iranian Constitutional Revolution in 1906 and its demise; and the 1908 Young Turk Revolution, which brought Turkists to power in the Ottoman Empire – increased Turkic national sentiments in Azerbaijan. Turkism in Azerbaijan emphasized its Turkic origins. The question was how to define this newly found Turkicness in relation to the Ottoman Turks? Əli bəy Hüseyzadə in his other leading literary journal *Füyuzat* (1906) defined both the Turkic population of the Ottoman Empire and in Azerbaijan as descendants of the Oghuz Turks, and he claimed that the difference between the two peoples were of minor significance. He called for some kind of unification with the Ottoman–Turkish realm. Publications such as *Açıq Söz* (1915–18), edited by

Məhəmməd Əmin Rəsulzadə (Mammad Amin Rasulzade, 1884–1955), also supported this Turkish cause. By contrast, writers in *Azərijilar* and other intellectuals such as Cəlil Məmmədquluzadə (or Jalil Mammadguluzadeh, 1886–1932) and his periodical *Molla Nasraddin* (*Molla Nasr al-Din*) argued that following its recent 'recovery' following Persian domination, the Azerbaijani identity had to flourish separately from the Ottomans. At the same time, there were some Iranian Azerbaijanis in Baku who were against this Turkish ethno-linguistic identity. They published *Azarbayjan, Joz'-e la-yanfakk-e Iran* which promoted a Persian territorial identity in Baku. At this stage, the Iranian identity still had a dynastic definition, and a non-Persian speaker could be easily part of this all-Persian identity (Atabaki 2006).

On May 27, 1918, the Democratic Republic of Azerbaijan (DRA) was declared with Ottoman military support. The rulers of the DRA refused to identify themselves as Tatar, which they rightly considered to be a Russian colonial definition. Instead, they defined the Turkic-speaking Muslim people of the south-east Caucasus as Turkic. In their native tongue they were *Azerbaijani Türk* or simply *Türk*, but with a broader meaning of the word. We understand the usage of this broader meaning from Russian texts of the same period where *Tiurk* or *Tiurkskii* (Turkic) was used. Officials of the DRA also frequently used 'Muslim' to identify the same group because the majority of the population still identified themselves by religion. Neighbouring Iran did not welcome the DRA's adoption of the name of 'Azerbaijan' for the country because it could also refer to Iranian Azerbaijan and implied a territorial claim. That is why the authorities in Baku also used these definitions with the adjective of 'Transcaucasian' (Russian: *Zakavkazskii*) (Stavrovskii 1920; for the minutes of the parliament in the Azerbaijani language see *Azərbaycan Xalg* 1998; for the minutes of the parliament in the Russian language see *Azerbaidzhanskaia Demokraticheskaia* 1998; Pashaev 2006). All these contradictory steps in the region were natural when Turks, Iranians and Azerbaijanis were all in search of national identities. The following two decades became an era of state-sponsored constructions of national identities. Once nation-states were established and started to operate, they consciously promoted their own brand of nationalism, while fighting against other conflicting descriptions.

In April 1920, when the Red Army entered Baku, the Bolsheviks followed the designation of the previous nationalist government and accepted *Türk* in the native tongue and *Tiurk* in Russian as the name for the titular nation. Azerbaijan was kept as the name of the territory and the republic. What were the consecutive developments that induced the Bolsheviks to replace this Turkic definition by an Azerbaijani definition seventeen years later? The following sections of this chapter aim to explain the multiple factors that forced the Bolsheviks to take this extraordinary step in 1937.

## Relations with neighbours

In the 1920s, the Soviet regime considered Azerbaijan a model of modernization and development that could be presented to the peoples of Iran and Turkey. If

Ukraine was the Soviet Piedmont on its western borders (Martin 2001), Azerbaijan played the same role on the southern frontier. Hence, before their fatal journey to Turkey in 1920, the founding leaders of the Turkish Communist Party were based in Baku. Also, when the Bolsheviks decided to summon 1,800 delegates from the colonial and semi-colonial parts of Asia for the Congress of the Peoples of the East in September 1920, Baku was the natural choice for the convention. When the First Turkology Congress was organized by Soviet authorities in 1926, the venue was again Baku (*Vsesoiuznyi Tiurkologicheskii s'ezd* 1926; Lenczowski 1949, 6–8). As long as steady modernization steps were being taken in Baku, Azerbaijani Bolsheviks felt comfortable comparing their achievements with the situation in Turkey and Iran (for the presentation of the commissar of the Narkompros AzSSR, M. Z. Kuliev, at the sixth congress of All Azerbaijan Soviets, on the tasks of cultural construction in the Republic, April 6, 1929 see VI-oi Vseazerbaidzhanskii sezd' sovetov 1929; *Azerbaidzhanskii gosudarstvennyi universitet* 1930; Bagirov 1934). Despite these comparisons, which aimed at demonstrating the desirability of the Soviet model of development to its neighbours, the first fifteen years of Soviet–Turkish and Soviet–Iranian relations were extremely positive (Rubinshtein 1982, 4–7). Turkey and the Soviet Union supported each other on different platforms. In order to improve relations, Soviet representatives including leading names from the arts and sciences visited Turkey, including composer Dmitrii Shostakovich (1906–75), Turkologist and linguist Aleksandr Samoilovich (1880–1938), linguist, historian, and orientalist Nikolai Marr (1865–1934), linguist and archaeologist Ivan Meshchaninov (1883–1967), Turkologist and historian Hadzhi Gabidullin (1897–1937), and also military figure Kliment Voroshilov (1881–1969), as well as various engineering brigades for construction works (Shostakovich 1995, 112–113; Aydoğan, 2007; Tahirova 2010).[1]

In 1934, the first signs of a changed policy came when Moscow sent Levon Mikhailovich Karakhanian (1889–1937) as the plenipotentiary Soviet representative to Ankara (an older account of the relations argues that they deteriorated in 1938–9; see Rubinshtein, 1982. However, the recent account of Dzhamil Gasanly (Cemil Hasanli), supported by primary sources, provides a more accurate view; see Gasanly 2008, 11, 12, 17). This decision was considered by the Turkish government as a signal that Soviet–Turkish relations were deteriorating. Apart from his ethnic Armenian origin and abrasive style, Karakhanian had been the secretary of the Soviet delegation at Brest-Litovsk in 1918 and had left a bad impression among Ottoman diplomats who had participated in the peace negotiations (Karakhanian remained in Ankara until 1937: Banac 2003, 54–55; Gasanly 2008, 20). At the same time, in anticipation of a military confrontation in Europe, Stalin began to consider an alliance with Turkey as an unnecessary liability (Banac 2003, 18). In Turkish foreign policy, the Soviet Union also lost its primary position after the Turkish state was admitted to the League of Nations in 1932 (Harris 1995, 3–6). In the following three years, and for a number of reasons, the gulf between Turkey and the Soviet Union only increased (Gasanly 2008, 22–49). The culmination of this new distrust between the two countries was reflected in the speech given by the first secretary of the CPA at the famous February–March plenum of the CPSU, in 1937. Bagirov claimed in his speech that Turkey supported the independence of the Turkic nations in the Soviet Union and that Ankara was trying to form a pan-Turkish state led by Turkey. It is quite clear that without the consent of Stalin, the first secretary of the CPA, Bagirov, could not have expressed these ideas at the plenum (for the speech of Bagirov see Materialy fevral'sko-martovskogo (1937g.) Plenuma 1994, 26). Finally, it should be noted that he gave this speech during the Great Terror in 1937–8 when thousands of Soviet citizens were prosecuted and shot as pan-Turkists or as the secret agents of Turkey.

Relations between the Soviet Union and Iran were not faring any better. In the 1920s Iran's primary foreign policy objective was the loosening of the economic grip of foreign powers, and in particular the dislodging of Britain from its dominant economic position in the country. To this end, from 1926 until 1932, Abdolhossein Teymuourtash, the powerful Minister of the Court of the Pahlavi Dynasty, orchestrated a foreign policy that sought to simultaneously improve economic ties with the Soviet Union, Germany, and the United States. From 1927, Iran slowly began to show increasing receptiveness to Germany's economic expansion and ties gradually intensified between the two countries. So long as there existed no serious political tensions between the Weimar Republic and the Soviet Union, the Soviet regime was not hostile to an increased German economic influence in Iran. From the Soviet perspective, the German factor could even be seen in a positive light as Germany could successfully compete with the British in the region. However, when the Nazis came to power, the Soviet attitude towards German activities in Iran changed. After 1933 Reza Shah pursued closer relations with Germany, inviting German experts and investments in order to break Soviet and British dominance (Lenczowski 1949, 151–158; Ramazani 1966, 277–288; Rezun 1981, 314–332; Rubinshtein 1982, 62). In the second half of the 1930s, there was a rapidly increasing fear in Moscow that a German-led crusade against the Soviet Union in the western borders was imminent. The Soviet Union considered heavy German investments in Iran and the growth of diplomatic traffic between the two countries as signs of an Iranian subjection to a fascist influence and even as encirclement. Nevertheless, as a result of economic interests Iran preferred Germany to the Soviet Union and the Iranians responded more and more negatively to the Soviet Union, bolstered in their stance by their strong relations with Nazi Germany (Ramazani 1966, 216–228; Volodarsky 1994, 100–120). As a result of this increasing tension between the Soviet Union and Iran, in mid-1938 all Iranian subjects were expelled from the Soviet Union. Parallel to the increasing rift between the Soviet Union and its southern neighbours, Turkey and Iran came closer. Perhaps as a consequence of this, Reza Shah made his only state visit during his reign to Turkey in 1934. Finally, in 1937, the Sadabad Pact, a non-aggression pact, was signed by Turkey, Iran, Iraq and Afghanistan.

The Soviet Union's souring relations with Turkey and Iran turned Azerbaijan from a showcase into a bulwark in the Middle East. Obviously, this change in the Soviet perception of Azerbaijan in the foreign policy arena cannot be the sole explanation for the dramatic change from a Turkic to an Azerbaijani identity. Additionally, nation-building policies in Turkey and Iran, which had ethnolinguistic and religious links and cultural proximity with Azerbaijan, should also be counted as important factors.

## Construction of homogeneous national identities in Turkey and Iran

Following the Ottoman defeat in the First World War and the fall of the empire, the Republic of Turkey rejected pan-Turkist ideas (Atatürk 1991, 251; 1995, 428–429; 1997, 216; *Gazi Mustafa*, 1996, 29; Poulton 1997, 92–94). In the 1930s the policy against the pan-Turkists continued and burgeoning pan-Turkist groups and publications were banned one after another (Landau 1995, 74–79; Önen 2005, 246–274.) A 'Turkey' nation-state (Turkish: *Türkiye*) was founded upon the principle that it was the only contemporary homeland of Turks (Poulton 1997, 112; Atabaki 2002, 219–236). In the 1930s, the republic became increasingly active in constructing a uniform Turkish national identity and culture across the whole of society (Ahmad 1993, 52–66, 76–90; Cağaptay 2006; Lewis 2002, 239–293, 323–361; Winter 1984; Zürcher 1997, 170–202; Arat 2010, 38–51; Bozdoğan 2001). However, the construction of Turkish national identity in Turkey posed problems for Azerbaijani Turkic identity. Both in Turkey and in Azerbaijan people were defined in their native tongues as *Türk*. In Azerbaijan this word was used as the equivalent of *Tiurk* in Russian, in other words with its broader meaning akin to Slavic, Germanic, etc. The usage of *Türk*, now possessing a narrow meaning, as the name of the titular nation of Turkey, made it complicated to also use in this broader meaning, as this would imply their belongingness to Turkey rather than to 'Turkicness'. Akin to Kazakhs or Uzbeks, if Azerbaijanis were Turkic speakers but did not belong to the Turkish identity of Turkey, the term *Türk* was rather a confusing definition. We can also find this concern in a report written by Zifel'dt-Simumiagi (1889–1939), an Estonian and a leading linguist and historian in Azerbaijan and in the Soviet Union, on the national identity problem of Azerbaijan. In his report written for the school and science section of the Central Committee of the CPA in the summer of 1937 in Baku, Zifel'dt-Simumiagi demonstrates that he was well aware of the recent nation-building policies in Turkey:

> In the old Turkey of sultans, the term '*türk*' was interpreted as 'uncultivated', 'redneck', 'yokel'; the opposed term '*osmanli*' was proclaimed proudly. The alteration of the Turkish identity, which was related to the overthrow of the caliphate-sultanate, the declaration of the republic, [and to] the consolidation of Balkano-Anatolian Turks into a nation (1908–1920) was accompanied by the refusal of the name of the dynastic past '*osmanli*' and legitimization of '*türk*' as a national name. That is why we henceforth have to name only Balkano-Anatolian Turks as *türk*, keep the term 'Ottomans' only to name

*The construction of Azerbaijani identity* 25

Turks in the epoch of the caliphate before the revolution, but 'osmanists' can be used only by those who try to depersonalize the Azerbaijani (or other) nation or its language, subjugate them to the old or new Turkish norms, which are alien to [Azerbaijanis].[2]

It is very likely that Mir Jafar Bagirov, the first secretary of the CPA, also read this report on such an important issue and the national identity was discussed in the inner circle of the CPA.

A possible solution would have been to remove the ethno-linguistic term *Türk* and Turkicness from the definition of 'Azerbaijani' identity. However, removing the Turkic element could turn the population into easy prey for the Iranian national identity that was already being promoted by Tehran at the time. As the transformation of 'Turkishness' in the 1930s into a national identity of a nation-state in Turkey produced an identity issue for the Azerbaijani Turkic population, the nation-building of Reza Shah also did so in Iran. After defeating the tribal uprisings and separatist movements, Reza Shah asserted central government control and re-established the territorial unity of Iran. This centralization and nation-building programme had to be accompanied by political discourse and cultural projects. To ensure territorial unity, the state attempted to bridge the differences among numerous identities through the homogenization of national culture. This attempt centred on achieving geographical unity through a shared understanding of patriotism, history, and mythology as well as through the dominance of the Persian language. National history and identity were constructed around the Persian language and Iranian history. While Hasan Pirnia, an old politician and a historian, wrote the three-volume *History of Ancient Iran* based on the superiority of Aryans, neo-Achaemenian architecture was used in public buildings. The leading officials and scholars genuinely believed in the Aryan superiority of the Iranian nation, and engineered a past by writing nationalist history as well as designing a vivid national spatial sense through architecture (Banani 1961; Cottam 1979, 23–205; Katouzian 1979; Clawson 1993; Ehlers and Floor 1993; Faghoory 1993; Matthee 1993; Chehabi 1993, 223; Vaziri 1993; Fisher and Ochseneald 1997, 414–418; Kashani-Sabet 1999, 180–216; Chehabi 1999; Atabaki 2000, 54–61; Cronin 2003; Grigor 2004; Marashi 2008, 86–133; Katouzian 2009, 200–228; Ansari 2012; Afra 1964, 114–143, 166–186; Trapper 1983; Amanolahi 2002; Abdi 2001; Grigor 2004; Atabaki 2009, 74; Safamanesh 2009). In the following years, nation-building policy was only accelerated. In 1934–5, the international usage of the country's name was changed from 'Persia' to 'Iran'. Iran was defined as the land of Aryans, the common ancestors of all contemporary Iranians. A temporal link among dynasties and a spatial link among geographies were constructed through the Persian language.

The nation-building policy in Iran was important for Azerbaijan because historical Azerbaijan, and the majority of Azerbaijani people, lived within the borders of Iran. For numerous reasons, historical Azerbaijan that was south of the Aras River was an inseparable part of the new Iranian national identity and history. In the medieval period, the historical Azerbaijani region was at the centre of Turco-Iranian states. Tabriz, the major city of the region, was the capital of Iranian states. Being a bulwark against the invading Ottoman and Russian armies also consolidated historical Azerbaijan's place within the imaginary borders of Iran. The region was the most receptive part of the country to the reforms and revolutions that took place in the neighbouring countries between 1890 and 1905, and it also became the stronghold of the Iranian constitutional revolution in 1906 (Atabaki 2001, 65–77). Thus, the success of the Iranian nation-building programme in the Azerbaijani region was particularly important. According to the official line, all Iranians were of one race (Aryan) and the Turkic speakers in Azerbaijan were also part of this Aryan family. However, they had been Turkified during an unfortunate period of history. Ahmad Kasravi (1890–1946) was a leading ideologist who articulated this Iranian theory of Azerbaijani identity. Kasravi, a Turkic-speaking native of the Azerbaijan province of Iran, was a linguist, historian and reformer. In his political views, he supported the modernization of Iran and the reformation and simplification of Persian language. He also embraced the construction of an Iranian nation-state by aiming to purify the Persian language from Arabic, Western and Turkic words. He was very conscious of the significance of a national language and its relation to a unified nation-state, which is why Persia had utmost importance for him as a unifying language of all Iran. According to Kasravi, the original language of Azerbaijan was a local Iranian language, *Azari*, which was related to Persian. This language nearly disappeared following the Turkification of the region, though remnants continued to exist in Khalkhal, Iran (for Kasravi and his ideas see Fathi 1986, 172; Swietochowski 1995, 121–122; Swietochowski and Collins 1999, 73; Vaziri 1993, 159–160; for the Azari languge, see Atabaki 2000, 7–10).

Before moving to the domestic factors in the Soviet Union, the adoration of Germany by certain circles in Turkey and especially in Iran should also be mentioned. In the first few decades of the twentieth century, both Turkey and Iran experienced foreign interventions, and the destruction and chaos of consecutive wars and domestic conflicts. There was a strong desire for centralization, stability and reform. Moreover, numerous officials and members of the intelligentsia in Turkey and Iran were fascinated by the fascist regimes in Germany and Italy and also Japan, admiring them for their unity, independence, and nationalist dynamism. The democracies of Britain and France, on the contrary, were seen as internally decadent and the archaic imperial enemies of national independence of Iran and Turkey (for Iranians, see Cronin 1999, 9). When the Nordic–Aryan racial theories gained ground in Europe and consequently became the official ideology of Nazi Germany, they added fuel to the clear references to the Aryan race in Iran. In the second half of the 1930s, Iranian–German relations improved not only in the economic sphere but also on the basis of a reference to common ancestors in prehistory (Lenczowski 1949, 158–162; Rezun 1981, 319, 333).

## Domestic dynamics

Domestic factors in the Soviet Union also played an important role in driving the change from a Turkic to an Azerbaijani identity. The writing of Soviet prehistory in the 1920s was under the influence of Nikolai Marr. In the 1930s, the strategies of writing national history shifted from the universalizing linguistic thesis of Marr to an increasingly primordial ethno-centric formulation. The search for the ethnic roots of nations was added to the task of prehistoric studies. Historians, archaeologists and ethnographers had to demonstrate that the contemporary inhabitants of each republic were descendants of the autochthonous people of those lands. Another important change in history writing in the Soviet Union was the denunciation of the Pokrovskiian school of historiography. From 1934 on, the priorities and concepts of the Pokrovskiian era were removed from the discipline of history.[3] A new linear trajectory of history followed the formation of national identities from antiquity until Stalin's 1936 constitution. The new national histories were closer to romantic narratives than to Marxist historiography. They had to define the ancient roots of nations, their golden ages and national heroes in antiquity (see the details in the introduction). These were all-Union policies that had an impact on every republic, including Azerbaijan, to varying degrees. Səməd Vurğun (1906–56), the famous Azerbaijani poet, also found himself in this spirit of the day when he protested the lack of an ancient Azerbaijani national history in 1936 in these verses: 'Let historians be blushed with shame!/Our history has not been written,/Had we been created without a history?' (Vurğun 2005h [1936], 238).

While contemporary linguistic evidence could be used to suggest the construction of national history and to explain the ethnogenesis of the titular nation of Azerbaijan on the basis of a Turkic identity, a Turkic identity would create more problems than it could solve. As in the national histories of other Turkic-speaking peoples, a Turkic identity posed a dilemma for Azerbaijani national history because the final Turkification of the territory happened between the eleventh and thirteenth centuries, which meant a non-indigenous origin of the people.[4] Russian historian Shnirelman summarizes this problem of Turkic peoples on the basis of Tatar-Chuvash history:

> A confirmed autochthonous origin serves as a basis for claims to territory, and a language with ancient roots encourages a feeling of pride in one's culture, since language is closely associated with culture in the minds of most people.... The Turkic languages were not of local origin but had come to the Volga region from elsewhere. Thus a choice had to be made: either an autochthonous origin and a language shift [to Turkic at some point in history] or an original Turkic language and a nonindigenous origin.
> (Shnirelman 1996a, 25–26)

In other words, Turkic ethnogenesis could provide a legitimate claim for the contemporary territory only after the eleventh century. For this reason, an emphasis on the Turkic roots could seriously hamper the primordial claims of the republic's titular nation to the same territory.

This brings us to a regional factor that turned the national claims concerning prehistoric and ancient times into a crucial issue. Complying with the new Soviet policy of national history writing, Georgia and Armenia, the other titular nations of the Transcaucasia, were also in the process of constructing their national narratives. Although the ancient Armenian speaking population arrived in today's Armenia from the Balkans in the middle of the second millennium BC (Russell 1997; Russell 2005) they had a comfortable position. As opposed to the Azerbaijani Turkic case, Georgians and Armenians could easily link their contemporary national identities with the peoples of ancient Iberia or Urartu respectively because both had long recorded pasts that had legends and historical events such as catastrophes and victories. Additionally, the absence of continuous secular polities and royal courts in Georgia and Armenia was filled by a tradition of chronicling within religious institutions that dated back to the fifth century (Suny 2001, 884). These particularities of Armenia and Georgia created disequilibrium in Transcaucasia that could have serious political implications. While the Turkic nation of Azerbaijan seemed to have appeared in the eleventh century as a latecomer or even as an occupier of the region, its two neighbours could pride themselves on being autochthonous inhabitants of the land. In the first two decades of the twentieth century, Transcaucasia experienced consecutive ethnic and religious clashes that resulted in ethnic cleansing, and deportations (Price 1918; Levine 2004 [1919]; Shklovsky and Sheldon 1968; Altstadt 1992, 39–44). After the establishment of Bolshevik rule, the region was in the process of reconciliation. The bloody memories of the recent past were quite fresh in people's minds. By presenting one side as latecomer-occupants and the other as ancient settlers, burgeoning national histories could provide a pretext for further ethnic tensions or territorial claims. For the Bolsheviks, this was the least desirable situation. They had to establish a balance among the identities and maintain peace in the region in order to implement their modernist projects. Indeed, various Bolshevik leaders, such as Stalin, Molotov, and Beriia, emphasized the importance of stability and inter-ethnic peace in the region. They underlined that the brotherhood of three nations (Azerbaijanis, Armenians, and Georgians) was an essential condition for the development of the region (Stalin 1934, 117; 1953a, 5: 97–98; Molotov 1936; Beriia 1934, 1936a, 1936b, 1937). The ethnogenesis and ancient history of the Turkic-speaking people of Azerbaijan had to be constructed in a way that would allow them to claim that they were indigenous alongside Armenians and Georgians. In order to connect Azerbaijani identity with prehistoric archaeological cultures in the Azerbaijani SSR, the Turkic ethno-linguistic identity had to be removed from the narrative.

It is not surprising then that until the Great Terror of 1937–8 there was no consensus on the ethnogenesis of the Turkic-speaking majority in Azerbaijan. Until the purges two approaches co-existed in academic circles. On the one hand, there was a group of scholars who supported a single ethno-linguistic interpretation of national history that insisted on a continuity based on the Turkic language. They accepted the thesis that their ancestors were relatively late settlers in Azerbaijan. These scholars argued that during the Turkification of the contemporary territories of the Azerbaijani SSR in the eleventh to thirteenth centuries, the influx of Turkic nomadic tribes was so high that these people quickly constituted a majority and established cultural dominance. For these historians, the roots of Azerbaijanis had to be traced to their Turkic past. Therefore, it was the Seljuk Empire that was singled out as the precursor polity of the Turkic people in Azerbaijan. The prominent historians and linguists of this group were Gubaidullin (1887–1937), Choban-zade (1893–1937) and Khuluflu (1894–1937) (for their views see Khuluflu 1930; Choban-zade 1926, 96–101; 1936; Gubaidullin 1994 [1924], 21–22; 1926, 39–57). We should note that all three leading figures were experts in the history or literature of Turkic nations.[5] They felt that this pro-Turkic approach could be a solution to the question of identity, given the contemporary Turkic linguistic identity.

However, Turkey's policies in the 1930s posed additional problems for the pro-Turkic national historiography of Azerbaijan. Although the government in Ankara did not support pan-Turkists, the nation-building policy of Turkey transformed the term *Türk* into a particular national identity and incorporated many figures and events of the past into the national narrative, including the Seljuks. If the national history of the Azerbaijani Turkic people was based on a Turkic past, Azerbaijani history could be reduced to merely an episode or a branch of the new Ankara-produced Turkish narrative. Following the crisis in Ukraine in 1932, any hint of shared identity by a cross-border national narrative was undesirable for a Soviet state (Martin 2001). Moreover, Soviet leaders assumed that a diaspora nationality could not be 're-invented' as a Soviet nation, because other states could have control over the histories and traditions that shaped the national consciousness (Hirsch 2002, 38).

Until 1937, another group of scholars co-existed next to the pro-Turkic group. These scholars refused Iranian or Turkic heritage and stressed the indigenous nature of the people based on territorially defined identity. These scholars based their approach on the theories of Nikolai Marr. They did not explain the ethnogenesis of the Azerbaijani nation by a common or predominant ethnicity. They considered the contemporary population to be an amalgamation of different ethnicities and cultures within territorial borders. They accepted the fact of a language shift but rejected the link to a Turkic legacy. Artur Zifel'dt-Simumiagi and Gulam Bagirov were members of this second group (Zifel'dt-Simumiagi 1926, 1927, 1930, 1936; Bagirov 1936).[6] Each group produced and published its own narrative. For example, in the history section of the article 'Azerbaijan' in the *Bol'shaia Sovetskaia Entsiklopedia* (the Great Soviet Encyclopaedia), which was produced by the second group, there is not a single word about Turkic dynastic states such as the Seljuks or the Iranic polities (Shmidt *et al.* 1926).

We can also find the argument of the second group of historians in Zifel'dt-Simumiagi's report, which I mentioned earlier. The report criticized the pro-Turkic thesis of the first group of historians by arguing that

[They] Turkified, Ottomanified, pan-Turkified Azerbaijani literature, grammar, terminology and orthography (at the behest of Rukh[ulla] Akhundov, Grinich, Khuluflu, Eminbeili and Co.). Choban-zade, in his work *Türk Grameri* went, shamelessly so far that he named all real Turkic-Tatar languages, including Azerbaijani language, not even as a 'dialect' but only 'accents' of some kind of a united Turkic language. The school of Chobanzade had something in common with classification of Prof. Köprülüzade of Istanbul and (until the last year) of A. N. Samoilovich in Leningrad.[7]

It is important to note that Choban-zade defined 'Azeri' as a dialect of a greater 'Turkic-Tatar language' among 'Kazak-kırgız, Karachay, Osmanlı (Anadolı)' dialects. According to Choban-zade, the complete crystallization of Azeri dialect separate from other Turkic branches can be first seen in the works of Molla Pənah Vagif (1717–97) (Chobanzade and Agazade 1929, 7–13).

Zifel'dt-Simumiagi also considered that referring to the Azerbaijanis as *Türk* (Turkic/Turk) in their native tongue would not be the right thing any more since *Türk* represented the national identity which was being constructed within the nation-state of Turkey. Furthermore, he criticized a similar approach that prevailed in the discipline of history:

> In recent years, B. Choban-zade advocated the 'theory' that all Azerbaijanis are direct descendants of those Seljuks who allegedly settled in large numbers in Azerbaijan at the end of the eleventh century. However, it is also believed that the Ottomans came out of the same womb as the Seljuks. So this theory seems to emphasize the 'historical foundations' of the fraternity of Azerbaijanis and the Ottomans in blood.[8]

According to Zifel'dt-Simumiagi, however, there was no ethnic connection between Azerbaijanis and Turks of Turkey because

> It is clear to everyone that the Ottomans were a mixture of Albanian [of the Balkans]–Slavic–Greek–Armenian–Laz–Kurdish–Assyrian and also Circassians, [while] Azerbaijanis were a mixture of Japhetic–Armenian–Iranian–Arabic.[9]

In other words, the Turkic element was insignificant in both cases and the ethnic make-up of the Turkic speakers of the Ottoman Empire (and contemporary Turks of Turkey) and the Turkic speakers of Azerbaijan was completely different. Under these conditions, to claim brotherhood was very difficult. Zifel'dt-Simumiagi further explained why the impact of the Seljuks was minimal in Azerbaijan and concluded that 'the role of 'Seljuks' [and] their various tribal mixtures come very close to zero in the Turkification of Azerbaijan'.[10] Considering the change of the meaning of *Türk* from a general ethno-linguistic term to a national identity in Turkey, Zifel'dt-Simumiagi suggested a de-Turkified Azerbaijani identity.

Though this de-Turkified Azerbaijani identity became official after 1937 and remained in place until the end of the Soviet Union, Zifel'dt-Simumiagi never witnessed it. At the end of 1936, parallel to the developments at all-Union level, Bagirov launched a campaign against the cadres in the higher institutions.[11] The initial wave purged the pro-Turkic group. On December 17, 1936, Rukhulla Akhundov, one of the chief ideologists of the CPA, the former secretary of the CPA and the vice-chairman of the AzFAN (Azerbaijani branch of the Academy of Sciences), was arrested in front of his house.[12] On January 4, 1937, the commissar of Narkompros AzSSR (the People's Commissariat of Enlightenment of Azerbaijan SSR), Shakhbazov, and his deputy Gasanov were removed from their posts and the latter was accused of being a former Musavvatist.[13] Within a single meeting of the Bureau of the Central Committee of the CPA, local historians V. Khuluflu and A. S. Bukshpan, who worked at the AzFAN and the API (Azerbaijan Pedagogical Institute), the director of the Azerbaijan State University, and chief of the AzGlavlit (Azerbaijani State Publishing House) Eminbeili were all dismissed from the CPA and removed from their posts. According to the customs of the day, they were accused of being counter-revolutionaries, Trotskyites, and nationalists.[14] On the same day that Bagirov launched these purges, a special detachment of the AzNKVD (the Azerbaijani branch of the Secret Police) arrived in Kislovodsk in order to arrest B. V. Choban-zade, the prominent Crimean Tatar linguist of Turkic languages who had worked in Baku since 1924 (Ashnin and Alpatov 1998, 127). On the night of March 18, 1937, Gubaidullin was also arrested in Baku. He was accused of organizing an anti-Soviet uprising, being a spy of Turkey, Germany, and Japan, and finally, of being a pan-Turkist (Ashnin et al. 2002, 88–93).

By the autumn of 1937, the Great Terror in Azerbaijan had removed the first group of historians who were Turkic by ethnic origin and proponents of a Turkic ethno-linguistic explanation. In 1938 some of the internationalist-Marrists, such as Gulam Bagirov and Zifel'dt-Simumiagi, were also arrested and, in a bitter irony, accused of being part of a pan-Turkist conspiracy against the Soviet regime. After their long interrogation, in 1939 both Gulam Bagirov and Zifel'dt-Simumiagi were sent to the notorious labour camps in Kolyma, Siberia. Zifel'dt-Simumiagi died there in the same year (Ashnin et al. 2002, 110–119, 125–130). When the carnage came to an end in 1938, there were no experienced historians left in Baku. It should be noted that the majority of victims were indigenous Turkic intellectuals whose intellectually most formative period was before the Revolution, and who aimed to construct a national history based on Turkic ethno-linguistic ancestors. Baku, an important centre of Turkology before 1937, was deprived of Turkologists.

## A new ethnogenesis for a new narrative

The first official attempt at building a national history in Azerbaijan was commenced by Mir Jafar Bagirov, the first secretary of the CPA before the Great Terror and the purges. Following the resolution of the CPSU on January 27, 1936 that organized the Zhdanov commission to write an all-Union history, on March 15, 1936, Mir Jafar Bagirov assigned an editing commission in Baku to write a history of the Azerbaijani nation of the Soviet Union. All prominent historians of the Republic – such as A. S. Bukshpan, Veli Khuluflu, Gaziz Gubaidullin, Zifel'dt-Simumiagi, and Pakhomov – were invited to join the editing commission.[15] The chair of the commission, Rukhulla Akhundov, had to identify the task of each member and distribute the burden of the creation of a national history. He was also charged with presenting the results of the work for the overview of the Central Committee of the CPA on May 15, 1936.[16]

The team in Baku wrote their contribution in a clear Pokrovskiian manner, most probably because they were not clearly informed as to how far Moscow had moved away from the Marxist writings of Pokrovskii towards a national narrative, and the last thing they wanted was to be stigmatized as nationalists or pan-Turkists. As planned, Bagirov received the draft of the national history from the commission. After examining it in June 1936, he instructed R. Akhundov and Usein Rakhmanov, the chair of the SovNarKom AzSSR (Council of Peoples' Commissars of the Azerbaijan Soviet Socialist Republic), to duplicate the material and distribute it among the members of the Central Committee of the CPA so that the text could be examined and discussed at the following session of the Central Committee.[17] The draft of the official national history had to be kept secret until receiving absolute sanction of the CPA. That is why Rakhmanov prepared only thirteen copies and sent them to the Central Committee.[18] Thus, only seven historians and thirteen Central Committee members knew the 'true' history of Azerbaijan. The Central Committee of the CPA discussed the draft history and approved it in August 1936 with minor amendments.[19] Finally, the materials on the history of the people of Azerbaijan were sent to Zhdanov in Moscow.[20]

This national history that was prepared in 1936 was never printed and, as I have explained above, nearly all its authors perished in the Great Terror. However, the project of writing national histories and the emphasis on ancient and prehistoric times raised the question of the ethnogenesis of the Azerbaijani people. Following the Great Terror, a new team continued to work on the construction of a national history in Baku. These new authors were not authorities on either Turkic or Caucasian history. They were a bunch of young graduates, party activists, and *vydvizhentsy*.[21] This was an age of opportunity for energetic and ambitious people, particularly those with 'good' working class or peasant social origins. It was the government policy to 'promote' young workers and peasants into higher education (Fitzpatrick 2000). The authors belonged to this upwardly mobile category, filling the vacancies following the Great Terror. Although they were not as experienced and competent as the ones purged in 1937–8, these *vydvizhentsy* were eager to learn on the job.

The first draft of this national history was prepared by three editors, and 100 copies were printed in 1939 for the historians and party *apparatchiks* responsible for constructing a national history of Azerbaijan (Dzhafarzade *et al.* 1939). The draft clearly defined people living in Soviet Azerbaijan as an autochthonous ethnic mixture that had been Turkified in the later stages of history. Following the Marrist approach, the text claimed that Azerbaijani tribes shared a similar language with Armenian, Georgian, and Dagestani tribes because they were all at a similar stage of economic and social development. In time, differentiation among them increased. Thus, there was no connection between the contemporary Azerbaijani nation and the rest of the Turkic peoples. Although the region was ruled by states that had been based in the Persian-speaking Iranian plateau for millennia, and the Azerbaijani population still included Iranian speakers such as Talysh and Tats, the Azerbaijani ethnogenesis did not contain any Iranian component either (Dzhafarzade *et al.* 1939, 4; on language: 14–15).

In order to achieve another element of primordiality, and to provide a golden age, the Medes were also integrated into the national history. This claim for the Medes found approval at the highest level in Moscow. In April 1938, a ten-day festival (*dekada*) of Azerbaijani art was organized in Moscow (Dekada azerbaidzhanskogo iskustva 1938). The festival aimed to present the achievements of Soviet Azerbaijan in the arts. On the evening of the last day of the festival an official reception was organized in the Kremlin's St George Hall. At this reception writers, composers, artists, musicians, and opera singers met with the heads of the CPSU; Stalin, Molotov, Kaganovich, Voroshilov, Kalinin, Chubar, Mikoian, Kosior, Zhdanov, Ezhov, and Bagirov also joined the reception.[22] It is claimed that at this reception Stalin honoured the Azerbaijani people by raising his glass for the 'Azerbaijani nation, who are the obvious descendants of the great civilization of the Medes'.[23] This was an astonishing definition. In those days, the Medes were considered a group of Aryans who had arrived in western Iran following the great Aryan exodus from the Himalayas (Vaux 1884, 15; Rawlinson 1871, 306–325; Bury *et al.* 1926b, 2, 209; Berr 1927; Huart 1927, 26; Bartol'd 1963b, 656). In fact, the first modern usage of history began in the eighteenth century when the French pioneer of orientalism, the first publisher of the Avesta, Abraham-Hyacinthe Anquetil-Duperron (1731–1806), made a connection between the name that Herodotus and Diodoros used for the Medes (Greek: αριοι), a self-designation in Avesta, and the country name Iran (Arvidsson 2006, 20). Moreover, the Media where the Madai or Medes lived was in the Iranian Plateau, far south of Azerbaijan (Frye 1983, 67; Diakonoff 1985, 36, 66, 67, and maps on 39, 99, 111; Dandamayev and Medvedskaya 2006; Brunner 2007, 762–763). Nevertheless, Stalin's interpretation of Azerbaijani history became a tenet, and in the coming years the Medes came to be thought of as the non-Aryan ancestors of Azerbaijanis (Conquest 1967, 8–9). The history of Azerbaijan was increasingly detached from a Turkic past, and the emerging gap was filled by the incorporation of hitherto Iranian past into Azerbaijani national history.[24]

The 1939 text was discussed at a conference organized by the history and philosophy section of the Academy of Sciences in Moscow on May 26–27, 1939 (Khronika 1939). The authors of the draft continued to work according to the comments that they had received at this conference. In 1941, two months before the German assault on the USSR, the national history of Azerbaijan was published (*Istoriia* 1941). This history was a collective work of all Azerbaijani historians at the Institute of History of the AzFAN. The authors argued that

## 34  *The construction of Azerbaijani identity*

Azerbaijani identity was primordial and that it had not changed over the past centuries. The peoples that had migrated to Azerbaijan for over millennia were small in number and primitive in their socio-economic structure. That is why they did not have a decisive impact on the autochthonous habitants of Azerbaijan. Obviously, these arguments cannot explain how Turkification started during – as defined by the authors – the invasion of Azerbaijan by the 'primitive' and 'small in number' pastoral nomads of the Seljuks. Additionally, the authors implied that even if there was a Turkification, this did not mean that the Azerbaijanis were of Turkic stock. By blood, they were the ancestors of the ancient Caucasians, the same primordial ancestors as Armenians and Georgians. Consequently, Marr's internationalist theories were used to construct a spatially defined primordial national identity (*Istoriia* 1941, 17–19). The 'indigenousness' of the nation and the friendship with two other Soviet nations (Armenia and Georgia) were both established in a single stroke.

Apparently, the draft of 1939 had been criticized in Moscow for its weakness in defending the Azerbaijani identity against the Turkic ethno-linguistic definition and its failure to emphasize the primordial brotherhood of Armenians, Georgians, and Azerbaijanis. When the final version of the Azerbaijani national history was published in 1941, the authors wrote an additional three-page argumentation, which started with Marr's internationalist theories and concluded with a spatially defined primordial national identity (*Istoriia* 1941, 17–19). The text, for the first time, incorporated the Medes as the great ancestors of the Azerbaijani nation from the first millennium BC, and explicitly pointed to Stalin as the source of this 'scientific truth':

> The only scientifically correct point of view on the descent of the Azerbaijani nation has been provided by comrade Stalin and it connects contemporary Azerbaijanis with their ancient ancestors – Medes.
> (*Istoriia* 1941, 19)

Once the Medes became part of the ancient roots of Azerbaijani national identity, the use of them in the national narrative continued in the following chapters in the official history. The chapter on the 'Beginning of the Median State' explained the foundation of the first mighty Azerbaijani state in antiquity. The 'Conquests of Media' illustrated the heroic deeds of Azerbaijani Median rulers. 'On the Culture of Media' examined the cultural achievements of early Azerbaijanis. Finally, the 'Fight [of Medes] against Persians' described the earliest clashes between the Azerbaijani Medians and the Persians, which was defined as the first episode in the centuries-long Azerbaijani struggle for freedom against the Persian yoke. Thus, the nationalization of the Median Empire extended the anti-Iranian stance and ethnogenesis well into the early pages of history (*Istoriia* 1941, 21–31). When Azerbaijani historians incorporated the Medians into the national narrative, they also included the Caucasian Albanians and Caspians to secure a primordial and autochthonous past to the north of the Aras River. In order to embrace both sides of the Aras River, the text described Azerbaijanis as a mixture of 'the Medes, [Caucasian] Albanians, and the descendants of the Caspians' (*Istoriia* 1941, 31). Turanian (Turkic) and Aryan (Iranic) components were carefully pushed away and turned into monstrous aliens. The territorially defined Azerbaijani nation gained a national past which started 2,500 years ago in the contemporary territories. We find Səməd Vurğun to be a proponent of this territorial identity from the beginning. In 1937, he wrote to his friend, 'Recently I have written a great epopee [i.e. epic poem] 'Azerbaijan'. Two thousand years of history of my fatherland has been presented in this work' (Vurğun 2005g [1937]). This independent territorial definition of Azerbaijani identity freed from any Turkic or Iranic elements can be seen in the above-mentioned poem by Vurğun. In this piece on the love of fatherland and national history in 1936, he equally distances Azerbaijan from the peoples of Turan and Iran who came to exploit Azerbaijan with their armies, even if they had friendly smiles (Vurğun 2005h [1936], 236). In 1940, when Vurğun opened his speech at the Military-Political Academy in Moscow on the heroic Azerbaijani history, he assured the audience that 'the Azerbaijani nation has a history older than two thousand years. Its ancestors were the heroic Medians' (Vurğun 2005b [1940], 42; also see the same emphasis in his article: Vurğun 2005c [1940], 54).

## Conclusions

It is an oversimplification to explain the change from an ethno-linguistic Turkic identity to a territorial Azerbaijani one in 1937 as a consequence of a Soviet 'divide and rule' policy for the Turkic peoples. The construction of a new Azerbaijani national identity, with its primordial roots in the contemporary territories of the Azerbaijan Soviet Socialist Republic, was a product of domestic as well as international factors. In the international dimension, nation-building policies in Turkey and Iran created alternative descriptions of national identities for the Turkic-speaking titular nation of Azerbaijan. Moreover, relations between the Soviet Union and these two countries increasingly deteriorated after 1934, which turned Azerbaijan from a 'red lighthouse' in the Middle East to a 'bulwark' against external enemies. These tensions were also connected to the developments in Europe, and the Nazis' coming to power in Germany had a domino effect. In domestic terms, the priorities of Soviet historiography changed and the new history paradigm demanded stronger national narratives with primordial descriptions of ethnogenesis. That is why the alteration of 1937 should be seen as a result of a combination of developments in Turkey, Iran, Germany, and the Soviet Union.

The third republic or the independent nation-state of Azerbaijan was founded in 1991. The contemporary territorial disputes over Nagorno Karabakh with the neighbouring Armenia raised the importance of primordiality which echoed the concerns in the 1930s. Azerbaijani territorial identity still functions and provides autochthonous roots back in history to compete with the claims of neighbours. The ideologists and historians of independent Azerbaijan kept the territorial definition that had been constructed in the 1930s. At the same time, a new Turkic ethno-linguistic dimension has been added to both the national identity and history. This duality of self gives Azerbaijan the flexibility to claim its share in the world of Turkic nations and in the geopolitics of the Caucasus. However, it is not easy to continue to have such a dual allegiance in history. That is why the scale of this Turkicness has been kept unclear. While sometimes it is increased to the extreme by the rather popular declarations of being 'one nation two states' with the Turks of Turkey, at other times the emphasis moves towards the ancient ingredients of the ethnogenesis such as the Caucasian Albanians. Thus, a territorial amalgamation of ethnicities and keeping Turkic as an ingredient among others is preferred.

## Notes

1 On the visits of Nikolai Marr and Aleksandr Samoilovich, Ivan Meshchaninov, and Hadzhi Gabidullin: RGASPI 17-163-966-51–53, November 28, 1932; RGASPI 17-163-969-145, December 23, 1932; RGASPI 17-163-981-288, May 10, 1933; RGASPI 17-163-1031-37–38, June 14, 1934; RGASPI 17-163-1115-92, June 15, 1936.
2 ARPİİSPİHDA,1–14–35–24, April 16–17, 1937.
3 A special collection of essays was printed to underline the change: Grekov 1939, 1940.
4 According to Bartol'd, Turkic peoples appeared in Azerbaijan and in Asia Minor during the Seljuk rule. At the beginning, they probably settled there for the protection of border zones against the Byzantine Empire and the Georgian Kingdom, which was a considerable force in those times (Bartol'd 2002a, 5: 590). However, Bartol'd is sure that the final Turkification occurred during the Mongol invasion (Bartol'd 2002b, 5: 96; 2002c, 5: 213; Golden 1992; 2009, 110, 118–119). During the reign of Hulagu, Kereits were settled in Azerbaijan. Kadyrbaev refers to Rashid-ad-din (Kadyrbaev 1993, 153).
5 For the biography of Gubaidullin, see Sumbatzade 1987, 84–85; Atakishiev 1989, 127, 201; GUBAIDULLIN Gaziz (Aziz) Salikhovich; Gubaidullin Gaziz Salikhovich; Pashaev 1996; Gubaidullin 1997. For his works in Uzbekistan see Shigabdinov 2002; Kerimova 2005, 78, 356–357. For Khuluflu, see *Azərbaycanda Sovet Hakimiyyəti* 1958, 229–230; Kerimova 2005, 512. For Choban-zade, see Atakishiev 1989, 127; Kerimova 2005, 516–518; Vasil'kov and Sorokina (n.d.).
6 For the biography of Zifel'dt-Simumiagi see Atakishiev 1989, 128; Kerimova 2005, 388–390; Lichnye Arkhivnye Fondy; ZIFEL'DT-SIMUMIAGI (Zifel'td-Simumiagi).
7 ARPİİSPİHDA, 1–14–35–21/22, April 16/17, 1937.
8 ARPİİSPİHDA, 1–14–35–22, April 16/17, 1937.
9 ARPİİSPİHDA, 1–14–35–22, April 16/17, 1937.
10 ARPİİSPİHDA, 1–14–35–19/24, April 16/17, 1937.
11 ARPİİSPİHDA, 1–14–33–17, January 1938.
12 Ashin and Alpatov relate these purges, especially the arrest of Akhundov, to the struggle between the groups of Bagirov and Akhundov (Ashnin and Alpatov 1998). On the purges and bibliographies of Turkologists in Azerbaijan, see Ashnin *et al.* 2002).
13 ARPİİSPİHDA, 1–74–453–330, January 4, 1937.
14 ARPİİSPİHDA, 1–74–457–7, January 28, 1937. The list of the scholars in the higher institutions occupying various positions included Gasanbekov, Chichikalov, Nikolaev, Tikhomirov, Khuluflu, Billiarli, Bukshpan, Tagi-Zade, Choban-zade, Azim Gasanov, Tagi Shakhbazov, Rizabeili, V. Mustafaev, Gubaidullin, P. Guseinov, and Vanandetsi.

*The construction of Azerbaijani identity* 37

Parallel to the purge of the scholars in the higher institutions, the cadres in the Narkompros AzSSR were also purged more than once. ARPİİSPİHDA, 1–14–7-79, April 17, 1937.
15 Gubaidullin stayed in Kazan, Tatarstan until 1936. His return to Baku must be related to his involvement in this project. Similarly, Zifel'dt-Simumiagi moved from Tbilisi to Baku in December 1935. The time of their return to Baku before the resolution of the Central Committee of the CPSU on the Zhdanov commission, and the resolution of the CPA on Azerbaijani history suggests that they were informed by the project of writing national history for Azerbaijan in December 1935. For the time of their return to Baku see Kerimova 2005, 357, 389.
16 ARPİİSPİHDA, 1–74–416–18, 19, 87, March 15, 1936.
17 ARPİİSPİHDA, 1–74–427–58, June 6, 1936.
18 ARPİİSPİHDA, 1–74–427–59, June 21, 1936.
19 ARPİİSPİHDA, 1–74–433–316, August 11, 1936.
20 ARPİİSPİHDA, 1–74–444–168, October 22, 1936.
21 A Soviet term used for the young appointees who were trained and nurtured in the first two decades of the Soviet rule. For the biographies of the editors of the new history, Isag Dzafarzade, Aleksei Klimov, and Zelik Iampol'skii, see Kerimova 2005, 372–373, 416–417, 541.
22 The *dekada* was organized from April 6 to 16, 1938 (Dekada 1938).
23 This anecdote was conveyed to me by Emeritus Prof. Süleyman Aliyarlı of Baku University in 2007.
24 A similar gap can be observed in the Tatar and Chuvash case, after 1944, when to construct a link between Tatars and the Golden Horde was forbidden by the Central Committee of the CPSU. For this issue see Shnirelman 1996a, 7, 22–24.

# 2 The miraculous return of Babak to Azerbaijan

Babak Khurrami (or Khurramdin) was a leader of an uprising which took place in AD 816–37 in today's Iranian Azerbaijan and parts of Armenia, against the Abbasid caliphate. The main reason for the uprising was the resentment of Persian speakers against Arab–Muslim invaders (Yarshater, 2007, 1004). The ideology of the uprising was a mixture of equalitarian neo-Mazdekism and pro-Persian sentiments. The uprising should be considered as part of successive revolts (Mukannaiyye, Fatimiye, Cavidaniyye, Khurremiyye) after the assassination of Ebu Muslim Horasani, the leader of the Persian population in the early Abbasids. This is why Babak had followers and sympathisers all around Iran, even in Horasan, the north-eastern region of Iran. It was only after twenty years of struggle that the armies of the caliph captured and killed Babak and his followers. He was brutally executed in Samarra under the revengeful eyes of the Muslim caliph (Yusofi, Babak Korrami; Sourdel, Babak). Many things had changed in the geography of Babak since the ninth century. In the following centuries, the predominant religion and culture moved from being Christian and Zoroastrian to Islam. Then the ethno-linguistic character also changed in the same territory and the population was Turkified. If anything remained in the popular memory of Azerbaijan or Iran in the nineteenth century, it did not go further than a cruel infidel waging an unholy war against Muslim believers. Yet, Babak is one of the most prominent national heroes in contemporary Azerbaijan. Babak, as a national leader, and his uprising as a national-liberation war can be found in contemporary Azerbaijani history textbooks with elaborate descriptions, pictures and maps. One of the main boulevards of Baku is named after Babak and there is also an administrative district and its central city in Nakhchivan region called Babak. It is normal for Azerbaijani families to name their baby boys Babak. However, Babak as a national figure is not a product of Azerbaijani national independence in 1991. His rise as an Azerbaijani national hero was part of a nation-building policy launched after 1937 under Stalin's rule. Since the nineteenth century, Babak emerged and re-emerged in different historical narratives and a few orientalists studied Babak. When the Iranian nation-builders launched their programme in the 1920s, they incorporated Babek into their national pantheon and based their arguments on the European orientalists. At the same time, on the northern shores of the Aras River, the Bolshevik rule popularized him by generating a standard and well-promoted narrative. It was a perfect choice because the profile of Babak complied well with the de-Turkified and de-Iranized Azerbaijani national identity and history after 1937. Among its European and Iranian rivals, Azerbaijani Soviet historiography succeeded in the most systematic construction of Babak as the national figure of Azerbaijan. The Soviet reconstruction of Babak was so successful that Babak still lives on in Azerbaijan. Hence, Babak is not only a sample of Soviet nation-building but also a brilliant example of how Soviet nation-building policies have had an enduring impact even after the official collapse of the USSR.

## White Babak: the birth of Babak as an Aryan hero

The towering figures of European orientalism were the first exhumers of Babak in the nineteenth century for multiple reasons. The ideology of Babak revived equalitarian Mazdakism, in new forms. Mazdak was an Iranian priest who established a new religion based on communal access to women and property by raising a peasant revolt in the sixth century (Guidi, Mazdak; for Mazdakism, Yarshater 2007; Crone 1991). Some European orientalists were interested in Mazdakites and Babakites for their communist or equalitarian principles along similar events of the medieval Middle East. These revolts seemed very similar to the European peasant revolts and religious movements for equality in pre-modern societies. The question was if these revolts could be assigned as the oriental version of communist movements in history (Flügel 1869; Nöldeke 1879a, 1879b; Von Wesendonk 1919; Christensen 1925; Yarshater 2007, 991–993; Daryaee 2009, 86–88).

Among the Western Orientalists of the second half of the nineteenth century, studying Iranian religious movements and their historical roots was the spirit of the day. This was a time when the Babais (or Babists), an Iranian religious sect which merged Shi'ite doctrine and non-Muslim elements was active, preaching from 1844. Babism was the last in a line of militant religious waves in Iran ranging from pre-Islamic ones to the extreme Shi'ite heresies. The following prosecutions, mass killings, and suppression of the Babais in Iran increased the attention of the Western Orientalists to Iranian religious and philosophical history. Increasing attention on Babists also turned the focus of the Western Orientalists towards either non-Muslim or Muslim heresies, including the neo-Mazdakism of Babak (Kazem-Bek 1865; Roemer 1912; Phelps 1912; Dreyfus 1909; Browne 1910, 1918. For a complete survey see Momen 1981, 1987).

European orientalists held the pre-Islamic period of Iran in high esteem. Also they read the antic past of Iran while searching Aryan civilization in Asia. The pre-Islamic Iran was interpreted as an Aryan cradle which struggled against the Semitic empires of Assyria and Babylonia and was devastated by the spread of Islamic conquest and Arabic/Semitic menace. These orientalists were mostly trained as classicists and looked at their subject from this perspective, through sources in Greek and Latin. Therefore, they had an aversion to Islam, seen as the phenomenon that put an end to eastern antiquity (Palmer

1867, xi; Justi 1879; Rawlinson 1871, 306–325; 1873, 19–26; 1876, 1878; Vaux 1884, 8, 17; Hoffmann-Kutschke 1925; Bury et al. 1926a, 13, 15; 1926b, 2,209; Berr 1927, xi–xvi; Huart 1927, 26, 32, 34, 136–138, 215; Zia-Ebrahimi 2011). Babak was the figure who organized resistance against the forces which ended the eastern antiquity. Since the arrival of the Muslim Arabs and the proselytization of Persian-speaking population to Islam, there had been consecutive religious movements embodying and reviving in the new forms of pre-Muslim and non-Muslim ideas or fusing these elements with Muslim creeds. European orientalists, who were looking for Aryan traces in Asia, readily interpreted these movements, including Sufism and the Shi'ite sect of Islam as, the remnants of the Aryan legacy in the East. Babak, an Iranian figure fighting against the Arab occupants for the re-establishment of Sassanid rule, fitted well into this bigger construction of the past. The writings of Comte de Gobineau, a seminal figure in the formation of European racist ideology, and an orientalist, is an example of the promotion of these ideas. Gobineau argued that Persian Shi'ism was a national and even racial (Aryan) riposte to the Arab conquest. The continuous and contagious heresies, and the sects including Sufism were the continuation of ancient doctrines and customs under the Islamic blanket. Persians were descendants of the prehistorical Aryan race following the great exodus from Inner Asia. Forgetting superior Aryan roots and culture was a consequence of mixing with inferior races. In this sense, the arrival of Semitic Arabs and their religion was a turning point in the history of Aryan Persians. Since then, the lost spirit of the Aryans has been trying to find a way out from the inferior Semitic culture and religion by various sectarian uprisings and denominations (Gobineau 2003, 30–31, 195–197; Biddiss 1970a, 1970b). The orientalists of the nineteenth century hoped 'to prove that Sufiism [sic] is really the development of the Primæval Religion of the Aryan race' (Palmer 1867, xi). This Aryanist language was also used by prominent western historians such as Ernest Renan and Edward G. Browne in their works (Nash 2009, 13–14; Browne 1902, 308–336; Bosworth 1995).

Understanding Iranian history based on Aryan race provided a comfortable starting point for the Iranian nation-builders at the beginning of the twentieth century. The western ideas of a lost golden age of Aryan past directly or indirectly had an impact on the Iranian iconoclastic secularists and anti-clerical nationalists such as Mirza Fatali Akhundov (1812–78), Mirza Aqa Khan Kermani (1853–96) and later Ahmad Kasravi. They defined the era before the Arab conquest and the spread of Islam as the golden age of the Iranian nation: the great Median, Achaemenian, and Sassanid Empires followed by the dark period of Arabization and Islamization of the ancient lands of Iranians. Islamic culture was qualified as foreign to Iranian traditions and was rejected. The Islamic period was accused of being the cause of ruin during several centuries of foreign domination when the Arab, Turkic, and Mongol conquerors controlled Iran successively. Under the Shah Reza Pahlavi, the national identity was constructed along the titular Persian ethnic group. In the national historical narrative, Arabs and Turks were often demonized as the perpetrators behind the demise of the glorious civilization of the Sasanid period. The leaders of uprisings against foreign invaders and despotic rulers became an important ingredient of the national narrative. These leaders were sometimes mythical figures such as Kaveh the Blacksmith. According to the legend, Kaveh was from Isfahan and his adversary was from Babylonia (Ridgeon 2004; Nash 2009, 13–14; Kian and Riaux 2009; Keddie 1980; Parsinejad 2003; Tavakoli-Targhi 2009; Zia-Ebrahimi 2011; Ansari 2012).

Babak and his uprising provided a romantic national narrative with a national leader who resisted a foreign invasion and religion. Babak's affiliation to the pre-Islamic religions in Iran and his strong anti-Arab and anti-Islamic attitude made him an idol of Iranian national awareness. In the following decades, under the nation-building policies of the Pahlavi dynasty, Babak, together with others such as Abu Muslim, Afshin, and Mazyar, became an Iranian hero within the Iranian national pantheon (Nefisi 1998 [1954]; Atabaki 2008, 142). This 'white Babak' can be seen in the works of Sa'id Nafisi, a nationalist historian and writer. Between 1933 and 1934, he published a series of articles in the journal *Mehr* in which he presented this romantic national picture of Babak as an ultra-nationalist who combined admiration for Iranian pre-Islamic beliefs with profound anti-Arab semtiments. Twenty years later, Nafisi published a book on Babak titled *Babak Khorramdin Delavar-e Azarbayjan* (Babak Khorramdin, the Hero of Azerbaijan) (Nafisi 1333 [1954], Nefisi 1998 [1954], 46–50; Atabaki 2012, 67). A similar Iranian national narrative could be found in official history textbooks of the time. In the history book of the sixth grade published in 1967, the uprising of Babak was glorified and portrayed as a movement aimed at 're-establishing the country's independence and restoring the Iranian kingdom of the Sassanids' (Khanlari 1967, 17–18. Cited by Atabaki 2012, 67).

## Red Babak: The re-birth of Babak as a Proletarian hero

While Western Orientalists and Iranian nationalists constructed Babak as the hero of the Aryan race or Iranian nation, the Azerbaijani Soviet historiography initially depicted him as a 'proletarian hero'. Ideological reasons behind Soviet preference for Babak can be traced back to Pokrovskiian historiography. Following the example of Marx and Pokrovskii, Soviet historians hastily looked for peasant uprisings and class conflicts in the ancient and medieval periods of every national history. On top of this, the neo-Mazdekite egalitarian tenets of Babak complied with the communistic ideals of the Soviet regime. Furthermore, his image of a 'simple peasant-shepherd transforming into a folk leader' had a great value for the Soviet modernization agenda. Parallel to Soviet modernization projects and *korenizatsiia* policies in Azerbaijan, thousands of young and poor villagers were educated and trained to become indigenous administrators, party officials, officers, teachers, engineers, and workers. These young *vydvizhentsy*, as they were called at that time in Russian, became active agents of Soviet modernity and aimed to eradicate their poor rural past and recast the world. Instead of a shah, bey, or sultan, the image of Babak becoming a legendary leader despite his simple roots was an ideal historical episode for the generation of *vydvizhentsy* to read. Historians were after 'folk leaders' with simple origins like Babak. Indeed, he did not inherit a principality from his predecessors. He was a member of the ordinary folk and lost his father when he was a child. His mother cleaned houses of well-to-do neighbours for a living. The Iranian and Azerbaijani nation-builders shared a bitterness and distaste towards the Arabs and their religion. This bitterness can be seen in the theatre play *Od Gəlini* of Cəfər Cabbarlı, the leading Azerbaijani writer and poet of the 1920s and 1930s. The original name of the play was *Babak* and it was written between 1924 and 1928. It was the first time in this play that the image of an Azerbaijani hero fighting against the Arab invaders stood in front of the contemporary Azerbaijanis (Cabbarlı 2005, 290–356, 358). After Cabbarlı, the poetry of Səməd Vurğun (the leading Soviet Azerbaijani poet, 1906–56) emphasized the same aspect. In his poem 'Gallows' that he wrote in 1935, he depicts greedy and hungry Arabs who left the deprived and infertile land and hostile climate of Arabia to colonize the green and fertile Caucasus. The occupants did not hesitate to enslave men and women and to destroy gender equality, and Babak led the struggle against them (Vurğun 1961, 195–199).

> One day the hungry hordes of Arabs
> A Sword in the right hand, the Quran in the left
> Launched an attack toward the north ...
> Bowed in front of it Iran
> ... Against this flow of humans only
> Stood the brave sons of the Caucasus
> (Vurğun 1961, 197–198)

In the first year of the Bolshevik rule in Azerbaijan, P. K. Zhuze (1870–1942), an orientalist and expert in Arab history, wrote about the history of Babak as an early communist movement (Zhuze 1921, 1: 204–216.). This work made medieval Arab sources narrating the uprising available to contemporary readers. In 1925, when Sysoev wrote his history of Azerbaijan, he also described Babak as 'a leader of a communist uprising' (Sysoev 1925, 48). Both of them clearly referred to the egalitarian aspect of this sectarian movement. In 1936, the first Soviet biography of Babak and the story of his uprising was published. In this account, he was again described as a leader of exploited classes (Tomara 1936). This book was part of a popular series of biographies with the title 'Life of Remarkable People' (Russian: *zhizn' zamechatel'nykh liudei*), initiated by Maksim Gorky.[1] According to this first Soviet account, Babak had been a leader of a class (peasant) uprising, and not an Azerbaijani national hero. He had mobilized the toiling peasants against the exploiting classes, landowners, and feudal lords for their class emancipation, but not for Azerbaijan (Tomara 1936, 26).

Babak was not alone in his post-mortem incorporation into the 'world history of toiling masses'. The uprising of Mazdak, an Iranian Zoroastrian prophet who stirred up a peasant revolt and led an egalitarian movement in the sixth century, was also incorporated into the Azerbaijani national narrative (Dzhafarzade *et al.* 1939, 42–43). It may be seen as contradictory to welcome Mazdak and Babak, with their strong religious motives, in a country where atheism was officially supported. However, referring to Engels and Marx, Soviet historians interpreted the religious aspect of these medieval uprisings as a progressive element. Religion in these movements was understood as peasant ideologies in a pre-capitalist society that mobilized masses for an uprising. Even the Babist sect and uprising in the nineteenth century was understood within the context of this economic determinism and centuries-old class struggles (Ivanov 1939). Azerbaijan was not the only example in the Caucasus. In Dagestani history, Sufism and Muridizm, led by Shamil, had already been described by Russian historian Bushuev as a progressive idea for the nineteenth century, and a way for peasant masses to resist the colonial expansion of the Russian Empire and her local agents – feudal lords – in Dagestan and Chechnya (Bushuev 1939). In neighbouring Armenia there were similar publications on Armenian peasant uprisings in the seventeenth century (Arutiunian 1939).

## Re-birth of Babak as an Azerbaijani national hero after 1937

In the second half of the 1930s, the teachings of Pokrovskii were gradually removed from history writing at the all-Union level. In the new formulation, histories came more in line with the romantic nationalism of the nineteenth century than Marxist interpretation of the past. National heroes were gradually restored to history (Merzon 1935; Konstantinov 1938; Ilichev 1938; Iudin 1939, 5: 45; Bernadiner 1939; Konstantinov 1939). When Pokrovskiian historiography was replaced by national narratives, however, Babak gradually transformed from a class hero to a national one. In this period of transformation, Babak was defined both as a national leader and as a class leader. For instance, at the fourteenth congress of the Communist Party of Azerbaijan (hereafter, CPA) in 1938, Mir Jafar Bagirov, the first secretary of the CPA, defined the uprising as a national-liberation struggle of Azerbaijani nation against the Arab occupants (Bagirov 1938). The draft of national history in 1939 defined the uprising as a revolutionary-peasant war against the Muslim–Arab exploiters (Dzhafarzade, Klimov, Iampol'skii 1939, 59–66). In the 1941 edition, Babak was both a peasant leader and the organizer of Azerbaijani national-liberation struggle. So, there was a gradual 'nationalization' of Babak in the narrative. In the neighbouring Dagestan Shamil also experienced a transformation. In 1940, when the twentieth anniversary of Soviet autonomy in Dagestan was celebrated, a series of works was published in Makhachkala depicting Shamil as a heroic national leader of the national-liberation struggle of Dagestani people and Chechens against the Russian colonial occupation (Magomedov 1939, 1940a, 1940b, Magomedov 1940c. Also see the publication on Shamil in Chechnya in autumn 1941: Kroviakov 1941). Akin to Babak, Shamil also exchanged his red banner for a national one.

Azerbaijani national identity constructed after 1937 was a territorial definition detached from other Turkic speakers and Iranian heritage (see Chapter 1). In a society where atheism was promoted by the state, Islam could not be part of the national definition. Yes, in the pre-modern times religion was a mobilizing ideology for peasants. When Turkic, Iranian, and Muslim heritages were removed, there were not many choices left for promotion. At this point Babak was a convenient choice because his profile was very adaptable to the national identity that was constructed after 1937. To start with, Babak was neither a Turkic speaker nor a Muslim and his affinity with the Iranian past was not clear. The conventional Iranian history had not incorporated Babak to the degree that it strongly embraced the Achaemenid and Sassanid Empires. Babak's uprising was organized in Iranian Azerbaijan. Considering that the new narrative was based on territoriality, the location provided a good justification to define him as an Azerbaijani hero. Moreover, he fought for his people and beliefs and against the Arabs from further south. This aspect was also convenient when the Soviet strategy positioned Azerbaijan as a defence barrier standing against any interventions from the south (see Chapter 1). Babak became a national leader who organized a national-liberation war against the Arab–Muslim occupants from the south. At the fourteenth congress of the CPA, in June 1938, Bagirov explained this interpretation to the delegates:

> In the middle of the eighth century, Arabs occupy Azerbaijan. They ruin [Azerbaijan]. They deprive them of their native tongue, forbidding the Azerbaijani nation to converse in her native language, they attach the Azerbaijani nation to the Arab language and Mohammad's belief by the force of their sword and whip. Azerbaijani nation upraised against the Arab oppressors more than once.... The uprising of the national hero Babak in the beginning of the ninth century covered all Azerbaijan and continued for approximately twenty years.
>
> (Kaziev 1942a, 11–12)

The CPA promoted the use of Babak as a historical-national hero to increase the public awareness and popularity. In the Soviet Union, it was a usual practice for the agitation-propaganda section of the Party to organize open letters from various sections of the population under the rubrics of 'kolkhoz workers', 'students', or 'intelligentsia'. These open letters were widely published to popularize a certain political message. When the intelligentsia of Baku sent such an open letter to Stalin in April 1939, on the anniversary of the Sovietization of Azerbaijan, national patriotic sentiments were framed with clear references to Babak:

> Babak rose, he urged his people to revenge thunderously,
> He is like lightning, his sword raised above an enemy's head
> To defend from foreigners the land of the fathers, dear land –
> Babak raging in the mountains gathered countless army
> Revolt resounded in the land like a flame in windy days
> And inextinguishable fires warmed our hearts
> When the children of his native country with a blade sit on horses –

Who can save the head from the rage of curved swords!
And sending sons off to the fight, the mother said:
– Well, good luck to my sons,
I wish I never heard,
That the enemy's arrow hit you in the back, not in the chest –
Then let the milk I fed you be a poison!
Arabs plundered the country, traces of their steps are everywhere,
But people rushed into battle and trembled enemy ranks.
We will never forget this day and the great year
The heroes who gave blood for our country and for the people
Years have passed, centuries have passed, but Babak is still alive.
(Kaziev 1942a, 19–20)

The following year, when Səməd Vurğun addressed the Military-Political Academy in Moscow in 1940 on the heroic Azerbaijani history, he echoed Bagirov's position: 'Babak, the great son of Azerbaijan, fought against the Arab caliphs, he numerous times defeated Arab armies and submerged them under the waves of the Aras River' (Vurğun 2005b, 42).

The love affair of the Azerbaijani Bolsheviks with Babak as a national hero continued even after a half century. For instance, when the communist regime wanted to emphasize Azerbaijani national identity on the eve of the Iranian Islamic Revolution, the Soviet rulers put even greater emphasis on Babak as a national hero. In 1978, the town of Təzəkənd in Nakhchivan exclave of Azerbaijan was renamed as Babak. In the following year, a movie on the life of this heroic figure was produced by Azerbaijani Soviet movie studios. Apparently the shooting of the movie was given high priority by the Azerbaijan Communist Party. It was the grape harvest time when the movie was shot in Nakhchivan. That is why, initially, it was not easy for the movie producers and local administrators to find enough figurants and workers to employ in the movie production. The movie shooting could jeopardize the grape harvesting and imperil annual production fulfillments. It was claimed that, at this moment, the first secretary of the Azerbaijan Communist Party, Haydar Aliyev, intervened in order to mobilize the local party administration to find the necessary labour force, despite the risk of lower harvest levels in that year (Qaraqızı 2003). Finally, in 1979, a ballet was composed on Babak by a leading Azerbaijani composer, Agşin Alizadeh, and staged in 1986.

## Green and blue Babak: Muslim and Turkic Babaks

The twentieth-century journey of Babak did not finish with Azerbaijani nation-building in the Stalinist Soviet Union and Iranian nation-building under the Pahlavis. New definitions of Babak appeared in both Iran and Azerbaijan. These new constructions are just as convincing as the previous ones. The 'green' Babak emerged after the Islamic Revolution in Iran. The new narrative in Iran did not (and probably could not) refuse Babak and omit him from the national narrative of the country. Instead, Iranian historians after the revolution added a 'Muslim flavour'. Babak continues to be a patriot of Iran opposing the Arab occupation. After all, this was a convenient interpretation during the Iran–Iraq War in the 1980s. At the same time Babak is the heroic defender of the 'true and uncorrupted' form of Islam against the Abbasid Caliphs. He was some kind of an early Shi'ite imam before Shi'a became the official denomination of Iran. The anti-Muslim image of Babak was a consequence of the Sunni court historians of the Caliphate (Najimi 1368 [1989–1990]; Mammadkhanly 1382 [2003–2004], 8–11). He was an important hero of the Iranian nation (Talibzadah 1381 [2002–2003], 5–9) who operated in the province of Azerbaijan. It was one of the greatest popular uprisings against the dominant system in Iran (Talibzadah 1381 [2002–2003], 136–141).

There is also an Azerbaijani national hero Babak, who experienced a transformation. After independence, Azerbaijani identity was increasingly redefined as Turkic and Muslim. In this new context, Babak was disturbingly a non-Turkic and anti-Muslim hero. However, it was not easy to remove such a hero overnight because the Soviet Azerbaijani narrative of Babak was already firmly rooted in the modern national identity. The Azerbaijani solution has been similar to the Iranian one with one difference. The official narrative defines his uprising as a powerful resistance of Azerbaijanis against the alien Arab exploiters. The multi-volume Azerbaijani history defines Babak's uprising as the 'Azerbaijani nation's liberation movement against foreign exploiters' (*Azərbaycan Tarixi* 2007, 211). Moreover, Babak's resistance inspired further uprisings against the Arab caliphs and even influenced the teachings of Sheikh Heydar, the founder of the Safavid dynasty in the fifteenth century (Vəlixanlı 2007, 203–213; *Azərbaycan Respublikası Naxçivan* 2010, 19; Nağıyev and Verdiyeva 2007, 46–47; *Azərbaycan Tarixi Atlası* 2007, 17). Babak has also been reproduced as a Turkic–Shi'a hero of Azerbaijan (Bayramlı 2011).

Another narrative of Turkic Babek was written by Muhammad Taqi Zahtabi (1923–98). Zahtabi was an Azerbaijani linguist and participant in the Azerbaijan Democrat Party, the political organization that declared the independence of Iranian Azerbaijan with the support of the Soviet forces in 1946. After the fall of the independence movement, he migrated to the Soviet Union. After spending three years in Siberian prison camps, he studied Azerbaijani philology and return to Tabriz during the Iranian Revolution (1978–82) (Atabaki 2008, 138–139). His *magnum opus* was the Ancient History of Iranian Turks published in two volumes (Zahtabi, 1382 [2003–2004]). This is an alternative narrative to the history that had been constructed under the Soviet rule in the north. Its principal argument is that the Turkic population of Azerbaijan has been an autochthonous people settled in the region before the arrival of the Aryan tribes. The gradual increase of the Altaic–Turkic waves increased their dominance and the Parthian Empire (247 BC – AD 224), essentially a Turkic rule, was founded in the following centuries. This Turkic heritage was challenged by the Sassanid rule and a Persianization began. Within this framework, Babak Khurrami stands as a Turkic hero, who resisted the Caliphate in Bagdad. Zahtabi, in his works, encouraged Iranian Azerbaijanis to celebrate the memory of Babak and visit Bazz, the mountainous fortress of Babak, to commemorate the heroic deeds of their forefathers. Every year, Azerbaijanis of Iran congregate in the fortress in increasing numbers. The cultural festival that is organized at the fortress and the size of the congregation underlines the collective national identity of the community and the sense of Azerbaijaniness (Atabaki 2008, 142).

## Conclusions

The nation-builders of the 1930s in Iran elevated Babak Khurrami to pan-Iranian level. According to their successful presentation, Babak was a brave national leader who fought for Iran and its ancient sedentary Aryan culture against the plundering nomadic Arabs and Islam (the new religion that was brought by them). After the Islamic revolution in 1979, the pre-Islamic period in the Iranian national history, constructed under the Pahlavi rule, was demolished. The right-hand man of Khomeini took this demolition literally when he tried to bulldoze the venues that had been promoted by the ancient regime as the symbols of the pre-Islamic Iran, such as the ruins of Persepolis and the mausoleum of Firdausi. While the country redefined itself, and references to the country's pre-Islamic past were destroyed, Iranian history writers of the new era could easily remove the Babak Uprising from the national narrative. Instead, they kept Babak but altered his content. Babak is still an Iranian national hero, but this time he is the defender of the 'true Islam' against the corrupt version of the religion that was cultivated by the Arab caliphs. The reconstruction of the narrative provided the new rulers of Iran with a historical beginning of the difference between their Shi'a denomination and their Sunni neighbours. It can also be argued that the secure position of Babak confirmed the success of the nation-builders in the 1930s. The Babak myth was so well established in the constructed common past that it was easier to keep him with a new content instead of bulldozing him to the ground.

The same conclusion can be made for the Azerbaijani case. The Azerbaijani nation-builders in the 1930s conveniently incorporated Babak into the new national history. Babak was not a Turkic speaker and he did not have to be anyway, because the Azerbaijani national identity and history was a territorial construction and it was totally freed from any ethno-linguistic limitations. The Bolsheviks were militant atheists and saw all religions as an obstacle against their modernization projects. In their fight against the local predominant religion (Islam), Babak provided them with a historical starting point. His inclusion was important because Babak was not an imported figure like the Bolsheviks themselves. The Bolsheviks knew well that, in the long run, the messages and ideas attached to a native figure (even if he lived earlier than a millennium ago) was always more effective than a Russian-speaking red commissar in a black leather jacket. When Soviet ideology left the stage for the sacred symbols and values of a nation-state in 1991, Babak did not disappear together with Marx and Lenin.

Rather, his story has been adjusted according to the new values and identity of the nation. The new ideologists and historians were happy to keep Babak, but this time as a national hero who might have even Turkic roots. One reason for this is that the Azerbaijani narrative still holds on to the territorial identity while borrowing from the ethno-linguistic definition. The secure position of Babak also implies the success of the Soviet constructors. The Azerbaijani Babak happened to be a success story as much as his twin has been in Iran. He is still a hero of the nation.

## Note

1 Some of the other biographies of this series were: Voronskii 1934; Vinogradov 1936; Gaisinovich 1937; Osipov 1939.

# 3 Pure Slavic blood for Ukraine

More than a decade ago, Mark von Hagen asked the following polemical question: what is Ukraine and who are the Ukrainians? He argued that

> The seemingly obvious categories of ethnicity and geography are of little help. Ukrainian history is being pulled in at least two major directions that had their parallels in the discussions on Ukrainian citizenship and that have their analogies in other post-Soviet states. Should citizenship and history be reserved for ethnic Ukrainians (however they might be determined in a long-time multi-ethnic population) or open to all ethnic groups on the territory of contemporary Ukraine? Given the especially large Russian population, but the historically large Polish, Jewish and German populations, a multicultural and territorial narrative of Ukrainian history that preserves the diversity and fluidity of identities [in the past and present] seems a more appropriate solution.
>
> (von Hagen 1995, 667)

Von Hagen was right to point to the fact that, only after the 'ethnic cleansings' and mass murders of the Second World War did Ukraine cease to be a multi-ethnic land and become a bi-ethnic, Ukrainian–Russian country with very small minorities. His next questions concerned what should be regarded as Ukrainian history. Should this history be preserved for ethnic Ukrainians or embrace all ethnolinguistic groups that inhabited the territory of contemporary Ukraine (Kappeler 2009, 56, 60–61)? Since the beginning of the recorded past the Iranic Scythians, the ancient Greeks, Germanic tribes, Finno-Ugric populations, the Jews, consecutive waves of Uralo-Altaic nomadic tribal federations, and the Western Slavs (the Poles) populated the Pontic Steppe in different periods (Magocsi 1996, 26–35). This heterogeneous ethno-linguistic mixture could have been defined as comprising the historical components of Ukrainianness, as was done in those years in Azerbaijan.[1] Territorial description of Ukrainian identity could cover both Slavic and non-Slavic elements. The allegiance of all ethnic or national identities in the Ukrainian Soviet Socialist Republic could be developed around this territorial identity. After all, 'Ukraine' was not an ethno-toponym referring to a particular race or ethnicity. However, the Soviets opted for a mono-ethnic definition.

The Soviet explanation of Ukrainian national genesis was based on two strong pillars. First, the Russians, Ukrainians, and Belarusians shared same ancestors in prehistory and antiquity, namely the Eastern Slavic nation, which was another construction of identity by its own. Second, Ukrainian genesis was mono-ethnic i.e. had pure blood. In the following years, this mono-ethnic definition of a Ukrainian nation evolved into an ethno-national identity.[2] This pillar attracted some attention from Ukrainian and Russian historians (for example Iusova 2005, 195–300; Dubrovskii 2005, 89–94). It also caused a widespread conspiracy theory generated in Russia which refuses to acknowledge Ukrainian identity as separate from Russian and sees it as nothing more than a fabrication in the 'secret laboratories' of Germans and Austrians in the nineteenth century (Ul'ianov 2004, 2007). Second, Ukrainian genesis was mono-ethnic i.e. had pure blood. In the following years, this mono-ethnic definition of a Ukrainian nation evolved into an ethno-national identity. The mono-ethnic definition of a Ukrainian nation was built in line with the mono-ethnic Russian and Belorussian identities. It is hard to find any Marxist ideology or Russo-centrism behind this preference. This chapter aims to shed light on the main reason behind the mono-ethnic (or ethno-national) definition of Ukrainian that prevailed in Soviet historiography. I will argue in this chapter that the political reason behind this pure blood definition was to answer a persistent narrative, one led by German historians, who looked upon the Slavs as 'inferior others' of Aryan Indo-European civilization, or a hybrid race of Indo-European and Asian components. According to this German-led 'orientalization'[3] of the lands and peoples in the east of the Vistula River, the Slavs were incapable of establishing durable polities and lacked the capacity for intellectual creativity.

## The peculiarities of Ukraine

Before going into the reasons behind the Soviet construction of a Ukrainian mono-ethnogenesis, three peculiarities of the Ukrainian case, compared to the other two cases, need to be addressed. First, in contrast to the Kazakh and Azerbaijani cases, Ukrainian historians had already developed national history writing at the expense of the Russian imperial and national identities, and there were already disputed and heavily politicized issues before the Soviet attempt to write a Soviet version of Ukrainian national history. Mykhailo Hrushevs'kyi played the major role in the pre-1917 construction of national history. He established a historical continuity from the earliest recorded period in the past until modern times. Ukrainians, thanks to Hrushevs'kyi, turned from a 'non-historical' to a 'historical' nation (Chlebowczyk 1980; Rudnytsky 1987a, 37–48; Plokhy 2005a).

Second, in Azerbaijan and Kazakhstan, the local communist parties initiated the process of construction of official national histories after 1936, when they received orders from the Zhdanov commission. In Ukraine, however, even before the Zhdanov commission in Moscow, the Institute of History of the VUAMLIN (All-Ukrainian Association of Marxist-Leninist Institutes, Ukrainian: *Vseukraïns'ka Asotsiatsiia Marksysts'ko-Lenins'kykh Instytutiv*) initiated the project of writing an official history of the Ukrainian nation, following the first signals from Moscow in 1934–5. In 1935, the Central Committee of the CPU (Communist Party of Ukraine) issued a resolution on this issue, and Mikhail Popov, the agitation-propaganda secretary of the CPU, became the chief editor of textbooks covering the history of Ukraine and Ukrainian literature. Initially, the textbook *History of Ukraine* was planned to be published in October 1935 (Iurkova 2001, 44, 52). Teachers and historians discussed the draft text at a special meeting as well as at a meeting of the presidium of the VUAMLIN in 1935 (Smolii 2006, 413). At the beginning of 1936, the Institute of History finished planning the four-volume national history.[4] The members of the editorial board commenced their work in order to publish the volume by July 1936.[5]

Finally Ukraine had a different starting point than either Azerbaijan or Kazakhstan because it had already experienced the first large-scale terror from 1929 to 1933, when the Ukrainization policy was amended. The schools of Hrushevs'kyi and his major Pokrovskiian opponent Iavors'kyi were removed from academic institutions. Many Ukrainian historians, both old specialists and Ukrainian national Bolshevik historians, were sentenced to long imprisonments, exiled or shot (Kostiuk 1960; Iurkova 2001, 5; Shapoval 2003; Plokhy 2005a; Lytvyn *et al.* 2007, 473–475).[6] Following the first purge, the figures who supervised history writing in Kyïv were young graduates, party officials, and *vydvizhentsy*.[7] These figures became Bolsheviks either before or during the 1917 Revolution, and they received their formal education in the new Soviet institutions. Moreover, almost none of them were Ukrainian.[8] Their plan of writing national history was ambitious, but institutional reorganization and the second large-scale terror campaign, i.e. the Great Terror (1936–8) in the Soviet Union, prevented them from taking any further steps.

## The constructors of the new national narrative

In the autumn of 1936, a wave of arrests among the former members of the VUAMLIN and the Institute of Red Professors was initiated and all the members of the history book's editorial board, which was writing the first volume, were arrested and subsequently shot. After the purges, the majority of the sixteen members of the Institute of History of Ukraine had no graduate degree. On November 23, 1936 Sergei Belousov (hereafter the Ukrainian version of his name Serhii Belousov will be used) was appointed as the new director.[9] According to the revised working plan in the report from Belousov to the Central Committee of the CPU, the textbook was to be prepared in three volumes.[10] However, in 1937, the campaign of terror was revived following a resolution of the Central Committee of the CPSU, targeting the first secretary of the CPU Postyshev and his team (Shapoval 1990, 14–20; Kas'ianov and Danylenko 1991, 87–91; Danylenko *et al.* 1991, 250–321; Bilokin' 2002; Shapoval 1993, 203–222; Shapoval 2003, 325–343, 343). During this wave of terror, the liquidation of historians at the newly founded Institute of History in Kyïv continued (Smolii 1996, 7–9; Iurkova 2001, 15–16, 48–49. Smolii 2006, 8–10. Also see Proty Burzhuaznykh

Natsionalistiv 1937; Yekelchyk 2004, 17–18). The figures who were involved in the writing of the national history in 1935–6 were accused of adding nationalist interpretations to the draft textbook and consequently arrested and shot.[11] In 1937, a mixture of apparatchiks, *vyvizhentsy* and 'old specialists' survived to continue the endeavour of writing the new history.

The new head of the Institute, Serhii Belousov (1892–1985), was a Russian from Tula (RSFSR, Russian Soviet Federative Socialist Republic, Russian: *Rossiiskaia Sovetskaia Federativnaia Sotsialisticheskaia Respublika*) and had been a member of the Communist Party since 1920. He was a party apparatchik first and then a scholar, and his knowledge of the Ukrainian language was poor. In 1930 he was one of the 100 successful party members who were sent to the Institute of Red Professors in Moscow to receive a higher degree in the history of the Party. After finishing his three years of education he was sent to Odesa as head of the political administration of the Grushov MTS (Machine-Tractor Station, Russian: *Mashinno-Traktornaia Stantsiia*) by the Central Committee of the CPSU, in 1933. He was probably very successful in implementing the government's policies in the rural areas during the *Holodomor*, for he was subsequently rewarded with the Order of Lenin. His later assignment was as secretary of the Bobrynets' *raikom* of the Odesa Oblast'. In January 1937, he started to work at his new office as the head of the Institute of History of Ukraine (Iurkova 2001, 14, 87, 88; Smolii 2006, 313–315).[12] Belousov was a *vydvizhenets*, similar to Buzurbaev in the Kazakhstan case. They both had working-class origins and had had no opportunities to receive a proper education. For them, the pre-revolutionary times represented barriers, repressions, and poverty. They believed in and supported the new system. The Party promised a new future and, moreover, provided them with a 'higher' education, though this education was in the domain of Party ideology and Party history. They were rapidly promoted to higher positions at academic institutions and in the communist parties of their respective republics as the purges unfolded. They were young and eager party bureaucrats who symbolized the new socialist era declared by the new constitution in 1936. Gradually, some experienced historians joined the team.

In particular, Mykola Petrovs'kyi, Oleksandr Ohloblyn, and Kost' Huslystyi, who survived the Great Terror, led the construction of the Ukrainian Soviet national narrative in the post-Pokrovskiian era. Mykola Petrovs'kyi (1894–1951) was Ukrainian from Chernihiv. His father was a priest, and he received his first education at a religious seminary in Chernihiv. Petrovs'kyi was considered an 'old specialist' and never became a member of the Communist Party. Yet he built his career in the Soviet period. He graduated from the Institute of Philology and History in Nizhyn (contemporary Ukraine) in 1919. At some point, he was a student of Hrushevs'kyi. He worked in his alma mater from January 1924 until December 1933 when he was removed from his post. The archival records inform us that the reason for his removal was 'nationalist ideas in his publications'. Of course, this was the judgement on his works when Pokrovskiian rules were still valid in history writing and such accusations were widespread when the Ukrainization policy was altered. When the emphasis in history writing moved from class to national, Petrovs'kyi found himself back in favour with the authorities. He started working in the Institute of History of Ukraine in Kyïv in January 1937. He received his doctoral degree in 1940 and he became the head of the Institute in 1942 and remained in this post until 1947 (Yekelchyk 2002, 61; Smolii 2006, 617).[13]

The other constructor of the new narrative was Kost' Huslystyi (1902–73). Both Petrovs'kyi and Huslystyi specialized in the medieval history of Ukraine and they worked together in the construction of the Ukrainian national history for the next decade. He was a Ukrainian from Zaporozh'e and educated in the Soviet institutions of the 1920s. Akin to Petrovs'kyi, Huslystyi was also accused of being a nationalist when Pokrovskii set the rules of the game (Smolii 2006, 527). The third historian was Oleksandr Ohloblyn (1899–1992). Ohloblyn was a Ukrainian from Kyïv. He enrolled at the University of Kyïv in 1917 but his education was interrupted in 1919. Nevertheless he was talented in history and educated himself, especially in the social and economic relations in the history of Ukraine. In the 1920s he worked at the University of Kyïv, and published various works. He participated in the rewriting of Ukrainian history within the Pokrovskiian–Marxist framework. Accordingly his doctoral dissertation was on the early capitalist industry in Ukraine. When the Ukrainization policies were slowed down, he was arrested for six months by the GPU (State Political Directorate, Russian: *Gosudarstvennoe politicheskoe upravlenie* (Secret Police)) in 1931. According to a report penned in 1940, 'in his old publications he made mistakes of nationalistic character'. In November 1937, he joined Petrovs'kyi and Huslystyi to re-write the national history. At the same time, he worked in the universities of Odesa and Kyïv (Plokhy 2012, 109–110).[14] These historians developed their careers during the Soviet Ukrainization policy in the 1920s. There were also others who participated in writing the new history. For instance, Fedir Iastrebov (1903–73) was a Russian originally from Ivanov Oblast, Russia. He moved from Vladimir to Kyïv in 1919, where he received his entire education in the new Ukrainian Soviet educational institutions. The works of these historians before 1934 predominantly reflected the Pokrovskiian approach. At the same time, these were the leading historians who managed to switch to the new line and wrote the new national history, which gradually moved from 'class analysis and class struggles' to 'national heroes and national struggles'.[15]

## The German orientalization of the Slavs and the response of Hrushevs'kyi

When these Ukrainian historians gathered to write the new history in 1937, the German orientalization of Slavs had already been on the table for a century. The German history thesis rotated around two migrations. There was a migration of Aryans and Indo-Germans towards the Asiatic east which brought civilization the semi-Asiatic Slavs. The other migration was of the Slavs from the Pripet marshes to fertile lands. However, this was not a conquest but a gradual dissemination to the fertile plains in the west and south when they met no resistance. Both theories were used for the German orientalization of Slavs.

In order to justify the Prussian occupation of Polish lands, conservative Prussian historians of the nineteenth century portrayed the German expansion beyond the Elbe River from the time of the Teutonic Knights as a historical mission to bring order, civilization, and government to their eastern neighbours. This high-medieval German colonization was also used as an argument for German eastward expansion during the First World War (Wipperman 1981; Liulevicius 2009, 71–129; Müller 2003, esp. 93–97). According to this messianic view, the eastward movement was an inescapable result of the German spirit and of the German nation, which was the conqueror, teacher, and discipliner of – in the words of Frederick the Great, the Prussian King – the 'imbecile crowd whose names end in -ki'. It was Frederick who 'resettled' German populations in the newly acquired Polish territories after the first partition of Poland in 1772. Although some German scholars referred in particular to Poles, and some of them to Russians, it was not hard to include Ukrainians when the last claimed their separate identity. Moreover, usually people think in ethnic totalities and this interpretation of history was easily transferable to all Slavs, including the Ukrainians. The 'industrious' Germans, who were the 'bearers of culture' (German: *Kulturträger*), were 'naturally' driven to the east as a consequence of a cultural gradient (German: *Kulturgefälle*) declining from the 'civilized Germanic' west towards the 'uncivilized Slavic' east. This orientalization of the Slavic lands was verbalized in the immortal phrase *Drang nach Osten* ('urge/drive towards the East') (Burleigh 1989, especially pp. 3–39; Rady 1999, 14). In the nineteenth century, these ideas were so widespread that even Karl Marx and Friedrich Engels saw the Germanic peoples, including Austrians, as civilizers of the Slavs, while considering Slavs, except for the Poles, as 'non-historical' peoples who lacked continuous statehood, elites and high culture (Rosdolsky 1986; Rudnytsky 1987a; Kappeler 2009, 51–80, 57). This century-old discussion was about the definition of European borders by particular ethnicities and nations, moreover, creating a less developed 'orient' beyond these borders. Germans had an important reason to be eager to establish such a border. The French, the 'archrivals' of the Germans in the nineteenth century, had already built a border and left the Germans out. The French had an easier time, since 'everyone knew' that they were the civilized people per se and they could claim to be the descendants of the Romans. When the Germans wanted to produce a history with a proud past, they only found savage Germanic tribes fighting against the civilized Rome. Germans had to find further evidence in the past to compete against such a claim. One way of this was romanticizing Germanic barbarian tribes as freedom loving, charmingly rough, and uninhibited (Arvidsson, 2006). The other way of remaining in the civilized world was finding their own 'orient' further in the Slavic east.

The orientalization effort was keen to dilute the 'Europeanness' of Slavs in prehistory. In the eighteenth century, before the rise of Slavic studies, there were already different theories on the origins of the Slavs.[16] The tension of placing the

Slavs on the western side of the delicate borderline between 'civilized Aryan-Europe' and 'inferior Asiatic lands' occurred in the nineteenth century when race, language, and culture were considered inseparable parts of one body. Early Slavists such as Pavel Josef Šafárik (1795–1861) aimed to describe the Slavs as an ancient nation in Europe, as old as the Germanic and Latin nations and even the ancient Greeks.[17] They connected the Slavs with the Scythians as well as with the Neuri, Budini, and Sarmatians of Herodotus (Minns 1913, 98; Czaplicka 1920; also see Rives 1999, 19–21; Tacitus 1999, 77; Jordanes 1960, 59). On the other hand, some German anthropologists of the nineteenth century thought that the ancient Slavs were connected to Finnic or Turanian groups (Niederle 1912, 8). The Slavs were latecomers to the Kyïv region, the lower banks of the Dnieper River, and Poland. They had originated in the Pripet marshlands, or (even worse!) stemmed from the Asiatic Scythians and gradually migrated to irrigable lands in the west and south at a later stage. Thus, the Slavs were not part of Indo-European or Aryan culture. The theory went that the Slavs had been unable to organize complex political structures such as states, and were incapable of creating a 'high culture' in history. It was the Germanic peoples who brought them civilization following their drive to the east.

Not surprisingly, the German orientalization created a domino effect among the Slavs. In Eastern Europe the radical Polish historian Franciszek Duchiński (1816–93) raised similar arguments when he looked upon Russians, seeing only a stock of Finnic and Tatar mixture speaking a Slavic language (Duchinski [Duchiński] 1855, 1864; Rudnytsky 1987b). According to the Russian imperial historian Pogodin, Ukrainians (*maloros*) were a mixture of Slavic–Turkic blood, while the ancestors of contemporary Russians (*velikoros*) kept their purity by evacuating the southern steppes towards the Oka–Volga region following the arrival of the Mongol–Tatar hordes (Andriewsky 2003, 203–207; Maksymovych 1876, 1: 5–92, 93–104; Tolochko 2012). Half a century later, it was Hrushevs'kyi's turn to make claims for purity and to define Russians as a mixture of Slavic–Uralic–Altaic people.

The identity of the Antes, a tribal confederation in the Pontic Steppe of the sixth century, was another battleground between the German orientalization of Slavs and Slavic historians. While German historians defined the Antes as Asiatic and even Circassian, their Slavic counterparts defined them as proto-Slavs.[18] When Ernst Eduard Kunik, a German–Russian historian–philologist and a member of the Russian Imperial Academy (1814–99; in Russian: Arist Kunik) defined the Antes as an 'Asian dynasty' ruling over Slavic tribes, other German historians did not hesitate to follow this example.[19] Theodor Schiemann (1847–1921), another German historian and publicist, a native of the Courland, worked in Russia until he was banished by the Russian Imperial authorities. After moving to Germany, he became the founder of scholarly research on Eastern Europe in Germany, and in 1906 he was appointed to the Professorship of Eastern European history in Berlin. Referring to Kunik, Schiemann argued that the Antes were Asians who ruled over Slavic tribes in contemporary

Ukraine, and he presented the ethnogenesis of the Slavs as an amalgamation of European and Asian elements (Schniemann 1886, 1: 1–22; on the Antes, 18–19). Another historian, Ernest Denis, in his account of the ancient Slavs claimed that although 'Slavs are Indo-European Aryans, some Slavic groups, especially the Russians, were a hybrid race mixed with non-Aryan elements' (Denis 1905, 689).[20] The Antes, according to him, were Asians who ruled the Slavic tribes at the shores of the Black Sea (Denis 1905, 691). The prominent German historian Albrecht Wirth (1866–1936), in turn referring to Denis (Wirth 1905, 248–253; see also Wirth 1904, 66) and the controversial Czech historian Jan Peisker (1851–1933) also supported the same theory (Peisker 1910, 4; 1913, 2: 418–419, 422–423, 426, 430–431, 436–437, 444–445). In a period when Indo-Europeans were seen as the only bearers of the torch of civilization in the history of humanity, these assumptions implied that the proto-Slavs were not among the elite members of mankind[21] (see also Kossinna 1919, 7).

Hrushevs'kyi fought against all those German and Russian-German historians who described all or a part of the Slavs as Asiatic peoples. The historiographical battle between Hrushevs'kyi and his German counterparts intensified when his first volume of the *History of Ukraine-Rus'* was published in German (Tel'vak 2008, 75–99). He viewed the Antes as forming part of the Slavic stock, and further attributed to them sole ancestry of the Ukrainians (Hrushevs'kyi [Hrushevsky] 1898; Hrushevsky 2005, 1: 6, 43, 130–134, 418–420. Plokhy 2005a, 121–127).[22] Defining the Antes as Slavs and sole ancestors of the Ukrainians underlined that Ukrainians had a mono-ethnic Indo-European ancestry; with their mono-ethnic Slavic ancestors, Ukrainians secured their place in the Indo-Aryan world. Hrushevs'kyi was not alone in his claim. His Ukrainian colleagues and the émigré historians in the interwar period such as Dmytro Doroshenko (1881–1951) (Doroshenko 1942, 11) agreed with him. This formula also complied with Doroshenko's historiography, which excluded non-Ukrainian elements (Prymak 2001, 39). The Ukrainian anthropologist and ethnographer Khvedir Vovk (or Fedor Volkov, 1847–1918) argued that the Ukrainian nation had ethnographic and anthropological unity and integrity which was distinct not only from non-Aryan races but also from other Slavic peoples (Volkov 1906; Vovk 1995). Serhii Shelukhin (1864–1938), émigré historian, consolidated the Europeanness of Ukrainians by arguing that the origin of the Ukrainians was a mixture of the Celtic tribes from the southern France and the Slavic Antes (Shelukhin 1929).

The German historians mentioned above, who defined all or part of Slavs as Asiatic, Turanic or 'Asiaticized', were also the ones who defined the Slavs as people unable to organize their statehood or to defend themselves against invaders. According to Wirth, for instance, 'the foundations of all Slavic states were laid by either German or Tatar leadership. Celts and Slavs were feminine peoples for centuries' (Wirth 1904, 65). This German approach to the Slavs was becoming so conventional that Peisker, who was commissioned to write the chapter on the Slavs in the 1913 edition of *The Cambridge Medieval History*, did not hesitate to depict the Slavs as

[a] weakly breed of men ... easily enslaved by a foreign yoke.... They were exceptionally unwarlike.... In summer, when suddenly attacked, they had to disappear like frogs into the water or into the woods.... But not even this wretched equipment [which they fought with] was Slavonic; it must have been borrowed from some German people.... The unwarlike inhabitants of the marshland can conquer nothing, and can only spread gradually where they meet with no resistance. This is upon the whole the difference between the expansion of the Germans and that of the Slavs.

(Peisker 1913, 2: 420–421, 424, 426, 438)

Peisker continued his description of the Slavs as a miserable folk who from early times filled the slave markets of Europe, Asia, and Africa, being ruled by warlike peoples such as the Celts (Venedi) in pre-Christian times, the Germanic Bastarnae and Heruli in the third century BC, the Goths in the fourth century, the Scandinavian Vikings (Varangians), and 'Altaian masters' such as Huns, Bulgars, Avars, Khazars, Magyars, Pechenegs, Cumans, and Mongols. There had never been a Slavic state in history, and Slavs could not maintain themselves without a German or Altaic warrior stratum (Peisker 1913, 2: 428–434; also see Peisker 1910, 4; Czaplicka 1920, 591; Dvornik 1956, 3). The Slavs, including proto-Ukrainians, were a passive race lacking political or military organizations. It was also argued that the Slavic title *kniaz'* (prince) originated in Germanic, and particularly Gothic, rule over the Slavs.

The German orientalization of Slavic peoples imputed a civilizing role to the Germans in the founding of the Kyïvan Rus' state, a polity that is considered the first state in Russian, Belorussian and Ukrainian national narratives. While the Normanist school of historians claimed that the founders of the Kyïvan Rus' were Nordic Germans, the anti-Normanist school saw the arrival of the Normans as a later stage that followed the foundation of Kyïvan Rus' by autochthonous Slavs. The first skirmishes began in the eighteenth century with the Normanist view of a historian of German origin, Gerhard Friedrich Müller (1705–83), who was the official imperial historiographer and a member of the Imperial Academy of Sciences in St Petersburg (Pritsak 1976, 5–10; Khlevov 1997; Plokhy 2008a, 23–33). In the second half of the nineteenth century, however, the controversy gradually became a battlefield of national or racial discourses. This was the outcome of the gradual crystallization of Russian and Ukrainian national identities, independent of the multi-ethnic imperial discourse. Following Müller, numerous scholars, many of them with German or Scandinavian origins, became adherents of the Normanist school: Ludwig Schlözer (Shletser, 1735–1809; Grekov 1945, 27); Ernst Eduard Kunik (Kunik 1903; Khlevov 1997, 22); Friedrich Westberg (Westberg 1899). August Wilhelm Schlegel (1767–1845), a key figure in German orientalist scholarship, argued:

Slavs everywhere and under all circumstances are destined to slavery (a word which derives from them, without a doubt) ... Slavic nation needs foreign infusions into the whole mass, just as the Germanic Norsemen had shaped the genesis of Russian statehood.

(Liulevicius 2009, 60–61)

The Scandinavian beginning of the Kyïvan Rus' was also taken for granted in English publications of the time (Peisker 1913, 2: 428–434, see especially 433; Toynbee 1916). While Hrushevs'kyi defined Kyïvan Rus' as a Ukrainian polity against Russian imperial and nascent national narratives, he also defended the Slavic character of Kyïvan Rus' against these German supporters of its Norman origins (Hrushevs'kyi [Hrushevsky] 1904,; Hrushevsky 2005, 1: 289–298).

Within this orientalization project, German linguists used comparative and etymological linguistics to show that the Slavic culture was underdeveloped and many items were borrowed from the Germanic neighbours. If there was a word in the ancient vocabulary, this indicated a knowledge of the thing. For instance, if 'sowing' had existed in the archaic form of a language, then those people must had been familiar with cultivation. German linguists argued that, since the Slavs were an incapable stock, similar words and terms with close roots in Slavic and Germanic languages could not be of Slavic origin. These various and numerous terms in Slavic languages must have been early borrowings from proto-German. The German side compiled a long list of items including plough, *tvarogъ* (a kind of cheese) and terms for milk, livestock, cattle, plough, bread, honey, wax, house, and *kniaz'* (prince). Hrushevs'kyi waged a battle against this orientalization of Ukraine (and other Slavic lands) by German historians (Peisker 1905; Hrushevs'kyi 1911; Hrushevsky 2005, 1: 187, footnote 1, 194–195, 203, 208, especially footnote 125).[23] In his history of Ukraine, Hrushevs'kyi also refuted the argument on the term *kniaz'* (for further German sources and Slavic replies see: Hrushevsky 2005, 1: 240, especially footnote 35; for the discussion on *kniaz'* 283; for Peisker's Uralo-Altaic higher stratum 280).

## Germany's Slavic orient in the interwar period

In the aftermath of the German defeat in the First World War, racist theories, that were founded earlier, continued to be represented by German scholars in the 1920s (Hertz 1928, 172–180). Moreover, both the postwar boundary changes and an urge to defend 'Germanness' (*Germanentum*) against the new neighbouring (Slavic) states accelerated the interpretation of Slavic history along the lines summarized above (Krüger 2003). *Ostforschung* ('East-research') as a multidisciplinary area of study played a key role in this post-1918 acceleration. *Ostforschung* researchers aimed to provide arguments and talking points for German demands for revisionist policies in the interwar period. Later, these experts of *Ostforschung* did not hesitate to work in the capacity of advisers when the German armies marched to this 'primitive orient' in 1939 and 1941. German scholars like geographer Wilhelm Volz (1870–1958) and the leading historian Herman Aubin (1885–1969) were in this movement, which aimed to promote German interests in the east by claiming that German settlers had shaped culture, social structure, and economic character in those Slavic regions for centuries (Aubin 1930, 56: 95–97; cited in Mühle 2003). The claims for German superiority in Eastern Europe continued during the Weimar Republic, which provided fertile ground for the racist discourse of Nazi rule after 1933 (Volz 1926, 5, cited in Burleigh 1989, 28; Wipperman 1981, 139; Burleigh 1989; Van Horn Melton 1994, 283–287; Liulevicius 2009, 158; Mühle 2003; Kossina 1932). The Nazis brought slight adjustments to the German orientalization of Slavs, such as biological differences that could not be solved by cultural assimilation. When it came to the imperialist geopolitical designs of Nazi ideology, there were few genuine points of disagreement between the Nazis and the German conservative historians who had developed the anti-Slavic German historiography.[24] In the new order envisioned by the Nazis, the Slavs simply had to evacuate the lands destined for the German people – the German *Lebensraum* – though after 1941, the 'hard-liners' including Hitler, Himmler, Bormann, and Erich Koch, aimed to exterminate most of the Slavic population in the occupied Soviet territories (Cecil 1972, 164–165, 190–214). The image of the German King Henry I, who 'drove back the Slavs', so impressed Heinrich Himmler that some thought that he came to regard himself as a reincarnation of the tenth-century hero (Cecil 1972, 70). In a typical case of orientalization, the Germans were 'great', as long as the Slavs were 'inferior'.

## German orientalization of the Slavs and the Soviet Union

In the Soviet Union, the 1920s constituted the high water mark for the opinions of Marr and Pokrovskii in history writing. For Marr, questions of ethnogenesis, proto-peoples or proto-languages were not a high priority because identities were fluid turning from one into another as a result of socio-economic transformations in a given geography. Pokrovskiian history, which was dominant until the mid-1930s in the Soviet Union, underlined that although Ukrainians, Belarusians, and Russians all spoke Eastern Slavic languages, they were composed of different ethnic mixtures and sprang from different roots. For instance, Russians, according to Pokrovskii, were a mixture of Eastern Slavs, Finnic tribes and other Asiatic elements such as the Chuvash. Probably, Pokrovskii continued, the Belarusians were the most isolated group, the remnants of those ancient Eastern Slavs who settled in Polessia and on the banks of the Dnieper (Pokrovskii 1967, 3: 24). Nevertheless, the exclusion of the non-Aryan/European elements from the Ukrainian ethnogenesis was so important that even in his Pokrovskiian–Marrist narrative of Ukrainian history, Iavors'kyi found it necessary to define Ukrainians as mono-ethnic Aryans: 'the Ukrainian ethnicity [*narodnist'*] belongs to Slavic tribes ... Slavic tribes are part of the great Aryan race' (Iavors'kyi 1928; 21).

After the Nazis came to power in Germany, the Communist Party leaders became increasingly aware of the German orientalization of Slavs and their prejudices.[25] After 1933, Soviet historians also observed with increasing attention how history teaching became racist, revanchist, and anti-Soviet in Germany. The directives and speeches of the Nazi ministers of education and interior affairs, German pedagogical periodicals, publications on geopolitics and history were closely monitored (Sokolova 1934; Fridliand 1934; Varga *et al.* 1934).

In February 1936, when the history faculty was re-established in Moscow following the demise of the Pokrovskiian history school, the primary task of scholars of the medieval period was to fight against German expansionist claims towards Eastern Europe and the USSR. The German racist interpretations of ancient and medieval history, and especially the usage of medieval expansion of the Teutonic Knights, had to be answered by Soviet historians. According to the language of the day, 'science had to be mobilized' (Russian: *mobilizatsiia nauki*) in order to prepare a strong rebuttal to the German claims. Historians had to promote 'the defence of the country in the sphere of ideas' (Russian: *ideinaia oborona*) in anticipation of a German attack. German expansion in the Middle Ages, as well as the German occupation of Ukraine in 1918, became major themes of historical research (Sharova 2004, 324). After 1936 the attention of Soviet historians to German racist historiography increased. Numerous books were published targeting German racist history writing and German descriptions of the Slavs as an 'inferior other'. These publications were a belated reply to the German orientalization of Slavs and aimed to show who the 'real barbarians' were (Gurevich 1936; *Protiv fashistskikh podzhigatelei* 1937; Kagarov 1937. Especially see: Udal'tsov 1937; Kazachenko 1937; Tarle 1937; Gratsianskii 1938; *Nauka o rasakh i rasizm* 1938; *Protiv fashistskoi fal'sifikatsii* 1939).

As I have mentioned above, the German history thesis rotated around migration. There was a migration of Aryans and Indo-Germans who brought civilization to others such as semi-Asiatic Slavs. The other migration was of the Slavs from the Pripet marshlands to the fertile plains in the west and south only when they found an opportunity. In other words, Slavs in Ukraine, Russia, and Poland were not autochthonous. The only 'prehistoric' homeland they could claim was the inhabitable and hostile marshes in the south of Belarus. The construction of an autochthonous and pure-blood Slavic identity in the valleys of the Dnieper and Dniester rivers was the only way out to reply to such an aggressive claim. It was in this context that, after a decade of silence, the Ukrainian Soviet historiography started to load the guns that were last fired by Hrushevs'kyi. The ethnogenesis of Slavic peoples including Ukrainians, the ethnogenesis of the Goths and other Germanic tribes, and also the prehistorical roots of other Soviet nations became an important research topic to answer the German claims. The consecutive meetings of social scientists to discuss the ethnogenesis issue and the establishment of a commission in 1938–9 headed by A. Udal'tsov, a Russian historian who had already worked in the field of Slavic ethnogenesis, signalled this new direction (Grekov 1937, 1102; Na sessii OON AN SSSR 1938; for further sources see Aksenova and Vasil'ev 1993; Shnirel'man 1993; Aksenova 2000, 150; Iusova 2006, 2007).[26] The famous solution of Soviet historians was the construction of the concept of 'Eastern Slavic people' in prehistory and ancient times which would provide a common ancestor with pure Slavic blood to Russians, Ukrainians, and Belarusians by one blow (Iusova 2000). Archaeologists came first to establish a link between the Antes, Eastern Slavs and the Kyïvan Rus' (Rybakov 1939; Tret'iakov 1939, 1940, 1941). According to Udal'tsov, the initial research plan of his commission was to answer the question of 'the origins of the [all] Russian nation, its ethnic relations with the Scythians, Sarmathians, Venethi (Sclaveni and Antes) Finns, Khazars, and with the other tribes of the

Eastern Europe, in the context of the Great Russians, Ukrainians, and Belorussians'.[27] The current literature is focused on the fact that the Soviet formula was based on the construction of the all-Russian or ancient East Slavic nation as being the common ancestors of the Great Russians, Ukrainians, and Belarusians. How Udal'tsov put the question in the beginning of the endeavour at the Institute of History in September 1938 gives us another detail with cardinal importance: this list was an incomplete one as if the ancestors of the three nations had lived isolated from the rest of the world since antiquity. Though the Finns and Khazars were mentioned, the Polish, Lithuanian, and Jewish elements were absent in the Belorussian case. In the Ukrainian case, there was no indication of the Polish, Germanic, and Altaic components. Finally, in the Great Russian case, there was no Altaic aspect in the list. The question was put from the beginning to achieve an autochthonous and mono-ethnic origin. Thus, the formation of the Eastern Slavs was completely isolated from the Asiatic elements. In time, this incomplete and inconsistent list of Sarmathians, Finns, and Khazars were clipped off, and the definition of the Eastern Slavic ethnic origins tied to the Antes. The consecutive articles on the Trypillian culture and proto-Slavs (Derzhavin 1939) and the Antes as the ancient Slavs (Mishulin 1939; Rybakov 1939; Gorianov 1939) were published by leading Slavists in Moscow. These publications claimed a direct line from Trypillian culture and the Antes to the Kyïvan Rus'. The archaeological excavations aimed to identify the ethnicity of the Trypillian culture and confirm what famous archaeologist V. V. Khvoika (1850–1914) claimed four decades earlier – that they were proto-Slavs four decades earlier (Passek and Bezvenglinskii 1939; Derzhavin 1939, 284).[28] They also answered the German orientalization. According to the leading archaeologist Passek, recent archaeological excavations 'expose racial migration theories of fascist "scholars" who tried to explain the emergence of settlements with painted ceramics in the Dnieper–Dniester basin by the penetration of Indo-Germans back in the Neolithic Era' (Passek 1938, 277).

While the romantic national historiography displaced the Pokrovskiian attempt of writing history from an orthodox Marxist perspective, both the ethnogenesis of the Ukrainians and the German orientalization of the Slavs rapidly regained their place as a primary issue for historians. As it happened before the Pokrovskiian interlude, the Ukrainian histories that were published in 1937 and 1940 aimed to rebut the German orientalization by presenting a mono-ethnic description of the Ukrainians. In other words, the post-1937 Ukrainian description of ethnogenesis was as pure as the definitions of Hrushevs'kyi and Iavors'kyi.

After the Great Terror, the first official history of Ukraine was the *Narysy z Istoriï Ukraïny*, which was published in autumn 1937, just after the publication of Shestakov's *Short Course of the History of the USSR*. The monograph was written by the survivors of the Great Terror, Iastrebov and Huslystyi, under the editorial supervision of Belousov.[29] Following this volume, in 1938, the Academy of Sciences of the Ukrainian SSR requested the permission of Nikita Khrushchev, the new first secretary of the CPU, to organize a competition to write a short textbook on Ukrainian national history and to establish an editorial board at the Institute of History of Ukraine at the Academy in Kyïv.[30] Following Khrushchev's approval, another history textbook, *Istoriia Ukraïny – Korotkyi Kurs* (History of Ukraine – Short Course), which covered the entire history of Ukraine, was prepared. The *Korotkyi Kurs*, which was published in 1940, was officially authored by Belousov, Huslystyi, Ohloblyn, Petrovs'kyi, Suprunenko,[31] and Iastrebov.[32] The Institute planned to publish it in October 1939 (Belousov 1938), but the unification of Ukraine in 1939 kept Ukrainian historians busy with some revisions of the text and this, with propaganda works, delayed the publication for a year.[33]

The preface of the 1937 edition put forward the ambitious task of the textbook as 'writing a Marxist history of the Ukrainian nation [and] Ukrainian statehood from ancient times up until our own times. This kind of Marxist history of the Ukrainian nation will arm the nation more and help reveal bourgeois-nationalist lies' (Belousov 1937a, 3). The prehistoric period still reflected a Marrist interpretation that eschewed explicitly identifying archaeological cultures with ethnicities. The Trypillian (*Trypil's'ka*) archaeological culture was praised as 'a highly cultivated artistic taste' and 'one of the brightest periods of the history of primitive society in East Europe'. Then the narrative explained the widespread geography of this culture, covering all contemporary Ukraine and even further in the west and south (Belousov 1937a, 10, 14–20). Detailed pictures of Scythian archaeological findings were added into the book. Although Scythian tribes were mostly nomadic, they could produce elegant artefacts and metalwork. The aim of the chapter was to demonstrate that Ukrainian lands had been inhabited by skilful craftsmen since the dawn of history: there was no need to wait for Germans to bring civilization to Ukraine. Following the skilful pastoral nomads, Greek colonizers from Miletus arrived in southern Ukraine. The Greeks possessed the most highly developed culture of the time and left footprints of their civilization in Ukraine. Thus Ukraine became part of the Mediterranean high culture (Belousov 1937a, 22–24). The first edition in 1937 represented Germanic Goths, an 'Asian' tribal federation, which arrived in contemporary Ukraine and moved to the West. The authors also cited Engels on this point to corroborate their view. The text emphasized that the Goths were unable to enslave the local tribes, who fought against them. This was a direct response to German depictions of the Slavs as a passive and pacific people. Next, the Goths were defeated with the help of the Huns (Belousov 1937a, 27). There could be no historical claim over Ukrainian lands by the Germans of the twentieth century referring to those days. Although Goths were described as 'Asiatic' in this narrative, 'Slavic tribes lived from time immemorial in Europe and occupied wide spaces'. The authors cited Engels to indicate that Slavic lands reached as far as the Elbe River and the Bohemian Forests (Belousov 1937a, 29). He stressed that, unlike the Goths, the Slavs were represented in a substantial part of Europe and had occupied Eastern Europe since the beginning of history. And the Antes, ancestors of the Eastern Slavs, who originally lived between the rivers Dniestr and Dniepr, by the sixth century had managed to Slavicize and 'colonize' contemporary Ukraine as far as the Don River in the east (Belousov 1937a, 30).

The revival of national histories also brought back the importance of the anti-Normanist arguments. While Russian historians were busy with anti-Normanist theories in Moscow, Ukrainian historiography also took it as a priority. The 1937 edition represented a challenge to the Normanist theory with a Marxist flavour. The text first described the emergence of Slavic towns and slave-owning society and agriculture in the seventh and eighth centuries. These socio-economic developments engendered the crystalization of classes, which in turn formed states as a polity, well before the arrival of the Normans. These states were small 'Eastern Slavic principalities' (Belousov 1937a, 36–41, 49). The Normans were plundering barbarians who sought slaves for trade, and attacked the rich and cultivated lands of Eastern Slavic principalities (Belousov 1937a, 50–51). In time, these Norman warlords were slavicized. After a mention of the Normanist and anti-Normanist theories, the authors of the 1937 edition followed the argument of Grekov, who claimed that there were two Rus' – the people in the Norman polity in Sweden in the north, and in the south – Slavic people. Kyïv was the point of convergence for these two Rus' (Belousov 1937a, 52; Grekov 1936, 169–171. Grekov refers to V. A. Brim). The point was that there was a Rus' or a Slavic state in the south before the arrival of the Varangians. The authors quoted the writings of Marx in order to avoid any 'misunderstanding' of Marx. To present Marx as a pro-Slavist was a hard task to accomplish. Marx had called the Kyïvan Rus' 'the Gothic Russia' or 'the Empire of the Riurikovich' and defined it as a Norman state during the epoch of Norman conquests all over Europe in the Middle Ages. Marx argued that although the Norman rulers were eventually slavicized, *druzhina*, the retinue or the military power base of these Norman princes, remained exclusively Norman. The reason for the demise of Kyïvan Rus', Marx continued, was the gradual disappearance of this superior warlike Germanic seed (Marx 1986, 75–76). The interpretation of Marx in the 1937 edition of the *History of Ukraine* was probably the most pro-Slav interpretation that one could squeeze out of his writings (Belousov 1937a, 81).

The subsequent edition, *Istoriia Ukraïny – Korotkyi Kurs* (1940), was the first history textbook published after the unification of Western and Eastern Ukraine. This newer text also confirmed that Ukraine possessed a high level of civilization in the early stages of its history. In the 1940 edition, however, non-Slavic peoples such as Sarmatians, Goths, and Huns were given short shrift. When the narrative explained the arrival of the Slavs in contemporary Ukraine, the troublesome word, Slavic 'colonization', of the 1937 version disappeared in 1940. This time the primordiality of Eastern Slavs in Europe was strongly emphasized from the beginning (Belousov *et al.* 1940, 18). The Antes were designated as the common ethnic origins of all Eastern Slavs including Ukrainians, and the text provided detailed information about them. The authors went on to explain that from the eighth and early ninth centuries, the Eastern Slavs were already known as *Rus'*. So the Rus' and Eastern Slavs were one and the same people. They inhabited the basins of the Western Bug, Dniester, Dnieper, Don, Western Dvina, and Volga, and the territories between these rivers (Belousov *et al.* 1940, 20). According to another account of Ukrainian history, published a few months before the German attack in 1941, the ancestors of Ukrainians, the Eastern Slavs, 'settled in the territory of contemporary Ukraine, Belarus, and Russia one and a half thousand years ago, in the eighth and ninth centuries' (Iastrebov 1941, 3). Iastrebov, a leading Ukrainian historian, explained at length how the Eastern Slavs resisted the Normans, as well as the political, military, and economic might of the Eastern Slavic Kyïvan state and the high level of its culture (Iastrebov 1941, 9–10).

## Conclusions

Since the nineteenth century, German orientalization had targeted the Slavic peoples including Ukrainians. According to this narrative, they were a hybrid race of Indo-European and Asian components. As a consequence of their hybrid origins, the Slavs were incapable of establishing durable polities, and lacked the capacity for intellectual creativity. The Slavs were 'inferior others' of Aryan Indo-European civilization. If Ukrainians, and Russians for that matter, had been described in terms of a heterogeneous mixture of ethnogenesis including Slavic, Finno-Ugric, and Altaic elements, then they could have been in danger of being expelled from the Aryan–European cradle of civilization to the barbaric lands of Asia. As well, this 'superior' Aryan–European civilization could claim to have right over its 'inferior orient' to fulfil its self-proclaimed historical civilizing mission. When Mykhailo Hrushevs'kyi constructed his monumental Ukrainian national history he fought against this German orientalization as much as he contested the Russian and Polish narratives. Part of his reply was to construct the Ukrainian national identity based on a mono-ethnic definition and to give up a territorial definition.

When the possibility of a German-led crusade against the Soviet Union increased after 1933, the Bolsheviks saw the German orientalization as an ideological challenge and propaganda item which had to be rapidly dismantled. The Ukrainian Soviet response was to follow the method of Hrushevs'kyi and other Slavic historians to construct a mono-ethic autochthonous origin and include only the Antes. Defining the nation based on mono-ethnic roots had nothing to do with Marxist ideology or Soviet rule in Ukraine. The theory of pure Eastern Slavic roots aimed to prevent the definition of the Ukrainians and the other two Eastern Slavic nations as inferior hybrid or Asiatic. The Ukrainian critique of the Soviet construction of the Ukrainian narrative has focused on the absence of an ethnogenesis separate from the Russians and Belarusians. However, the mono-ethnic autochthonous definition, a cardinal choice that had been made in the 1930s, has had an enduring impact on the formation of the Ukrainian national identity.

The Soviet construction of the Ukrainian mono-ethnic national identity is still valid and the competing definitions are at the centre of the Ukrainian question today. Since the independence of Ukraine, the ethnic definition of the nation has been inapt and incapable to embrace the minorities of Transcarpathia, the Tatars of the Crimea and the Russians of the Eastern provinces. A territorial definition of Ukraine would be a melting pot of the Scythians, Greeks, Poles, Jews, Germanic tribes, and various Altaic tribal confederations in the past. Moreover, it could be a remedy for the ethnic issues in Ukraine by turning 'Ukrainian Tatars' or 'Ukrainian Russians' into natural identifications. Avoiding a narrow Slavic definition and embracing various ethnic ingredients in the past and present would not only enrich the domestic content of the national identity, but Ukraine could have been more successful in establishing the difference between the Ukrainian Russians and the Russianness of Russia. Finally, by avoiding pure Slavic ethnonational definition, Ukrainian narrative could also liberate itself from the rivalry with Russian history writing and it would consolidate its genuine claim.

## Notes

1 A historian of antiquity, Michael Rostovtzeff defended this territorial approach (Rostovtzeff 1922); also see Plokhy 2005a, 117–118.
2 Kappeler 2009, 58. Kappeler argues that multi-ethnic definition of Ukrainian identity and history was represented by Drakhomanov and Kostomarov, who already propagated a multi-ethnic, federalist approach to Ukrainian history (p. 61). What Kappeler refers to is more of a diversity within all-Russian imperial identity or ideas of romantic enlightenment. Their description of this multi-ethnicity of Ukrainian identity covered *Malorus'* and *Velikorus'* but excluded the Poles, Jews, Germans and Turkic peoples.
3 For orientalism, see Said 1991. This orientalism was part of a bigger picture. In the eighteenth and nineteenth centuries, geographers, historians, travellers, and the intellectuals of the Enlightenment 'invented' Eastern Europe, a term that designated the east of Germany including the Russian Empire. For a broader view of the invention of 'Eastern Europe', see Wolff 1994.
4 K. G. Huslystyi, T. T. Skubyts'kyi, G. D. Lukonenko, F. O. Iastrebov, Senchenko, and Mezhberg prepared the draft of the first volume. Iurkova 2001, 6–8. The last two historians, Senchenko and Mezhberg, are mentioned in the list provided by Belousov. *TsDAHOU* 1–20–4291–189, and *TsDAHOU*, 1–20–7092–86/89 (June 19, 1937).
5 The board consisted of A. K. Saradzhev, V. M. Smol'nyi, O. P. Dzenis (the president of the VUAMLIN) and N. M. Voityns'kyi (the director of the Institute of Red Professors in Kyïv) (O. V. Iurkova, *Dokumenty*, pp. 6–8). Even though the tasks were successfully executed, the VUAMLIN and its Institute of History were liquidated by the decree of the Central Committee CPU of 23 July, 1936. The historians in the VUAMLIN were moved to the Department of the Social Sciences of the Academy of Sciences of the Ukrainian SSR (consequently the Institute of History of Ukraine), which had previously gained a new status by the resolution of the Party in February 1936. *TsDAHOU*, 1–20–6851–15/22 and 15, 16 and 18, July 23, 1936; *TsDAHOU*, 1–20–7092–32, April 2, 1937. This was done in order to centralize scholarly institutions and intensify control over them. A. K. Saradzhev was appointed as the first director of the Institute of History of Ukraine before his arrest a few months later. The historians affiliated with the Institute of History of Ukraine were V. V. Hurystrymba, K. G. Huslystyi, I. M. Premysler, T. T. Skubyts'kyi, M. F. Tregubenko, and the younger scholars F. E. Los' and F. O. Iastrebov (Smolii 2006, 8).
6 The terror against the historians of Slavic peoples was not limited to Ukraine. There were also purges in academic institutions in Moscow, Leningrad, and other cities against the Slavists in 1933–4 and 1937–8. See Ashinin and Alpatov 1994.
7 A Soviet term used for the young appointees, who were trained, nurtured in the first two decades of the Soviet rule.

8 Mikhail Popov (1891–1938), the agitation-propaganda secretary of the CPU and the editor of the first commission for writing the history of Ukraine in 1935 was a Russian party official (Iurkova 2001, 44; Lozytskyi 2005, 245); Osval'd Dzenis (1896–1937) was a Latvian from Riga and a Bolshevik since 1915, who became the president of the VUAMLIN and a member of the TsIK Ukrainian SSR in 1934. During the Civil War, he was a commissar in the Red Army and stayed in the Army until 1923 (Iurkova 2001, 21–22); Artashes Saradzhev (1898–1937) had been a Bolshevik from Armenia since 1917 and worked as a party bureaucrat in Baku before becoming the scientific secretary of the VUAMLIN in 1934. Later, he was appointed as the head of the Institute of Philosophy and the Institute of History of the VUAMLIN (Smolii 2006, 307–309); Zarmair Ashrafian (1898–1937), who was also a party bureaucrat from Armenia, became the director of the Institute of Red Professors in Kyïv and at the same time the head of the agitprop section in CPU. He was appointed to these posts when he arrived in Ukraine in 1934, after the purges conducted by Postyshev (Iurkova 2001, 20).
9 The secretary of the CPU Kosior also informed this decision to Malenkov in Moscow. *TsDAHOU*, 1–20–6851–137, November 23, 1936 (Smolii 2006, 310–311).
10 The remaining historians, Huslystyi and Iastrebov, worked on the first volume, Tregubenko on the second volume, and Hurystrymba and Premysler on the third *TsDAHOU*, 1–20–4291–189, and *TsDAHOU*, 1–20–7092–86/89, June 19, 1937.
11 The leading figures were Vasyl' Hurystrymba, Heorhii Lukonenko (Lukanenko), Trokhym Skubyts'kyi, and Mykola Tregubenko. For the collection of archival documents and protocols of the NKVD see Iurkova 2001, 49–65. *TsDAHOU*, 1–20–7092–33, April 2, 1937.
12 NAIIU, (P-251)-1l-24, January 15, 1940.
13 He received his PhD on 'the Liberation War of Ukrainian Nation against the Polish Landed Gentry' in 1939. NAIIU 1–1-463–1/112.
14 NAIIU 1–1-463–1/112.
15 For a summary of this period by Iastrebov and Huslystyi see: *TsDAHOU*, 1–70–753–104–9 and 246, April 29, 1947.
16 For the ideas of travellers and historians in the eighteenth century on the origins of the Slavs, see Wolff 1994, 285–305.
17 The Slovak scholars of the eighteenth century defined the cradle of all Slavs as the Tatra Mountains (Kirschbaum 1962, 43: 7, 19). Another early theory pointed to the Danubian region as the birthplace of Slavdom (Dvornik 1956, 3). For a short explanation of early historiography of Slavic ethnicity see Curta 2001, 6–10.
18 Russian historian Aleksandr Pogodin (1872–1947) claimed that the Antes were the ancestors of the Eastern Slavs (Pogodin 1901, 27). There is also abundant evidence that the Antes could also be the ancestors of the Crimean Goths rather than Slavs (Strumins'kyj 1979–1980; Magocsi 1996, 39–40).
19 Ernst Kunik was also a proponent of the Normanist theory (Kunik 1844, 1878). For Hrushevs'kyi's account of Kunik and German historians see Hrushevsky 2005, 1: 418. For earlier discussions on the Antes and Arist Kunik see Plokhy 2005a, 121.
20 This work was translated into Russian by Russian historian Tarle.
21 Some European historians who did not want to leave Slavs and especially Russians in the wilderness of the 'orient', which was created by their colleagues, opposed these claims (Rambaud 1898, 34). This work is an English translation of his earlier history (Rambaud 1878).
22 In addition, he refused the German claims of Gustaf Kossinna positioning the cradle of Indo-European race in Germany. He secured a safe place for proto-Slavs by asserting that the 'the original home of the Indo-European tribes was eastern Europe' (Hrushevsky 2005, 1: 45–47 and especially footnote 91).
23 On German works and the view of Hrushevs'kyi see Hrushevsky 2005, 1: 189–90, especially footnote 16.

24 For more details see Liulevicius 2009, 171–202. For the continuity of this Germanic West/Slavic East dichotomy in a different form during the Nazi regime, see Mühle 2003, 107–130; on the relationship between the Nazi regime and German historians and scholars in humanities see Bialas and Rabinbach 2007, especially 212–218; Mess 2008, 5.
25 Khrushchev recalls that Hitler had both anti-Bolshevik and anti-Slavic ideology. The translation of Hitler's *Mein Kampf* was distributed for the higher party members and he also had a copy (Khrushchev 2004, 1: 216).
26 Arkhiv RAN, 394–13–1-7/35 (Winter 1939).
27 Arkhiv RAN, 1577–5-143–47, September 10, 1938.
28 In the Imperial period, V. V. Khvoika (1850–1914), a Ukrainian archaeologist of Czech origin, discovered the Tripolye culture. He interpreted the Tripolye–Zarubintsian–Chernyakhovian cultural sequences as consecutive stages in the development of Slavic ethnicity.
29 The volume covered the pre-Slavic period of Ukraine, Eastern Slavs and their settlement in Ukraine, Kyïvan Rus', and the first century of Tatar rule (Belousov 1937a, 3).
30 *TsDAHOU*, 1–20–7240–2, February 20, 1938.
31 Mykola Suprunenko was a Ukrainian from Poltava, a member of the Communist Party since 1925, who graduated from the Institute of Red Professors in Kyïv in 1937.
32 Belousov *et al.* 1940. However, various historians in Kyïv had worked on this textbook since 1935, and historians who were purged in 1936–8 had written some sections. *TsDAHOU*, 1–70–753–254, April 30, 1947.
33 *TsDAVOU*, 3561–1-237–26; *Naukovyi arkhiv Prezydiï NAN Ukraïny* (The Scholarly Archive of the Prezidium of the Ukrainian National Academy of Sciences), (P-251)–1–81–46/47, February 15, 1940.

# 4 The adventurous lives of Bohdan Khmel'nyts'kyi

Bohdan Khmel'nyts'kyi was a hetman of the Zaporozhian Cossaks and the leader of a popular uprising (1648–57) against the Polish–Lithuanian Commonwealth. The uprising linked peasant fury to political, social, and religious grievances. It was nearly suppressed by the Poles when he turned to the tsar. He agreed with the representatives of the Principality of Muscovite in the town of Pereiaslav in 1654, and the Cossacks swore an oath of allegiance to the ruler in Moscow. Many on both sides opposed it. Within a few years of having proclaimed it eternal, both signatories contravened its stipulations. One declared it null and void, and then both declared war on each other. Bohdan Khmel'nyts'kyi never disseminated his copy of the treaty, while the Council of Officers in Moscow did not ratify it (Velychenko 2005, 97). In the following decades after the death of the famous hetman, the Ukrainian Church scripts mostly blamed his leadership and the Cossacks for the war and the widespread misery and destruction that he initiated.

The Khmel'nyts'kyi cult depicting him in positive terms re-emerged and begun to flourish in the eighteenth century. The Cossack elites, the promoters of the cult in written panegyrics and histories, used it to secure for themselves the privileges once granted by the tsar to the famous hetman but curtailed or abolished in the following century. The image of Khmel'nyts'kyi was an ideal historical example for the Cossack leaders to show the loyalty of the Cossack elites to the tsars as well as their desire to preserve the office of hetman (Plokhy 1992). In the nineteenth century, Khmel'nyts'kyi remained a popular anti-Polish hero among the laypeople of Ukraine well before his promotion within the modern notion of national identity. A Western visitor to the Polish Ukraine in 1919 noticed that, the Ukrainian population in the region had been brought up on stories about Bohdan Khmel'nyts'kyi (Goodhart 1920, 147–148).

When homogeneous narratives were constructed in the twentieth century, Bohdan experienced consecutive but contradictory reconstructions. As also happened with Babak of Azerbaijan, his final and most successful regeneration was that of the Bolsheviks. The Bolshevik reconstruction of Khmel'nyts'kyi after 1937 has been so successful that he is one of the rare historical figures who is still considered as an all-national Ukrainian hero. This chapter will focus on the reconstruction of Bohdan Khmel'nyts'kyi as a Ukrainian national historical figure after the turn in 1937 and the political reasons behind this reconstruction.

## Competing constructions at the turn of the twentieth century

The first modern constructors of the Khmel'nyts'kyi narrative were the Russian imperial administrators who elevated him as an all-Russian imperial figure with a Little Russian origin, targeting the Poles. In this Russian imperial discourse, 'Russian' and 'Russia' had been used not as an ethnicity or nationality in the narrow sense, but as a broader dynastic and statist concept (Velychenko 1992, 80–96; Bushkovich 2003; Plokhy 2008a, 19–33). The Russian historiography in the last decades of the Empire also wanted to supplement traditional dynastic identity with modern ideas of nationalism. (Rogger 1960; Saunders 1982; Velychenko 1992, 97–110, 134; Carter 1990, 16–42; Pelech 1993, 2–4; Hosking 1997, 367–396; 1998; Tolz 2001; Yekelchyk 2003; Miller 2003; Miller 2008; Plokhy 2008a, 19–23).[1] Khmel'nyts'kyi was useful at this junction of ideas. He was praised as the defender of the Orthodox Church and as an all-Russian hero against the Catholic Poles and the Jews. This definition was not too far from the reality. The records of the Orthodox Church in the heyday of Khmel'nyts'kyi praised him as the liberator of the Orthodox folk from the rule of the Polish Catholic nobility, akin to Moses liberating the children of Israel from the Egyptian Pharaoh. His Cossack Army butchered Catholics on its way from the Dnieper up to the Vistula. At the same time the Khmel'nyts'kyi Uprising was notorious for its Jewish pogroms. The Jewish annals of his time branded him as 'Chimel the Wicked' (Nadav 1984; Kohut 1998; Hrushevsky 2002, 8: 516–519; Hanover 1950; Svod znanii o evreistve 1913, 646; Das Judentum 1930; Ettinger 2007, 654–656; Zhydy 1955, 671; Weinryb 1977; Aster and Potichnyj 1983, 23–24, 38–39; Kubijovyč and Markus 1988, 386; Pelenski 1990; Sysyn 1990; Klier and Lambroza 1992; Fonberg and Liubchenko 2005, 51–55; Kappeler 2009, 52). The promoters of this all-Russian narrative erected a monument to Khmel'nyts'kyi, mounted on his rearing horse, with his hand holding his *bulova* pointing to the east – Moscow – which was inaugurated at St Sophia Square in Kyïv in 1888. The monument was designed after the Polish uprisings in the nineteenth century against Russian imperial rule. It stands at the centre of Kyïv as the epitome of the all-Russian imperial hero. The inscription on the monument reads: 'To Bohdan Khmel'nyts'kyi from one and indivisible Russia'. In the initial plan of the monument, the hind legs of the horse stood on bodies representing a Pole, Catholic priest, and a Jew.

By the beginning of the twentieth century, Khmel'nyts'kyi and his uprising was already considered a contested historical topic (Basarab 1982; Plokhy 2005c, xl). Decaying Russian imperial identity and an emerging Russian national narrative had to struggle against the emerging Ukrainian nationalism and Ukrainian national narrative. The increasing bifurcation of an all-embracing imperial Russian culture and identity into Russian and Ukrainian sent a clear message that Russian culture and history was destined to retreat from Ukraine into its ethnic borderlands (Ilnytzkyj 2003, 301; Luckyj 1956; Shkandrij 1992; Mace 1983).[2] The Ukrainian narrative nationalized Bohdan Khmel'nyts'kyi together with the Cossackdom. However, the founder of the Ukrainian primordial national history,

Hrushevs'kyi, was not a strong supporter of Khmel'nyts'kyi. The reason behind the distance of Hrushevs'kyi towards Khmel'nyts'kyi can be found in his populist (*narodnik*) ideas. Hrushevs'kyi criticized Khmel'nyts'kyi for his indifference towards the masses and his failure to turn to them as his base of support. Khmel'nyts'kyi achieved personal power at the cost of terrible suffering by the Ukrainian masses; he destroyed half of the Ukrainian population and most of the economy. Hrushevs'kyi judged the uprising to be a 'complete fiasco' in the long run, because it did not bring any benefits to the masses; and the alliance with Muscovy, which was intended to be temporary, came to determine Ukraine's political fate in the following centuries. According to Hrushevs'kyi, Khmel'nyts'kyi lacked strong political orientation, constantly fluctuated, and sought a way to shake hands with the Poles. The only solid line he held was the preservation of his personal power. Hrushevs'kyi, nevertheless, also considered the Cossack uprisings of the Khmel'nyts'kyi period as a turning point in the development of Ukrainian nationhood and in the awakening of a national consciousness (Prymak 1981; Sysyn 1999; Basarab 1982, 129–133; Sysyn 2000; Sysyn 2002, xlvii–xlix; Plokhy 2005b, 347–348; Plokhy 2008b, xxxvi–xliv). The conservative Ukrainian historian V. Lypyns'kyi, who was a member of the statist school, had a different interpretation.[3] He idealized Khmel'nyts'kyi as a statesman of genius, who sought to create a hereditary monarchy and a Ukrainian state. The Pereiaslav Agreement, according to Lypyns'kyi, was an agreement between equals, which also functioned as the first constitution, akin to the *Magna Carta* (Basarab 1982, 134–140; Lypyns'kyi 1954 [1920]; Sysyn 2002, xxxvi; Motyl 1980, 25–28).

## Khmel'nyts'kyi: a merciless exploiter

The description of Khmel'nyts'kyi dramatically changed when Soviet rule was established in Ukraine. In the 1920s, the early Soviet interpretation of the Khmel'nyts'kyi era was based on a desire to dismantle the Russian imperial narrative. Nobody needed a historical figure polished by the ancient regime as the defender of the Orthodox Church against the Catholics and Jews. The Pokrovskiian Soviet accounts of Khmel'nyts'kyi emphasized his class interests as an exploiter (Kappeler 2009, 73). According to Pokrovskii, the events of the Khmel'nyts'kyi era were a consequence of two competing exploiting classes: Polish magnates on the one hand, and Ukrainian burgers and Cossack landowners on the other. The Khmel'nyts'kyi uprising was a 'revolution' of the latter against the former. The uprising was a revolution of commercial capital and its agents, the Cossacks. Kheml'nyts'kyi was far from being the saviour of the true belief, leader of freedom-loving Cossacks, a hero of toiling masses, or the liberator of the Ukrainian nation. He represented the Cossack bourgeoisie. After 1649, he abandoned the toiling masses; that is why he had no choice but to go for an alliance with Muscovy to secure his role. Khmel'nyts'kyi and his cohort signed the Pereiaslav Agreement not because of religious or national brotherhood. The common interests of the same classes in two societies were the major factor. In this sense, he was little different from a Russian boyar or a Polish magnate (Pokrovskii 1966, 474–495). As a consequence, until the mid-1930s, the Soviet authorities saw the monument of Khmel'nyts'kyi as an embarrassment. During the mass celebrations of Soviet holidays, the monument was boarded up with wooden panels and the Ukrainian Communist Party leaders even considered demolishing it altogether (Yekelchyk 2004, 17). When the relevant volume of the first edition of the Great Soviet Encyclopaedia (*Bol'shaia Sovetskaia Entsiklopediia*) that covered the Khmel'nyts'kyi uprising was published in 1935, it described him as 'a traitor and ardent enemy of the revolting Ukrainian peasantry' (Shmidt *et al.* 1935). In *Ukraïna v ogni* Dovzhenko explains that the sabre of Khmel'nyts'kyi was exhibited in the museum of Chernihiv and the description beneath it said: 'This is the sabre of the famous butcher of the Ukrainian nation, that he suffocated the [Ukrainian] national revolution with' (Dovzhenko 2010, 265). The only point in common between the interpretation of Pokrovskii and the imperial narrative was their refusal to define the uprising as a 'Ukrainian national liberation war', and Khmel'nyts'kyi as a 'Ukrainian national hero', but each for its own ideological reasons.

In line with the approach of Pokrovskii, in the 1920s, Marxist Ukrainian historians aimed to reconstruct history based on reading classes as the main agents of history and class struggles as its motivating force. M. Iavors'kyi was a leading ideologue and historian of Soviet Ukraine in the 1920s, who represented the Pokrovskiian historiography. Iavors'kyi called the uprising a revolution of landed aristocracy (Iavors'kyi 1926, 48–50). At the end of the revolution, the feudal order was abolished and centralized Muscovite serfdom with its commercial capitalism was established (Iavors'kyi 1926, 51–54). The treaty of Pereiaslav, in the history of Iavors'kyi, was briefly mentioned as an agreement of autonomy for the Cossacks. Iavors'kyi did not favour Muscovite rule over Polish rule. He even mentioned that seventeenth-century Ukrainians did not know that a fate worse than that under the (Polish) landed aristocracy awaited them at the hands of the Muscovite *dvorianstvo* and its autocrat. In the final analysis, instead of being the leaders of their nation, they were the representatives of the Cossack exploiting classes, betraying their people for their class interests. Iavors'kyi did not refrain from belittling their role in history, complying with Pokrovskiian rules (Iavors'kyi 1926, 13). Within the Pokrovskiian school, there were other Ukrainian historians – Sukhyno-Khomenko, Karpenko, and Iastrebov – who presented various interpretations within the walls of this school. They called the uprising a 'Ukrainian bourgeois revolution', 'Cossack War' and 'the Peasant War of 1648 in Ukraine'. Needless to say, these interpretations diminished the role of any figures such as Khmel'nyts'kyi to mere executers of the interests of the exploiting classes that they represented. While noting that the ideology of the struggle was one of a religious conflict between Catholicism and Orthodoxy, Iavors'kyi argued that this only 'masked the real motives of the struggle, the economic and social liberation of the masses'. The Pereiaslav Agreement with the Principality of Moscow was a pact between Ukrainian landowners and the representatives of the big landowners or commercial capitalists of Muscovy, in order to keep the popular demands of the labouring masses under control (Iavors'kyi 1927, 22–81; 1926, 58, 61; 1928, 52–59. For other interpretations of the Khmel'nits'kii uprising fromf the Pokrovskiian era historians of Ukraine see Mace 1983; Plokhy 2005b).

In 1929, Pokrovskiian historians launched an attack against Hrushevs'kyi and criticized him for describing the revolution of 1648–54 as a national revolution that aimed to liberate Ukraine from Poland. According to Iastrebov, Hrushevs'kyi intentionally obscured the class struggle in Ukraine because, as a 'bourgoise nationalist' historian, he wanted to deny the existence of class differentiation and class conflict within the Ukrainian nation. (For a review of Pokrovskiian historians in Ukraine who criticized Hrushevs'kyi in 1929–34, see Plokhy 2005c, lviii–lxii; 2008b, xlv–xlvii.)

## Poland: the launchpad of anti-Bolshevik crusade

Why did Khmel'nyts'kyi, the defender of the Orthodox faith and all Rus' at the turn of the century, and then the bloody hangman of greedy landowners and commercial capitalists, come to be re-born as the national hero in Stalin's Ukraine after 1937? This reconstruction was a consequence of the new Ukrainian national narrative which was constructed around anti-Polish antagonism. What were the consecutive developments that induced the Ukrainian Soviet national history writing to be so anti-Polish? The answer, as in the Azerbaijani case, can be found in international relations. The relations with Poland, the biggest western neighbour of the USSR, were neither stable nor beneficial from the beginning. Both Poland and the Soviet Union were founded in the ashes of consecutive armed conflicts which were fought on every inch between Warsaw and Kyïv in 1918–21 (Hunczak 1977; Szporluk 1992; Garlinski 1992; Kuchabsky 2009). In the years following the peace agreement, every prospect for improvement in the relations was halted by a deep crisis.

General Józef Pilsudski, the national leader of Poland until his death in 1935, strived to keep a balance in Poland's relations with its two powerful neighbours, Germany and the USSR (Brzoza and Sowa 2009, 469). At the same time, he believed that Poland could only be seriously threatened by Russia (Buell 1939, 324–330; Budurowycz 1963, 19–20). Although a non-aggression pact was signed between Poland and the Soviet Union in November 1932, Pilsudski did not modify his belief in the Soviet threat to Poland's independence (Polonsky 1972, 200, 381; Budurowycz 1963, 47–49; Brzoza and Sowa 2009, 163–164; Budurowycz 1963, 13–19; Roszkowski 2006, 60). After the death of Pilsudski in 1935 Polish–Soviet relations went from bad to worse. Until 1939, Polish foreign policy remained exclusively under the control of Colonel J. Beck, the man Pilsudski had long designated as his successor in this field (Harley 1939, 24; Roberts 1953). Though Beck was loyal to the Non-Aggression Treaty with Moscow, he regarded the Soviet Union as Poland's principal enemy. He was hostile to Soviet attempts to build up a system of collective security against Germany, which he regarded as a pretext for increasing Soviet influence in

Europe. He refused to join the Franco-Soviet and Czechoslovak–Soviet alliances. He acted in concert with Hitler over the re-militarization of Rhineland, in relation to the Czechoslovakian crisis, and in the *Anschluss* with Austria. Parallel to the demands of Hitler, he demanded that Prague cede the tiny Tans-Olza area. He put strong pressure on the Romanians to refuse the French demand to permit the free passage of Soviet troops (Debicki 1962, 80–81; Budurowycz 1963, 51–72; Roos 1966, 133–134; Brzoza and Sowa 2009, 484).[4] Consequently, in the second half of the 1930s, the Soviet rulers became increasingly suspicious that Berlin, Warsaw, and Budapest were pursuing a coordinated anti-Soviet policy (Polonsky 1972, 470–484; Budurowycz 1963, 73–126, 195).

The Soviet leaders mistrusted Pilsudski's Poland as much as the Poles were suspicious of their eastern neighbour. The Bolsheviks studied both the French Revolution and the Paris Commune and came to the conclusion that the only socialist country in the world had to expect an intervention in the near future. These historical examples aside, that they had personally struggled through the foreign intervention during the Russian Civil War (1917–20) was a good example. After the Polish–Soviet War, the Bolsheviks saw Poland as a tool or vanguard of Western imperialism pointed like a dagger at the heart of world communism (Stalin 1954a, 307–309). The Soviet Union suspected that Pilsudski's *coup d'état* in 1926 had been inspired by Britain as a first step in Western intervention against the USSR. When the Soviet envoy to Warsaw, Petr Voikov, was assassinated by a young Russian émigré in 1927, Moscow again saw evidence of a conspiracy by the West. The Soviets defined Pilsudski's Polish government as fascist before the Nazis came to power in Germany (Zaretskii 1935, 1936; Sonov 1938; Dimitrov 1939, 31, 137).[5] After the Nazis came to power in Germany, the Bolsheviks saw Poland as a member of fascist block along with the Nazi Germany, Hungary, and Bulgaria. With the days of the Civil War and the intervention in mind, Moscow concluded that Poland was again the springboard for an intervention, this time in the form of German eastward expansion. Moreover, the Soviet leaders were well aware of a widespread rumour that the Nazi officials had offered the Soviet Ukraine to the Poles, while they would take the Polish Baltic cost, following a victorious German–Polish military attack against the USSR (Radek 1933, 54; Antisovetskaia politika 1933, 10; Literatura germanskikh fashistov 1933; Gal'ianov 1938; L'vova, 1938; Tul'skii 1938; VII Congress 1939, 315, 323, 402–405, 424–425, 588–589. Also, see: *Kommunisticheskii International* 1969, 369).

In addition to the balance of power politics, the ideological tenets of Bolsheviks also increased the anticipation of war at the Polish–Soviet border. The Soviet leadership led by Stalin placed the rise of fascism within the Leninist doctrine of imperialism and understood the rise of fascist regimes as a consequence of global economic crisis and internal contradictions and conflicts in the capitalist world which could be ended only by a total war (Kuusinen 1933, 1934a, 1934b, 1935; Dvorkin 1933; Knorin 1933, 1934, 382–384; Dashinskii 1934; Rikhter 1935; Kongress edinstva 1935; Manuil'skii 1935a, 1935b, 1937; Levi 1936; Ivanov 1936; Dengel' 1937; Gofman 1938; Liubimov 1938; Ustinkin

1941). Lenin saw the First World War as such and defined it as 'the first imperialistic war'. The theory claimed that the global economic crisis in 1929 and the nature of the capitalist economy had brought the world to another total war. Such a war meant both 'a new round of imperialistic war and military intervention against the USSR' (Mad'iar 1933, 20). The Japanese occupation of Manchuria and China in the Far East, the Italian occupation of Ethiopia, the Spanish Civil War, and the German occupation of Austria and Czechoslovakia were considered as the first episode of this second global imperialistic war. In 1938, Stalin concluded that the 'second imperialist war' had already been started a long time ago. His interpretation became a canon to be followed by the party ideologists (Kratkii kurs 1938, 318; Vtoraia imperialisticheskaia 1938; Gal'ianov 1939; Dvadtsatipiatiletie pervoi mirovoi 1939; Varga 1939). This mixture of ideological interpretations and escalating tensions in international relations pointed to the Polish–Soviet border as the gateway of an anticipated attack. Such an anticipation of war on the western horizon was well propagated (Vudman 1935; Geiden 1935; Ivanov 1936; Litvinov 1938; Natisk fashistskikh 1938; Ul'brikht 1938; Bor'ba protiv fashistskikh 1938; Molotov 1938) and also widespread among the man on the street (Shostakovich 1995, 233; Roberts 2000; Fitzpatrick 2000; Broekmeyer 2004).

The deterioration of Polish–Soviet relations and the anticipation of war with Poland can be observed in different Soviet acts. The resolutions of the Politburo of the Central Committee of the CPSU further limited border crossings to the USSR from Poland from 1934 and closed the Polish consulates in Kharkiv, Leningrad, and Tbilisi in 1937.[6] While the war was looming, Stalin feared a 'fifth column', manipulated by the 'country of the main enemy', Germany, and other states which bordered on the USSR, especially Poland. His policies after 1937 targeted the Polish minority in the Soviet Union. In 1937, the Polish population in the USSR was 636,220 and 417,613 of them lived in the pre-1939 borders of Ukraine (*Vsesoiuznaia perepis'* 1991, 83–94). In 1936, 36,000 Poles within the western borderland districts were sent to Kazakhstan (Bugai, 1992, 1995). In 1937 and 1938, more than 50,000 Poles in Ukraine were sentenced. Out of this total, 47,327 were shot and 8,601 were sent to the Gulags. In all territories of the USSR, 139,835 Poles were sentenced; out of this number 111,091 were shot and the rest were sent to the Gulags (Khaustov 1997; Petrov and Roginskii 1997; Poland and Ukraine 2012, 127–242). After the Polish (Western) Ukraine became part of the Soviet Ukraine the persecution and forced migration of the Poles in these territories (also in neighbouring Belorussia, and after their Sovietization in the Baltic Republics) continued (Gorlanov and Roginskii 1997; Gur'ianov 1997; Poland and Ukraine 2012, 243–348). Poland was also constantly depicted in the fabricated cases and show trials of the 1920s and 1930s (such as the Industrial Party (Russian: *Prompartii*) and Toiling Peasants' Party (Russian: *Trudovoi krestianskoi partii*)) as the external base of counter-revolutionaries, military interventions, and other conspiracies (Lih *et al.* 1995, 192–196, 208–209).[7] During the show trials in the days of the Great Terror, many members of the so-called Block of Rights and Trotskyites were accused of being spies working for the Polish and/or German intelligence agencies. These accusations aimed to provoke Soviet people against the Poles and show ordinary people who the enemy was. After 1938, some scholars of Slavic languages were accused of being pro-Polish in their interpretations and a war against the Polonization of Ukrainian and Belorussian languages was declared (Aksenova 2000, 103–104).

## Anti-Polish account in Ukrainian nation-building

After 1937, Soviet historiography shifted emphasis from the class conflict of revolutionary masses to national romantic narratives and national heroes. In the second half of the 1930s, in increasing anticipation of a Polish–German attack, the bottom line of the new Ukrainian history became anti-Polishness. The whole history was constructed against the Poles and pointed out where the enemy was. At the same the new national history aimed to bring Ukrainian and Russian identities as close together as possible. The aim was to mobilize the population who would fight together when Polish–German occupation forces would cross the Soviet border in the near future. Nevertheless, the narrative of common roots was utilized for the first time when the Red Army crossed the same border in the opposite direction and annexed Eastern Poland in 1939.

When Ukrainian historians prepared the first edition of national history in 1937, they found the first anti-Polish account in the tenth century, when the Riurik Prince Sviatopolk (the accursed) (980–1019) became the ruler of the Kyïvan Rus' with Polish support. In the narrative, he was described as a betrayer and a puppet prince of the Poles, and the coalition that supported him was a bunch of looters and occupants of the fatherland, who did not have any popular support. The Kyïvan people rose up against Sviatopolk and expelled him and his Polish allies from the city.[8] However, this is not the only interpretation of Sviatopolk. For example, Lypyns'kyi, who aimed to construct a Ukrainian lineage of statehood, described Sviatopolk as a westernizer and the first prince with 'Ukrainian' tendencies. In fact, in the absence of a strong central structure, the Kyïvan throne could be obtained and kept only by a coalition.[9] Increasing ties with the Polish or Hungarian monarchial families demonstrates that, in the eleventh century, part of the Kyïvan dynasty was gradually joined to the complex European system of aristocratic family networks. However, in the Soviet narrative, every attempt at this westernization was presented to the reader as a betrayal to the nation. After the disintegration of Kyïvan Rus', anti-Polish enmity continued and the narrative described Galicia-Volhynia as a target for the Poles and Hungarians (Belousov 1937a, 118–124).

In the history that was published in 1940, out of the first nine chapters, three were allocated for the fight of Ukrainians against their eternal enemies, the Poles. According to the narrative, the western bastion of the Eastern Slavs, the Principality of Galicia-Volhyinia had struggled against the Poles and Hungarians since the twelfth century (Belousov *et al.* 1940, 36–37). When the Ukrainian lands transferred to the Poles following the Lublin Agreement in 1567, the narrative suddenly recognized the 'Ukrainian nation' as a different identity and its struggle against the 'national-religious' yoke imposed by the Polish *szlachta* (landed aristocracy) (Belousov *et al.* 1940, 78–93). The narrative incorporated at this point the uprisings of Cossack hetmans Kryshtof Kosyns'kyi, Hryhorii Loboda, and Severyn Nalyvaiko. Instead of defining these events as the uprisings of higher echelons of Cossacks for more payments and privileges from the Polish Crown, they are described as Ukrainian peasant uprisings or national uprisings against the Polish szlachta. The long list of uprising Cossack hetmans continued in the following pages. 'The struggle of the Ukrainian nation against Polish rule in the 1630s and 1640s' was led by the Cossack leaders Taras Fedorovych (1630), Ivan Sulym (1635), and Pavlo But (1637–8) (Belousov *et al.* 1940, 82–84). The narrative constantly reminded readers of how terrible it was for the Ukrainians to live under the Polish yoke. In some cases, the authors did not hesitate to provide dreadful details:

> The Polish nobles and soldiers were constantly in Ukraine, brutally treated with the population of Ukraine: ... blinded them, cut their beards, raped the women, cut off their breasts, and murdered them; children were thrown into cauldrons of boiling water.
>
> (Belousov *et al.* 1940, 84)

## Bohdan Khmel'nyts'kyi the Ukrainian national hero

Naturally, the culmination of this anti-Polish discourse was the Khmel'nyts'kyi Uprising. Khmel'nyts'kyi, the defender of the Orthodox Church against the Catholics and Jews, or the greedy exploiter and manipulator of peasant masses who signed the Pereiaslav Agreement to protect his class privileges, now became the great national hero of Ukrainian nation. Ukrainian history had the special attention of the Bolshevik leadership in Moscow for its historical closeness to Russia. When Stalin, Zhdanov, and Kirov defined their 'lesser evil formula' in 1934 they had Ukraine and Georgia in mind. In fact, the annexation of Ukraine and Georgia by Russia was the only example of the lesser evil formula until 1950. The first signs of the reconstruction of 'Khmel'nyts'kyi – the national hero' appeared with the lesser evil formula. Bohdan Khmel'nyts'kyi preferred the suzerainty of the Muscovite Principality to the Polish Kingdom or Ottoman Empire at Pereiaslav. The lesser evil formula accepted him, despite a feudal suzerainty and loss of independence. Yet, among three choices, being the vassal of the Muscovite Tsar was comparatively better for Ukraine than accepting the Polish and Turkish lordship (Znat' Istoriiu Narodov SSSR, 1937). In August 1937, an article by Belousov, the head of the Institute of History, publicized the new interpretation in Ukraine. The article was published on the same day as the manuscript by Shestakov's team under the supervision of Zhdanov was declared in Moscow as the official history textbook of the USSR. Belousov warned that

> the Polish pans [feudal lords] have been the worst enemies of the Ukrainian nation who enslaved [Ukrainians] for centuries and they are dreaming about it again. Contrary to this well-known truth, false-historians and Trotskyites

falsifiers ... tried to present Bohdan Khmel'nyts'kyi only from a negative perspective, they did not want to see that he played a certain role in the all-national struggle against the Polish nobles.

(Belousov 1937b)

While Belousov was an apparatchik appointed by the Communist Party to supervise the Institute of History in Kyïv, it was M. Petrovs'kyi, the Ukrainian historian of the medieval period at the Insitute, who developed the new interpretation in Kyïv and re-constructed Khmel'nyts'kyi as a national hero.[10] Petrovs'kyi wrote his doctoral dissertation on the Khmel'nyts'kyi uprising and his conclusions were in line with the spirit of the time. The uprising, he argued, was an all-national movement because the yoke of the Polish nobles targeted all aspects of the life of Ukrainian nation. The all-national movement enjoyed the support of extreme majority. Petrovs'kyi continued to acknowledge that Khmel'nyts'kyi aimed to establish a feudal system and hereditary monarchy. However, his place in the Ukrainian national history had to be defined according to his role in uniting the Ukrainian people for the anti-Polish struggle for independence and establishing a union with the 'fraternal' Russian nation.[11] The following year (1938) was commemorated as the 300th anniversary of the anti-Polish uprising of 1637–8. Petrovs'kyi published an article in *Bil'shovyk Ukraïny*, the periodical of the CPU, on the liberation struggle of the Ukrainian nation against Poland in the seventeenth century, where he depicted Khmel'nyts'kyi as a national leader (P[etrovs']kyi, 1938). When his next account of Khmel'nyts'kyi was published in 1939, he continued the approach. After referring to Stalin's conversation with the German correspondent E. Ludwig on the role of leader in history, the text attacked both the Ukrainian émigré nationalist interpretations and the Pokrovskiian Soviet interpretations of Khmel'nyts'kyi. Petrovs'kyi argued that the émigré nationalist groups, as the collaborators of Poland or other imperialists, could not be genuine in their claim for Khmel'nyts'kyi as their own hero. He then criticized Pokrovskiian historiography:

It is not possible to downplay the role of Bohdan Khmel'nyts'kyi in the history of Ukraine, in the struggle of the Ukrainian nation against the Polish gentry, or to vilify Bohdan only because he was a leading feudal lord and did not completely destroy feudal exploitation in Ukraine. This is a hypocritical [*dvorushnyts'ka*], 'leftist' [*'livats'ka'*], and anti-Marxist approach. Historical figures should be evaluated only within the historical conditions of their time. Therefore, we must place Bohdan Khmel'nyts'kyi side by side with the heroes of our nation, such as Alexander Nevskii, Minin, Pozharskii, and others, who fought against the occupation of our country by all kinds of foreign invaders.

(Petrovs'kyi 1939, 254–255)

The narrative that followed was strongly anti-Polish and emphasized the fraternity of Moscow and the Ukrainians at every possible opportunity. Petrovs'kyi underlined that, by deciding to declare war against Polish rule and ally the nation to Russia, Khmel'nyts'kyi achieved the best situation under the given conditions.

Some of the Cossack military leaders who led anti-Polish uprisings were also added to this series of national leaders and heroes. These included Maksym Kryvonis, with his infamous anti-Jewish violence, and Khmel'nyts'kyi's army commanders, Danylo Nechai and Ivan Bohun (Podorozhnyi 1940; for Kryvonis: Weinryb 1977; Nadav 1984; Plokhy 2001, 195).

This new narrative also found a place in the performing arts. Stalin was keen to use new historical narratives in arts and popularize them. In the first half of the 1930s, he encouraged and supervised Aleksei Tolstoi to write a play on the life of Peter I and portray him as a national hero (Dubrovskii 2005, 137–155). Akin to this earlier example, the Ukrainian playwright Oleksandr Korniichuk (1905–72)[12] wrote a play called *Bohdan Khmel'nyts'kyi*. Historians of the Institue of History in Kyïv provided consultancy to Korniichuk (Santsevich and Komarenko 1986, 40). Based on this play, film director Ihor Savcheko directed a film of the same title, which was screened in 1941. K. Dankevych composed an opera based on the same story. Korniichuk, with his wife Wanda Wasilewska,[13] a Polish communist writer, also wrote the libretto of this opera (Wasilewska, Wanda 1993, Yekelchyk 2004). Nothing could shadow the rise of Khmel'nyts'kyi, even the most famous Ukrainian poet of all times, Taras Shevchenko. When some his poems were published in 1939 in *Vybranykh Tvorakh* (selected works) they did not include the ones that criticized Khmel'nyts'kyi (Shevchenko 1939; Odarchenko 1994, 236).

## The Red Army crosses the Polish border

Originally the anti-Polish national narrative was pitched against a possible Polish–German invasion. In this sense, this narrative was built to defend Soviet Ukraine. After multiple bargains and overtures, the unexpected happened and the German–Soviet (or Molotov–Ribbentrop) Pact was born. When Moscow sent a strong Red Army contingent of half a million soldiers and officers for the occupation of the eastern provinces of Poland (Krivosheev 1997, 57) under the command of Timoshenko, a Ukrainian General, the anti-Polish historical narrative continued at full speed. This time, however, the narrative was used for the new offensive policy and to justify an unholy alliance with the fascist regime in Germany (Plokhy 2011). The popular series of biographies initiated by Gorky, under the title 'Life of Remarkable People' (Russian: *zhizn' zamechatel'nykh liudei*), published volumes on various historical figures, including Babak (1936) and Pugachev (1937). In November 1939, following the occupation of the Polish Ukraine and Belorussia, another volume appeared – a biography of Bohdan Khmel'nyts'kyi (Osipov 1939).[14] The narrative was strongly anti-Polish and emphasized the fraternity of Moscow and the Ukrainians (Osipov 1939).

The national aspect was obvious in historical works as well as in the official declarations of the time. Molotov underscored on the day of the Soviet invasion of Poland that

> the government considers helping the Ukrainian and Belorussian brothers living in Poland as a sacred duty. It is impossible to ask from the Soviet

government to be indifferent to the destiny of consanguineous [*edinokrovnykh*] Ukrainians and Belarusians living in Poland who were nations without any rights [before the war] and now [after the occupation of Poland by Germany, they] were left in the midst of events.

'Considering all these facts', Molotov continued,

> today [17 September], in the morning, the government of the USSR handed a note to the Polish Ambassador in Moscow, which announced that Soviet government has instructed the High Command of the Red Army to order troops to cross the border and take the life and property of the population of Western Ukraine and Western Belorussia under its protection.

The same arguments had been repeated earlier in the Soviet note handed to the Polish Embassy (Molotov 1939a, 1939b). In the interwar period, nationalist regimes in Europe were keen to use their kinsmen in other countries as a tool in international relations. They used the pretext of 'protecting the lives of consanguineous nationals' for intervening in domestic policies of or attacking neighbouring countries. That is why it was also common practice to see national minorities as potential invitation cards for a foreign intervention, and why governments pursued assimilation policies. Nationalism was not the official ideology in the USSR and the Soviet Union was not a nation-state. Nevertheless, the Soviet explanation of the occupation in 1939 was a nationalistic one. The nationalistic propaganda was so strong that some villages welcomed the representatives of the new order with bread and salt, and blue and yellow national flags (Krawchenko 1990). The first days of annexation in Ukraine witnessed demonstrations of Ukrainian nationalism. Ukrainian and Russian writers followed by thousands of others visited the grave of Ivan Franko in L'viv after a demonstrative march, to lay wreaths. When the Ukrainian Supreme Soviet was summoned in Kyïv, Petro Franko, the son of Ivan Franko, came to the tribune as the voice of Western Ukraine for the unification of Ukraine. In Dovzhenko's propaganda movie on the unification of Ukraine, the narrator used phrases like 'the ancient Slavic Carpathian Mountains joined the Great Soviet Ukraine'. In the homogenizing manner of a nation-state, Gutsyls, an ethnic group, were defined as the Ukrainian mountaineers. Even British and French newspapers suggested that Soviet foreign policy moved towards Panslavism. In May 1940, these arguments were strongly rejected by Moscow (O panslavizme (Istoricheskaia spravka) 1940). But still, the occupation and annexation was based on ethnic ties. One month later, on 28 June 1940, the Red Army crossed the Romanian border and the Soviet Union occupied Northern Bukovina and Bessarabia using the same ethnic and historical arguments. Soviet authors underlined that Northern Bukovina was predominantly populated by Ukrainians. In Bessarabia, the region was considered as having been part of the historical Slavic lands since the tenth century. On top of this, the Soviet-nurtured Moldavian identity card was also used to explain the annexation (Mikhailov and Orlov 1940).

## A double-sided axe: nation and class in one narrative

Yet, the Marxist ideology dictated that the Soviet narrative had to include a 'class element' next to the romantic national narrative. Since 1937, Soviet historians had already been seeking a way to merge 'national' and 'class' in one pot. When the historians at the Institute of History in Kyïv constructed their anti-Polish historical narrative they wanted to describe this double-sided axe with the following common theme: the 'Struggle of the Ukrainian Nation against the Poland of Pans'. They demonstrated 'the centuries-old Polish yoke' from the Kyïvan Rus' until the twentieth century. The formulation of the antagonism covered both class struggle and national conflict (Ukrainian peasants v. Polish landed gentry). This double yoke became the historical explanation of the Soviet annexation of the Polish Ukraine and Polish Belarus (Spravochnik agitatora: Bor'ba 1939a; Petrovskii 1939; Huslystyi 1939; Petrovs'kyi 1939; Podorozhnyi 1940; Picheta 1940; Belousov, Petrovskii, Iastrebov, and Premysler 1940a; Belousov, Petrovs'kyi, Iastrebov, and Premysler 1940b; Belousov and Ogloblin 1940; on the Khmel'nyts'kyi uprising: Petrovs'kyi 1941). The historical narrative of this merge argued that 'The struggle of Ukrainian and Belorussian nations reached to the zenith under Bohdan Khmel'nyts'kyi in 1648–54. His closest companions-in-arms were Maksym Kryvonis, Ivan Bohun, [Danylo] Nechai and other dozens of brave sons of Ukrainian nation'. The same text then emphasized that this was 'a struggle of Cossacks and peasants against the Polish landlords under the leadership of Bohdan Khmel'nyts'kyi' (Spravochnik agitatora: Bor'ba 1939a, 32). Merging both national and class aspects was a common issue for the historians in Kyïv as well as in Moscow. In 1940, when Boris Grekov, the head of the Institute of History in Moscow, requested the Ukrainian historians in L'viv to write a short narrative on the first half of the nineteenth century, he clearly defined this double-sided axe. On the one hand, '"it was important to show [Austrian] feudal-serfdom exploitation [of Ukrainian peasants]' and 'the mass scale of the Ukrainian peasant movement'. On the other hand, the same text had to show the 'Ukrainian national movement'.[15] The atrocities that were committed against the Jewish population of Ukraine in the Khmel'nyts'kyii uprising were also explained by the 'class dimension'. The apologetic explanation published in 1940 'revealed' that there was a class struggle against the Polish lords and Jewish exploiting classes, while there was class solidarity between the Jewish and Ukrainian toilers against the former (Boroboi 1940). The propaganda activities which used historical narratives also aimed to merge class and nation (Akt istoricheskoi vazhnosti 1939; Aleksandrov 1939; Tikhomirov 1939; Spravochnik agitatora: Bor'ba 1939a, 31–33; Spravochnik agitatora: Zapadnaia Ukraina 1939b; Radetskii 1939; Na osvobozhdennoi zemle 1939; S kremlevskoi tribuny: Vyderzhki 1939; Krainov 1939; Komu my idem pomoch' 1939; Gol'dshtein 1939; Min 1939; Egorov 1939; Kammari 1940; Varga 1940). This was an easy task because national divisions overlapped with the class identity in the annexed territories. While the overwhelming majority was consist of peasants and only a small fraction of the population lived in towns and cities. At the same time, the urban dwellers were predominantly Polish and Jewish while nearly all rural population was Ukrainian (Jackson Jr 1960, 182–183). The Ukrainian history writing and political propaganda reflected this reality on the ground.

## The row between the Orthodox Marxists and the authors of the new history

The question of how to establish the 'right' balance between Marxist class struggle and national unity in history continued in different episodes of history. According to the new framework, Khmel'nyts'kyi was the leader and he was anti-Polish. But who were the uprising people? Peasants? Cossacks? Ukrainians? The definition of the uprising population would indicate the social or national character of these events. A similar discussion was recorded among the Ukrainian historians on the uprisings and the Cossack leader Semen Palii in right-bank Ukraine in the second half of the seventeenth century. Huslystyi suggested that the period should be named 'the struggle of Ukrainian peasants and Cossacks against the Polish pans in the right-bank Ukraine'. This title certainly underlined a class conflict. O. Ohloblyn and M. Marchenko were for the title of 'struggle of the Ukrainian nation [*narod*] against the Polish yoke in the right-bank Ukraine'. According to M. Marchenko, a historian of the feudal period at the Institute, terms like 'national-independence struggle' [*natsional'no-vyzbol'na*] should be avoided.[16] Marchenko was still a follower of the Pokrovskiian–Marxist history writing and felt uncomfortable with 'national' dominating a class warfare. The final title was somewhere in between: 'struggle of the Ukrainian nation against the Polish pans in the right-bank Ukraine' (Ohloblyn 1939, 16). The same issues were also raised at the meeting of the historians at the Institute of History when they discussed the rule of Peter the Great.[17] The shift in Ukraine was too obvious to be missed by historians, who kept an orthodox view and considered history writing without class struggles as a deviation from the Marxist–Leninist course. Both the theatre play of Korniichuk and Petrovs'kyi's book were criticized by the orthodox historians and officials at the agitation-propaganda department of the Central Committee of CPSU. These Russian and Ukrainian historians and ideologues accused both authors of showing Khmel'nyts'kyi as a leader of the Ukrainian nation instead of a defender of the Ukrainian feudal class (Yekelchyk 2002). The Soviet annexation of Polish Ukraine in 1939 did not stop the hardline Marxists. A critique which was published in the primary history journal of the Soviet Union voiced these concerns (Baraboi 1940).

M. Marchenko, the head of the feudal period section of the Institute of History in Kyïv, was also against the view that was represented by Petrovs'kyi, Huslysytyi, and Ohloblyn. Marchenko (1902–83) was a Ukrainian historian. He actively participated in the Russian Civil War on the side of the Bolsheviks when he was a teenager. In 1923, he was enrolled in the artillery school in Kyïv. He became a member of the CPSU in 1927 and during the Holodomor, he worked as the head of rural Soviet of Novo-Petrivs'k in Kyïv oblast (1930–2), then he enrolled at the Institute of Red Professors in Kharkiv. After the graduation in 1937, Stanislav Kosior, the first secretary of CPU, sent him in August to work at the Institute of History. Without any academic career, he administered the section of feudalism and supervised experienced historians such as Ohloblyn and Petrovs'kyi.[18] In autumn 1939, when the Soviet Army crossed the Polish border, he worked as a senior propagandist in Western Ukraine and fulfilled some additional tasks that were assigned by Khrushchev. In October 1939, the secretary of the CPU for propaganda offered him the opportunity to be the first Soviet rector of L'viv University, and Marchenko accepted this position. His primary task was the Sovietization and Ukrainization of this institution.[19] In the meantime, he published historical articles (Marchenko 1940, 1941) and received his doctoral degree on 'the struggle of Russia and Poland for Ukraine in the first decade after the annexation of Ukraine by Russia 1654–64', which was published in Kyïv (Rubl'ov 1996). In short, he was a *vyvizhenets* and the Party trusted him until 1941. According to Marchenko, the new narrative 'simplified and vulgarized' the Khmel'nyts'kyi Uprising and the Pereiaslav Agreement, and defined the individual role of Khmel'nyts'kyi 'from a subjective-idealistic point of view'. By whitewashing the Russian tsarism, this new narrative diminished the role of the October Revolution. If the colonial policies of the Russian state were denied, then where was the 'prison of the nations' that the Bolsheviks fought against in the later episode of history? Yes, Russia and Ukraine were fraternal nations 'with close cultures and relatives by origin'. However, this did not change the character of the Pereiaslav Union, which turned Ukraine into a suzerain of the 'autocratic Russian state of feudal lords and serfdom'. This was a 'lesser evil' which was not presented as such by Petrovs'kyi. Marchenko also questioned whether Khmel'nyts'kyi wanted a union with Russia from the beginning, or whether the conditions brought him to this point later (Marchenko 1938a, 1938b, 1938c, 1939a, 1939b). He also found the new history to be too ethno-centric. He questioned the term 'consanguineous' [*edinokrovnye*] because 'there is an abstract biological side [of it] but social, class [-oriented] and historical character of the union and fraternity of nations is absent'.[20] The term 'biological' was used in the lexicon of Soviet humanitarian studies to refer to the racist theories and strongly denounced. Marchenko felt that this propaganda word in historiography had nothing to do with the Marxist interpretation of history. The clash between the historians who wrote the new history after 1937 and the ones who refused this interpretation in the name of Marxism was not soft. When Marchenko accused Petrovs'ky and Ohloblin of idealization of Khmel'nyts'kyi, his uprising, and the Pereiaslav Agreement, and opposed the disputable term *edinokrovnye*, he implied that this narrative was closer to nationalist than Marxist and those historians were disguised nationalists. The constructors of the new national history did not fall short in their accusations. Belousov, the director of the Institute, supervised the construction of the new narrative and he protected Petrovs'kyi and Ohloblyn against Marchenko. In 1939, he threatened the Marxist opposition that he would go and talk to Khrushchev, the first secretary of the

CPU.[21] Ironically, Marchenko was vilified and arrested for being a 'nationalist' on 22 June 1941. He was imprisoned and interrogated in Toms'k and Novosibirsk and released in February 1944.[22] He worked at the Novosibirsk Pedagogical Institute and returned to Kyïv in 1945.

While Marchenko answered the questions of NKVD interrogators in the prisons of Siberia, the fight between the two camps continued. Ohloblyn, already disillusioned by his arrest in 1931 and the politicisation of history writing, remained in Kyïv and defected to the Germans when the latter entered the city in September 1941. Marchenko's former opponents did not waste time in slandering him by using the defection of Ohloblyn. The following year, Petrov'skyi wrote a letter to the President of the Academy of Sciences of Ukraine to use the situation to meet his personal goals. He described Marchenko and Ohloblyn as two close nationalists and added Suprunenko, another proponent of pro-Marxist history writing, to this evil tally. According to Petrov'skyi all three historians were nationalists who sabotaged the Institute before the war and committed all kinds of crimes from plagiarism to bribery. Pointing to the defection of Ohloblyn and the imprisonment of Marchenko as evidence supporting his arguments, Petrovs'kyi asked the President of the Academy for the purge of Suprunenko, the academic secretary [*uchenyi sekretar'*] of the Institute. Positioning himself as the 'real' Marxist historian in the Institute, he accused Belousov, the chief apparatchik and the head of the Institute, of tolerating the actions of 'nationalist' historians and being 'liberal' towards them, a word which was used to accuse individuals in the Soviet Union of not having solid ideological convictions.[23] There is no evidence of whether Petrov'skyi wrote any other letters of denouncement but this one ended up in the hands of K. Lytvyn, the secretary of propaganda and agitation of the CPU.[24] In the midst of the struggle between two groups, Petrovs'kyi became the head of the Institute in 1942. After the Second World War, the discussion between the two groups continued when Petrovs'kyi accused these hardliner Marxist critics of having 'dirty hands'.[25] It is interesting to see that the post-independence reviews classified these historians and their relations and disputes according to the Soviet accusations of the time. Petrovs'kyi and other constructors of the new history were closer to the romantic national narratives; nevertheless they are seen more like 'perpetrators' or the compromising figures who accommodated the demands of the Soviet system. Marchenko and Ohloblyn with their Marxist interpretations in their early careers became the defenders of the national legacy and values against the Red Empire just for the fact that they were jailed or defected at some point for absolutely different reasons.

## Conclusions

The Soviet government in Ukraine did not wait until the Second World War to increase the nationalistic narrative in history writing. When the emphasis moved from class conflicts and consciousness to national struggles and the heroic past after 1937, the Ukrainian narrative was written in an anti-Polish spirit. This preference was not based on Marxist ideology or alleged Russification policies. The anticipation of war with a Polish–German alliance was the main motive behind this narrative. Accordingly the Cossack uprisings were described as 'national-liberation wars of the Ukrainian nation against Polish oppressors'. Military leaders have always been essential parts of romantic national narratives and Bohdan Khmel'nyts'kyi, the leader of the biggest anti-Polish Cossack uprising, became the embodiment of this strong anti-Polish narrative.

The Soviet usage of Khmel'nyts'kyi differed from the Russian imperial narrative. First of all, he was not defined as the defender of the Orthodox Church in an all-Russian narrative derived from an age-old imperial-dynastic identity. The narrative also did not cover how Khmel'nyts'kyi's armies massacred the Jews on their way. Finally, the Soviet narrative defined Khmel'nyts'kyi as a Ukrainian leader, and his uprising as a Ukrainian uprising. The proponents of the new history built their narrative, which was utilized in two years, when the Red Army crossed the border westwards and occupied the Polish Ukraine and Belorussia.

The founders of this new narrative had aimed to mix class and nation in one melting pot since 1937, well before the Second World War. However, from the beginning they had opponents among the orthodox Marxist interpreters. Mykola Petrovs'kyi, Oleksandr Ohloblyn, and Kost' Huslystyi led this construction of the new narrative which tried to find a place between Marxist and romantic national narratives. While Petrovs'kyi and his team were active participants in the new construction of the past, Marchenko, Suprunenko, and others considered themselves proper Marxist historians, defended the class narrative and awkwardly found themselves in opposition to what was apparently a Marxist state. Although it is beyond the scope of this chapter, it may worthwhile to say that their struggle continued until 1947. Inevitably, historians were influenced by the surrounding events. For instance, Ohloblyn started scholarly activities and publications following Pokrovskiian interpretations in the 1920s, then participated in the construction of the new national narrative from 1937 to 1941. By the time the German armies crossed the Soviet border he was disillusioned with the sharp political turns in Soviet historiography. In 1941, he changed his direction for the third time and worked for the Nazi occupants in Kyïv and finally migrated to the west at the end of the war.

Anyone who deals with Ukrainian national history and national identity detects very soon that there is a lack of consensus on some important national symbols and the national past among the Ukrainian population (Khineyko 2005; Velychenko 2005, 117–122). There is also an inability of nationalized history to create a fully functional 'all-Ukrainian pantheon' as part of an integrative civic mythology. Unfortunately, this inability undermines the realization of the task of creating an imagined civic nation in Ukraine. The figures of Ivan Mazepa, Stepan Bandera, or even Mykhailo Hrushevs'kyi lack such broad appeal. However, Taras Shevchenko, Lesia Ukraïnka, and Bohdan Khmel'nyts'kyi may be acceptable to most of the population as symbols representative of the whole nation, not only because of their 'universality' but also because they belonged to the Soviet pantheon (Kasianov 2009, 20). In other words, the success of Khmel'nyts'kyi as a national leader owes much to the Soviet efforts of establishing him as a national hero.

## Notes

1 For the major historians who constructed the imperial narrative successfully, see Karamzin 1833–35; Solovev 1893–95. The earliest history textbooks in Russia that explained this narrative were Kaidanov 1832; Ustrialov 1839–41; Ilovaiskii 1876–99. We should note that Ilovaiskii wrote numerous influential textbooks.
2 The initial and prominent work that defended this interpretation was the monograph *Istoriia Rusov*. The author and the exact dates of its creation are under dispute; however, historians of Ukraine propose different years in the period between 1775 and 1825 (Basarab 1982, 76–77; Plokhy 2012. The copy that I referred to was Koniskii 1846). M. A. Maksymovich (1804–73) and M. I. Kostomarov (1817–85) were the founding fathers of the modern Ukrainian national history in the nineteenth century. On Hrushevs'kyi and his vision of the Ukrainian Past, see Sysyn 2001.
3 V'iacheslav Lypyns'kyi (1882–1931) was a Ukrainian historian, political activist, and ideologue of Ukrainian conservatism. As a historian, he was the founder of the statist school of Ukrainian history writing and he was the main ideological rival of Hrushevs'kyi. He accused the latter of neglecting the role of the state in the Ukrainian history. Especially after 1917, he was a conservative historian who supported the regime of Hetman Skoropadsky. Under the government of the Hetmanate, he served as the ambassador of Ukraine to Austria. After the Sovietization of Ukraine, he lived as an exile in Berlin and Vienna. His monograph *Ukraine on the Break of 1657–69* was published in 1920. In this work, Lypyns'kyi analysed the historical process of the creation of the Ukrainian state in the fifteenth to seventeenth centuries (Plokhy 2005a, 24, 144, 222, 286).
4 It was not only the Soviet government that thought that Colonel Beck was an instrument in the hands of Berlin. In order to convince the English audience, the account in *Colonel Beck and His Policy* was written during the Second World War (Mackiewicz 1944).
5 RGASPI, 495–3-134–2/5, February 29, 1932. Also see Iz Rezoliutsii Politsekretariata 1998. For the difference between Stalin and Zinoviev on what the Party policy should be after the military intervention of Pilsudski see Lih *et al.* 1995, 110–111.
6 RGASPI, 17–162–17–84/85, November 23, 1934; RGASPI, 17–162–19–1/4, December 1, 1935; RGASPI, 17–162–21–86, 114, June 28, 1937; RGASPI, 17–162–21–149, August 13, 1937.
7 RGASPI, 17–162–3-74–5, May 20, 1926; 17–162–3 77/79, May 27, 1926.
8 Although Iaroslav is positioned by Belousov as an anti-Polish leader, Dobronega, his sister, marries the Polish King Kazimir, and the latter's sister Gertrude marries Iziaslav, the son of Iaroslav. In the next account, the Poles again intervene in the rivalry between the candidates for the throne and the Polish King Boleslav II supports his son-in-law Iziaslav. However, this intervention is pictured again as another chance 'to rob the population of Kyïvan Rus' … by Polish occupants' See Belousov 1937a, 90–91. For the account of Sviatopolk also see Belousov *et al.* 1940, 30.
9 Even Belousov provides an example. Sviatopolk II, the son of Iziaslav and Gertrude, was the Kyïvan Great Prince thanks to the support of the Princes of Chernigov, the Poles and Hungarians. See Belousov 1937a, 100.
10 *TsDAHOU*, 1–70–753–171, April 29, 1947.
11 Arkhiv RAN 1577–2-23–1-11, June 25, 1939.
12 Oleksandr Korniichuk was a dramatist and prominent Soviet Ukrainian political figure. He worked as a screenwriter at the Kyïv, Kharkiv, and Odesa artistic film studios. In 1934, he became a member of the executive of the newly created Writers'

Union of Ukraine and became the head of the Union (1938–41, 1946–53). He held numerous positions in the Supreme Soviet of the Ukrainian SSR. His plays were formulaic and written in conformity with the Party's political imperatives and propagandistic needs (Korniichuk, Oleksandr, 1988).
13 Wanda Wasilewsa was a Polish communist writer. She moved to Kyïv from L'viv in 1939 (Wasilewska, Wanda 1993).
14 In order to emphasize the Russocentric aspect of Soviet historiography, J. Basarab, in his account, erroneously argued that Khmel'nyts'kyi was the only non-Russian popularized figure in this series before the Second World War. As we mentioned in the chapter on Azerbaijan, the biography of Babak was also published within the same series. For Basarab's argument, see Basarab 1982, 172.
15 Letter from Boris Grekov, the head of the Institute of History, Academy of Sciences of the USSR to M. Marchenko, the Rector of the L'viv State University, *Arkhiv IU im. Krip'iakevycha NAN Ukraïny*, op. VI-f, No. G-4, ark. 84, July 13, 1940.
16 *TsDAVOU* 3561-1-240–1/5, January 3, 1938.
17 *TsDAVOU* 3561-1-240–13/15, May 31, 1940.
18 In those days, there were three sections in the Institute of History in Kyïv: history of feudalism, history of capitalism, and history of the Soviet period.
19 HDA SBU spr. 31982FP, ark. 91–125, May 30, 1943.
20 HDA SBU spr. 31982FP, ark. 58–63, June 2–3, 1943; HAD SBU, spr. 31982FP, ark. 69–72, June 7, 1943; HAD SBU, spr. 31982FP, ark. 73–75, June 11–12, 1943.
21 HDA SBU spr. 31982FP, ark. 58–63, June 2–3, 1943.
22 HDA SBU spr. 31982FP, ark. 150151, February 8, 1944.
23 *TsDAHOU* 1–70–48–2/4, February 25, 1942.
24 *TsDAHOU* 1–70–48–1, April 10, 1942.
25 *TsDAHOU*, 1–23–1652–18/19, March 10, 1945.

# 5 The rise of red batyrs in the Kazakh steppe

Although full-scale national histories were written in Baku and Kyïv, the construction of a primordial past was not a priority for the Kazakh case. The discussions over the ethnogenesis of the Kazakh nation continued until the publication of the 1943 edition of the Kazakh national history. While the ethnogenesis of the Kazakh nation remained obscure, the most important step towards a national history in Kazakhstan occurred in the definition of national heroes. The Soviet Kazakh nation-builders elevated prominent batyrs attached to particular tribal unions and territories to all-national heroic figures. This chapter examines this important milestone in Kazakh nation-building.

A batyr is a folk hero among pastoral nomadic Kazakh tribes, who achieved the title through his heroic deeds. In most cases, these heroes were prominent figures only in a particular region of the vast Kazakh steppe. When Kazakh national history was constructed under Soviet rule, batyrs were incorporated into the narrative as national heroes. Although there were numerous batyrs in the long history of the Kazakh steppe, the national history focused on those who led uprisings against Russian colonial expansion in the nineteenth century. Current literature, however, does not explain how Soviet nation-building in Kazakhstan used these batyrs. Instead, it is assumed that nineteenth-century anti-Russian uprisings that took place on the Kazakh steppe were undesired and even prohibited topics in the Soviet historiography. In the post-Soviet period, Kazakh scholars have been 'recovering' and disseminating this 'lost chapter' of national history (Sabol 2003a, 231–232).

There were two developments in the Soviet Union that support these assumptions. The first development was the strong emphasis on Russian national identity after 1936. This emphasis also brought the famous 'lesser evil' formula, which explained the Russian expansion in Ukraine and Georgia as a better option for these territories than for them to be incorporated into Poland or Turkey respectively (see chapters that discuss this in Black 1962; Keep 1964; Tillett 1969; Mazour 1971; Heer 1973; Dubrovsky 1998, 873–892; Brandenberger 2002; Markwick 2001). This shift in the western borders of the Soviet Union was extrapolated into Kazakh history writing. It is assumed that anti-Russian uprisings were removed from the Kazakh national narrative in order to establish an imaginary Russian–Kazakh friendship in history. Second, this position of the literature is also based on the condemnation of Kazakh historian Ermukhan Bekmakhanov (1915–66). Bekmakhanov was a bureaucrat and historian who was denounced as a nationalist and jailed in 1951 for writing on an anti-Russian uprising led by the Kazakh Khan Kenesary Kasymov in the nineteenth century (Tillett 1969; Kozybaev 1992, 44–96; Gurevich 1992, 63–95; Diskussia 2000; Sizov 2001; Kapaeva 2004; Bekmakhanov 2005; Mazhitov 2005). This literature on the Soviet treatment of batyrs complements the post-Soviet Kazakh narrative, which defines the Soviet period as merely a repressive period for the Kazakh nation, and the independence period after 1991 as the sole episode when its national heritage was promoted.

This chapter, however, argues that Kazakh Soviet historians used batyrs and other heroic figures of anti-Russian uprisings in the nineteenth century in order to construct a national narrative. This usage continued after 1936, parallel to the union-wide emphasis on Russian identity. Moreover, Kazakh historians transformed these batyrs from obscure local figures into national heroes. In other words, folk narratives on some regional figures were collected, codified, and homogenized on a pan-national scale. Finally, these tribal or local figures and events were turned into an all-national heritage, transcending strong tribal or regional affiliations. This aspect of Soviet modernization and its construction of Kazakh national history (and identity) in Stalin's time had a lasting impact, even up to today.

## The batyrs of the nomadic world

Individual courage and charisma were important elements in the pastoral nomadic peoples of Central Asia. In the absence of a bureaucracy or institutions, a central figure was essential in the nomadic states (Barfield 1989, 5). Nomadic leaders had to possess particular features to hold together numerous tribes and clans of the steppe. An heroic warrior-leader was blessed by heaven with luck and charisma and showered his followers with gifts (Barfield 1989, 3, 5; Skrynnikova 1997, 149–200). Among other titles indicating personal charisma and courage in the Central Asian steppes, a frequently occurring one has been *batyr*. Batyr is the Kazakh form of a word that can be found in other languages of Asia and Europe. Although the etymological roots of batyr are not clear, most probably it has Mongolic or Turkic origins, and the ancient Turkic word *batur* or *bağatur* describes a courageous, decisive, virile, bold, valiant hero or leader.[1] These heroes were mounted warriors, who became renowned for their heroic deeds on the battlefield and were hence given this name on merit. This word was also used to praise the courage of a group of warriors (Blake and Frye 1949, 343; Cleaves 1949, 435.) It was so prestigious to bear that in many nomadic empires it became also a title or a rank in the army. In pastoral nomadic societies, batyrs frequently played military (in some cases legal or spiritual) roles for one or two clans. Famous batyrs would become protagonists of folk stories and songs. Akyns (poet-bards) and zhyrshys (epic singers) of the Turkic nomadic world conveyed batyrs' heroic deeds to the next generations by travelling long distances and narrating these stories and singing songs with their instruments, the dombyra (dombra) or kobyz (long-necked lutes popular among Turkic peoples: Reich 2000; Aca 2002, 5–93). Batyrs were mounted warriors; that is why epic tales of heroic batyrs always included their horses as dominant figures in the narrative: Manas and his horse Ak-Kula; Jangar and Aranzal; and Alpamysh and Baichibar (Lipets 1984).

There are legendary batyrs, such as Alpamys (Alpamysh) or Shora (Shura or Chora), who lived before the formation of the Kazakh Khanate but were incorporated into Kazakh heroic epics. These legends were also famous among other Turkic peoples. There were many other batyrs, such as Er-Targyn, Er-Sayn, and Kambar, who were protagonists of legendary tales (Batyrlar Zhyry 1939; Orlov 1945; Alpamys 2004, 192). The Jungar–Kazakh conflict in the eighteenth century was the source for a series of Kazakh batyrs not shared with any other Turkic people (Valikhanov 1984; Galiev 1998; Kazakhsko-Zhongarskie voiny 2004, 71; Edilkhanova 2005; Kasenov 2006; Karasai Batyr 2004, 149; Bogenbai 2004, 429–430; Mukanov 1991, 19; Er-Kabanbai 2005, 248; Kabanbai Kozhakuly 2005, 5–6; Nauryzbai 2004, 111; Otegen 2004, 246; Sarghozhaev 1998).[2] The last wave of batyrs appeared as the leading figures in the nineteenth-century uprisings against Russian colonial expansion in the Kazakh steppe, such as Syrym (in the 1783–97 uprising), Isatai (in the 1836–8 uprising), Eset Batyr (in the 1847–58 uprising) and Beket (in the 1855–8 uprising). Batyr Zhankozha, a leader of the Shekti clan, fought against the khanates of Kokand and Khiva in the south between 1835 and 45, and Russian forces in the north from 1856 to 1857 (Zhankozha 2005, 298). The impact of these batyrs and the uprisings was limited to a particular region but they were later to be promoted by the Soviet nation-building programme in Kazakhstan.

## The reasons behind the Soviet promotion of batyrs

The ideological reasons behind the Soviet promotion of batyrs can be traced to Pokrovskiian historiography. Pokrovskiian history de-emphasized historical personages, such as kings, princes, sultans, emperors, generals, and their ideologies, and their national identities. Instead, he looked for folk leaders with humble origins and backed by popular support. In a pastoral nomadic society anyone potentially could become a batyr. In other words, every single shepherd could become a king. This egalitarian fact was related to the socio-economic structure of these societies. In pastoral nomadic societies, tribal membership imposed strong bonds of communal obligations and loyalties on every individual. However, owing to the inherent mobility of a nomad's life, which required self-reliance and the ability to take responsibility for decisions, individual nomads remained autonomous agents, who if dissatisfied could move with their household and flocks to new locations (Akiner 1995, 8; Golden 1998, 10). Every nomad was at the same time a shepherd, artisan, hunter, and warrior. In the absence of a landed aristocracy, even a simple member of the society could become a batyr by his deeds. Hence, many batyrs had been simple shepherds.

Batyrs were therefore self-made men for whom personal charisma and skills were key factors in their ascent. Nomadic culture glorified military adventure and heroic personal achievement (Barfield 1989, 2; Barfield 1993, 131). In fact, taking personal initiative to gain a place in society was an ancient Turkic tradition. Each member of a tribe, after the age of fifteen, received a new and permanent name reflecting his birth, deeds, or abilities in his youth (Fazlallakh 1987). For example, Kabanbai Batyr was named wild boar (from the Kazakh *kaban*), because as a teenager he had protected a herd of horses from a wild boar attack (*Kabanbai Kozhakuly* 2005, 5). This image of a 'simple labourer transforming into a folk leader' and the egalitarian system of a nomadic society were invaluable assets for the Soviet Kazakh literature and for national history writing. The Soviet system in Kazakhstan literally aimed for something similar. Parallel to the modernization project, thousands of young shepherds were educated to become administrators, teachers, engineers, or workers on the railways and in factories. These were simple people who were turned into batyr-like heroes and active agents of Soviet modernity. For this epic modernization project, the batyrs of popular folk tales offered a local theme and symbol that could be incorporated into the Soviet narrative in fine arts, national history, and political propaganda. As the epic tales of batyrs were always the most popular and well-known themes among the Kazakh population, batyrs could be held up as admirable examples and propaganda items among the population in order to convey the message of the Soviet rule in local symbols.

However, not every Kazakh batyr was incorporated into the national narrative. Surprisingly, Kazakh batyrs who fought against the Jungars in the eighteenth century were absent from early Soviet historiography.[3] In the Soviet Kazakh national history construction, the emphasis was given to the batyrs who led the nineteenth-century uprisings against the Russian forces in the North Caspian plateau. Again, this was a consequence of Pokrovskiian history writing. First, Pokrovskii was interested in the rise of the working class and class struggles in the history of Soviet peoples, and was looking for an analogy of the Jacquerie in France, the Hussite War in Bohemia, and the peasant wars in sixteenth-century Germany.[4] The Kazakh uprisings in the north Caspian plateau against Russian colonization in the nineteenth century could therefore possibly reveal that Kazakhs also had a revolutionary spirit, and that they were part of the materialist development pattern in history. Second, these anti-Russian uprisings occurred within the historical time frame that Pokrovskii and his colleagues found most relevant. They saw the French Revolution and the following centuries as the period most deserving of study. While the French peasants were attacking the Bastille and Napoleon's career was unfolding in Europe, the only significant thing occurring in the Kazakh lands was Russian colonization and the resistance of Kazakh tribal confederations. Kazakhs seemed to appear for the first time in modern world history with their anti-colonial uprisings. Third, Pokrovskii described Russian rule over non-Russian peoples (Poles, Jews, Ukrainians, Caucasians, Siberians, etc.) as a ruthless force of oppression, plundering, and mass killings. He categorically refused to acknowledge any progressive aspect to this relation. The Kazakh resistance, led by batyrs, against the Russian expansion in the nineteenth century fits well into this paradigm. Kazakhs as an oppressed nation were opposed to their Russian oppressors/colonizers. Thus, it was a moment in history that could be depicted both as a class struggle of the labouring masses and as an anti-colonial movement. The Russian Empire was both the colonizing power and the prison of the peoples of Central Asia, and the Kazakh tribal uprisings were against this reactionary power. Consequently, the Russian colonial expansion became a popular theme for the Central Asian historians in this period (Galuzo 1928; Galuzo 1929; Lavrent'ev 1930). These priorities could also be seen in the resolution of the first All-Union Turkology Congress in 1926. The congress called for closer attention to the modern epoch, economic and social history, and popular and revolutionary movements within the Turkic nationalities (Rezoliutsii 1-go Vsesoiuznogo 1926, 403). According to Asfendiiarov, a leading Kazakh historian and adherent of Pokrovskii, the character of Kazakh liberation movements in the period of the conquest of the Kazakh steppe by tsarist Russia was spontaneous peasant uprisings against colonial theft and against the feudal yoke (Asfendiiarov 1993 [1935], 171). They also constituted a distinctive part of the global resistance of labourers against the imperialist colonizers. He connected the Kazakh revolts to those in other colonial territories: India, Malaya, Sudan (led by the Mahdi), and recent developments in the Middle East. In all these revolts, the common fact was that local peasants raised the flag of liberty against European capitalism and the indigenous feudal aristocracy collaborating with the colonizers (Asfendiiarov 1993 [1935], 172). Lastly, the preferences of Soviet Kazakh historiography in the 1920s and 1930s were also a result of easily available written records. The indigenous source for the batyrs who fought against the Jungars or Central Asian khanates or emirates was folklore passed down by zhyrau or akyns (Turkic bards). However, the nomadic tribes of the Desht-i Kypchak (the steppe stretching from Ukraine to Central Asia) did not leave written records of the events. Because of their proximity to Russia, there were many more written records in Russian archives on the social and political structure and economic developments in the Small Zhuz, one of the three great unions of tribes that for centuries divided the Kazakhs. The Small Zhuz (Kishi Zhuz) was located in the north-west and western territories of the Kazakh steppe, near the Russian territories. The other two zhuz were the Great Zhuz (Uly Zhuz) in the south and south-east, and the Middle Zhuz (Orta Zhuz) in the centre and north-east (*Zhuzy* 2005, 345–346). In the first half of the nineteenth century there was also an autonomous khanate of the Small Zhuz known as the Inner Zhuz (Bökei Zhuz) that also attracted the attention of the Russians. As a result, the uprisings in the Middle and Inner Zhuzes and their struggles against Russian–Cossack forces were well recorded by the Russian bureaucratic apparatus, and most of these records were housed in the Orenburg archives.[5]

## The batyrs of the anti-Russian uprising become Soviet heroes

A. F. Riazanov was the first historian who used the Orenburg archives in order to write a Marxist–Pokrovskiian history of the Kazakhs (Riazanov 1927; Riazanov 1928).[6] His works on the revolts of the Small and Inner Zhuzes between 1797 and 1838 also elevated the tribal or regional events onto an anti-colonial *and* all-national scale. These uprisings were described simultaneously as 'progressive peasant' revolts against foreign and local exploiting rulers, and as 'national independence struggles' against a European colonial power and local collaborators. The final claim of the title – and of the whole book – was that these uprisings caused a chain reaction. From Syrym to Kenesary, all leaders were representatives of one idea, one goal, over half a century. Isatai Taimanov was an illiterate batyr challenging the khan in an attempt to eliminate the exploiting classes of landowners as well as the despot (Riazanov 1927, 6–15, 82; 1928, 288–298). In the narrative, Isatai was placed on the imaginary line drawn by Soviet historiography from Spartacus to the Bolsheviks as a leader of the labouring classes. Before the revolt, Isatai Batyr had been confined in a Russian prison for murder and burglary. According to Riazanov, this experience was 'an inescapable school of all great revolutionaries'. Here we are invited by the author to recall the Russian revolutionaries who 'sacrificed' their lives and spent years in prisons and in exile for the sake of the labouring masses. Though Riazanov wrote according to the Pokrovskiian rules, he successfully constructed a national history and identified Kazakh revolutionary figures by using regional figures and events (Riazanov 1927, 16–17).[7] This was the first construction of the past towards a national narrative. In fact, the Russian imperial administration in Orenburg preferred to label Isatai and his followers a 'disturbance' (*vozmushchenie*) (Riazanov 1927, 82, footnote) instead of an 'uprising' or 'revolt' (*vosstanie, miatezh*). Most probably, the Russian imperial administration did not assign a political character to this movement. The second nationalization attempt of batyrs came from Sandzhar Asfendiiarov (1889–1938) a Kazakh historian, national Bolshevik, party official, and a public figure who occupied important party and public posts. Asfendiiarov was the author of one of the first national histories of the Kazakhs, which was written according to the principles of Pokrovskii (Asfendiiarov 1993 [1935]).[8] In Asfendiiarov's history, Syrym Batyr (Datov) appeared as the first Kazakh hero and a significant leader in the history of Kazakhs. Syrym was described as 'the leader of the movement, the chief enemy of sultans [aristocrats], and the popular leader of the masses'. Moreover, this movement was 'a revolutionary movement of masses' (Asfendiiarov 1993 [1935], 156–157). Isatai Batyr (Taimanov) was described as a leader of 'the struggle of enslaved masses against 'white-bones' [Kazakh feudal aristocrats]' and, later, 'against tsarism' (Asfendiiarov 1993 [1935], 163–166).

## The Great Terror in Almaty

The reaction of Almaty to the resolution of the Central Committee of the CPSU in January 1936 was similar to that of Baku. The Council of People's Commissars of the Kazakh ASSR (Kazak Autonomous Republic, a union-republic after 1936) and the Bureau of the Kazkraikom (Kazakh Autonomous Regional Committee) of the CPSU issued a joint resolution on writing the history of Kazakh literature. In accordance with this resolution, a committee was formed within the Narkompros (The People's Commissariat of Enlightenment of) Kazakh ASSR for writing a book outlining the history of Kazakh literature and a textbook on Kazakh literature for secondary schools. The commission, chaired by the Narkompros Kazakh ASSR Temirbek Zhurgenev, was a mixture of eminent writers, intellectuals, pedagogues, and *apparatchiki* such as Saken Seifullin (1894–1938), Mukhtar Auezov (1897–1961), Gabbas Togzhanov (1900–38), Moldagalii Zholdybaev (1887–1937), Telzhan Shonanov (1894–1938), Arystanov (most probably an apparatchik), Sultan Lepesov (1904–1937), and Sabit Mukanov (1900–73).[9] This resolution of 15 March 1936 was the first step towards the penning of a national history. A month after ordering the production of a textbook on the history of national literature, the first secretary of the Kazkraikom CPSU, Levon Mirzoian (1897–1937), was eager to expedite the writing of a Kazakh national history. At this stage, the history was named 'The History of Kazakh People and Kazakhstan'. There was an intended implication in this title. The geographical emphasis (Kazakhstan) would embrace other peoples of these lands (Uygurs, Dungans, Uzbeks, Russians, etc.). Archival documents suggest that from the beginning the agitation-propaganda department of the CPK (Communist Party of Kazakhstan) in Almaty was intensively involved in writing this national history. However, insufficient preparations on the part of the agit-prop department and the historians in the region repeatedly delayed its presentation to the Bureau of the Kazkraikom. In fact, the real reason for the delay was the initial measures of the Great Terror.

After the official demise of Pokrovskii, the historian Semen Tomsinskii, who was a leading figure in the Leningrad branch of the Pokrovskiian school, was drawn away from Leningrad (Vanag and Tomskinskii 1928; Tomsinskii 1925, 1927, 1932, 1934a, 1934b). It is not widely known that he was sent to Almaty as the first director of the history section, which had recently been founded within the KazFAN (Kazakhstan branch of the Academy of Sciences). Tomsinskii was responsible for history writing in the republic, but he did not have enough time to satisfy the demands of the Bureau of the Kazkraikom. Soon after his arrival in Almaty, he was arrested on 29 April 1936. The Bureau of the Kazkraikom, however, was keen to discuss the topic of writing a history and to issue a resolution.[10] The Zhdanov Commission was not the only reason. Another reason was peculiar to Kazakhstan. In the spring of 1936, the all-Union constitutional commission in Moscow prepared a draft of a new constitution, which would be called Stalin's constitution, and submitted it for a nationwide discussion. According to the new constitution of 1936, Kazakhstan would become a union-republic.[11] With this elevated status, it became more important for Kazakhs, as a titular nation of a union-republic, to possess a national history.

After the arrest of Tomsinskii, Sandzhar Asfendiiarov became the head of the history section of the KazFAN.[12] Subsequently, it took more than a month to reorganize responsibilities at the KazFAN and prepare a draft. Finally, at the end of May 1936, the Bureau of the Kazkraikom received the structure of the textbook's draft and instructed historians on further steps. According to the resolution of the Bureau of the Kazkraikom, a history textbook on Kazakh people and Kazakhstan for the final year students of secondary schools had to be ready by September. As the resolution concluded, historians had serious issues to face. They had to work out the different periods, sources, and materials of Kazakh history. The task was mainly given to the history section of the KazFAN. The abstract of the Kazakh national history textbook that was prepared after the resolution of Moscow in January 1936 recalls the preferences of Pokrovskii. In order to write the national history, a permanent commission of historians and *apparatchiki* was appointed. The commission was headed by the experienced Turkmen Bolshevik Khalmurad Sakhat-Muradov, the secretary of the school and science department of the Bureau of the Kazkraikom, who would organize and manage the project. The task of working out the textbook was given to Asfendiiarov. Also, some prominent members of Kazakh intelligentsia, such as Saken Seifullin and Turar Ryskulov, were asked to participate in this colossal work. The issues for further investigation were so enormous and complicated that it would be impossible to finish the task within three months.[13] Asfendiiarov quickly prepared and presented the structure of the textbook to the Party. He was consistent with his previous approach in 1935. For one thing, the great bulk of the book (three out of four chapters) was devoted to the Russian period commencing in 1717. This book would be a shorter form of Asfendiiarov's history, published in 1935. In the chapters on Russian domination, the leaders of tribal revolts were counted as the leaders of 'nomad-peasant' uprisings. Syrym Datov of the Small Zhuz was one of them. The planning of the textbook suggested that further research had to be done on the revolts of Eset Batyr, Beket Batyr, Dzhangodzhi, and Sadyk, and on the uprising in western Kazakhstan of 1869–70.[14] Although their revolts never spread to all three zhuzes, again these figures were elevated to a national level.

After receiving the sealed letter of 29 July 1936 from the Central Committee of the CPSU, the Bureau of the Kazkraikom CPSU met twice to discuss the purges in the Party. These meetings launched the first wave of the Terror.[15] We should note that at this point the purges had not yet reached an intense level.[16] However, it was enough to prevent Kazakhstan from sending a national history to Moscow, because the Terror commenced before the history was completed. Using inexperienced local graduates or calling for more experts from Moscow were the only proposed solutions.[17] The local graduates were not only young, but also lacked knowledge, because the teaching of the history of Kazakhstan in the local university was merely an experiment.[18] The arrests were a sustained process in 1937. The plenum of the Kazkraikom CPSU on 16–23 January 1937 demanded that the Party revealed more counter-revolutionary terrorists, Kazakh nationalists, and Trotskyites, who were also the agents of Germany and Japan, within its own organization.[19] The February–March plenum of the Central Committee of the CPSU in 1937, in Moscow suddenly increased the speed of the

Terror in Kazakhstan.[20] In this plenum, Stalin publicly criticized Mirzoian for transferring his protégés from the Caucasus and Ural and employing them in Kazakhstan (Stalin 1937, 20). Mirzoian had to show his capacity and diligence as first secretary after his return to Almaty. According to Mirzoian's report to Stalin at the end of July 1937, there were already 400 unveiled members of the 'National-Fascist Organization' who were also Japanese agents, led by Ryskulov, Nurmakov, and Khodzhanov. These arrests included important public figures, party and state bureaucrats, and technocrats.[21] Apparently these arrests were not enough. In September 1937, an article in *Pravda* criticized Party organization in Kazakhstan for being incapable of revealing the enemies of the people in Kazakhstan (Karaganda 1937). After the article, arrests and executions accelerated. From 22 September to 14 November 1937 hundreds of party members in Kazakhstan were arrested. Among the accused were the commissars of agriculture, finance, etc.[22] At the beginning, the Great Terror targeted party and state bureaucrats. In the summer and autumn of 1937, however, leading Kazakh writers Beimbet Mailin, Il'ias Dzhansugurov, Gabbas Togzhanov, Saken Seifullin, Sabit Mukanov, and Mukhtar Auezov were condemned, and in the following months most of them were arrested.[23] The figures involved in the first project of history writing disappeared one by one. The commissar of the Narkompros KazSSR, Temirbek Zhurgenev, was removed in August 1937.[24] Asfendiiarov was also arrested on 22 August 1937 and accused of being a spy for Germany, Japan, and Britain, and spreading anti-Soviet, pan-Turkist ideas. Together with other Kazakh intellectuals and public figures, he was shot following the last show trial in Moscow, in February 1938.[25] In the first half of 1938, another local historian and secretary of the KazFAN, L. P. Mamet, temporarily headed the history section, but soon he was also arrested and shot.[26] Within three years (1936–9) the chair of the Institute of History in Kazakhstan changed five times, three of them ending up in unknown graves.[27] The witch-hunt during the Great Terror had a peculiar logic for purging historians. There was a campaign of unveiling and removing 'nationalists'. While historians had to escape from being 'nationalists', there was not much room left to be internationalist either. The Pokrovskiian school, the only available Marxist interpretation in the Soviet Union, was also denounced. Those who believed that they hitherto wrote a Marxist history such as Asfendiiarov were now accused of being anti-Marxist 'falsifiers' of history. The arrested historians were denounced as being both Pokrovskiian falsifiers and nationalists. For example, Asfendiiarov was accused of being an anti-Marxist Pokrovskiian, but he was at the same time indicted for being a leader of a counter-revolutionary nationalist organization.[28]

## Constructors of national narrative and batyrs after the Great Terror

The Great Terror wiped out thousands of local communists including the first secretary Levon Mirzoian. The purges also opened the way for *vydvizhentsy* eager to fill in the new vacancies. These new Soviet cadres including historians, ethnographers, archaeologists, party propagandists and ideologues constructed further Kazakh national history. Although there are numerous examples of this wave of new nomenklatura, one of them deserves mentioning in detail. Abdulla (Gabdulla) Urazbaevich Buzurbaev (1908–43) was a young and energetic Kazakh who had a meteoric career, representing the new Soviet generation. Before his education at the *rabfak* in Omsk (1927–31), he was a peasant and later a lower-rank worker at a dam construction site. He became a party member in 1928. After the *rabfak*, he worked as a teacher at the *Medrabfak* in Omsk. Further, he graduated from the Institute of Marxism–Leninism in Novosibirisk (1932–7). During the purges, he moved upwards (1937–40) in administrative positions very fast, and finally, in 1940, he became the vice-secretary of the agitation-propaganda department of the CPK. In the summer of the same year, he also became the vice-chairman of the KazFAN. Two weeks before the German attack on the Soviet Union, he became the Kazakhstan party secretary for agitation and propaganda.[29] Additionally, in 1941, he became a member of the editorial council of the KazOGIZ (Kazakh Branch of State Publishing House).[30] He was only 32 but he had high-ranking positions in both the Party and the academy. The example of Buzurbaev is an important one for two reasons. First, Buzurbaev was a typical *vydvizhenets* of the 1930s and he was involved in national history writing. This was a general pattern that we can also see in Azerbaijan and Ukraine. After the Great Terror, the majority of party officials and historians involved in history writing were *vydvizhentsy*. Second, the chief propagandist and ideologist of Kazakhstan also occupied a leading role in the construction of history. The young Buzurbaev was the harbinger of practices in the following decades. His two consecutive successors as head of the agitprop department were also the co-authors of the first and second official national histories of Kazakhstan, published in 1943 and 1947. This involvement of the party secretaries responsible for agitation and propaganda activities was also a general pattern that was shared by Azerbaijan and Ukraine.

Nikolai Skvortsov (1899–1974), the new first secretary of the CPK after the Great Terror, got off to a vigorous start, including resuming the writing of a national history. In the summer of 1938, the school and science department of the CPK issued an order that asked for intensive cooperation between the history sections of the Institute of Marxism–Leninism and the KazFAN, the KazPI (Kazakh Pedagogical Institute), and the KazGU (Kazakh State University) in order to write the 'History of Kazakhstan'. A working plan had to be prepared by 20 September 1938, and preliminary texts had to be presented by 1 January 1939.[31] Nothing came out in 1938, because all these institutions were affected by the purges.[32] According to official reports, in 1935, 51 per cent of the Kazakh population was illiterate and the educated elite comprised a very small portion of the Kazakh population.[33] Before the Great Terror, there were already very few trained local cadres, including historians. In terms of quantity of cadres, even Azerbaijan was in a better position. Hence, the impact of the Great Terror on the Kazakh intelligentsia was worse than in the Azerbaijani or Ukrainian cases. At the end of 1938, A. Baimurzin, who was an apparatchik in the CPK and did not have an academic status in history, became the new head of the history section.³⁴ In May 1939, the CPK renewed the task of the history section, which was the preparation of a textbook of the history of Kazakhstan for higher education institutes by 1 July 1939.³⁵ However, when the deadline came, the history section could not even provide a date for the conclusion of writing of a national history. There was not a single chapter on the desk. In order to overcome the lack of experienced historians, assistance was requested from institutions in Leningrad and Moscow. In 1939 and 1940, the Institute of History in Moscow was involved in the project of writing the national history of Kazakhs (Iaroslavskii 1939, 8; Shunkov 1941). Prof. Viatkin was invited from Leningrad to Almaty in February 1939, in order to organize the work. His team in Leningrad prepared the structure of the history from ancient times until the 1870s.³⁶ The local historians N. T. Timofeev, E. Fedorov, A. P. Chizhov, and A. F. Lakunin were supposed to contribute only to the chapters covering 1870 to 1936. These historians were mostly experts on Party history and the twentieth century of Kazakhstan and were not themselves Kazakhs.³⁷ In the following months, the performance of the KazFAN in general, and the history section in particular, did not satisfy the Party. The twentieth anniversary of Soviet rule in Kazakhstan had to be celebrated without an official national history. That is why the Bureau of the CPK again asked for support from the Academy of Sciences of the USSR in providing qualified specialists, parallel to the reorganization in Almaty.³⁸

In the mid-1930s, Soviet historiography experienced a great shift and the principles of Pokrovskii were left behind as a vulgar interpreter of Marxist history. This anti-Pokrovskiian wave had a profound impact on national historiographies of the Soviet Union. Some folk leaders were kept in the narrative and steadily transformed from 'class leaders' to 'leaders of their nations'. Some of the local rulers (princes, khans, emirs, etc.) were transformed from being 'ruthless exploiters' to 'wise leaders' who had sought the unification of the nation and the establishment of a centralized state. The Russian imperial expansion, considered as a 'lesser evil', at least in Ukrainian and Georgian territories, and a mythical friendship between Russians and non-Russian nations of the union, was underlined by the new narratives. Russian national history, with its great heroes and events, gained an emphasis that had been absent in the previous decade. Considering these changes, one may assume that anti-Russian uprisings in the Kazakh steppe in the nineteenth century became undesired themes in Kazakhstan. However, the nineteenth-century anti-Russian uprisings and their leading batyrs continued to be a dominant narrative and a very popular research subject. Kazakh tribal uprisings against the Russian Empire were not considered off-limits as subjects. Likewise, the thirty-first volume of the Great Soviet Encyclopaedia (*Bol'shaia Sovetskaia Entsiklopediia*), which covered Kazakhstan and was published in 1937, was written according to the Pokrovskiian approach. The article did not mention a single national leader or hero before the anti-Russian uprising of Syrym Batyr (Datov) at the beginning of the nineteenth century. Syrym was presented as 'a popular leader of a big movement of the Kazakh masses'. Other anti-Russian uprising leaders, Isatai Batyr (Taimanov), Mukhambet Utemisov, and Kenesary Kasymov, were also mentioned. The expansion of the

Russian Empire towards the Kazakh steppe was explained as being motivated by 'the demands of commercial capitalism'. All uprisings were also defined as 'class struggles of the masses against the Kazakh feudal rulers' (Shmidt *et al.* 1937). In the meantime, Shestakov's history of the Soviet Union (1937) was published, written under the control of the Central Committee of the CPSU in Moscow. It mentioned only one Kazakh figure, 'the fearless leader' Syrym Batyr, while the khans of Small Zhuz were accused of betraying their own people by assisting the Russians in conquering Kazakh lands (Shestakov 1938, 73–74). In the narrative, there was no difference between Russians, Central Asian khanates, and China. They all represented rivals who wanted to rule the Kazakhs. However, after the publication of his book, Shestakov added that the Russian conquest of the Kazakh steppe could be defined as a 'lesser evil' for the Kazakhs (Shestakov 1937, 91). The impact of Russian colonial expansion in the Kazakh steppe was still a subject of debate but it was not denied.

When the Great Terror was unleashed, many Kazakh historians who wrote in Pokrovskiian style were arrested and shot; however, studying the nineteenth-century anti-Russian uprisings was not interrupted. During the Great Terror, V. F. Shakhmatov and L. P. Mamet, both young Kazakh historians who were influenced by Pokrovskiian historiography, continued to work on 'The revolt of Kazakhs under the leadership of Isatai Taimanov in Bukei [Inner] Zhuz, in 1836–38'.[39] The year 1936 or 1937 could have been declared the centennial of the uprising of Isatai Taimanov; however, the continuous reshuffling and uncertainties as a result of purges in the academy and in the Party did not permit this event to be celebrated on a grand scale. Nevertheless, the history section of the KazFAN prepared a draft for the celebrations and sent it to the Central Committee of the CPK and the Council of Peoples' Commissars of the Kazakh Soviet Socialist Republic (SSR).[40] Following the Great Terror, the emphasis on the batyrs who led anti-Russian uprisings was not weakened. Kazakh historians continued to collect documents about 'The people's uprisings of Isatai Taimanov and Makhambet, and the Adaev uprisings', and also worked on 'the history of the [Russian] colonial seizure of Semirechie'.[41] After his colleague Mamed was purged, V. F. Shakhmatov continued to work on 'The revolt of Kazakhs under the leadership of Isatai Taimanov in 1836–38'.[42] In the following year, the title of the manuscript was altered to 'The uprising of Kazakh toilers in 1836–9 under the leadership of Isatai Taimanov and Makhambet Utemisov'. The theme was described as 'one of the glorious pages of the revolutionary national independence struggles of Kazakh toilers against the colonial yoke of tsarism and its agents – bais, mullas, sultans'.[43] In 1940 historians in Kazakhstan continued to work on the Russian colonial expansion in Kazakhstan and the local insurgencies by batyrs and published their preliminary findings (Shakhmatov 1940; Iakunin and Shakhmatov 1940; Baimurzin 1940). In 1941, history classes on the anti-Russian uprising of Isatai Taimanov were still in the lecture lists of the local party organization.[44] Even on the eve of the war with Nazi Germany, the agitation-propaganda section of the Communist Party of Kazakhstan was using the theme of anti-Russian uprisings. It employed propagandist lecturers for every region of the republic who would conduct courses and lectures in step with Party policies. There was a long list of lectures, and two of them were on the heroism of the Kazakhs: 'Hero of Kazakh nation Amangel'dy Imanov' covered the Soviet-made hero of the 1916 uprising, and 'The uprising of Kazakh labourers under the leadership of Isatai Taimanov and Makhambet Utemisov' described the anti-Russian popular 'nomad-peasant' uprisings led by batyrs in the nineteenth century.[45]

While young Kazakh historians worked on the batyrs of the anti-Russian uprisings in the nineteenth century, M. P. Viatkin and his team in Leningrad and Almaty wrote the first official version of Kazakh history 'from ancient times until the 1870s', which was published in 1941 (Viatkin 1941). He devoted a long chapter to the nineteenth-century anti-Russian uprisings, and interpreted most of them as 'anti-colonial', 'nomad-peasant' uprisings. According to Viatkin, Syrym Batyr's movement could not fully possess the characteristics of a peasant war because the leaders of the movement were elders and notables of different clans within the Small Zhuz. The elders simply wanted a submissive khan and they manipulated the masses for 'a good khan'. Viatkin pointed to similarities with the peasant uprisings in Russia for 'a good tsar'. Syrym Batyr, however, wanted the liquidation of the khanate as an institution. At a later stage, after 1791, he fought against the khan and Russian colonial rule. The progressive side of the movement was a liberating movement of 'nomad peasants' against the colonial aims of tsarism, with Syrym leading the labouring masses (Viatkin 1941, 197–203). Syrym never aimed to abolish the existing patriarchal-tribal structure. However, he acted against the elders and notables, and according to Viatkin, this was enough for the Kazakh masses to remember him as a hero (Viatkin 1941, 210–212). Another anti-Russian uprising by the Inner Zhuz was led by Isatai Batyr (Taimanov). Although Viatkin identified the previous events as 'movements', he named the case of Isatai Taimanov an 'uprising'. Moreover, this uprising was 'unique in the first half of the nineteenth century of the history of Kazakhstan, for clearly bearing the characteristics of a peasant war' (Viatkin 1941, 257). Viatkin explained this 'uniqueness' with 'socio-economic change'. The oppressed and exploited peasant masses were opposed to the feudal sultans and the despot Zhangir. The revolt provided an image of uprising peasants burning down the lord's manor and grabbing his land. This image convinced Viatkin to conclude that 'all of these were typical for a peasant war' (Viatkin 1941, 258).

## The imaginary unification of the Kazakh steppe under the batyrs

The Soviet propaganda of batyrs as historical leaders of all Kazakhs helped to establish a unified and common past and to construct a modern Kazakh national identity. The gathering of local information was followed by the creation of a coherent pan-national narrative and the construction of a category or identity that we call 'national' in a territory where such an identity was absent. The lack of unification or homogeneity was not only to be found in the nineteenth century as the Kazakhs were for centuries divided into the three zhuz, the great unions of tribes, the Small Zhuz, the Middle Zhuz, and the Great Zhuz. As mentioned above, each zhuz possessed a section of the Kazakh steppe, and travelled according to the annual nomadic cycle within this territory (Zhuzy 2005). In the earlier episodes of history, the regions of Kazakhstan followed completely different trajectories.

After the Mongol invasion in the thirteenth century, important events took place in western Kazakhstan, south-east of Aktöbe and north-west of South Kazakhstan, in the territories where the Small Zhuz would be formed in the coming centuries. The formation of the Golden Horde, its struggle with Tamerlane and eventual demise, the emergence of the Kazan, Astrakhan, and Crimean Khanates, and their competition for the legacy of the Golden Horde all created great turmoil, wars, destruction, and migration in the fourteenth to sixteenth centuries. In this sense, the history of the western territories of Kazakhstan was separate from the rest of contemporary Kazakhstan and constiuted the history of the eastern Desht-i Kypchak where Mangyts (Nogays) lived (Vasary 2009, 76–85). Hence, the epics of 'Edyge Batyr', 'Ormambet-bii', 'Er-Kokche', and 'Shorabatyr', that reflect this period, were well-known tales in the North Caucasus, Crimea, and among Bashkirs and the Kazakhs of Small Zhuz, but not in eastern Kazakhstan and Zhetysu. The task of constructing a national history – tying together various figures, events, and tribes – meant carving out the eastern section of Desht-i Kypchak and attaching it to the history of the rest of the Kazakh steppe. Asfendiiarov, in his article on Kazakh Epics in *Kazakhstanskaia Pravda* rightly comments:

> Kazakhstan is a vast country stretching for hundreds of thousands [*sic*] of kilometres. That is why, in the past, its separate regions had their own history. This situation is also reflected in the folk poetic works of Kazakhs. Historical events, for which one or another region of Kazakhstan was an arena, had impact on folklore. In this regard, we have a great difference between western and eastern Kazakhstan. Folk epics (tales on batyrs etc.) developed in western Kazakhstan (previous Small Zhuz) and in 'Middle Zhuz', [but] we have a very weak adoption of the development of epics from 'Small Zhuz', and in the 'Great Zhuz' (Almaty oblast and eastern section of southern Kazakhstan) folk epics do not exist at all. In our opinion, the reason behind this situation is the difference in the developments of historical events within three divisions of Kazakhstan.
>
> (Asfendiiarov 1934)

This historical divisions can also be seen in the regional customs and rites in the regions of Zhetysu, eastern Kazakhstan, the Syr Darya region, and Mangystau (Kurmangali 2001, 99–172).

Moreover, there was no political unity to establish such a cultural unity. It was very rare that one khan could organize the three zhuzes into a single political and military unit.[46] Kazakh khans had nominal powers in peacetime. Their authority increased at the time of mobilization against a common enemy. Even in this case, some tribes could refuse to obey the call of khan for the front line. Those tribes could not be punished for their absence (Logutov 2007, 191–192). Tribal leaders were always more powerful than sultans or khans (Krasovskii 2007, 13). Although khans considered themselves descendants of Genghis Khan their power was very limited. (Konshin 2007, 69). They could not recruit soldiers and intervene in the internal relations of tribes (Chuloshnikov 1924, 215). Each tribe or zhuz very often had its own khan. For instance, the Argyns recognized Ablai Khan as their khan, but the Kypchaks of Kazakhs never saw him as their khan and were against him. For the Naimans, Barak was the khan, while other Kazakhs considered him as merely a sultan (prince) (Masanov 2007b, 79). Khans vied with each other in order to gain as much control as possible over tribal unions. In the socio-political structure, Kazakh nomads never had a single khan ruling all Kazakhs. Similar to other nomadic states, there was no centralized structure and the Kazakh khans never enjoyed the power of absolute monarchy as nomadic life constantly favoured centripetal forces. The khans could not exert absolute control on the economy, means of violence, and ideology (Golden 1998, 14). Similarly, tribal aristocracies (in Turkic, *beg, bey* or *bii*) existed, but their role in this highly mobile society was more limited than that of the landed or service aristocracies in the sedentary world (Radlov 2007a, 9–10; Masanov 2007b, 116–118; Golden 2009, 110). The Russian emissaries of the beginning of the nineteenth century describe clearly how these titles had very limited political and judiciary power. At the end of the eighteenth century, the Great Zhuz did not even have a khan but loosely connected to the ruler of Tashkent (Pospelov and Burnashev 2007, 10–17; Nazarov 2007, 90; Meindorf 2007, 196–197). A nineteenth-century Russian Turkologist, Vasilii Grigoriev, noted:

> Nowhere in the world had the heads of the nation and the aristocracy of birth so little meaning, so little real strength, as the Kirghiz [Kazakh] Khans and Sultans. If any of them attained any influence, so as to be able to draw a crowd after him, he reached this not because of his 'white bone', but on account of his personal worth, and personal qualities have gained exactly the same influence for simple Kirgiz [Kazakh] of the 'black bone'.
> (Sabol 2003b, 18)

Kazakhs strongly detested any idea of settlement which would end their freedom (Lewshin 2007, 22–23). They considered settled dwellers of villages or towns insane (Vamberi 2007, 225). To force them to stay between walls was like torture (Geins 2007, 111). In short, the uprisings of the nineteenth century were not all-Kazakh movements, simply because there has not been a unifying Kazakh national identity or polity. Rather, these revolts were confined mostly to a single zhuz. Even some of these resistance movements were organized by a section (one or two tribes) of a zhuz. The batyrs that were mentioned in the national history could not control all people of a single zhuz, let alone the whole Kazakh steppe.

Originally, these events were sporadic disagreements between various tribes or their conflict with local Russian authorities. These batyrs and their uprisings were events that held limited impact and participation. The Kazakh steppe, equivalent in size to Western Europe and divided by vast and empty deserts, hosted three separate zhuz, loose confederations of independent tribes. Except for the Mongol invasion of Genghis Khan and the Jungar expansion in the eighteenth century, there was not a single event that was experienced by the whole Kazakh steppe and its inhabitants. Memories, traditions, and narratives were divided and developed independently for centuries. When Kazakhness was promoted as a modern national identity within the Soviet modernization project, batyrs and their uprisings became part of a constructed common past. The verbal narratives and written records on these local figures and events were collected. Following this, they were defined and codified as 'national', 'anti-colonial', or 'liberation movements'. Subsequently, they constituted an important part of the first all-national narrative of the Kazakhs: pan-national Kazakh uprisings against an imperial-colonial power.

## Kenesary Kasymov's revolt

The Soviet attempt to build a modern Kazakh national identity and construct a homogeneous national history successfully incorporated regional or tribal batyrs and their anti-Russian uprisings. However, Kenesary Kasymov, the khan of the Middle Zhuz, and his uprising (1837–47) presented a controversial issue for Soviet Kazakh historiography right from the beginning. On the one hand, the uprising targeted colonial expansionist Russia. It was a popular movement covering large sections of the Kazakh steppe. On the other hand, the uprising was led by a khan, an exploiter by class origin. This was far from an analogy with Pugachev or Razin. Nevertheless, the Kenesary Uprising was too prominent in the Kazakh steppe to be omitted. In the 1920s, Riazanov worked on the uprising and prepared a monograph. Another work on Kenesary by A. Bokeikhanov, a former Alash-Orda leader, was published in Tashkent, the academic centre of Central Asia (Bokeikhanov 1923). In 1924, M. Auezov, a young and promising Kazakh writer, wrote a play, *Khan-Kene*, apparently following the example of another historical play, *Pugashchevchina* by K. A. Trenev.

While these affirmative works were conducted, there was also an opposition to this theme. Auezov and his play were denounced for favourably presenting the khanate as an institution. According to critiques, nineteenth-century Kazakhstan was full of popular anti-tsarist movements, and they could be studied, but to present a khan as the leader of the Kazakh nation was not acceptable. When discussions of this issue flared up in the summer of 1934, an article appeared simultaneously in the newspapers *Kazakhstanskaia Pravda* and *Sotsialdy Kazakstan*. The article warned:

> In the play *Khan-Kene*, the class nature of this last khan is obscure – he moves on stage as the leader and commander of the Kazakh nation and dies

as a hero, suffering for the nation, but the nation, especially the Dulats, appear in the role of betrayers of their hero.

(Za proletarskii internatsionalizm 1934)

Another newspaper article critical of the play appeared the following month. This article, written by Kabulov, the head of cultural and propaganda affairs of the Kazakh branch of the Communist Party of the Soviet Union, said that the 'class' dimension clearly demanded that the fine arts reflect socialist realism. Among other features, the aim of socialist realism was:

> Education of labouring masses in the spirit of socialism, [it should bear] 'objective' depictions, snapshots.... Let us take, for example, the last work of our playwright comrade [Mukhtar] Auezov, *Khan-Kene*. This work contains idealisation of heroism and boldness of the khan's descendants, and together with this, there is an attempt at reconciling this boldness and heroism with the dominant contemporary worldview. There is a fabrication of fraternisation in the Kenesary movement.... In general, the play *Khan-Kene* ... provides an idealisation of the khanate's social system [*khanskii stroi*].
>
> (Kabulov 1934)

These comments on the play also provided an idea of how national history was supposed to interpret Kenesary Kasymov and his uprising. Kazakh playwrights and historians were free to produce works on anti-Russian uprisings of the nineteenth century. Anti-colonial uprisings led by batyrs were good examples of the struggle of the Kazakh nation against both foreign exploiters and their local collaborators. However, Kenesary Kasymov was a khan. His class origin did not fit into this epoch of proletarian struggle against their exploiters.

When historians started constructing the Kazakh national narrative, they aimed to show that the characteristics of the popular revolts of the batyrs and the Kenesary Uprising were not the same, though they both were anti-Russian. Asfendiiarov, the leading Kazakh historian and follower of Pokrovskii, did not sympathise with Kenesary Khan. According to Asfendiiarov's national history (1935), Kenesary Kasymov initiated a revolt because of the circumstances. In other words, he did not have a 'progressive political agenda'. He escaped from the pressure of the Khanate of Kokand in the south by moving towards the northern territories of the Middle Zhuz, where his winter pastures were located. However, other sultans who had close relations with the Russian administration had already occupied these territories. Kenesary could see no alternative but to revolt. It was not about ideology, toilers, or nation. He simply found himself at a dead end. Eventually the revolt gained its own momentum and Kenesary conducted a 'partisan war.' The movement expanded and gained new recruits and supporters (Asfendiiarov 1993 [1935], 167–170). Asfendiiarov was aware of the fact that, unlike Isatai Batyr, Kenesary was a khan. That is why he added in his book this note:

It is absolutely clear that Kenesary, as a distinct feudal, tried to secure the seat of khan[;] the reactionary side in his actions and in the motives of his policies (especially the fight against Kyrgyz) can be easily seen. However, this circumstance in any case does not minimise the revolutionary character of the movement of Kazakh masses.

(Asfendiiarov 1993 [1935], 170)

In the following pages he added that Kenesary merely wanted to be khan, attacking the clans that did not accept his rule, such as the Dzhappas, and occupying neighbouring Kyrgyz lands. In other words, the leader could be reactionary or may have had personal interests. At the same time, the uprising was a popular revolt and in time the massive participation of peasant-nomads changed the revolt from a reactionary-monarchical to a progressive-peasant class struggle.

In 1936, when the Soviet authorities of Kazakhstan wanted to prepare a book on their republic for the next Congress of the Soviets of the USSR, the theory of Kazakh 'voluntary subjugation' (*'dobrovol'noe poddanstvo'*) to Russia in the nineteenth century was labelled a 'fabrication.' Tsarism was depicted as 'military-feudal imperialism' and was vilified in order to emphasize the achievements of the new regime in the successive pages. The anti-colonial fighters Syrym Datov and Isatai Taimanov were on the list as usual. However, Kenesary Kasymov was left out at the last moment.[47] It was good to criticize the tsarist period and depict the tribal uprisings against Russian forces as glorious days, but the leading figure could not be a khan. This policy continued in the following years. When Shakhmatov worked on the revolts of 1840–50 with his colleague A. Iakunin in the first half of 1939, Kenesary Kasymov and his uprising were still off the list. It seems that historians did not want to emphasize this problematic figure.[48]

In the second half of 1939, the Kazakh historian A. Margulan, an assistant at that time, began to work on 'the uprising of Kazakhs in 1837–47 (Kenesary Kasymov)' by collecting archival materials. These archival sources were supposed to be added to the collection of materials prepared by the Institute of History in Moscow and the KazFAN on the history of Kazakhstan. That is why the materials collected by Margulan were immediately sent to Moscow for analysis.[49] However, the collection on the history of Kazakhstan printed in 1940 did not include these materials on the revolt of Kenesary (Materialy po istorii 1940). Though the materials on 1830–40 were ready for publication, the scope of the volume ended at 1828. It was a well-known fact that Kenesary fought against the Russians, yet this aspect of his resistance cannot be taken as the reason for its exclusion, because all the other uprisings mentioned in the text were also against the Russians.[50] By being a khan with a strong character, and unifying different clans through his personality, he could have easily been elevated to a leader of the national independence movement against a non-Kazakh state. However, with the abundance of batyrs, it would have been controversial to show a khan as a leader of the labouring masses. That is why Viatkin described Kenesary's movement as merely an anti-colonial national-liberation movement against 'Russian tsarism' and 'the khanates of Kokand and Khiva', leaving out any dimension of a 'revolutionary struggle of the working class' (Viatkin 1941, 286–290.) Nevertheless, the controversial position of Kenesary continued and when the Society of Studying Kazakhstan was founded under the Council of Peoples' Commissars of the Kazakh SSR in February 1941, the planned publication on 'legendary national heroes' still included Kenesary Kasymov.[51] This wavering continued until the German invasion of the Soviet Union in June 1941. The scope of this chapter does not cover further developments. However, it is important to mention that during the Second World War, Kenesary was promoted as a national leader next to the batyrs, whose images had already been cultivated to be all-national heroes. Following the war, the dispute over how to interpret the Kenesary Uprising was renewed and continued until 1951. The condemnation of Bekmakhanov is usually pointed to as an example of how Soviet historiography treated anti-Russian uprisings of the Kazakhs. Long before the Bekmakhanov affair in 1951, Kenesary was a controversial topic among Kazakh intellectuals and Party officials. Although it was a popular revolt and he was a well-known figure among the Kazakhs, the class character of Kenesary raised eyebrows among the local Bolsheviks from the beginning. In the midst of other popular anti-Russian uprisings, which were studied and published by the Soviet historians, Kenesary's revolt was the only controversial event, and that was because, instead of being led by a batyr, the uprising was led by a khan.

## Conclusions

In the post-Soviet period, Kazakh scholars have been 'recovering' a past and disseminating a 'lost chapter' of national history (Sabol 2003a, 231–232). One of these 'lost chapters' involves the anti-Russian uprisings of the nineteenth century. There are two important assumptions in this understanding of the Kazakh past. First, it is claimed that the nineteenth-century uprisings were 'national-liberation movements'. Second, it is assumed that these national-liberation movements (or nineteenth-century anti-Russian uprisings) that took place on the Kazakh steppe were undesired and even prohibited topics in the Soviet historiography. In fact, the reality was the other way around: these uprisings did not have a national character and it was the Soviet history writing which promoted the Kazakhness of these uprisings in a territory where kinships and tribal and regional affiliations were the only motives that unified individuals for a common cause. The nineteenth-century anti-Russian uprisings among Kazakh tribes were popular themes for Kazakh historians who aimed to write a Marxist history of Kazakhs in the 1920s and 1930s. The reawakening of the Russian national narrative after 1934–6 did not constitute a barrier for Kazakh national history writing in emphasizing the anti-Russian uprisings of the nineteenth century. Historians in Almaty continued to study and publish on these uprisings. The national history textbook, which was published in 1941, extensively covered these events. Soviet nation-building policies translated regional anti-Russian uprisings led by their batyrs in the nineteenth century into pan-national figures and events. This Soviet instrument of building a homogeneous national past and identity was not abandoned after 1991 when Kazakhstan became an independent nation-state. More and more batyrs of earlier centuries were added into the national history as national heroes. Although new interpretations of the batyrs downplayed class struggles and underlined national motives, batyrs were kept as essential instruments of nation-building. This continuity attests to the success of Soviet policies in choosing the right instruments for building modern national identities. It also demonstrates how much the modern national identities of Central Asia owe to Soviet nation-building policies and to the state-driven modernization programme in Central Asia.

## Notes

1 For a detailed explanation, variants in different Turkic languages and dialects and a discussion on the origin of the word, see Drevnetiurkskii slovar' 1969, 89; Sevortian 1978, 82–85. For the evolution of the word in Mongolian: Cleaves 1949, 436. The Russian *bogatyr'*, Ukrainian *bohatyr*, and Persian *bahadur* come from this Turko-Mongolian word. Also see Mel'nychuk 1982, 220; Fasmer 1986, 183.
2 Jungars (Oirots) were western Mongolian tribes that established a strong federation in the seventeenth century, also known as the Jungar State.
3 Three Kazakh researchers worked between 1917 and 1941 on the Jungar attacks and batyrs of this period. However, all three were former members of Alash-Orda and were purged. Their works were republished only after 1991: Dulatov 1994; Bokeikhanov 1996; Tynyshpaev 1997. This absence continued in the following decades (Erofeeva 2007, 141).
4 The Jacquerie was a popular revolt by peasants, which took place in northern France in the summer of 1358. The Hussite War was the rebellion of Jan Hus and his followers against the Roman Catholic Church in the Kingdom of Bohemia from 1419 to 1434. The Peasant War in Germany was described by Friedrich Engels in his writings on the peasant uprisings of 1525 in Germany. Engels downplayed the importance of political and religious causes of the war and focused on materialistic and economic factors.
5 Some of these documents were published as the first volume of a planned multi-volume collection (Materialy po istorii 1940). M. P. Viatkin prepared this volume. However, the editor of the volume (otvetstvennyi redaktor) was V. I. Lebedev. See for a detailed explanation on the sources Kozybaev 2006.
6 To write these works Riazanov extensively used the archives of the border department of the Orenburg Governorship.
7 There were two other figures in this narrative, who experienced similar elevation: Mukhamed Utemisov and Sultan Kaip Gali Ishimov.
8 The references are from the 1993 edition. Sandzhar Asfendiiarov was the head of the section of the socio-economic disciplines at the KazPI. At the same time, he was the vice-chairman of the KazFAN, a member of the Scientific Council and of the Presidium of the KazFAN until autumn 1937. See: KRPM, 141–1-10598–4/5, November 11, 1936; KRPM, 708–1-39–117/118, November 10, 1937. For a detailed biography, also see Tokenov 1993; Degitaeva 1998, 265–266.
9 In fact, the poet, writer, and public figure Saken Seifullin had already written a textbook on the history of Kazakh literature. Apparently, this book was not valid any more. The members of the commission, Togzhanov together with Sabit Mukanov and Saken Seifullin, actively participated in the organization of the SSPK (Union of the Soviet Writers of Kazakhstan). In 1937, he was the chair of the SSPK. For the commission see KRPM, 141-1-10583–268/270, March 15, 1936.

10 KRPM, 141–1-10585–377, April 15, 1936; KRPM, 141–1-10586–471, May 4, 1936.
11 KRPM, 141–1-10598–4/5, November 11, 1936; KRPM, 708–1-39–117/118, November 10, 1937.
12 Apparently, the initial opinion of Stalin was different. In 1934, he preferred that Kazakhstan should remain as an autonomous republic within the RSFSR. The elevation of Kazakhstan to a union-republic was decided at a later stage. See RGASPI, 81–3-100–67/71, August 28, 1934.
13 The other members of the commission were the head of the agitprop section I. Kabulov, the Commissar of Narkompros Kazakh ASSR Temirbek Zhurgenev; the historian of the Communist Party E. G. Fedorov: KRPM, 141–1-10587–323, May 28, 1936. In the meantime, the Institute of the National Culture merged with the Institute of History and the Institute of Language and Kazakh Literature.
14 KRPM, 141–1-10587–324, May 28, 1936.
15 KRPM, 141–1-10592–430, August 5, 1936; KRPM, 141–1-10599–501/503, November 1, 1936.
16 During the August–October period, 43 'counter-revolutionaries Trotskyites-Zinovievites' were unveiled: KRPM, 141–1-10599–501/503, November 1, 1936.
17 KRPM, 141–1-10620–46, 64, September 25, 1936. The repressed historians were not only leading ones such as Tomsinskii and Asfendiiarov. Numerous assistants such as Butovskaia, Palamarchuk, and Prusak also disappeared in 1937. See: KRPM, 141–1-11793–45, Autumn 1936.
18 KRPM, 141–1-11792–3 (1936). According to the document Asfendiiarov had to conduct these lectures eight hours per week.
19 For the plenum of the Kazkraikom on January 16–23, 1937, KRPM, 141–1-12801–8/21, January 22, 1937; and also see KRPM, 141–1-12811–377, February 4, 1937.
20 The plenum of the CPSU met from February 23 to March 5, 1937. Following Moscow, the Kazkraikom CPSU also organized a plenum for March 19–20, 1937. In this plenum the Party organization in Kazakhstan was informed that the list of the enemies that had to be revealed was extended by adding Bukharin, Rykov, and their supporters: KRPM, 141–1-12801–179/180, January 20, 1937. For the denouncements of the writers-poets, following the plenum in February–March 1937: KRPM, 708–1-604–35/41, July 13, 1937.
21 KRPM, 708–1-82–24/27, July 30, 1937.
22 KRPM, 708–1-106–176, 177, November 14, 1937.
23 Only Mukanov and Aezov remained after the purges of 1937 and 1938.
24 KRPM, 708–1-25–2/4, August 1–5, 1937.
25 According to the archive material in Almaty, he was shot on February 23, 1938. KROMM, 2178–1-12–1. However, according to the KGB archives in Almaty, he was shot on February 25, 1938. See Ashnin *et al.* 2002, 237.
26 KRPM, 708–2.1–752–6 (1937); KRPM, 708–2.1–752–15 (the first half of 1938).
27 Tomsinskii, Asfendiiarov, Mamet, Baimurzin, Shakhmatov.
28 Following the January 1936 resolution of the Central Committee CPSU on history writing, Kabulov, the head of the agitprop department in Kazakhstan, accused Asfendiiarov and Fedorov of being the representatives of Pokrovskii in Kazakhstan and at the same time of being Kazakh nationalists (Kabulov 1936) The next year, before his arrest, he was again accused of being a Kazakh nationalist (Isakov 1937).
29 In July 1941, Buzurbaev became the head of the agitprop section and was freed from his position in the KazFAN. However, as a history teacher and head of the agitprop department, he continued to be involved in the formation of national history: KRPM, 708–5.1–77, July 8, 1941.
30 KRPM, 708–4.1–170–68, May 29, 1940; KRPM, 708–5.1–13–58, January 4, 1941.
31 KRPM, 708–2.1–752–6, August 16, 1938.
32 Other planned publications of historians in Kazakhstan were also not published. Most of them waited for a decade before publication. For example, the work of M. P. Viatkin on

Syrym Batyr was planned for publication in 1938, but was only published in 1947. In 1938, research prepared by Apollova, M. P. Viatkin, and Bekenbaev had the following title: 'National-colonial policy of tsarism in Kazakhstan in the 1750–70s of the eighteenth century' (Khronika 1937). Following the alterations in history writing in the following decade, the monograph of N. G. Apollova published in 1948 was *Kazakhstan's accession to Russia in the 1730s of the eighteenth century* (Apollova 1948).

33 KRPM, 141–1-11661–3, October 26, 1936.
34 Following the purges, A. I. Baimurzin, who had no academic status in history, headed the section. After May 1939, he was appointed as head of the Kazakh branch of the Glavlit (State Publishing House).
35 KRPM, 708–3.2–136–45, May 10, 1939.
36 KRPM, 708–3.1–789–24, the first quarter of 1940; KRPM, 708–3.2–136–4, May 10, 1939; KRPM, 708–3.2–137–42/43, July 26, 1939.
37 The Presidium of the Academy of Sciences of the USSR of November 5, 1938 and the resolution of the Council of People's Commissars of the Kazakh SSR on December 13, 1938, were the administrative steps behind the assignment of Bernshtam and the invitation for M. P. Viatkin to Almaty. See KRPM, 708–3.1–789–24, the first quarter of 1940; KRPM, 708–3.2–136–4, May 10, 1939.
38 KRPM, 708–4.1–138–105/108, May 20, 1940.
39 KRPM, 708–2.1–752–30 (the first half of 1938).
40 KRPM, 708–2.2–66–2ob, 9 April 1939.
41 KRPM, 708–2.2–66–2ob, 9 April 1939.
42 KRPM, 708–3.1–788–43/45, 31 May 1939.
43 KRPM, 708–3.1–789–25/26 (the first quarter of 1940). In order to create a feudal period, Bais (or Bei/Bey in other Turkic dialects and languages) played the role of feudal seniors in the Kazakh Soviet historiography, while Sultans were designated as aristocrats.
44 KROMM, 1692–1-514–1 (1941).
45 KRPM, 708–5.1–570–38, 39, 11 April 1941.
46 After the rule of Shygai Khan (r. 1581–3) there are no khans who ruled the three zhuzes at the same time. See the genealogy chart of Kazakh and Astrakhan khanates (Togan 1942–47; Sabol 2003b, 18–19).
47 KRPM, 141-l-10592–158, September 1936.
48 KRPM, 708–3.1–788–43/45, 31 May 1939.
49 These materials and the text on the uprising were supposed to constitute a separate book, and they were included in the project of the four-volume history of Kazakh SSR for the future: KRPM, 708–3.1–789–26, first quarter of 1940.
50 In addition to the Kenesary revolt, the history section had other purely anti-Russian themes for research such as 'The colonial seizure of Priirtysh and Semirech' and 'The uprising of Kazakhs in 1916'.
51 KRPM, 708–5.1–673–15, 16, 15 February 1941.

# Introduction to the war period

In the Second World War, there cannot be a better example than the eastern front for how each nation's full human, material, and moral resources were thrown into the battlefield (Mawdsley 2007). The mobilized Soviet manpower during the war surpassed all belligerents and reached 29.5 million. If we add the men already under arms in June 1941, the total manpower was more than 34.5 million. Women also made an enormous contribution both at the front lines and on the home front. The number of mobilized women was close to half a million. Out of this mobilized population, 8,668,400 Red Army members were killed or lost. Of this loss, 66.4 per cent were Russians by nationality (5,756,000). With 1,377,400 dead and lost, Ukrainians came the second in the rank. Considering their population in 1941, Kazakhs and Azerbaijanis also lost immense amounts of their manpower during the war, 125,500 and 58,400 respectively. The total demographic loss of the Soviet Union during the war was beyond the figures of other belligerents, reaching 26.6 million.

This was also a war of machines. For instance, the Soviet military industry produced more than 100,000 warplanes and 98,000 tanks and self-propelled guns during the war (Krivosheev 2009, 36, 38, 42, 45, 52, 333; Simonov 1996, 169–180). This was also a propaganda campaign on a huge scale. Within the five years of war, Soviet publication organs printed 255,659,800 copies of books and brochures for the Red Army (*Partiino-politicheskaia* 1963, 9).

As Shostakovich puts it, at the time of the Great Terror before the war, 'everyone had someone to cry over, but you had to cry silently, under your blanket.... And then the war came and the sorrow became a common one' (Shostakovich 1995, 135–136). The common sorrow united the population and provided a fertile ground for the patriotic wartime propaganda. The pre-war society, divided along class lines, such as kulaks, bourgeois specialists, workers, peasants, and intelligentsia, and terrorized by a continuous hunt for 'wreckers', 'saboteurs', and 'spies', gave way to national unification to drive out the foreign invaders. The Soviet government mobilized the population of the Soviet Union to fight and to labour on for years of struggle. The literature on the Second World War emphasized the Soviet mobilization of Russians and Ukrainians by using national and religious values in propaganda activities. To a certain extent, the non-Russians in this literature have been largely limited to the anti-Soviet collaboration of non-Russians with the Germans and the tragic and deadly deportation of certain nationalities that were accused by the regime of treason to Central Asia (Garthoff 1954, 227–228; Barber and Harrison 1995, 68–72, 104–108, 112–115; Miner 2003).

In fact, Soviet wartime propaganda was more complex than utilizing Russian national and religious sentiments. To begin with, there were two layers of allegiance that the Party recognized and utilized: 'Soviet patriotism' and national patriotism or 'national pride'. The ideal Red Army soldier and Soviet citizen had to have these two qualities at the same time (Kalinin 1943b, 29–31). Soviet patriotism was a common theme that was amplified *both* at the central and the republican levels. This patriotism was based on the official Marxist ideology and class solidarity. The Second World War was a collision of ideologies and this was also true at the eastern front. Propaganda work and lectures focused on ideological themes such as 'fascism – fierce enemy of humanity', 'fascism – rabid gang of adventurers', 'fascism – worst enemy of culture' (Iudin 1941b; Aleksandrov 1941; Komkov 1983, 87 for the detailed list see Burdei 1991, 201–202). In his order on 23 February 1942, when the enemy was at the gates of Moscow, Stalin explicitly pointed out that the war was against the fascist regime: 'It would be ridiculous to identify Hitler's clique with the German people, [and] German State. Historical experience suggests that Hitlers come and go, but the German people and German state remains' (Stalin 1953b, 46).

The concept of Soviet patriotism was also a consequence of multi-national reality in the Soviet Union. The Red Army was a multi-national force, as was the country. From 1941 to 1945, recruits came from all nationalities and more than eighty national divisions were established within the Soviet Army (Zakharov and Kumanev 1974). Every Soviet soldier, regardless of his or her nationality, took a special oath of allegiance upon entering the armed forces. The military oath which was in power since 1939 emphasized this unifying Soviet patriotism:

> I swear ... to my last breath to be devoted to my people, to my Soviet Motherland and the Government of Workers [and] Peasants. I am always ready at the order of the Government of Workers [and] Peasants to rise to the defence of my Motherland – the Union of Soviet Socialist Republics.
> (Prikazy 1994, 89)

The collective struggle of all Soviet nations against the common enemy was constantly published during the war (Zaslavskii 1941; Velikaia otechestvennaia 1941; Za rodinu 1941; Pavlenko 1941a, 1941b; Vasetskii 1941; Cheburakov 1941; Shcherbakov 1941, 1944; Vasil'ev 1941; Varga 1941; Kalinin, 1943a; Karpinskii 1943; Manuil'skii 1944). When Krushchev addressed the delegates of the Ukrainian Supreme Soviet at their first convention after the German occupation in Kyïv, he did not avoid counting one by one the nationalities of soldiers and officers who became the Heroes of the Soviet Union, the highest distinction in the USSR for liberating Ukraine (Khrushchev 1944, 10). The proletarian–internationalist content which underlined the union of Soviet nations continued in the following months after the speech of Stalin on 7 November 1941 (Kalinin 1941; Vyshinskii 1943; Genkina 1943). Stalin was not behind his team in emphasizing this ideological and multi-national aspect. In his first speech after the German attack, Stalin defined the latter as a common enemy of all nations of the Soviet Union. He even named a long list of nations to emphasize his case (Stalin 1941a).

The second and louder side of Soviet wartime propaganda was national patriotism. The all-Union propaganda used the Russian heroic past and Russian culture. Molotov, in his famous speech on the first day of the war, which was edited with Stalin, could not avoid referring to the Patriotic War waged against Napoleon (Molotov 1941). On the same day, the Russian Orthodox Church provided an even longer historical list. The metropolitan bishop Sergei in his sermon on 22 June and later in his letter talked of the fight against the Swedish king, Karel XII, and about the war with Napoleon, and also spoke of historical heroic figures such as Aleksandr Nevskii, Dmitri Donskoi, Alesha Popovich, and Ilia Muromets (Korolev 1990; Ganichev 1995). A little later, old national and military traditions also resurfaced in the union-wide propaganda. Stalin in his speeches on 6 and 7 November 1941 at the anniversary celebrations of the October Revolution increased the volume of Russian nationalism by reference to carefully selected Russian historical figures. These figures became part of the wartime propaganda materials (Stalin 1941b, 1941c). At the famous 7 November parade in 1941 in Red Square, Stalin addressed the troops:

> The war you are waging is a war of liberation, a just war. May the encouraging example of our great forefathers – Aleksandr Nevskii, Dmitri Donskoi, Kuzmina Minin, Dmitri Pozharskii, Aleksandr Suvorov, and Mikhail Kutuzov – inspire you in this war. May the victorious banner of the great Lenin light your way.
>
> (Stalin 1941c)

Although historians were in touch with the agitation-propaganda department from the first day of the war, in 1941 the historical-propaganda texts seemed more like academic lectures than easily intelligible propaganda materials. They did not focus on bright historical figures or heroic deeds. In April 1942, the agitation-propaganda department of the Party held a meeting with the prominent historians of the country. A new course was defined and the Central Committee of the CPSU asked the state publishing house to print a series of short stories of Russian military leaders Nevskii, Suvorov, Kutuzov, and others (Istoriia Velikoi 1961, 571). Central organs in Moscow addressed the Russian majority and referred to Russian national pride and the victorious military past of Russians. Same nationalist propaganda included a pan-Slavic aspect (Tarle 1941b; Leonidov 1941; Iaroslavskii 1941; Iovchuk 1941; Obrashchenie uchastnikov 1941; Fadeev 1941; Iudin 1941a; Derzhavin and Konstantinov 1943; Barushin 1943; Geroicheskoe proshloe 1943; Pigarev 1943; Tarakanov 1943; Korobkov 1944; Savushkin 1990, 58, 63, 64; Barber and Harrison 1995, 68–72, 104–108; for a detailed list see Burdei 1991, 227–229). In the meantime, the enemy was defined as 'German' or within national terms (Braithwaite 2007). In December 1941, Lazar Zakharovich Mekhlis, the head of political affairs in the Red Army, changed the slogan on the masthead of *Pravda* from 'Proletariat of all countries, unite' to 'Death to German occupiers'. Consequently, in 1943 a German propaganda specialist reported on Soviet propaganda that, following the failure of Marxist doctrine in the conditions of the war, the Soviets substantially borrowed German nationalist methods of propaganda (Bezugol'nyi 2005, 179–181).

Soviet propaganda based on national patriotism was not limited to Russians. This was not a German–Russian war and the Soviet Union was a multi-national union. While the central party and state propaganda played on the Russianness, the republican authorities used their titular-national pasts, which had been constructed since 1937, for the wartime mobilization campaigns at the republic level. There was a division of tasks in drumming up national pride. The war chapters of this book cover how the party and state officials in Soviet republics of Ukraine, Azerbaijan, and Kazakhstan used indigenous national identities and national heroic pasts for the agitation-propaganda campaigns of their republics. Local historians had to provide 'ideological ammunition' to the nations of the Soviet Union. Ukraine was on the front line and Ukrainian national patriotism was a key discourse in the wartime propaganda. The same intensity of nationalist propaganda can also be seen in Azerbaijan and Kazakhstan. These republics were part of the home front. As in the other unoccupied territories, they had to provide recruits for the army, raw materials, fuel, food and clothes, and industrial outputs. Moreover, there were millions of evacuees from the territories that fell under the German occupation. These people either lost their homes or came along with the dismantled and evacuated factories and plants. The republican communist parties and local administration had to find sufficient accommodation and food for these millions, organize a local auxiliary labour force for the reconstruction of evacuated factories, and construct additional infrastructure. After August 1943, another burden, mobilization for the reconstruction of liberated territories, was added on top.

The party apparatchiks of Ukraine, Azerbaijan, and Kazakhstan, without any clear signals from the centre, organized this second layer of propaganda themselves in order to increase the fighting spirit of non-Russian soldiers and meet the wartime targets of production and recruitment. During the first years of the war, the role of the agitation-propaganda section of the all-Union Communist Party and the Central Political Administration of the Red Army was limited merely to sending general guidelines to the communist parties of union-republics (Bezugol'nyi 2005, 189). This was partly because Mekhlis did not pay enough attention on the multi-national character of the Red Army and the adaptation of non-Russian soldiers. Although the Caucasian and Central Asian recruits were brought to the front line from the first months of the war, the political administration in Moscow did not work on the regulation of international relations within the Army. The nationalist propaganda in the union-republics was a product of local teamwork. The first secretaries and agitation-propaganda workers of local communist parties, movie artists, theatre players, composers and musicians, painters, writers, and historians worked as an organized team to provide agitation-propaganda brigades, lecturers with slogans, leaflets, booklets, periodical papers and journals, drawings, paintings, posters, theatre plays, and movies which reflected the heroic past of each nation.

When Aleksandr Shcherbakov replaced Mekhlis the adaptation of non-Russian soldiers and political propaganda works to avoid conflict between different nationalities became a priority. Fifteen months after the beginning of the war, in September 1942, Shcherbakov, the new head of the Political Administration of the Red Army, issued the first order on 'educational work of non-Russian Red Army members and junior commanders'. Shcherbakov ordered political workers in the Red Army to pay attention to the cultural differences of non-Russians (and especially Central Asian and Caucasian contingency), to organize enough agitators with native languages, to publish newspapers, leaflets on the friendship of peoples of the USSR, and the racist essence of Nazism (Bezugol'nyi 2005. 195–203). Numerous papers and journals were published for the Red Army and Fleet soldiers in their native languages, including in Azerbaijani, Kazakh, and Ukrainian. The non-Russian soldiers were encouraged to learn Russian for effective communication of orders, instructions and training. Nevertheless, as Kalinin acknowledged, the best propaganda-agitation could only be done in one's own language with native themes (Kalinin 1943a; 1943b, 29).

# 6 Soviet and Iranian Azerbaijan at war

In all Soviet lands, including Azerbaijan, the wartime propaganda was a special issue to be carefully handled. The Bolshevik leadership in Azerbaijan was well aware of its importance. The Party organization in Azerbaijan received clear instructions from Mir Jafar Bagirov, the first secretary of the CPA, at the end of the first week of the war. In his directive, Bagirov underlined the importance of mobilization and propaganda activities.[1] In October 1941, Bureaus of the Central Committees of three Caucasian communist parties (Azerbaijan, Georgia, and Armenia) adopted detailed regulations to strengthen discipline and morale, and improve training of the Caucasian contingents.[2] Later on, at the seventh plenum of the Baku Committee of the CPA, in November 1941, he emphasized that propaganda-agitation work had to be conducted at every moment in the daily lives in the kolkhozes and towns of Azerbaijan (Azərbaijan K(b)P Baki Komitetinin 1941). Furthermore, this propaganda had to be built on heroic national history. In another Party meeting, Bagirov warned that

> The workers of ideological front have urgent tasks. One of them is to reveal different periods of Azerbaijani history, and to conduct research of the centuries-old fight of Azerbaijanis against foreign occupants.
> 
> (Bagirov 1944, 32)

In their wartime propaganda, the local Bolsheviks repeatedly used Azerbaijani nationalist sentiments and national historical themes. To this end, the Azerbaijani Bolsheviks further promoted the new Azerbaijani national identity and history that was constructed after 1937. Besides, this nationalist message had to be propagated in both Russian and Azerbaijani. According to one report, 34 per cent of Azerbaijani recruits in 1941 did not know Russian (Bezugol'nyi 2005. 47). According to another account, in 1941, out of 25,788 Azerbaijani recruits 20,967 did not know Russian.[3] This official rate was higher among the recruits in the following years. The unofficial figures must have been even higher. Azerbaijani leaders were not alone in their nationalist propaganda activities. Historical figures and heroic episodes were used in propaganda activities in all three Caucasian republics. Armenian historians in Erevan produced a similar series of publications. The series had the title *Boevye Podvigi Synov Armenii* (the feat of arms of the sons of Armenia). In my comparative work Azerbaijan stands as an example from the Caucasian region (Arakelian 1941a, 1941b; Shaldzhian 1941, 1942; Muradian 1943; Iusian 1943; Dzhanpoladian 1943; Eremian 1944; Kikodze 1945; Grigorian 1946).

## War propaganda and national history

Although the German occupation did not reach Transcaucasia, the wartime mobilization of the Azerbaijani population was still extremely important. First of all, Azerbaijanis were recruited for different units of the Red Army, including the Black Sea Fleet, the South Front, the South-West Front (the Crimea, North Caucasus, Lower Don region, and Ukraine), and also in reserve units located in Georgia and Armenia.[4] In addition, during the first months of the war, eight Azerbaijani national infantry divisions were formed.[5] During the war, 623,096 Azerbaijanis were recruited for the Army. If we add officers in the reserves (21,043) and the ones already enlisted on active duty before 21 June 1941 (75,579), the total number reaches 719,718.[6] By the summer of 1943, the war had depleted the human resources of the Caucasian and Central Asian republics. On 9 October 1943, the recruitment of titular nationalities in the Caucasus and Central Asia was halted. Instead, the local authorities were asked to focus on Slavic populations of these republics (Bezugol'nyi 2005, 89–91). During the war 58,400 Azerbaijani Red Army soldiers lost their lives (Krivosheev 2009, 52). The Azerbaijani contingency under the red flag can be counted as half of the story. The Azerbaijani émigré population that gathered on the German side of the front and fought for the re-establishment of the Azerbaijan Democratic Republic (1918–20) as an independent state reached 70,000 (Yaqublu 2005; Mamulia 2011, 22–23). The Soviet Azerbaijani propaganda had to provide a nationalistic reply to the political propaganda activities of the émigré circles.

The German danger was not that far from the Caucasus either. In 1942, the German invasion already stretched to the North Caucasus. Until the Battle of Stalingrad, the Germans considered the occupation of Baku for its oil reserves within their immediate war targets. German reconnaissance and surveillance aircraft flew over Azerbaijan and even parachuted in agents to collect information and sabotage transportation and production.[7] In August and September 1942, fifty German agents were caught in the Caucasus and nineteen parachutists were detected.[8] The wartime national propaganda aimed to secure the allegiance of Azerbaijani citizens when they were asked to be alert against German intelligence infiltration into the region.

The civil population had to be mobilized for higher production levels in severe conditions. At the production front, the oilfields of Baku supplied approximately 75 per cent of the Soviet oil in 1939 (Trofimuk 1939). Despite the increasing demands of war, Azerbaijan kept providing between 60 and 70 per cent of Soviet oil production between 1941 and 1945. The supply rate of aviation fuel was even higher, reaching 80 per cent (Beliaeva 1957, 37; Abasov *et al.* 1990, 64). The Baku oilfields were so important that the British military experts planned to send an army for the defence of Baku in case of a Soviet failure in Stalingrad. Without sufficient oil from the Baku fields, it would be nearly impossible for the Soviet Union to continue fighting.

The Soviet wartime propaganda used four main tools to convey the heroic national past. Special bulletins or newspapers for Azerbaijani soldiers came first. Single-sheet newspapers, such as *Sovet Vətəni Uğrunda*, *Döyüş Zərbəsi*, and *Hücum*, had already been printed in the Azerbaijani language since 1942.[9] Similar to the Kazakh case, another medium for patriotic propaganda activities was the theatre. The war affected the list of plays that were staged at Azerbaijani theatres in 1942. The Bureau of the Central Committee of the CPA recommended that heroic figures of the Azerbaijani people should be memorialized in operas. The programme of the Azerbaijani state opera included some new plays with national or heroic themes, such as *Aslan Yatağı* (the Lion's Bed), *Nizami*, *Dumanlı Tabriz* (Foggy Tabriz), and *Babak*.[10] The third patriotic propaganda tool was agitation-propaganda lectures. The historians of the AzFAN contributed to agitation-propaganda initiatives by organizing lectures, in cooperation with the agitation-propaganda section of the CPA both in Baku and other regions of Azerbaijan. Lectures were organized on Javanshir, Babak, Koroğlu, Qaçaq Nəbi, and Ibrahim Shirvanshah, further positioning these figures as national heroes.[11] The local historians Iampol'skii, M. Vekilov, Kaziev, and Ismail Guseinov addressed themes such as 'The heroic past of the Azerbaijani nation', 'Patriotic ideas in the history of Azerbaijan', and 'Babak – warrior for the liberation of the Azerbaijani nation'. Petrushevskii conducted lectures on 'The heroic history of the Azerbaijani nation' and 'The joint struggle of Transcaucasian nations against foreign occupants'.[12] The historical heroic episodes such as those of Babak and Koroğlu were also used in radio broadcasts in the Azerbaijani language (Bayramov 2006, 144–145). Finally, to spread the message of these lectures, the same themes were immediately prepared and published as booklets both in Azerbaijani and Russian from the first months of the War. By 1945, the members of the Institute of History and the Institute of Language and Literature of the AzFAN had written more than sixty texts on historical themes, revealing the patriotism and heroism of the Azerbaijani nation in history.[13]

In October 1941, the first booklet by M. Vekilov, a historian of the AzFAN, was published in the Azerbaijani language. This booklet described the heroic deeds of the Caucasian Albanian prince Javanshir against Arab armies (Vəkilov 1941; Huseinov 1941). The second booklet was hastily prepared by Iampol'skii in December 1941 on the Babak Uprising (Iampol'skii 1941). Later, his booklet was republished in Azerbaijani under the pseudonym 'Lənkəranlı', which means 'from Lənkəran' of Azerbaijan, in order to disguise his ethnicity but underline his native region in Azerbaijan (Lənkəranlı [Iampol'skii] 1943a). Another small booklet prepared in the autumn of 1941 was 'From the Heroic Struggle of the Azerbaijani Nation in the Thirteenth and Fourteenth Centuries' by I. P. Petrushevskii and published in both Russian and Azerbaijani (Petrushevskii 1941; Petruşevski 1943).

In 1942 and 1943 propaganda materials using national history continued to flourish. Booklets were published and distributed in both Azerbaijani and

Russian 'on the bravery and courage of Azerbaijanis' in the national history. These episodes included 'the leadership and military bravery of Ibrahim of the Shirvanshah, and Shah Ismail', 'the history of struggle of the Azerbaijani nation against foreign occupants', historical examples of bravery and courage in the medieval epics of Koroğlu, Kitab-ı Dede Korkut, and patriotic poems of Nizami Ganjavi of the thirteenth century. In order to address the female labour force who replaced the male army recruits in industry, transportation, and agriculture, historical examples also included female characters, such as Tuti Bike of Darband from the eighteenth century (Petrushevskii 1942; Kaziev 1942a, 1942b; Hüseynov 1941a, 1942, 1943, 1945; Şükürzadə 1943a, 1943b; Rəhimov and Hüseynov 1944; Petruşevski 1943; Lənkəranlı [Iampol'skii] 1943b; İbrahimov 1942, 1944; Şərifli 1944).[14] Some historical accounts that had been originally written in Russian were also translated into Azerbaijani for the wartime propaganda (Altman 1941; Taşçiyan 1941; Tarle 1941c; Qorodetski 1941; Levin 1941; Pisarevski 1941; Osipov 1942; Ter-Qriqoryan 1942).

The local historians were not alone in mobilizing their kinsmen using national narratives. Indigenous poets, writers, and experts in Azerbaijani folklore and literature, such as Səməd Vurğun (1906–56), Məmmədhüseyn Təhmasib (1907–82), Məmməd Arif Dadaşzadə (1904–75), Həmid Araslı (1909–83), and Süleyman Rəhimov (1900–83) were also involved in propaganda activities using the national history which had been constructed since 1937 (Axundov and Rəhimov 1941; Axundov 1942a, 1942b; Təhmasib 1941, 1942, 1943a, 1943b, 1943c; Təhmasib and Araslı 1941; Dadaşzadə 1941a, 1941b, 1942, 1945; Hüseynov 1941b; Paşayev 1941; Araslı 1942a, 1942b; Cəlal 1942; Rza 1942; Rahim 1942, 1946; Vurğun 1941a, 1941b. Also Vurğun mentioned Babak in his wartime poems: Vurğun 2005a, 41, 58, 140. For a list of other writers see Vurğun 2005f [1942]). These authors also worked at the army newspapers published for Azerbaijani soldiers in their native tongue (Vurğun 2005d [1942], 79). The use of heroic motives from the national history can also be documented in the speeches of Azerbaijani intellectuals. When the anti-fascist demonstration of the Caucasian peoples was organized in Tbilisi on 23 August 1942, Səməd Vurğun, the leading poet of Azerbaijan, added historical accounts of all three Caucasian nations into his speech. He vowed that

> The foot of fascist occupants will not step on the land that created [the poet] Nizami Ganjavi.... Let our grandfather Tariel [legendary hero in the epic tale 'The Knight in the Panther's Skin' of Georgian poet Rustaveli], David of Sasun [legendary Armenian warrior], Babak, and Koroğlu [national heroes of Azerbaijani] resurrect in our minds.
> (Orucov 1984, 21–22)

As happened with historians, most of these writers were *vydvizhentsy*, who received their vocational education in the 1920s and 1930s, thanks to the new Soviet regime. They climbed the career ladder during the Stalinist modernization of Azerbaijan. When the war broke out they were ready to defend the system and its values against the German aggressors. There was also continuous collaboration between the Party, historians, and writers. Some of them had overlapping tasks in arts, academia, and politics. For instance, Süleyman Rəhimov was a writer, historian, the secretary of the Union of Soviet Writers of Azerbaijan, and also the deputy director at the agitation-propaganda department of the CPA. These patriotic works were distributed among Azerbaijani soldiers to raise fighting spirit (Vurğun 2005f [1942], 109).

The wartime propaganda, which used the national heroic past as a frequent theme, increased the importance of national history. Thus, despite the severe conditions of the war, the construction of a national history continued after 1941. The agitation-propaganda section and even Bagirov, the first secretary of the CPA, were personally involved in how national history should be written. On 25 June 1942, the AzFAN sent two draft copies of *The History of Azerbaijan* to Gazanfar Mamedov, the agitation-propaganda secretary of the CPA, to receive his and Mir Jafar Bagirov's comments. Unfortunately, these copies are not located in the archive file, but the cover letter gives evidence of a revised text in 1942.[15] In light of the war, the prospective text had to 'reflect the heroic traditions of Azerbaijani history'.[16] In the meantime, the 1941 edition of the national history was still valid for the promotion of Azerbaijani national feelings. An Azerbaijani translation of the 1941 edition was published in 1943 in order to convey the nationalist message to the majority of Azerbaijanis who did not know Russian (*Azərbaycan tarixi qısa oçerk* 1943). In 1943, the local historians received various comments from Bagirov and edited their texts accordingly. On 12 January 1944, the authors met with Bagirov. Apparently, the first secretary of the CPA asked the historians to finalize their texts. Two days later, a report sent to Bagirov informed him that the new text would be ready at the end of January.[17] From 28 January to 4 February 1944, the chapters of the textbook were reviewed and discussed at a committee of historians.[18] The book was scheduled to be published for the twenty-fifth anniversary of Soviet rule in Azerbaijan in the following year.[19] However, the text remained unpublished because of disputed issues. Chances are that the unpredictable situation in the Iranian Azerbaijan kept the whole project in the freezer. It was in 1946 when the history textbook of Azerbaijan was finally published (Istoriia 1946). Along with these efforts, Sysoev's history of Azerbaijan published in 1928 was banned and removed from the public libraries.[20] The older accounts were contradicted by the newer ones, so they had to be removed in order to avoid confusion in the public.

The lectures and booklets of the wartime, and the textbook that was published in 1946, were authored by the same group of historians, who prioritized wartime propaganda efforts. In all cases, the agitation-propaganda section of the local communist party was deeply involved. The local historians continued the construction of a national narrative which had been initialized in 1937. The authors further developed the primordial and ancient roots of Azerbaijanis. They increased the number of national figures and leaders, as well as elaborating further the ones that had been incorporated into the narrative since 1937. Finally, historians continued to emphasize the friendship and fraternity among the South

Caucasian nations (Azerbaijanis, Armenians, and Georgians), and the common struggles of the three fraternal nations against foreign occupants, particularly Mongols and Arabs.

The Azerbaijani national identity that had been constructed since 1937 was based on a territorial definition. The new national history defined all ancient polities located in the south-east Caucasus and western Iran (the ancient Caucasian tribes, Caucasian Albanian Principality, and the Median Empire) in antiquity as the forefathers of the Azerbaijani nation. The propaganda activities for the wartime mobilization used this identity and history which had been constructed since 1937. The editorial remarks at the beginning of Iampol'skii's booklet *Babak* explained that, 'By publishing this brochure, the Institute of History of the AzFAN announces the necessity of broad propaganda of the heroic traditions of our Soviet nation, whose beginning lies in deep antiquity' (Iampol'skii 1941). In *From the History of Struggle of the Azerbaijani Nation against Foreign Occupants* Kaziev added that 'The Azerbaijani nation is one of the ancient nations of the world. Its history covers approximately three thousand years' (Kaziev 1942a, 7). The primordial claims continued in the 1946 edition. The ancient Caspians, the Median Empire (Istoriia 1946, 28–32), and the Caucasian Albanians were positioned as ancient Azerbaijanis. It referred to the Caucasian Albanian alphabet, a source of curiosity in the 1940s, as 'an ancient Azerbaijani Albanian writing' (Istoriia 1946, 38). In other words, the ancient Caucasian Albanian scripts were defined as the earliest Azerbaijani national alphabet. Claim for the ancient Albania was so important that, despite the severe conditions of the war in 1944, the AzFAN decided to conduct an archaeological expedition in the ancient capital of Caucasian Albania, the town of Qabala (Qəbələ).[21]

Another recurring theme was the national heroes of the Azerbaijani people since ancient times. While the figures incorporated to the national narrative since 1937 were utilized, new faces were included in the national history. At the beginning of his narrative Kaziev declared:

> The centuries-old history of the Azerbaijani nation is full of names of patriots: fighters for the people's happiness. Legendary Babak, self-asserted Mazdak, the hero Javanshir, Kör-oğlu, Gachak Nabi [Qaçaq Nəbi], his comrades in arms Khadzhar, Gachak Kiaram, Katyr Mamed, and others.
>
> (Kaziev 1942a, 3)

Kaziev then described the anti-Arab struggles of Javanshir and Babak, who by this point were already incorporated names as Azerbaijani national heroes (Kaziev 1942a, 12–18). Iampol'skii published a short book on Babak, continuously labelling him an 'Azerbaijani leader', his uprising an 'Azerbaijani uprising', and the people living in the Caucasian Albania and Iranian Azerbaijan in the ninth century as 'the Azerbaijani people' (Iampol'skii 1941).[22] Compared to the previous edition, the episodes on the struggle of Azerbaijanis against Sassanid and Arab rulers were described in much more colour and detail in the edition of national history which was published right after the war (Istoriia 1946: 40).

Babak was positioned as a national leader who fought against Arab exploiters (Istoriia 1946, 51–57). Another figure who was turned into a national hero after 1937 was Ibrahim of Shirvanshah. The title of the booklet by Petrushevskii, *The Great Patriot Ibrahim of Shirvanshah*, implied that Ibrahim was far from being a 'feudal lord' or the 'hangman of feudal exploiters'. In line with the history that was constructed before the war, Ibrahim was described as a national leader. He was a 'talented orator and diplomat', 'talented ruler', and 'great military leader' who wanted to liberate and unite Azerbaijani lands under a centralized state (Petrushevskii 1942, 16–38, also see Istoriia 1946, 89–91).

There were also new names that were added to the pantheon during the war. A contemporary and unexpected military hero was General Əliağa Şıxlinski (or in Russian: Aliaga Shykhlinskii, 1865–1943). Originally from the Kazakh district of Elizavetpol Guberniia (in contemporary Azerbaijan), Şıxlinski was an artillery officer with a brilliant career, being promoted to the rank of lieutenant-general (1917) in the Russian Imperial Army. He participated in the Russo-Japanese war (1905) and the First World War and was known among his colleagues as 'the god of artillery'. Following the 1917 revolution and the independence of Azerbaijan, he moved back to his native land. He was promoted by the new regime to the general of artillery and participated in the foundation of the first national army as the first deputy of the ministry of war (1918–20). When the Red Army occupied Democratic Republic of Azerbaijan (DRA) in April 1920, he considered resistance against this gigantic force as a futile bloodshed of his people and ordered his subordinates not to detonate the explosives planted on bridges along the route of the Red Army. In the following months, he did not participate in the Ganja Uprising organized by the nationalists and officers of the DRA against the Soviet occupation forces. After the establishment of Bolshevik rule in Azerbaijan, Azerbaijani Bolshevik leader Nərimanov Nəriman (Russian: Nariman Narimanov, 1870–1925) sent Şıxlinski to Moscow for his expertise in artillery which could be used in the ongoing Soviet–Polish War (1919–21) (Şıxlinski 1944, 177). Later on his involvement in the Army was curtailed and he devoted his attention to the writing of the Russian–Azerbaijani military dictionary, which was published in 1926 (Şıxlinski 1926). He resigned in 1929 and lived as a forgotten figure until his death in 1943. However, in 1943, the propagandists of the CPA, most probably following the directives of Bagirov, decided to utilize his profile as a patriotic propaganda item. On his deathbed Şıxlinski dictated his memories to the party officials. These memories were most probably heavily edited by the party propagandists and immediately published as a valuable patriotic propaganda item in Azerbaijani. Evgenii Barsukov, another Russian general who fought together with Şıxlinski in the Russian Imperial Army, wrote a preface for the memories (Şıxlinski 1944). Barsukov's preface was so appreciated by the propagandists in Baku that it was published in 1944 as a separate booklet in Azerbaijani (Barsukov 1944; Ibragimov 1975: 122–123).

The struggle of the Azerbaijani nation against the foreign invaders was also a repeating theme in the wartime propaganda. For instance, at one of his public speeches, Səməd Vurğun emphasized the struggles of the Azerbaijani nation for freedom and liberty in its millennial history. He also counted Babak, Koroğlu, and other figures as the leaders of national-liberation struggles (Vurğun 2005e, 80). Kaziev underlined that 'Hordes of Romans, Parthians, Khazars, Arabs, Mongols, and other occupants one after another trampled across the beautiful fields of Azerbaijan, ransacked and destroyed its towns and villages. The Azerbaijani nation fought against all these intruders' (Kaziev, 1942a, 7). Moreover, this struggle was frequently presented as a struggle of three South Caucasian nations in order to intertwine the national struggle with regional solidarity. Since the beginning of the Soviet rule in 1920–1, the Bolshevik leadership in the region had emphasized the 'historical friendship' of Armenians, Azerbaijanis, and Georgians in order to maintain inter-ethnic and inter-religious peace. The region experienced numerous clashes between ethnic and religious communities which resulted in ethnic cleansing and deportations in the first two decades of the twentieth century. Maintaining inter-ethnic peace was cardinal for the success at the front and home front. The Germans counted on the region's ethnic diversity and saw the Soviet Union as an artificial patchwork of national identities which would dissolve following the initial military defeat. Goering, in his 'Green Folder', an instruction that was distributed to the officers in the wake of the German assault on the Soviet Union, advised his subordinates that 'the contradictions between natives (Georgians, Armenians, Tatars [Azerbaijanis], etc.) and the Russians should serve our interests' (Ibrahimbeili 1977, 278). The historical fraternity of the three South Caucasian nations continued to be an important theme both in the speeches of the Bolshevik leaders and in historical accounts. For instance, at the end of his speech 'Let us turn the Caucasus into a grave for the Hitlerites', Bagirov defined Georgians, Armenians, Azerbaijanis, Dagestanis, the peoples of Checheno-Ingushetia and Ossetia as 'proud and freedom-loving sons of the Caucasus and fraternal nations' (Bagirov 1942, 16). M. Kaziev's *From the History of Struggle of the Azerbaijani Nation against Foreign Occupants* emphasized over and over again the friendship of the Georgian, Armenian, and Azerbaijani nations in ancient times and the Middle Ages (Kaziev 1942a, 6–14, 18, 19). Kaziev explained how the fraternal nations of the Caucasus – Azerbaijanis, Armenians, and Georgians – fought together against the Romans, who were the 'ancestors of contemporary fascist Italians'. Moreover, the Roman legions contained Germanic peoples, the predecessors of contemporary Hitlerites. Thus, Azerbaijanis had been fighting against Italians and Germans since the dawn of history. As a continuous theme, the Azerbaijani nation also fought against the Arab–Muslim invaders (Kaziev 1942a). Petrushevskii's book was devoted to the national resistance against foreign occupants. In particular, Petrushevskii covered the struggle of the nation against Mongol invasion in the thirteenth century (Petrushevskii 1941). The account covered the period when the Seljuk Empire lost its power and former governors of this empire emerged as regional rulers. Thus, there was no centralized polity in western Iran, including Azerbaijan, that could resist the Mongol forces. In the thirteenth century, the whole territory was a patchwork of various dynastic polities based around major trade cities such as Ganja, Shamakhi, Ani, and Sheki, and the Mongol Hordes were unstoppable. It is not a surprise that Petrushevskii could not name a single great battle between an Azerbaijani leader and the Mongol forces of Subutai, Dzhebe, or Ögedei. However, he had the task of constructing a heroic national struggle out of this patchwork. That is why his account created an imaginary unity among various khanates, principalities, and individual cities under the name of 'Azerbaijan', and called their individual confrontations with the Mongols an 'Azerbaijani struggle' against foreign invaders (Petrushevskii 1941, 44–45). The 1946 edition of the national history followed the example of historical accounts that were published during the war. It emphasized the ancient fraternity of Azerbaijani, Armenian, and Georgian tribes (Istoriia 1946, 28). The ancestors of Armenians (Urartians) and Azerbaijanis (Medians) fought together against the Assyrian 'slave owners'. The Persians, as the historical enemies of the ancient Azerbaijanis, were depicted as culturally inferior and former vassals of the Medes. The ancient Armenians were allies with the ancient Azberbaijanis (Medians) against the revolting Persians; however, the struggle ended in a victory for the latter (Istoriia 1946, 30–32). In order to present the situation in a dramatic tone, the history added:

> The Persians, led by Darius, defeated the Medians, enslaved Fraourt [*sic.*, the Median king], cut off his nose and ears, gouged his eyes out, and completed [this torture] by impaling him.
>
> (Istoriia 1946, 32)

The Romans and Sassanids were the enemies of the nation as it was depicted in 1941. Soon, ancient Armenians and Georgians joined this force of 'ancestors of Azerbaijanis (Albanians and Atropatenes)' to fight against the Romans (Istoriia 1946, 37). When the Arab–Muslim armies appeared on the horizon, Azerbaijanis, led by their leaders Javanshir and Babak, fought together with Armenians and Georgians against the invaders (Istoriia 1946, 43–45).

## Fine-tuning from Moscow

In the first two years of the war, Azerbaijani Bolshevik leadership and the local historians and writers disseminated nationalistic and historical accounts for the war efforts. When Shcherbakov replaced Mekhlis and became the head of the Political Administration of the Red Army, the attention of Moscow to the wartime nationalistic propaganda among the non-Russian nations increased. On 11 August 1943, A. Shcherbakov ciphered a telegram to Bagirov on measures for (1) consolidating ties between Azerbaijani soldiers of the Red Army and Azerbaijani people and (2) strengthening their education in Soviet patriotism. Sherbakov's suggestions included:

> The publication of small booklets for agitators and soldiers on the heroic traditions of Azerbaijani people, on the Azerbaijani nation in the fight for its fatherland, a collection of selections from national epic tales and from the

works of the best writers of Azerbaijan, and on the Russian nation – the elder brother of the Azerbaijani nation.[23]

Shcherbakov's message made it clear that the Bolshevik leaders of Azerbaijan had to keep propagating the heroic deeds of the Azerbaijani nation. It also emphasized the Russian position among the other nationalities. The Bureau of the Central Committee of the CPA issued a decree based on Shcherbakov's message. Bagirov immediately sent a copy of the message to Gazanfar Mamedov, the agitation-propaganda secretary, in order to summon Azerbaijani writers and prepare texts for this purpose.[24] Three days later, the Bureau of the CPA charged the historians of AzFAN

> with the organization of popular booklets with the topics 'on the Stalinist friendship of nations', 'on the great Russian nation', 'on the heroic past of Azerbaijani people', 'on the historical friendship of the Azerbaijani nation and the great Russian nation', and 'on the great military leaders of the Azerbaijani nation' for Azerbaijani agitation-propaganda officers in the military units.[25]

Additionally, Bagirov ordered Gazanfar Mamedov and Ali Hassan Shakhgeldiev, the agitation-propaganda secretary of the Baku Committee of the CPA, to send 5 to 10 per cent of the printed materials on popular political fiction and military publications (*massovaia politicheskaia khudozhestvennaia, voennaia literatura*) in the Azerbaijani language to the soldiers and to organize lecturers for the army divisions with Azerbaijani soldiers. The lecturers included Ismail Guseinov, the director of the Institute of History of the AzFAN, to disseminate the heroic past of the nation among Azerbaijani soldiers.[26] In the following year, the editorial board of the *Boets RKKA*, a Red Army newspaper for the Transcaucasian front, asked the agitation-propaganda section of the CPA for 'texts about the historical friendship of the Azerbaijani nation and the great Russian nation'.[27] In order to satisfy these propaganda needs the Azerneshr (in Russian *AzGlavlit*, The State Publishing House of Azerbaijan SSR) published *Velikaia Druzhba* (the Great Friendship) by historian Z. Ibragimov in 1944, who explained the historical solidarity of the two nations (İbrahimov 1944).[28] It is no surprise that the historical friendship of Russian and Azerbaijani people had to be emphasized in the army divisions in which Azerbaijanis and Russians fought together. In a multi-national army, the propaganda of historical friendship of participants was very important. Shcherbakov's message can be understood within a greater context of fighting against mistrust and rumours in the army barracks. There were already reports on the table on the discriminative and nationalist attitude of Russian officers towards Azerbaijani and Caucasian recruits. Moreover, there was a prevailing negative attitude towards the Caucasian soldiers after the evacuation of the Crimea, where they fought. In order to fight against the Great Russian chauvinism, special divisions of the NKVD prosecuted chauvinist officers (Bezugol'nyi 2005, 192–194). Shcherbakov's telegram can also be read as an initial step in a new recruitment policy. By the summer of 1943 the war had depleted the human resources of the Caucasus and Azerbaijan. In October 1943, the republics of the Caucasus were asked to stop recruiting titular nationalities and divert their attention to Russians, Ukrainians, Belorussians, and other non-Caucasian nationalities (Bezugol'nyi 2005, 89–91). The new emphasis on Russian–Azerbaijani brotherhood might have aimed to ease this new recruitment target. Nevertheless, Azerbaijani historians followed this new line of friendship and solidarity when the new national history was published in 1946. The warriors of the Kyïvan Rus', who ransacked towns located in modern Azerbaijan more than once in the tenth century, disappeared from the national narrative. The 1941 text explained in detail how the Rus' warriors, 'the ancestors of Russians, Ukrainians, and Belorussians', sailed in their boats all the way from Kyïv, arrived in Azerbaijan (Arran), and plundered the region. The destruction was so massive that, following this disaster, the city of Barda, the ancient centre of Arran that had survived previous invasions, disappeared from the pages of history (Istoriia 1941, 76–77). In 1946, however, this account was completely removed from the official history of Azerbaijan. Clearly, the authors were anxious not to damage the mythical fraternity of Russians and Azerbaijanis in history.

## Azerbaijani national identity and history exported

The Red Army crossed the Soviet–Iranian border on 25 August 1941, occupying northern Iranian territories, while the British occupation forces took the southern regions of Iran. The Soviet occupation ended in May 1946 after causing the initial crisis of the Cold War (Fawcett 1992; Hasanli 2006). This was also the time when the national history constructed in Baku was utilized and even exported southwards. During these five years, Bolsheviks in Moscow and Baku tried to use in their own interests the nationalist sentiments of Azerbaijanis on both sides of the border. The Azerbaijani communists led by Bagirov beat the drum of Azerbaijani nationalism in both Soviet and Iranian Azerbaijan. Today some Azerbaijani authors present Bagirov as a nationalist leader who used the moment for the unification of his nation between 1941 and 1946 (Əhmədov 2004; Qurban 2006; Məmmədov 2007a, 2007b, 2008). While aiming at an 'acceptable' version of the Soviet past, this interpretation bestows too much credit on Bagirov. The occupation of Iranian Azerbaijan was an all-Union policy directed from Moscow. In August 1941, the pronounced reason for the Anglo-Soviet occupation was to maintain Iran as a safe corridor through which western supplies and aid could be transported to the Soviet Union. These supplies from the western allies were crucial for the Soviet Union to fight against the German forces.

There are other explanations that suggest that Moscow already had additional concerns beyond the 'safe supply corridor'. In fact, Soviet preparation for a possible invasion of the Iranian Azerbaijan had started more than a year earlier in the autumn of 1939 when Ukraine and Belarus were united under the red banner

(Hasanli 2006, 2–3). The Soviets had recently annexed neighbouring territories (Polish Ukraine, Polish Belarus, Northern Bukovina, and Bessarabia) in 1939–40 based on the 'reunification' of cross-border ethno-linguistic populations. A southern expansion of Soviet territory playing the Azerbaijani national card would be a concurring act of the same policy. Demanding a strip of adjacent territories for security reasons was also a practice that Moscow was already familiar with. The territorial demands from Finland caused by the security concerns for Leningrad as an important port and industrial region triggered the Winter War (1939–40) between Finland and the Soviet Union. The annexation of the Iranian Azerbaijan could secure the Caucasian flank and the Baku oilfields in particular. The Soviet concerns over the Baku oilfields were based on the recent past. The Soviet leadership still had a fresh memory of how the Ottoman Turks, the allies of the Germans in the last World War, had simultaneously occupied Tabriz, Baku, and Makhachkala in 1918. After two decades, in 1939–41, the British, French, and Germans had serious military plans to annihilate the Baku oilfields by aerial bombardment, land operations, or subversive attacks which could be launched either from Turkey or Iran. The British and French aimed to interrupt the oil flow to the Nazi Germany when the Second World War broke out. In the following year the same plans were still on the table to support the Finnish struggle against the Soviet occupation (Ibrahimbeili 1977, 24, 28–30, 56; Cherniak 1969, 432–433; Sovremennye mezhdunarodnye 1974, 56; Nekrich 1963, 185; Grechko *et al.* 1974, 44–47; Darabadi 2008). There was already an escalating tension between Iran and the USSR in the second half of the 1930s. The Soviet government was worried by the increasing political influence and economic investments of the Nazi regime in Iran (see Chapter 1) (Minaev 1941). When German armies crossed the Soviet border in 1941, Soviet leaders considered a German–Iranian assault in the Caucasus as a possibility. The readiness of the Soviet Army for a cross-border operation since 1939 can be a consequence of these concerns. Finally, Moscow showed serious interest in Iranian oil and the invasion of Northern Iran could force Tehran to give some concessions to the Soviet Union.

The preparations for the invasion of Iran were started in 1939 and accelerated in 1941. From June to July 1941, the 47th Army, stationed in Transcaucasia, was relocated to the Iranian border and Azerbaijani Bolsheviks were also involved in the preparations. When the Red Army contingency marched into Iran, it included Azerbaijani national infantry divisions that were formed in the first months of the war (Buniatov and Zeinalov 1990, 32). In May to June 1941, before the Soviet invasion, 3,816 people (fifty-two brigades) were organized in Baku to be sent to Iranian Azerbaijan. This included eighty-two Azerbaijan Communist Party functionaries, 100 employees of various Soviet organizations, 200 security service officers, 400 militiamen, seventy procurator officers, ninety court officers, and 150 printing and publishing employees. The Azerbaijani team also included 245 railroad workers and geologists. Aziz Aliyev, the third secretary of the Central Committee of the CPA, was appointed to head the mission ready to be sent to Iran. Süleyman Rəhimov, the secretary of the Baku organization of the

CPA, was the head of propaganda workers in this mission. Aziz Aliyev's mission was to ripen Iranian Azerbaijan for a unification which was staged earlier in Western Ukraine and Western Belarus. When the Soviet occupation was launched, Bagirov was stationed in the border regions to supervise the operation and report to Moscow. Furthermore, he left the Soviet Union for the first and last time in the capacity of the first secretary and visited Tabriz in 1941 (Hasanli 2006, 3–6).

After the entry of the Red Army, Soviet Azerbaijan exerted great influence over Iranian Azerbaijan to the south. The resentment among the population in Iranian Azerbaijan was high as a result of the economic decline of the region and the homogeneous nation-building policy which had been pursued since the 1920s. The Azerbaijanis of Iran welcomed the foreign occupation as an opportunity to free themselves from the Pahlavi authoritarianism, Iranian nationalism, and economic problems. In order to win the hearts and minds of their kinsmen, Azerbaijani brigades dispatched by Baku were instructed to distribute grain, sugar, kerosene, and manufactured wares to the towns of Tabriz, Pahlavi, Ardabil, Resht, and Astara. In September and October the members of Aliyev's mission were dispatched to the regions of Iranian Azerbaijan and the first food and medical services and aid arrived from Baku. In November 1941, the first newspaper in Azerbaijani language was published in Tabriz, after twenty years of prohibition (Atabaki 2000, 4, 5, 59–65, 89). Aziz Aliyev's mission's objective was to disseminate the success of Soviet Azerbaijan in the field of literature, art, culture, and economics. At the same time, Aliyev's group started their propaganda and cultural activities in the entire territory of Iranian Azerbaijan. As Bagirov instructed Aliyev, 'It is essential to create the best impressions about our theatre, actors, and the art of Soviet Azerbaijan among the population' (Hasanli 2006, 13). Baku artists performed in Tabriz and other towns of Iranian Azerbaijan the fine examples of Azerbaijani musical comedies and operas. These examples of Azerbaijani classical music were developed in the 1930s and some of the themes – Shah Ismail, Koroğlu – were from the national history (Rüstəm 2005, 267–273; Hasanli 2006, 5, 6, 9). Beyond the demonstration of Soviet cultural revolution in the north, these plays also aimed to popularize these title figures as Azerbaijani national heroes and spread the national identity and history which had been produced in the north since 1937. There was a parallel theme which merged national and class conflict, as it happened in western Ukraine. Azerbaijani Soviet poet Səməd Vurğun covered the love of Azerbaijani fatherland, Tabriz, Iranian Azerbaijan, the division of Azerbaijan along the Aras River and the historical moment of anticipated reunion (Vurğun 2005a, 40–43, 88–93, 96–98, 108–110, 148, 150, 155–157; Bayramov 2006, 260–270) and Süleyman Rüstəm wrote poems on the fraternity and blood kinship of Azerbaijanis of the Soviet Union and Iran, the love of Tabriz (the capital of the Iranian Azerbaijan), the freedom, liberty, and union of Azerbaijani people, and national and class oppression that the Azerbaijani toiling poor faced in Iran (Sharif 1976; Rüstəm 2005).

The radio broadcasting from Baku was established to deliver the message of the Soviet government. A Soviet printing press was established in Tabriz, printing two newspapers in Azerbaijani, *For Fatherland* and *The Red Soldier*.[29] The leading writers of Soviet Azerbaijan[30] worked at the *For Fatherland*, which was published in Azerbaijani and widely distributed in Iranian Azerbaijan (Hasanli 2006, 17). While busy with exporting the national identity that was constructed earlier in Baku, the Azerbaijani team had local aides. Thousands of people were exiled from Soviet Azerbaijan to the south shortly before the war, in 1937. They had lived in Soviet Azerbaijan for nearly two decades, becoming exposed to the cultural revolution on the Soviet side of the border. These ex-Soviet citizens were inclined to help the Soviet Army and its agents. With the support of Baku, they also gained control of the local organizations of the all-Iranian leftist Tudeh Party (People's Party of Iran) and labour unions in the Iranian Azerbaijan and helped the Communist Party of Azerbaijan to influence the decisions of these organizations.[31]

In order to establish control in Iranian Azerbaijan, the Communist Party of Azerbaijan established contact with the intellectuals of Tabriz, the chiefs of Kurdish tribes, and Turkic Shahsavan tribes. The Shahsavan tribes were a number of tribal groups of migrant shepherd pastoralists who formed part of the Turkic population in north-west Iran. They opposed the constitutionalists following the 1906 revolution and constituted an important part of Royalist troops (Tapper 1966). The Iranian army armed Shahsavan tribes in 1941 while leaving the region for the Red Army, which was a serious concern for the Azerbaijani Bolshevik leadership in Baku. That is why the conservative chiefs of the Shahsavan tribes, who were part of the Azerbaijani population in Iran, were invited to Baku. They arrived on 16 November 1941. In order to establish stronger ties with the kinsmen in Iranian Azerbaijan the representatives of the Tabriz intelligentsia arrived in Baku on 20 November 1941. Bagirov received both delegations. During this visit, the rulers of Soviet Azerbaijan did their best to impress their kinsmen from Iran and to show the benefits of Soviet rule in the north. Attending the talks were prominent Azerbaijani Soviet writers and poets such as Süleyman Rüstəm, Süleyman Rəhimov, and Məmməd Ordubadi. At the meeting with the Tabriz intelligentsia, Bagirov stressed that they were all the children of Azerbaijan, and the duty of Soviet Azerbaijanis was to help their brothers in their struggle to demand from the Iranian government their cultural rights and their share of the riches of Azerbaijan (Hasanli 2006, 14).

By the end of 1941, the developments in Iranian Azerbaijan started to receive increasing reactions from Tehran. For the Soviets, the uninterrupted carriage of western military aid through Iran was vital when the Germans rapidly advanced towards Moscow. The Soviet leadership was unwilling to deteriorate relations with Iranian authorities and the western allies while this transportation needed further cooperation with them. For this reason, Moscow became discontent with the activities of Soviet Azerbaijani envoys and gradually withdrew them from Iranian Azerbaijan in 1942. This left Bagirov with a *fait accompli*. After the Red Army changed the course of the war at Stalingrad, Soviet leaders felt more confident to apply pressure on Iran for oil concessions and Azerbaijani national identity once again became a bargaining chip (Hasanli 2006, 15–22). Moscow ordered geological prospecting work and oil drilling in Northern Iran. In February

1944, the geological group from Baku discovered great reserves of oil near Ordubad, Gorgan, Tashabad, and Semnan, and gas reserves on the Resht plain. Bagirov reported these discoveries to Beria and Stalin. Strangely enough, research in the following decades, including extensive ones in the 1990s, never confirmed such oil and gas fields in Iranian Azerbaijan (Hasanli 2006, 26; Mamedova *et al.* 2010, 265–314, 310). It can be argued that Bagirov applied pressure on the geologists to write such reports in order to keep the Red Army in Iranian Azerbaijan and present Azerbaijani national union as an attractive option to Moscow. That means that Azerbaijani Bolsheviks were not merely 'objects' of the central policy but 'subjects' in their own right. It is also plausible to think that Bagirov was under enormous pressure, as were the geologists. Moscow wanted to hear that there was oil in the Northern Iran and Bagirov gave what the centre passionately wanted. In any case, Moscow and Baku returned to the course of 1941. In March 1944, Moscow asked Bagirov to send the Azerbaijan State Theatre and a concert group to perform in Tabriz and other towns of Iranian Azerbaijan. With the purpose of increasing its influence in Iranian Azerbaijan, the CPA adopted a decision on 20 March 1944 to urgently set up a Department of Religious Affairs of Caucasian Muslims (Hasanli 2006, 29–32). A printing house was established in Tabriz to print popular and periodical literature in Azerbaijani language with Arabic script.[32] Azerbaijani Soviet cadres were sent again to Iranian Azerbaijan to raise the feeling of national identity among their kinsmen, persuade them that they were not isolated from their brothers beyond the border, and that their brothers to the north had a much higher standard of living. This policy continued incessantly until May 1946.

The activities to win the sympathy of Azerbaijanis of Iran were based on Azerbaijani national identity. The increasing nationalist tone can be seen in Bagirov's speeches in this period. He shared his view on this issue at various meetings of dispatched workers before their departure for Iran:

> In some places of the city [of Tabriz] I met seven to eight boys and girls and wanted to talk with them. However, when my car stopped, they were about to run away. I addressed them in Azeri, saying 'Come here'. Having heard their native tongue, they returned.... The land of South Azerbaijan is our motherland. Citizens living on the border of our Republic are those separated from their relatives.... Historically, these are Azerbaijani lands. The largest towns of Iran, including Qazvin, Urmiyeh, Miyaneh, Maragha, Tabriz, Ardabil, Salmas, Khoy, Enzeli, etc. are the motherland of our ancestors. To tell the truth, Tehran is an ancient Azerbaijani town.... I would like to add that while the Red Army is still there, we could not leave hundreds of people starving to death. If your Azerbaijani blood still boils, we should strive for the unification of a once divided people.
>
> (Hasanli 2006, 5, 6)

Indeed, these were strong Azerbaijani nationalist declarations. The speeches of Mir Jafar Bagirov, the first secretary of the CPA, provided clear indication as to how historians had to interpret the past.

## The impact of the Soviet occupation on the national narrative

In the 1930s, Soviet Azerbaijan was a bastion of the Soviet Union when relations with Turkey and Iran became increasingly tense. The national history was written in a defensive spirit. The builders of the Azerbaijani nation separated it from the Turkic and Iranian past and moved it closer to a territorial identity and built fraternity with the two other titular nations of the South Caucasus – Armenians and Georgians. This identity and narrative aimed to build a defensive line without any claims for the Iranian Azerbaijan across the border. That is why it did not seek for a proper balance between the past of the Soviet Azerbaijan and the Iranian Azerbaijan. For instance, the famous castle of Babak and the epicentre of the uprising was located in the Iranian Azerbaijan. When Azerbaijani historians included Babak in national history they could use this fact in order to depict the Iranian Azerbaijan as 'a lost fatherland beyond the contemporary borders'. Yet, the 1941 edition avoided such a formula and moved the centre of the Babak Uprising to the vicinity of Lankaran within the Soviet Azerbaijan (Istoriia 1941, 67). Another figure promoted by the national history was Ibrahim of Shirvanshakh (1382–1417). He gained the favour of the nation-builders partly because Ibrahim was the ruler of Shirvan, the northern territories of the Soviet Azerbaijan and his bitter enemies, the Ak-Koyunlu and Kara-Koyunlu States, ruled in the Iranian Azerbaijan. In the first edition of the national history in 1941, these contemporaries (and enemies) in the Iranian Azerbaijan were not incorporated into the narrative. They were Turkic nomadic tribal federations and depicted as the feudal plundering rulers and the enemies of the Azerbaijani nation (Istoriia 1941, 121). Thus, the epicentre of the historical narrative was kept to the north of the Aras River and two important polities in the south were excluded.

During the war, however, political priorities changed. While Moscow had its own calculations, at the local level, the Azerbaijani intellectuals from the Soviet Union were excited at the possibility of a national union (Rüstəm 2005, 213–217). Until the withdrawal of the Red Army from Iran in May 1946, the anexation of the Iranian Azerbaijan and the unification with the Soviet Azerbaijan was highly possible. As Bagirov summarized to the Azerbaijani workers who were about to cross the border:

> Your task is of great responsibility and honour. Should you succeed, your service to the Azerbaijani people would be immense. Success on this track means the fulfilment of century-long dreams of a people partitioned. You will thus unite partitioned hearts, loves and feelings. This is a matter of honour, fidelity and love.
>
> (Hasanli 2006, 5, 6)

Even after the evacuation of the Red Army, the short-lived Azebaijani government in Tabriz kept many Azerbaijanis in the north waiting for a unification.

The history which was published in 1946 reflects these hopes. Instead of the defensive narrative which demonstrated a careful approach to the Iranian

Azerbaijan since 1937, the new narrative tried to strike a more equal balance between these two territories. That is why the Kara-Koyunlu and Ak-Koyunlu states that ruled the Iranian Azerbaijan for a century were incorporated into the national history (Istoriia 1946, 91–96). The 1941 edition depicted them as enemies of the nation and of Ibrahim of Shirvan and despised the Kara-Koyunlu Turkic nomadic tribal federation as 'Turkmen feudals'. The 1946 edition affirmatively called them 'Azerbaijani nomadic tribes' (Istoriia 1941, 121; 1946, 91). Although they bitterly fought against each other, both the rulers of Shirvan and the Kara-Koyunlu sultans were described positively. This affirmative approach continued in the narrative of the Ak-Koyunlu period. Given the possibility of unification between Soviet and Iranian Azerbaijan, the national history had to reconcile this historical conflict, build a historical fraternity around the national ideals and embrace the territories in the south.

In order to keep a balance between both sides of the Aras River, a long and colourful description of Tabriz was included in the newer text. The account of the occupation of Tabriz by Ibrahim of Shirvan also changed. The earlier text merely stated that Ibrahim conquered Tabriz (Istoriia 1941, 120). This was a trivial development because Ibrahim could hold the city only for a month. The 1946 edition, however, turned this ephemeral episode into a cardinal step in the historical struggle for the unification of Azerbaijan:

> [Ibrahim] as a ruler was the protector of crafts and trade; he sought to maintain peace in Shirvan and [that is why] he was very popular in all of Azerbaijan. The people of Tabriz felt sympathy for him precisely because of these features.... When] Ibrahim crossed the river of Aras [and] in May 1406 occupied Tabriz, the population of the city hailed the Shirvanshah. The annexation of Tabriz was another step towards the creation of the great Azerbaijani state.
>
> (Istoriia 1946, 91)

The reason for this amplification was obvious. The Soviet forces who came from the Soviet Azerbaijan (historical Shirvan) to Tabriz in 1941 repeated this historical episode in 1406 to unite the brothers of one nation.

Although the Ak-Koyunlu, Kara-Koyunlu, Shirvanshahs, and later the Safavids were all defined as Azerbaijanis in the new narrative, they were bitter enemies of each other and belonged to different denominations. The Sunni Ak-Koyunlu ended the rule of the Shi'ite Kara-Koyunlu and expelled the ancestors of Safavids from Ardabil. The Sunni Shirvanshahs defeated and killed the heads of the Safavids in two consecutive generations. In their turn, the Safavids attacked Shirvan for three generations. The army of Safavids was dominated by devoted Turkmen Shi'ite warriors which concluded a series of wars by ending the rule of the Sunni Shirvanshahs in the Caucasus and the Ak-Koyunlu in Iran. The antagonism between the Safavids and Shirvanshakhs was so high that when the Safavids took Baku in 1501 it included some extraordinary images. As the 1941 edition rightly conveys '[The Safavids] exhumed and burned the bones of the members of Shirvanshahs family, who were buried in Baku' (Istoriia 1941, 132). Indeed, even today, visitors are surprised to see the empty chambers of mausoleums at the Shirvanshakh Palace in Baku. Thereafter, most of the Baku population was forcibly converted to the Shi'ite denomination (Mitchell 2009, 20–24). This exhumation episode was removed from the 1946 edition in order to conceal the sectarian conflict and establish a national brotherhood. In addition, the 1946 edition solved these complex dynastic and religious wars by providing an anti-Turkish teleology. The struggle among different dynasties and denominations was for a centralized state against Turkey since the Ak-Koyunlu State (Istoriia 1946, 97) and Safavids were the winners and organizers of this state.

> The Safavid sheikhs who led the Shi'ite movement, moved forward with the claim of uniting the territories of neighbouring countries. The foundation of a new centralized state completely answered the urgent demands of the population, and at the same time, it [complied with] the duties of defending the country [Azerbaijan] first of all against Turkey in the west.
> (Istoriia 1946, 104)

At the same time, the text was careful on the Shi'ite–Sunni schism and downplayed this division within the population. The denominational division was emphasized only in the conflict against the Sunni Ottomans (Istoriia 1946, 106).

The post-1937 national narrative had an anti-Persian aspect. The struggle of the ancient Azerbaijani Medians against the Persians was recorded as the first episode of Azerbaijani–Iranian struggle for the centuries to come. The wartime narrative also continued to emphasize the difference between the Azerbaijanis and Iranians. Contrary to the claim of Tehran, the Azerbaijanis of Iran were not Turkified Persians. They were the proud members of an Azerbaijani nation separate from the Iranian or Turkish identity. For instance, in 1941, the booklet of Iampol'skii on Babak underlined the difference between Azerbaijani and Persian-speaking Iranian nations. Iampol'skii first pointed out that 'sources do not say anything about the language in which Babakites conversed'. He then continued with a questionable point:

> It can be confidently argued that the language of the majority of Azerbaijani Babakites was an ancient Azerbaijani-Japhetic [read Caucasian] language at a particular stage of its development. [Although] we cannot provide here materials that would characterize this language, we note that, in any case, the language they spoke at that time was a separate language (ancient Azeri), differing from all languages of the peoples of the Near East and particularly from Persian.
> (Iampol'skii 1941, 33)

Although the argument of Iampol'skii could be valid only in the north of the Aras River, the author aimed to underline the difference between Persians and autochthonous Azerbaijanis and answer the Iranian claims developed by Kasravi (see Chapter 1).[33]

This argument found a convenient milieu when the representatives of Soviet Azerbaijan moved to Iran with the Red Army troops. When Bagirov addressed the intelligentsia of Tabriz who arrived in Baku in 1941, he declared: 'First we are Azerbaijanis, we know we are Azerbaijanis. We know what honour is. Enough of being slaves for decades, centuries, the Azerbaijani people have been under [Iranian] slavery' (Hasanli 2006, 14). The struggle of the Azerbaijanis in Iran with the assistance of their Soviet kinsmen in the north was the last episode of a long fight against the Iranian yoke. They were one step away from national liberation from the Persians.

## Conclusions

Azerbaijani national identity and history, which was constructed after the Great Terror, was fully utilized during the war. The Azerbaijani Bolsheviks planned and launched the wartime nationalistic propaganda campaign from the first days of the war. The local historians wrote accounts on heroic and patriotic themes. These historical accounts went hand in hand with popular-historical works and poems. After 1943, Moscow followed and backed this campaign more closely. There are two main reasons why the local Bolsheviks played the Azerbaijani nationalist card during the war. Obviously, Azerbaijani Bolsheviks aimed to increase the fighting spirit of soldiers and mobilize the civilian population for higher level of productions under severe living conditions. The second reason was the Soviet occupation of Iranian Azerbaijan, or Southern Azerbaijan, and the possibility of the annexation as happened with Western Ukraine and Belarus. Soviet leaders, both in Moscow and in Baku, tried to use the nationalist sentiments of Azerbaijanis on both sides of the border in their own interests. Since the independence of Azerbaijan in 1991, there has been a tendency to present Bagirov as a national leader who strived for the unification of his nation. It is true that Azerbaijani Bolsheviks were not merely 'objects' of the central policy but 'subjects' with their own agenda. Yet, Bagirov and others did not share the political aims and ideology of the Azerbaijani émigré leaders in Berlin or Ankara. They were first and foremost Bolsheviks and they were after a united and socialist Azerbaijan. At the same time, the Soviet Union utilized Azerbaijani national sentiments in order to guarantee a bigger stake in the Middle East at the end of the war (Ismailov 2003, 273–274; Hasanli, 2006).

As had happened before the war, the relations between the USSR and Iran continued to influence the Azerbaijani national history writing. The Soviet occupation of Iranian Azerbaijan had various impacts on the construction of national history in Azerbaijan. Instead of defending the Soviet borderline, now the national history could justify the expansion of the Soviet rule in the south. The narrative incorporated the past of the Soviet and Iranian Azerbaijan with a greater balance. At the same time, to the south of the Aras River, the Iranian Azerbaijanis were exposed to the Azerbaijani historical narrative and became familiar with the national identity which had been built since 1937 in Baku. For the first time in modern history, one administration produced and propagated a homogeneous Azerbaijani national identity on both sides of the Aras River. When the war ended in 1945, the national administration in Tabriz formed a sense of the motherland and a system of national values in the minds of the Iranian Azerbaijani population for another year. It can be claimed that the promotion of Azerbaijani national identity from 1941 to 1946 has had a lasting impact in establishing values shared by the Caucasian and Iranian Azerbaijanis.

## Notes

1 ARPİİSPİHDA, 1–153–11–21, June 28, 1941.
2 RGASPI, 17–22–532–187 (October 1941).
3 ARPİİSPİHDA, 1–26–39–42 (1941)
4 ARPİİSPİHDA, 1–253–9–104 (in the second half of 1942); Bezugol'nyi 2005, 22–23.
5 The numbers of these nation divisions were: 77, 223, 271, 396, 400, 402, 404, and 416 (Buniatov and Zeinalov 1990, 15; Bezugol'nyi 2005, 126).
6 ARPİİSPİHDA, 1–26–239–1/3.
7 ARPİİSPİHDA, 1–26–53–24/25; ARPİİSPİHDA, 1–26–135–63/64; ARPİİSPİHDA, 1–168-6-311/315; ARPİİSPİHDA, 1–168–6–311/315 (second quarter 1942); ARPİİSPİHDA, 1–26–69–138, May 26, 1942.
8 ARPİİSPİHDA, 1–153–262–1/2; ARPİİSPİHDA, 1–153–222–1/6 (September 1942).
9 See a copy of the newspaper, ARPİİSPİHDA, 1–238–109–10, March 12, 1942. Also, for the military publication section in the Azerbaijani language at the Transcaucasian Front in Tbilisi, see: ARPİİSPİHDA, 1–238–109–97, November 8, 1942.
10 ARPİİSPİHDA, 1–103–64–138/140, March 18, 1942.
11 ARPİİSPİHDA, 1–238–156–31/31ob (January 1943).
12 ARPİİSPİHDA, 1–238–156–36 (January 1943).
13 ARPİİSPİHDA, 1–29–344–39 (1944).
14 ARPİİSPİHDA, 1–238–140–5 and 11 (1942); ARPİİSPİHDA, 1–238–141–10 (1942).
15 ARPİİSPİHDA, 1–238–109–40, June 25, 1942.
16 ARPİİSPİHDA, 1–238–222–1/2 (1943).
17 The historians were Z. I. Iampol'skii, V. V. Leviatov, E. B. Shukur-Zade, E. A. Tokarshevskii, G. N. Guzeinov, and M. A. Kaziev. ARPİİSPİHDA, 1–29–237–8/10, January 14, 1944.
18 ARPİİSPİHDA, 1–29–400–14, February 5, 1944.
19 ARPİİSPİHDA, 1–29–400–44 (1944).
20 ARPİİSPİHDA, 1–238–109–125 (1942).
21 ARPİİSPİHDA, 1–29–400–42/43, April 3, 1944.
22 Soviet poet Il'ia Sel'vinskii also wrote a theatre play on Babek during the war which was published in 1946 (Sel'vinskii 1946).
23 ARPİİSPİHDA, 1–28–30–73, August 11, 1943.
24 ARPİİSPİHDA, 1–28–30–72, August 11, 1943.
25 ARPİİSPİHDA, 1–28–30–65, August 14, 1943.
26 ARPİİSPİHDA, 1–103–84–31, October 19–30, 1942. Ismail Abbas Ogly Guseinov (Hüseynov) was born in 1910 and became a member of the CPSU in 1940. He graduated from the Institute of Nationalities at the Central Committee CPSU. See ARPİİSPİHDA, 1–253–1-5 and 35 (1941).
27 ARPİİSPİHDA, 1–29–384–31, May 13, 1944.
28 ARPİİSPİHDA, 1–29–387–144.
29 ARPİİSPİHDA, 1–238–141–12/17, January 30, 1942 (Atabaki 2000, 212, footnote 100 and 101).

30 Such as Mirza Ibrahimov, Suleyman Rustam, Israfil Nazarov, Osman Sarivelli, Mehtikhan Vekilov, Gylman Musayev, and Shamsi Badalbeyli.
31 The Tudeh Party was the strongest leftist opposition party in Iran with the support of labour unions.
32 ARPİİSPİHDA, 1–206–21–4, November 4, 1945.
33 If there was a 'Japhetic' (read Caucasian) language, it was certainly in the Caucasian Albania or Arran but not in the historical Azerbaijan. According to Bartol'd, before the Arabs 'ethnographical difference [between Arran and Azerbaijan] was not eliminated; even in the Islamic period Iranian language of Azerbaijan (azeri) differentiated from Arranian language (arrani) [which was] most probably [a] Japhetic [language]' (Bartol'd 1963a, 777).

# 7 Kazakh batyrs marching in Stalingrad

Kazakhstan seems to be a remote corner of the Soviet Union far from the struggles of the Second World War. However, the Kazakh lands were not totally isolated from the war. This chapter explains the impact of wartime propaganda on the development of national history writing and how the Kazakh Bolsheviks utilized the national history that has been constructed since 1937 to mobilize millions of Kazakhs for the survival of the Soviet regime. The national history book (Pankratova and Abdykalykov 1943) which was published in the midst of the war became a topic of research for the discussions around this work in the following years. This history book has already been reviewed and historical debates which ensued after its publication have been recounted (Tillett 1969; Kozybaev 1991, 74–84; 1992, 44–96; Gurevich 1992, 63–95; Olcott 1995; Diskussia 2000; Siov 2001; Brandenberger 2002, 123–125; Kapaeva 2004; Bekmakhanov 2005; Mazhitov 2005). Nevertheless, a short outline of the story of the history book can be useful for readers unfamiliar with it before moving into the primary topics of the chapter. The national history of Kazakhs was written by Kazakh Soviet scholars, their Russian colleagues, who were evacuated from Moscow, and by Kazakh Communist Party officials in Almaty in 1942 and 1943.[1] Following its publication, the book became an object of ideological discussions among Russian historians in Moscow in 1944. After the war, political priorities in the Soviet Union gradually changed and some sections of the book were discussed and criticized by historians and party officials – including Kazakhs. The book was republished in 1947 and 1956. Bekmakhanov, who authored the chapter on the Kenesary Kasymov[2] uprising in the first and second editions, was demoted in 1951 and jailed from 1952 to 1954.

## The war reaches the Kazakh steppe

From the first weeks of the war, enormous numbers of people evacuated the occupied territories and ended up in the far corners of Siberia or Central Asia. While recruits crowded wagons and freight cars to the west, factories, plants, and institutions were relocated to Siberia and Central Asia, behind the Ural Mountains. Soon all Central Asian towns and cities, including Almaty, were filled with hundreds of thousands of evacuees from the western regions of the

USSR. They were mostly women, the elderly, and children, who were all exhausted and in terrible condition after travelling for nearly a month. The local state bureaucrats and the officials of the Communist Party of Kazakhstan (hereafter CPK) had to find food and shelter for these endless waves of migrants (Likhomanov 1974, 188; Druzhinin 1990, 230; Kobylyanskiy 2003). The authorities had even bigger issues to tackle. The war efforts had clear aims, and recruiting soldiers came first. Up to 1 May 1945, the mobilization for the Red Army in Kazakhstan SSR amounted to 935,725. In addition, 245,054 individuals were mobilized for industrial production.[3] Among them the number of Kazakh Red Army soldiers who lost their lives during the war was 125,500 (Bezugol'nyi 2005, 98; Krivosheev 2009, 52). If we consider the population of the republic on the eve of the war (4,820,000 in a 1937 source: Vsesoiuznaia perepis' 1991, 28), the ratio was significant. The Second World War was a total war in which mobilization of the home front had utmost importance. People behind the front lines had to be mobilized for the production of weapons, food, and clothes for an expanding army, and for transporting troops and goods to the west. As all of Ukraine and Belorussia, as well as numerous industrial centres and some black earth districts of Russia fell into the hands of the enemy within a matter of a few months, Soviet food production, industry, and mining suffered simultaneously (Harrison 1985, 1996). All this meant a sharp increase in Moscow's demands on Kazakhstan in these sectors (Shaiakhmetov 1942; Velikaia 1970, 180, 183; Kozybaev 1991, 46, 49, 51, 55, 60, 63; Olcott 1995, 188–191).[4] The coal mines (Donbas and Moscow basin) in the occupied territories produced 63 per cent of the whole of Soviet coal production (Sovetskaia 1970, 85). All this meant a sharp increase in Moscow's demands on Kazakhstan (Shaiakhmetov 1942; Olcott 1995, 188–191). For example, during the war, Kazakhstan produced 30 per cent of all smelted copper production in the Union, 50 per cent of copper ore, 60 per cent of manganese ore, 86 per cent of lead and 70 per cent of polymetallic (complex) ore. Compared to 1940, Kazakhstan provided nearly three times more meat in 1943 and the production at the Karaganda coal mines increased 179.3 per cent by 1945. In 1943, machinery production in Kazakhstan and Central Asia, thanks to the evacuated production lines from the west, increased fourfold (Velikaia 1970, 180, 183; Kozybaev 1991, 51, 55, 60, 63; Zakharov and Kumanev 1974, 110; Pervukhin 1974, 18–19; Sovetskaia 1970, 54, 91). As a propaganda memo summarized, there were diverse needs:

> The task of the Kazakh nation is ... to provide the necessities (more cotton, beetroots, grain, leather, meat, warm clothes, [and] industrial products) to the glorious Red Army for the complete defeat of the hated invaders.[5]

The Bureau of the Central Committee of the CPK also made decisions in the sphere of agitation-propaganda and mobilizing people in Kazakhstan. During the war, agitation-propaganda workers of the CPK and Komsomol organizations in the Kazakh SSR increased instead of shrinking and reached up to 60,000. In the first year of the war, the party lectures and propaganda speakers increased to

5,000 (Kazakhstan v pervyi 1943, 43–44; Komkov 1983, 88). This army of propagandists were employed to ensure the following dictum of the wartime in the Kazakh steppe: 'political work among the population must be implemented every day and night'.[6] Moreover, the Bureau quickly became aware of the importance of the Kazakh language and the Kazakh national heroic past in agitation and propaganda activities among the Kazakh population. The reports of the Kazakh propagandist-lecturers on the different regions of the republic confirmed this view. The Party urged local historians to produce the necessary pamphlets and construct a heroic past. Historians who already incorporated tribal uprisings or nomadic coalitions into the national history used the same narrative for the wartime patriotic propaganda. Buzurbaev and Abdykalykov, the consecutive secretaries of the CPK for agitation and propaganda, as well as local historians and writers, played a leading role at this stage. During the war, the agitator was not only responsible for organizing talks; he also had to convince people to provide practical support to the front (Kozybaev 1991, 87). Buzurbaev, at a meeting of Almaty intelligentsia on 22 September 1941, demanded that the intelligentsia – including historians – act as ardent agitators and increase vigilance among the masses (Buzurbaev, 1941; Abdykalykov 1997).

## Kazakh Bolsheviks commence the wartime campaign

The CPK's intention of using a heroic past in agitation-propaganda and increasing vigilance can be seen in the first days of the war. On the third day of the war, experienced lecturers were dispatched by Buzurbaev to the main regions of the republic in order to convey new instructions to the regional party organs and conduct propaganda meetings for the collective farm workers and town dwellers. These propaganda trips to the regions were also a good opportunity to assess the state of public opinion, local rumours, and the issues to which the attention of agitation-propaganda had to be directed. Typically, the propagandists would note down the questions posed by the audience and report them to the centre, so that appropriate answers and further instructions could be prepared for lecturers before the next talk.[7] In June and July of 1941, when the first wave of propaganda activities concluded, the reports started to flow to the centre. According to these reports, both agitator-propagandists and audiences urged the Party to conduct more activities in the Kazakh language. It is not surprising that lectures delivered to Kazakhs in their native tongue were more effective in mobilizing them for the tasks of the war period.[8] After conducting activities in different regions of Kazakhstan during the first weeks of the war, the propagandists also suggested that the lecturers had to be much better prepared for questions and examples on 'the heroic past of our fatherland'.[9] According to the report of another propagandist, a lecture in the Kazakh language would have a greater impact if the message was conveyed by reference to 'a heroic past'. The same agitator in his report suggested that, Kazakh heroes such as Amangel'dy Imanov, the leader of the 1916 uprising, Edyge Khan of the fifteenth century, Bugenbai Batyr, a hero against the Jungars in the eighteenth century, and Batyr Syrym,

Isatai Taimanov, leader of anti-Russian uprisings of the nineteenth century should be used in the propaganda activities as examples of heroic deeds for the contemporary Kazakh population. The agitator continued:

> As [in the case of] the Russian comrades [agitators], Kazakh comrades are also very much in need of materials on the heroic deeds of the forefathers of the Kazakh nation and their military traditions. I consider that it is high time for us to organize two to three of these kinds of brochures with high circulation and in a small format.[10]

Thus, within the first two months of the war it became apparent that in order to convey its message and to mobilize the Kazakh people, the CPK had to use Kazakh packaging. The Party decree on the wartime propaganda emphasized more than once that activities among the Kazakh population had to be conducted by Kazakh agitators in the Kazakh language. Moreover, the agitation-propaganda section had to assist the *agitpunkty* (political agitation-propaganda centres) in factories and collective farms, and to prepare newspaper boards, slogans, posters, and exhibitions that would reflect the heroic past of *both* the Russian and the Kazakh nations. Finally, this struggle was not a Russian–German affair and the Party wanted to make sure that the masses understood that point well.[11] The agitation-propaganda section of the CPK even sent propagandists to the Urals and the central and Siberian regions of the RSFSR, where approximately 200,000 Kazakhs were working in production lines, mines, and construction sites during the war period. It should be noted that Kazakhs were not alone. Among the multi-national territories of Kazakhstan, such as in Dzhambul oblast, talks were conducted in Dungan, Uzbek, Russian, and Kazakh (Kozybaev 1991, 72, 87; Adambekov 2001, 134). There were also Tajik, Uzbek, Turkmen, and Kyrgyz workers transported to the industrial centres of Ural and Siberia (concentrated in Sverdlovsk (Ekaterinburg), Chel'iabinsk, and Novosibirsk) in the RSFSR. Kazakh agitation-propaganda workers organized propaganda activities in native languages among these Central Asians workers (Rozhin 1943).

One of the 'national' themes in propaganda campaigns was the national divisions formed in the autumn and winter of 1941. These divisions demonstrated the kind of reaction the people could have when an endeavour was formulated in 'Kazakh'. At the meeting of the Bureau of the Central Committee of the CPK, Aleksei Babkin, the commissar of the KazNKVD, noted that after the announcement of the formation of Kazakh national divisions, even 'people who are excluded from military service wanted to be conscripted into the national formations [of troops]'.[12] At the end of 1941, the Kazakh national military division contained 13,622 soldiers, hardly a significant number. The political and propaganda purposes of these national units were more important than recruitment numbers. Nikolai Skvortsov, the first party secretary of the CPK, wanted to utilize this aspect by emphasizing that these were 'national divisions': 'More than anything, it must be said [to Kazakh collective farms] that Kazakhstan is forming its own divisions; our divisions are participating in the fight'.[13] The enormous loss of the army divisions in the first months of the war asked for more national divisions. Two infantry and two cavalry regiments had to be formed urgently when the enemy was at the gates of Moscow. Every collective farm had to provide clothes for soldiers as well as horses, fodder, and saddles for the cavalry. These national divisions, in turn, engendered more need for agitation-propaganda that used the national heroic past. Skvortsov concluded at the fifth plenum of the Central Committee of the CPK that 'It is necessary to significantly intensify the [propaganda] efforts among the Kazakhs in our republic, to bring out their rich traditions of heroism.'[14] Parallel to these efforts, in September 1941 the Party decided to celebrate the anniversary of the 1916 uprising.[15] When Shaiakhmetov, the second secretary of the CPK, referred to the heroic past of the Kazakh nation in his patriotic speech for the occasion, he went beyond the 1916 events and referred to anti-Russian uprisings of the nineteenth century.

> The warlike Kazakh nation since time immemorial has enjoyed courage and bravery, and highly appreciated feats of arms. The leaders of national-independence uprisings, Batyrs Beket, Kenesary [Kasymov], and Nauryzbai [Batyr], Isatai [Taimanov], and Makhambet [Utemisov] were distinguished by their extraordinary courage and fearlessness, and they have always served as an example for future generations.[16]
>
> (Shaiakhmetov 1941a)

In the Kazakh version of the text, Shaiakhmetov provided a similar argument:

> In all national-liberation wars, the sons of the Kazakh nation became examples of bravery and sacrifice. It had to be like this. From ancient times, the Kazakh nation has loved to be a batyr. Beket [Batyr], Kenesary [Kasymov] and Nauryzbai [Batyr], Isatai [Taimoanov] and Makhambet [Utemisov], Amangel'dy [Imanov] – batyrs of the Kazakhs – fought for freedom and independence. They defeated their enemies numerous times.
>
> (Shaiakhmetov 1941b)

These figures lived through and led particular events which had occurred among particular Kazakh tribes and in certain areas of the great Kazakh steppe before the concept of a nation was introduced. The nation-builders or historians had already incorporated these figures and events in the previous two decades. This construction of national history accelerated after 1936. Shaiakhmetov's statement demonstrates how the national history that was constructed in the 1930s was used for the wartime mobilization among the indigenous people. It was also the next stage of the construction of a homogeneous national identity that had already began before the war because the national wide usage of this constructed past during the war disseminated this official history to the remote corners of Kazakhstan. After the publication of Shaikhmetov's speech in the republic's daily papers, the propagandists of the CPK strongly advised that the speech be printed and distributed as agitation-propaganda material. Leading Kazakh Party officials and bureaucrats continued to use the same heroic and legendary Kazakh past until the end of the war. The list of national heroes included Edyge, Koblandy, Kambar, Syrym, Kenesary, Eset, and Isatai (Kenzhebaev 1943; Undasynov 1944; Tolybekov 1944; Abdykalykov 1944).

The nationalist propaganda of the Kazakh communists was not limited to lectures or speeches of the officials. It can also be easily traced in the sphere of arts and popular writings. The annual programmes of theatres and cinemas were refashioned according to the needs of the war. This meant that theatres had to show patriotic plays and movies. In a similar vein, the publication plans of the state publishing house of the republic, the KazOGIZ, for the second half of 1941 were altered. The Bureau of the CPK asked the KazOGIZ to publish collections of Kazakh folk epics and Kazakh proverbs and sayings on heroism. This list offered broad coverage of the struggles of different Kazakh tribes or clans against Jungar-Oirots, Russians, and Central Asian khanates. These included publications such as 'Zhangozha Batyr [an epic hero] against the Central Asian Khans', 'The Kazakh Nation against Zhongar Khans', 'Bolat Tondy Batyrlar' by Kazakh bard Dzhambul Dzhabaev, and 'Isatai [Taimanov] Makhambet [Utemisov]'.[17] During the first year of the war, the KazOGIZ published heroic materials as booklets in the Kazakh language, thereby popularizing figures such as Bazar Batyr, Isatai, Makhambet, and Koblandy Batyr.[18] Prominent Kazakh writer Mukhtar Auezov created a new Kazakh opera on the heroic past of the Kazakh nation. The topic was the uprising of Beket Batyr in the eighteenth century (Dva primera 1942).[19] In 1941 and 1942, the theatre play *Isatai i Makhambet*, which narrated the uprising of Isatai Taimanov against the Russian imperial forces, was staged in various Kazakh theatres in Kazakhstan (Kino, Teatrlarda 1941).[20] Nevertheless, the agitation-propaganda department of the CPK criticized the repertoire of Kazakh theatres and demanded:

> There have to be more plays on the heroic past of the Kazakh nation and the civil war. [These plays should] demonstrate epic and romantic heroes, who are closer and more familiar [*blizkie i znakomye*] to the Kazakh nation, such as 'Mak-Pal', 'Kambar-Batyr', 'Isatai and Makhambet', 'Kozy Korpesh', and 'Baian Slu' in opera.[21]

Traditional forms of art were also used to convey the same message. By the end of 1942, Kazakh folk bards (*akyns*) had composed more than 300 patriotic songs to be used in agitation-propaganda works among Kazakhs. The songs of prominent akyns Dzhambul Dzhabaev and Nurpeis Baiganin depicting Kazakh heroes at the front lines gained overwhelming popularity (Mezhrespublikanskoe 1943).

These efforts did not come to an end in 1942. Kazakh writers continued to write on historical themes with the encouragement of the Party. In February and March 1943, Auezov wrote the play *Kara-Kypchak Koblandy* based on an epic tale, and depicted the Kypchaks as ancient Kazakhs. According to a CPK report, 'The play deals with the struggle of the Kazakh people and its batyr Koblandy against foreign enemies [and] oppressors.' Khazhim Zhumaliev wrote a play on

Edyge Batyr, incorporating him into Kazakh national history. The play was about 'the struggle of Edyge Batyr for the independence of his people during the expansion of the Golden Horde'. These and similar works were under the control of and encouraged by the secretary of the agitation-propaganda section of the CPK.[22] Both plays were first staged in 1944. However, the Bureau of the Central Committee of the CPK was still dissatisfied and appealed to the directorate of arts at the Council of People's Commissars of the Kazakh SSR to prepare even more plays and operas in 1944 that would cover 'the heroic past of the Kazakh nation'.[23]

All these efforts were part of a general approach that involved a mixture of Kazakh patriotism and allegiance to socialism. This discourse can also be observed in various articles or speeches published in *Kazakhstanskaia Pravda* and *Sotsialistik Kazakstan* after June 1941 which explained in detail the heroic deeds of Isatai Batyr, Kenesary Kasymov, and Nauryzbai Batyr (Biz Zhenemiz 1941). In October 1941, another article, entitled 'Military Traditions of the Kazakh Nation', again explained in detail the heroic deeds of Isatai Batyr, Kenesary Kasymov, and Naurizbai Batyr (Kazak khalkynyng 1941). Figures from national history were used for the conscription and preparation of Kazakh soldiers. The speech of a Kazakh soldier at an agitation-propaganda meeting held at the army recruiting centre in Kökchetau (a regional centre in the north of Kazakhstan) in July 1941 clearly demonstrates the line of patriotic propaganda conducted among Kazakh recruits:

> The peoples of the Soviet Union constitute a single family. Each of our nations has a heroic past. We [Kazakhs] are the people brought up by Lenin and Stalin [who] will fight for the fatherland like a tiger, as our forefathers Amangel'dy [Imanov], [Batyr] Syrym [Datov], [Batyr] Isatai [Taimanov], [and] Edyge [Batyr fought], until the destruction of the enemy of our people – Hitler.[24]

These historical figures furnished the image of 'batyr' as a folk hero, a figure of valour, and a defender of his people. Subsequently, military propaganda publications such as *Otandy Korghauda* in the Kazakh language constantly called Kazakh soldiers 'batyrs', associating them with the heroic-epic figures of the past. Although the historical batyrs belonged to tribes or tribal confederations (Kazakh: *Zhuz* or *Orda*), contemporary history writing after the 1930s elevated them to a national level. The contemporary batyrs of the Red Army were at the same time batyrs of the Kazakh nation and the Soviet Union (Kaz. *Sovetter Soiuzynyng batyry*) (Otan 1942; Kazaktar 1942; Byzdyng 1943; Kazakstanda 1943). In some cases, the materials printed for Kazakh soldiers explicitly referred to the heroic leaders Edyge, Er-Targyn, Syrym Batyr, Kenesary Kasymov, Nauryzbai Batyr, Isatai Taimanov, and Akyn Makhambet (Batyrlar 1943).

In brief, both the Kazakh language and heroic themes were important for the agitation-propaganda section of the CPK. The majority of the Kazakh population lived in rural areas and could not understand Russian. This was the same for the Kazakh recruits and even for the Kazakh propagandists, who were supposed to convey the message of the Party to the masses. According to an internal report of the CPK, in 1943, there were 45,000 Kazakh agitators in Kazakhstan and in most cases their level of Russian was either bad or insufficient.[25] Moreover, the level of education among the Kazakh population was very low. In order to establish communication with this rural population, the usable past, which was constructed to increase the fighting spirit, had to be familiar to them. The stories transmitted by *zhyraus* or *akyns* (bards) as folk tales or narratives about the nineteenth-century uprisings and their leaders Syrym and Kenesary were well known, especially in the regions where uprisings had occurred. Agitation-propaganda workers were therefore accompanied by folk bards such as Dzhambul Dzhabaev, Nurpeis Baiganin, and Shashubai Koshkarbayev, who addressed the Kazakh people in poetic forms of verbal literature and conveyed a heroic narrative (Kozybaev 1991, 87).

## Local historians and wartime propaganda

The history section of the Kazakh branch of the Academy of Sciences of the USSR, the KazFAN immediately reacted to the needs of the front and to the CPK's call for publications addressing the heroic national past. Local historians prepared a series of 'booklets dedicated to the heroic past of the Kazakh nation'. Al'kei Margulan prepared three of these volumes with the goal of increasing the fighting spirit of the soldiers and helping propaganda activities in Kazakh towns, mines, and collective farms. The first booklet was about the uprising of Syrym Batyr. It described the uprising as 'one of the most important events in the history of the Kazakh nation' and highlighted 'how the heroic Kazakh nation, under the leadership of its beloved hero Syrym [Batyr] Datov, selflessly fought against the oppressors of peoples, khans and tsarism'.[26] Margulan's second booklet was about the Kypchaks, who were defined as the ancestors of the contemporary Kazakhs, Karakalpaks, and Nogais. Moreover, these ancestors of Kazakhs had demonstrated a heroic resistance against the 'ancestors' of fascist Italians (colonist Genoese and Venetians) on the southern shores of the Crimea and in the Azov Sea.[27] Margulan's final booklet was entitled *The Struggle of Edyge against the Order of Magistrate*. In this booklet, the author described the struggle of Edyge Batyr against the combined forces of European feudal lords and their defeat at the Battle of Vorskla River (1399). In the second part of the booklet the figure of Edyge is depicted as a wise folk hero, a freedom fighter, and a great patriot who dedicates himself to the happiness of the people. His heroic merits and deeds 'became an example for many Kazakh fighters for freedom in the following centuries (Syrym Datov, Kenesary [Kasymov], Isatai Taimanov)'.[28] Thus he found a historical struggle of Kazakhs against feudal invaders from the west. Both booklets were very similar to the propaganda initiated by Moscow which used the Battle of Ice[29] in order to mobilize the Russian population of the Union. The other texts that Margulan worked on were *The role* of *Ablai [Khan] in the Struggle of the Kazakh Nation for Independence*, *The Heroic Fighters of the Kazakh Nation Seiten and Taizhan*, and *Edyge Batyr in History and Legends*.[30] Another historian, Viatkin, covered other heroic episodes with the last volume in the series, which included the nineteenth-century uprisings, *From the Struggles of the Kazakh Nation for Independence*. Viatkin aimed to cover all the events that could be presented as part of a struggle for national independence, from the Kypchaks up to the twentieth century.[31] All these efforts took place before the arrival of Moscow's historians, and before the project of *The History of the Kazakh SSR* was launched in 1943. By the time that members of the Institute of History of the Academy of Sciences arrived in Almaty on 10 November 1941, the agitation and propaganda section of the CPK and Kazakh writers and historians had already been using this heroic past for the mobilization of the Kazakh population. After the arrival of Russian historians in Almaty from Moscow on that date, the efforts of the Kazakh historians continued. For example, the Kazakh branch of the Institute of Marx, Engels, and Lenin (IMEL) prepared the booklet *From the Heroic Past of the Kazakh Nation* and the KazFAN worked on '*The Military Legacy of the Kazakh Nation*: A collection of articles and outlines dedicated to portraying the heroic deeds of the Kazakh batyrs in the past and in the days of the patriotic war'.[32]

As I have noted earlier (Chapter 5), the uprising of Kenesary Kasymov had been a sensitive issue since the 1920s. The public declarations of politicians and intellectuals and the publications of historians very often included the name of Kenesary along with other historical figures. Yet, the Kazakh writers knew that emphasizing Kenesary could have unintended results and they were not sure how far the name of Kenesary should be popularized. On the one hand, the uprising was the most formidable and well-organized uprising of the nineteenth century. This heroic past could provide valuable material for wartime propaganda. On the other hand, in the absence of a class dimension, this uprising could only be interpreted as a national conflict between Kazakhs and Russians. With Kazakhs and Russians fighting together under the red banner, this example could hardly promote international comradeship at the front or on the production lines. Initially, Auezov intended to write a script about Kasymov but later changed his mind for this reason. In December 1941, when writers and film studio representatives discussed projects for 1942, they worried about precisely this issue. The uprising of Isatai Taimanov and Makhambet Utemisov was considered appropriate. However, Kazakh writers objected to Kenesary Kasymov. M. Auezov, S. Mukanov, A. Tazhibaev,[33] and Musrepov argued:

> The main theme of the biography of this hero was a struggle with Russian oppressors, and this may be understood as fighting between Russians and Kazakhs, which is particularly harmful at a time when we need to show the unity of the nations of the Soviet Union.[34]

They worried that the uprising may not have been the best story for fulfilling the aims of wartime agitation-propaganda when Kazakhs and Russian were fighting in the same trenches. Mentioning his name here and there was one thing, but writing a screenplay and making a movie would be too much. While Kazakh historians and writers were worried about the ambiguous impact of Kenesary as a propaganda figure, the periodical of the Institute of History of the Academy of Sciences in Moscow published an article in 1942 on this uprising. The author defined Kenesary as a national-liberation leader against Russian colonial expansion and exploitation (Steblin-Kamenskaia 1942).

## Historians from Moscow join the team

Initially, Buzurbaev considered the arrival of historians from Moscow to be a great opportunity, because the CPK could employ them as high-quality lecturers and speakers for agitation-propaganda purposes, or as tutors at local institutes. Even though there was a shortage of accommodation, Buzurbaev insisted that some of them stay in Almaty. There was a reciprocal need. While some other historians went to Tashkent, Anna Pankratova, the head of the group of historians, had asked in her letter to Buzurbaev for permission for the historians to stay in Almaty and deliver lectures and presentations.[35] In the following days, the historians delivered lectures according to the needs of the agitation-propaganda section. Within the first month of their stay, a group of fifteen historians had prepared a booklet entitled *Teaching History under the Conditions of the Great Patriotic War* (Prepodavanie 1942).

In the meantime, hundreds of thousands of refugees were already overcrowding Central Asian cities, and the Kazakh authorities were unable to cope with the wave of refugees in Almaty. The historians were dismayed to learn that they would soon be sent to regional towns as lecturers. At this point, Anna Pankratova met with the leading members of the Ministry of Education and learned that the Kazakh administration had made a decision long ago to prepare a textbook on the history of the Kazakh SSR. She then prepared a working plan and proposed the project to the CPK and the Narkompros KazSSR (People's Commissariat of Enlightenment of the Kazakh SSR). The Bureau of the Central Committee of the CPK and the Narkompros KazSSR saw this as an opportunity to gain additional agitation-propaganda material and approved Pankratova's working plan. Consequently, none of the historians were sent to the towns and eleven of the scholars from Moscow began to work with their local colleagues in Almaty.[36] Kazakh leaders continued to support the project and did their best to provide comfortable conditions for the historians (Druzhinin 1990, 111, 228–231). Pankratova's working plan was adapted according to the directives of the Narkompros KazSSR.[37] The writers comprised three different contingents. First, there were evacuated historians from Moscow, Leningrad, and Kharkiv, such as Pankratova, Grekov, Druzhinin, and Viatkin, whose history of Kazakhstan had been published earlier in 1941. There were also the Kazakh writers Mukhtar Auezov and Sabit Mukanov, as well as Kazakhstani historians of Russian or Kazakh origin, including Fedorov, Timofeev, Al'kei Margulan, and Ermukhan Bekmakhanov, who was a junior historian at the KazFAN and a director at the Narkompros KazSSR (Druzhinin 1990, 231). Finally, there were leading Party members and administrative representatives of the CPK and Kazakh SSR. Some of them, such as Buzurbaev and Abdykalykov, the consecutive secretaries of agitation and propaganda, were co-editors of the book. When Buzurbaev lost his life in an accident and Abdykalykov became secretary, it was Skvortsov who named him a co-editor (Abdykalykov 1997).[38] The political supervision and endorsement of the CPK was crucial for this agitation-propaganda work. As historian Anna Pankratova put it, 'It would be appropriate to entrust to the propaganda section of the Central Committee of the CPK overall political control.'[39] Others, such as Shaiakhmetov, the second secretary of the CPK, were involved in the project from behind the scenes (Druzhinin 1990, 243–244). In the autumn of 1942, the draft of the textbook was discussed at a special editorial commission organized at the agitation and propaganda section of the CPK.[40] It was also reviewed twice at a special commission of the NarkomprosKazSSR, in 1942.[41] Following this, the draft was discussed again by historians. One of the topics of discussion was the uprising of Kenesary Kasymov. This section was initially written by Viatkin, but the local historians criticized the draft, and the task of rewriting was delivered to Bekmakhanov, who was working on the chapter 'The Establishment of Soviet Rule in *Zhetysu* (Russian: *Semirechie*) of Kazakhstan'. After the discussions among historians, the Central Committee of the CPK also reviewed each chapter of the history book over the course of two months (Kozybaev 1992, 28). Finally, *The History of the Kazakh SSR* was published in 1943, with 10,000 copies printed, under the co-editors Anna Pankratova and M. Abdykalykov (Pankratova and Abdykalykov 1943). The textbook covered consecutive heroic episodes of the Kazakh nation in history. Articles celebrating the publication appeared in both *Kazakhstankaia Pravda* and the all-Union *Pravda*. The initial reaction was positive (Zasluzhennyi deiatel' 1943; Viatkin and Kuchkin 1943; Piaskovskii 1943). The CPK was keen on using the publication for continuing efforts in agitation-propaganda. The best way of disseminating the heroic past of the Kazakh people as it was described in the textbook was to reprint the relevant sections in daily newspapers. *Kazakhstanskaia Pravda* and *Sotsialistik Kazakstan* started to publish a series of articles under the general title 'Hero-Batyrs of the Kazakh Nation' (Geroi-Batyry 1943; Ablai 1943; Srym Datov 1943; Isatai 1943; Kenesary 1943; Zhankhozha 1943). According to Abdykalykov, the copies of the book were sent to the front and distributed to the agitation-propaganda section of the CPK (Abdykalykov 1997). We should also note that in addition to the history of Kazakhstan, Pankratova and other Russian historians in Almaty continued their efforts in publishing patriotic texts, just as their Kazakh colleagues did.[42] All of the historians were involved in organized lectures for the public on contemporary issues and heroic episodes from Kazakh national history.[43] One of the works by Russian historian Orlov, which was written 'to popularize the heroic themes in Kazakh folklore'[44] was published at the end of the war. This work portrayed various batyrs and heroic leaders of Desht-i Kypchak as Kazakh heroes, including Er-Targyn and Edyge (Orlov 1945).

## Conclusions

The Second World War was a devastating experience for the USSR and involved a total mobilization of society for the war effort. The republican communist parties were aware of the fact that national sentiments and narratives, which were constructed before the war, were important for mobilizing millions. While the propaganda-agitation of Moscow focused on the Russian population of the multi-national union, Kazakh communists initiated a very strong nationalist propaganda campaign by using their indigenous heroes and events in Kazakhstan. This policy became the leitmotiv of the public speeches of the Kazakh Party officials and lecturers, the publications of daily papers, propaganda leaflets, and the repertoire of performance art.

Soviet historiography had already transformed tribal or regional nomadic heroes into national figures in the 1930s. This was done under the principles of Pokrovskiian history writing and did not aim to construct a romantic national narrative. Yet, historians collected the figures of the past which had an impact on tribal or regional level and attached to these figures a national value. Then, these nationalized figures and the events that they were involved were disseminated by publications to construct an all-national homogenous history. Most of these figures who were amplified up to the national scale were batyrs. These 'national' batyrs were intensively utilized in the wartime propaganda. This usage, in turn, increased the homogenization of the past with its figures and events. In other words, while the wartime propaganda used the national narrative that was worked out in the 1930s, it also participated in the popularization of this narrative and further homogenization of the Kazakh identity. The 1943 edition of the Kazakh national history is a good example of this two-way relation between the wartime propaganda campaign and the construction of national history.

## Notes

1 Previous histories were written by Chuloshnikov (1924), Asfendiiarov (1993 [1935]), and Viatkin (1941).
2 Kenesary Kasymov (1802–47) was a Kazakh sultan (inherited aristocratic title) from the Middle Horde (Kazakh: *Zhuz*) and the leader of an anti-Russian uprising in the Kazakh steppe (1837–46).
3 *KRPM*, 708–9–1363–2, May 31, 1945.
4 KRPM, 708–5.1–596–157 (Summer–Autumn 1941).
4 KRPM, 708–5.1–596–157 (Summer–Autumn 1941).
6 KRPM, 708–5.1–146–85 (1941).
7 See the report of the propagandist-lecturer after his trip to Akmola, Karaganda and Balkhash on June 24, 1941; KRPM, 708–5.1–588–2/5 July 17, 1941.
8 KRPM, 708–5.1–601–19, September 25, 1941; KRPM, 708–5.1–601–36 (November 1941).
9 KRPM, 708–5.1–588–99, July 21, 1941; KRPM, 708–5.1–79 (August 1941).
10 KRPM, 708–5.1–601–20, 24, September 25, 1941. Syrym or Srym (Batyr) Datov (1723–1802) was the leader of an anti-Russian uprising of the tribes within the Small Horde (Kazakh: *Zhuz*) between 1783 and 1797. The territory of the uprising was north of the Caspian Sea. Edyge Khan (1340 or 1352/56–1419), the Amir of Ak-Orda and

the Beklerbek of the Ulus of Dzhuzhi, was the founder of the ruling dynasty of the Nogai Horde. Edyge is also a protagonist of a widespread epic tale and variants of it can be found in the folk narratives of Turkic peoples in Central Asia, Middle East and Siberia. The importance of Edyge epos is akin to the *Slovo o Polkulgoreve* of the Eastern Slavs, or the *Manas* of Kyrgyz.

11  KRPM, 708–5.1–596–97ob, 98 (Summer–Autumn 1941).
12  KRPM, 708–5.1–144–67, December 8, 1941.
13  KRPM, 708–5.1–144–121, December 17, 1941.
14  'Ne obkhodimo znachitel'no usilit' rabotu sredy Kazakhskoi chasti naseleniia nashei respubliki podnimat geroicheskie traditisii kazakhskogo naroda, kotorymi on tak bogat'; see KRPM, 708–6.1–602–134.
15  During the First World War, Russian imperial administration increased the financial burden and began the conscription of the Muslim population in the Empire. Consequently, in 1916, a widespread anti-Russian uprising and ethnic violence broke out in modern-day Kazakhstan and Uzbekistan.
16  KRPM, 708–5.1–603–73.
17  KRPM, 708–5.1–80–1, 47, 54, 55, 56, June 14–17, 1941.
18  KRPM, 708–6.1–661 (June 1942).
19  The libretto of the opera was written by M. Auezov and the music was composed by A. Zil'ber.
20  Ural'skii Oblast' Kazakh Theatre, Enbekshi-Kazakh Kolkhoz-Sovkhoz Theatre, Semipalatinskii Oblast' Kazakh Theatre, Turgaiskii Oblast' Kolkhoz-Sovkhoz Theatre. KRPM, 708–6.1–559–1/12, January 16, 1942.
21  KRPM, 708–6.1–559–19 (February 1942).
22  KRPM, 708–7.1–90–17/18, December 16, 1943.
23  KRPM, 708–7.1–90–14, December 16, 1943.
24  KRPM, 708–5.1–601–17; the date of the meeting was July 25 or 26, 1941.
25  KRPM, 708–7.1–198–3 (10 June 1943).
26  KRPM, 708–5.1–151–78 (December 1941).
27  KRPM, 708–5.1–151–79 (December 1941).
28  KRPM, 708–5.1–151–79 (December 1941).
29  The battle between the Republic of Novgorod and the Teutonic Knights in 1242 which resulted in the defeat of the latter. Since the nineteenth century, German nationalists had used the medieval eastern expansion of the Teutonic Knights as a historical example for the *Drang nach Osten*. The Soviet propaganda used the Battle of Ice as an example of Slavic and Russian superiority. Sergei Eisenstein's film *Aleksandr Nevskii* (1938) was part of the Soviet propaganda campaign, which was intensified during the Second World War.
30  KRPM, 708–6.2–104–99, 99ob (January 1942).
31  These included: (a) the struggle of ancient Kypchak heroes (batyrs) for the destiny of ancient Kazakh tribes until the formation of Kazakh state; (b) the struggle of the Kazakh nation against Jungars (seventeenth century); (c) the Kazakh nation at the uprising of Pugachev; (d) the uprising of Syrym Datov; (e) the uprising of the Kazakh nation under the leadership of Kenesary Kasymov and Isatai Taimanov; (f) the uprising of Kazakhs in connection with the introduction of new provisions (1868); (g) the uprising of Kazakhs in 1916 and the role of the legendary hero Amangeldy Imanov in this uprising. KRPM, 708–5.1–151–80 (December 1941).
32  KRPM, 708–6.1–590–30, March 25, 1943; KRPM, 708–6.1–591–19, August 15, 1942.
33  The secretary of the presidium of SSPK.
34  KRPM, 708–5.1–645–77, December 5, 1941.
35  KRPM, 708–5.1–561–7, 9–11, November 10, 1941.
36  Some of the historians, including Grekov, went back to Tashkent. KRPM, 708–5.1–562–41, December 13, 1941.

37 KRPM, 708–5.1–562–11, December 12, 1941.
38 KRPM, 708–5.1–562–37; KRPM, 708–6.1–449–30b, January 1, 1942; KRPM, 708–6.1–85a-73, December 11, 1942; KRPM, 708–7.1–652–120ob, March 6, 1943. Following Buzurbaev's accidental death in the winter of 1942, Abdykalykov became the secretary.
39 KRPM, 708–6.1–449–1, January 1, 1942.
40 KRPM, 708–7.1–652–120ob, March 6, 1943.
41 KRPM, 708–6.1–449–30, 31, October 14, 1942.
42 KRPM, 708–6.1–469–77, December 3, 1941.
43 KRPM, 708–6.1–469–91, December 22, 1941; KRPM, 708–6.1–602–129/134, November 5, 1942.
44 KRPM, 708–6.2–104–97 (January 1942).

# 8 Bohdan Khmel'nyts'kyi fighting against the Germans

This chapter explains how Ukrainian communists used the national history, which was written since 1937, for wartime propaganda, and the impact of the Second World War on the further construction of the Ukrainian national narrative. The eastern front was not only a battlefield between two regular armies. During the War, Ukraine became home to different armed units, including regular troops of the German army, and the Red Army, which included Ukrainian recruits. There were also Soviet and non-Soviet partisan groups: the Red partisans, who were Soviet forces acting behind enemy lines, *Polis'ka Sich*, the Ukrainian paramilitary formation of Otaman Taras Borovets (Bul'ba-Borovets), the Ukrainian Nationalist Organization and its military branch, OUN-UPA, which fought against the Germans and the Soviets, and the Polish underground movement, which was known as the Home Army (*Armia Krajowa*, AK). Finally, there were various Ukrainian military units that were initiated or supported by the Germans: the Ukrainian Legion (Ukrainian: *Druzhyna Ukraïnskykh natsionalistiv*), the *Nachtigall* and *Roland* units within the *Wehrmacht*, and the Waffen SS 'Galicia' Division. There were also Ukrainian Police units organized by the Nazis (Kamenetsky 1956, 69–71; Pan'kivs'kyi 1983; Armstrong 1990, 37–43; Bul'ba-Borovets 1993; Bihl 1994, 138–162; Chaikovs'kyi 1994; Bolianovs'kyi 2000; Serhiichuk 2000, 2003; Kentii, 2008; Gogun and Kentii 2006).[1] Ukraine was not only a battlefield of regular or irregular combatants, but also a field of ideological competition to win the hearts and minds of Ukrainians. The OUN-UPA leaders were well aware of the ideological front. One of the internal pamphlets of the OUN-UPA in 1943 warned the leaders of the movement, 'Fire must be fought with fire. The Bolsheviks have been striking at us throughout the Soviet Union, primarily with their ideology. We must turn their methods and ideology against them' (Shakhai 1986, 285). The Soviet propagandists were also aware of this propaganda war. Soon the ideological competition turned into a race of capturing and nourishing national feelings.[2]

Both the Ukrainian nationalists and the Ukrainian Bolsheviks had their own national narratives and propagated them to mobilize Ukrainians on their side of the battle. When the Germans invaded Ukraine, there was an upsurge in Ukrainian national feeling (Basarab 1982, 173) fuelled by both sides. The Ukrainian nationalists, naturally, were against the Soviet construction of national history.

The Soviet version of the Ukrainian history was a falsification of the past events by Moscow. According to the pamphlets of the OUN, 'Marxist ideology has become a tool of Russian imperialism', and 'the Communist Party has quietly transformed itself into a red Ivan Kalita'. The Russians, under the disguise of international Bolshevism, Russified 'the glorious era of old princely Ukraine'; 'The aim of the Soviet education in Ukraine was the destruction of the historical memory of Ukrainian youth' (Khersonets 1986, 232, 234). After twenty years of Bolshevik rule, the Ukrainian nationalists were eager to disseminate an alternative understanding of Ukrainian's past and present in response to the Ukrainian Soviet national history. When new recruits joined the nationalist organization, the first thing they had to learn was the OUN version of Ukrainian national history. Ideological or organizational instructions would come afterwards (Pyskir 2001, 11–12). For the Soviet authorities, the nationalist upsurge in the occupied lands was not merely a *fait accompli* with which they had to contend or fight against. In fact, the Ukrainian Bolsheviks used Ukrainian national identity and national history that they constructed since 1937 (Lystivky 1969). Moreover, we might even argue that it was the Soviet Union that used Ukrainian national history as propaganda-agitation material with the greatest success.

## Construction of a national narrative in Ufa

During the German occupation of Ukraine, the members of the Ukrainian Academy of Sciences in Kyïv were evacuated to Ufa, Bashkiria in July and August 1941 (Santsevich and Komarenko 1986, 46). For most of the war period they stayed there and continued to write the national history with active involvement of the agitation and propaganda section of the CPU. In addition to the wartime propaganda publications, the institute was eager to publish national history textbooks – a four-volume history for universities and a single volume short course for schools.[3] In fact, the Ukrainian historians (M. Petrovs'kyi [ed.], L. Slavin, S. Iushkov, and K. Huslystyi) had started to work on the multi-volume history in Kyïv in 1940,[4] and had prepared a text by April 1942.[5] At the same time, Prof. Petrovs'kyi worked on an abridged textbook for the third and fourth grades.[6] Once the draft was printed, in a very limited circulation, the Presidium of the Academy of Sciences of the Ukrainian SSR sent two copies to Lytvyn, the secretary of the agitation-propaganda section of the CPU, on 14 January 1943.[7] This textbook was read and evaluated by K. Lytvyn,[8] the secretary of the agitation-propaganda department of the CPU, M. Bazhan, a prominent Ukrainian Soviet writer and poet, and the Ukrainian playwright Oleksandr Korniichuk. Bazhan and Lytvyn examined the text in terms of political appropriateness, and for editorial purposes. Their comments give us a clear idea of their political priorities and the level of intervention of the CPU in history writing.[9] First, Bazhan noted,

> It was impossible to simply ignore the legend of the Varangians. The fascists are making a lot of noise about this 'Nordic element' in our history. We have to give a scientific answer to their noise – we should not take the position of an ostrich.

He also criticized the authors who omitted the fact that the head of Vladimir Principality ransacked Kyïv in 1169. As he saw it, 'The ransacking of Kyïv by Bogoliubs'kyi should not be ignored.... What is this sensitivity over Bogoliubs'kyi?' He also suggested that the fraternity of the Eastern Slavs, the struggle of Galician princes against the Germans and their efforts to construct a centralized state, and the anti-Polish struggle had to receive more emphasis. A delicate balance of different topics had to be found. On the one hand, the fraternity of Russians and Ukrainians against Germans had to be emphasized: 'It would be easy to record Aleksandr Nevskii as a hero of Ukraine; however, this is not correct. The common defence of eastern Slavdom against German aggression should be demonstrated – if Russia has Aleksandr [Nevskii], we [Ukrainians] have Danylo [Halyts'kyi].'[10] On the other hand, this friendship should not become the sole aim of history: 'It is not possible [to interpret] all anti-Polish uprisings and struggles of labourers as a desire for the unification of Ukraine and Russia – this is too much simplification.' There were also new sensitivities over western Ukraine. The reviewers warned that it was inadvisable to show all members of the Greek Catholic Church as traitors and 'it is wrong and offensive to the population of western Ukraine'. To portray an important part of the western Ukrainian population as a fifth column would be a crucial mistake while the Soviet authorities sought the support of all Ukrainians. The review covered Khmel'nyts'kyi too:

> It was not enough to describe Khmel'nyts'kyi as a talented leader; his talents also had to be described. There should be more emphasis on Bohdan and on his generals.... The chapter on the annexation of Ukraine by Russia has to be expanded. The tsarist policy should be mentioned.... In general, ideas should be elaborated [on the following]: What were the reasons that stipulated such an important historical act? It is impossible to forget the Stalinist formula of the 'lesser evil'.

At the same time, the rich Ukrainian cultural heritage had to be emphasized: 'All chapters on the [Ukrainian] national arts, culture, and literature from the middle ages until the Soviet period must be expanded and substantiated.'[11]

The first volume of the four-volume history of Ukraine for higher institutions and universities was published in 1943. This volume covered the national history until 1654 (Petrovs'kyi 1943a).[12] As the authors stressed in the preface, they believed that 'studying the history of our nation would increase even more the Soviet patriotism of Ukrainians on the battlefields or working at the home front for the defence' (Petrovs'kyi 1943a, 3). This text, as in the previous histories, did not define Trypillian culture as Eastern Slavic. However, the authors increased their primordial claims on the contemporary Ukrainian fatherland. The text underlined that Slavs already existed in Ukraine during the time of the Scythians and Sarmathians: 'The indigenous population, who were the direct ancestors of the Slavs, continued to grow steadily during the hard times of the consecutive Sarmathian, Gothic, and Hunnic tribal federations' (Petrovs'kyi

1943a, 32). Departing from the previous histories, the text also connected these indigenous Slavs with the field burial urns of Bronze Age (*polia pokhovan*). This attachment of archaeological cultures to a specific (in this case Eastern Slavic) ethnos was a gradual return to the pre-Marrist approach of V. A. Gorodtsov (1860–1945), A. A. Spitsyn (1858–1931), and V. V. Khvoika (1850–1914) at the beginning of the twentieth century (Spitsyn 1898/9; Gorodtsov 1901, 1908; Dolukhanov 1996, 2–5; Shaw and Jameson 1999, 135, 166–167). The primordialization of Slavic existence in Ukraine continued in the next chapter on the Slavic tribes by mixing the primordial claims using the Marrist theory:

> The Ukrainian, Russian, and Belorussian nations are descended from the Slavic tribes in Eastern Europe, and, in particular, in contemporary Ukraine in the first millennium C.E. These [Slavic] tribes were mostly composed of descendants of the local sedentary population of the Scythian and Sarmatian periods, who previously lived in this territory.
> (Petrovs'kyi 1943a, 32)

Following this claim of Slavic primordialism in Ukraine, the history emphasized that the Antes, as 'early Slavic tribes', lived between the Dniestr and Don and that these early Slavs were freedom-loving and bellicose peoples. The narrative avoided mentioning that the earliest ancient writers actually described the original habitat of the Antes as being between the Dniester and Bug rivers and that they moved to contemporary Ukraine at a later stage. Finally, the connection between the Antes and Eastern Slavs was firmly established in the subsequent pages.[13] In the chapter on the Kyïvan Rus', the 1943 history integrated the discussion on the role of the Normans in the formation of the Kyïvan Rus'. The text outlined the discussion starting in the eighteenth century, conveying each point of the Normanist theory in detail and providing a response to each argument (Petrovs'kyi 1943a, 39–44). It was clear that Ukrainian historians in 1943 did not want to give any ground at all to the historical front; either to the Normanist theory or to the German claims of the Germanic origin of the Kyïvan Rus'. On the emergence of the Ukrainian nation, the history of 1943 was not clear. It noted that 'Ukraine' as a term was first recorded in a chronicle in 1187. The text identified the appanage principalities of the Middle Ages as part of Ukrainian territory. The development of the Ukrainian language and Ukrainian identity were described as processes that started in the thirteenth century and 'took a step forward in the fourteenth and fifteenth centuries' (Petrovs'kyi 1943a, 180–183). The next chapter described the Ukrainian nation stepping onto the stage of history in the sixteenth century through the uprising against the Poland of Lords. The Polish–Ukrainian conflict was not only based on class struggle between Polish owners of great estates and Ukrainian peasants or poor Cossacks. It was at the same time a Ukrainian struggle against national and religious oppression (Petrovs'kyi 1943a, 183–202). Although the text initially named these uprisings 'Cossack peasant uprisings', the narrative described them as part of a national-liberation struggle. According to the authors, 'The struggle of the Ukrainian nation against the overlordship [*panuvannia*] of the Polish nobility was a just and progressive one' (Petrovs'kyi 1943a, 210). The description of the Khmel'nyts'kyi uprising as 'The Liberation War of the Ukrainian Nation against the Yoke of the Poland of Lords' in the textbook (Petrovs'kyi 1943a, 260) conveys this merge of 'class' and 'national' struggle. The first volume of the history criticized previous historians for depicting these uprisings as a national struggle and avoiding mentioning the class interests of different groups in Ukrainian society. The authors did not want to echo the interpretation of nationalist historians, and aimed instead to emphasize class struggle as the motivating force behind historical events. Yet, their own interpretation in this first volume was far from being a Marxist narrative. The final section of the text summarized various interpretations of the Khmel'nytsk'yi Uprising and explained the Soviet 'lesser evil' formula, referring to the review of Stalin, Kirov, and Zhdanov in 1934 as the correct explanation of the era (Petrovs'kyi 1943a, 307).

## Emerging revisions

While Ukrainian historians were writing the first volume, the necessities of the war altered the ways in which Ukrainian history was constructed. The construction of the national past moved further from Marxist guidelines towards romantic national narratives. Consequently, some elements in the first volume became obsolete six months after its publication. The first trend had to do with the interpretation of the prehistoric period and primordialization of national histories. During the period of the war, we can observe the first signs of a departure from what had been the dominant reading of prehistoric times, which rejected the concept of archaeological cultures as an equivalent of ethnicity. Derzhavin's *Proiskhozhdenie Russkogo Naroda: Velikorusskogo, Ukrainskogo, Belorusskogo*, published in 1944, signalled this policy change (Grekov 1942; Derzhavin 1944). N. S. Derzhavin, in his work on the origins of the Russians, referred to Russian archaeologist V. V. Khvoika, who located Trypillian culture at the end of the nineteenth century and defined this Neolithic culture as proto-Slavic. Derzhavin, after giving lip service to the Marrist–Marxist view by using familiar terminology such as 'matriarchal society' and 'patriarchal-tribal relations', openly affirmed Khvoika's conclusions. The Trypillian culture that continued from the Neolithic to the Copper and Bronze Ages and expanded from the Dnieper River basin to the Carpathians presented a culture with features that recurred in archaeological excavations. Derzhavin concluded that the people of the Trypillian culture were ancestors of the three Eastern Slavic nations (Derzhavin 1944, 5–6). This primordialization of the Eastern Slavs, including Ukrainians, soon found its way into Ukrainian national history writing. Though this campaign of primordializing Eastern Slavs went into top gear after 1945, the first signs had emerged by the end of the war (Tret'iakov 1948; Artamonov 1950). Huslystyi, one of the Ukrainian authors of the 1943 volume, reiterated this primordiality at his lecture on the 'Heroic Past of Kyïv' on 29 March 1945 in Kyïv. He started with a reference to the archaeological excavations of the Paleolithic Age by Khvoika in

1893 in Kyïv. He then continued by tracing a linear progression from the Antes to the Polians to the Kyïvan Rus' (Huslystyi 1945, 3).

The Slavicization of the prehistory went hand in hand with the expansion of Ukrainian identity in history writing. In April 1944, F. Enevych, the director of the Institute of History of the Communist Party, wrote a report to the agitation-propaganda section of the CPU on the insufficiencies of the Institute of History in Kyïv and severely criticized Ukrainian historians. Enevych started his attack by targeting the interpretation of Ukrainian prehistory and the period of pre-Kyïvan Rus'. The German orientalizaton of the Slavs, an overly politicized historical discussion and a German political propaganda material (see Chapter 3) still kept this Soviet ideologist's mind busy. The author of the review warned that the pre-Kyïvan Rus' period could be used by the German historians. In the narrative of the Ukrainian historians,

> the political history of our ancestors before the Kyïvan Rus', i.e. the period until the ninth century, has not been shown. This gap [that was left by] our historians has been used by Germans who 'prove' that allegedly their ancient predecessors dominated Eastern Europe until the ninth century and established the basis for the emergence of the Kyïvan Rus'.

The reviewer criticized the authors for not studying the recent work of Grekov, *Bor'ba Rusi za Sozdanie Svoego Gosudarstva* in 1942. In his work, Grekov demonstrated, 'on the basis of factual materials', that the Eastern Slavs had already established their political unity and agricultural economy before the arrival of the Riurikovichs (Varangians), as early as the sixth century. Enevych accused the 'scholars of the Institute of History' of not using Grekov's findings. 'Even the first volume of the History of Ukraine, edited by Prof. M. N. Petrovskyi [Petrovs'kyi] and published one year after the work of Grekov, did not cover this issue' (Grekov 1942).[14]

The Party reviewer Enevych was also critical of the Ukrainian historians for being ambiguous as to when exactly the formation of the Ukrainian nation began and was completed. In various publications, including the History of Ukraine published in 1943, the Ukrainian historians made contradictory statements on this issue.[15] Again, for Enevych, this issue had contemporary political importance:

> After the unification of Western Ukraine with Soviet Ukraine and Western Belorussia with Soviet Belorussia, Władysław Sikorski, the former Prime Minister of the Polish government in exile in London announced that the Soviet Union continues the policy of Catherine II and partitioned Poland for the fourth time.

Naturally, neither Ukrainians nor Moscow officials would refer to the Molotov–Ribbentrop Agreement as the fourth partition of Poland. Enevych was eager to re-write history in order to justify the annexation of the Eastern Poland (Western Ukraine and Western Belorussia) and fight back against the Polish claims.

According to Enevych 'the thesis of the partition of Poland [was] ... an old, outworn, and wrong statement and [it should be] replaced by a new scientific statement. Instead of doing this, our historians blindly accept this old definition and create confusion]'. Accepting the 'partition of Poland' implied that the eastern territories were Polish before the partition. However, Enevych wrote, Galicia, Volhynia, Kholm (Chelm), and the right bank of the Dnieper had never belonged to Poland 'because these territories had never been ethnographically Polish'. If the Ukrainian historians continued to argue that Ukrainian identity did not exist in the fourteenth century (when the Polish Kingdom annexed Galicia) then one would conclude that these lands were taken from the local Galicians but not from the Ukrainians. This narrative defines Galicia as a legitimate province of Poland from 1387 until the partition of Poland in 1772 and jeopardizes the Ukrainian and Soviet claims for these territories as historical Ukrainian fatherlands. For Enevych, the solution was simple. The official history had to move the emergence of Ukrainian identity backwards to the fourteenth century and it had to emphasize that Galicia had been a Ukrainian land. Finally, there had to be clear emphasis on the struggle of Ukrainians against Polish expansion in the fourteenth century.[16] Thus, in order to claim Western Ukraine as a historical fatherland, Ukrainian national identity had to appear in the history earlier. Enevych's demands contradicted the arguments of Marxist interpreters. Earlier in 1941, Picheta and Krut' criticized the Ukrainian historians for artificially moving the formation of Ukrainian identity backwards in history. The Ukrainian lands of the fourteenth to sixteenth centuries were not and could not be seen as one united body because the Marxist understanding of the feudal system could not permit such a national union. They had to be named 'Galician Rus'' and 'South-Western Rus'' (referring to the right-bank) instead of Ukraine (Picheta and Krut' 1941, 103).

Enevych was not alone in his uneasiness at expanding Ukrainian identity backwards into the past, and probably he acted according to the directives of his party boss, Nikita Khrushchev; because there was another Bolshevik who aimed to expand Ukrainian national identity into the past. Joseph Stalin ordered in 1944 that Ukrainian district, town, and city names that seemed Polish, German, or anything other than Ukrainian had to be renamed in a Ukrainian form. This changing of toponyms and spatial construction of the national past aimed to retrospectively endorse the primordiality of Ukrainian or East Slavic habitation in these territories. In other words, this was a construction of a national history and national fatherland by changing toponyms.[17] As Ukraine was liberated, numerous names were changed into forms that seemed more Ukrainian or East Slavic, based on the toponyms found in medieval records. If a record of an old name could not be found, the authorities simply made it up. For example, the Polish 'Lipitsa Dol'na' in L'viv became 'Nizhnaia Lipitsa'; the Turkish 'Akkerman' became 'Belgorod-Dnestroevskii'. This renaming was even done for previously Bolshevized place names, if the place bore historical importance. For example, Pechersk, part of the historical city of Kyïv and also a district of contemporary Kyïv, was named Kirovskii after the famous Bolshevik Sergei Kirov. In 1944, the name of the district was changed from Kirovskii to Pecherskii or Pechersk.[18] While the Red Army moved westward and liberated the Soviet territories, the Soviet annexations of 1939 and 1940 became an international issue. Where would the new Polish–Soviet borders be drawn? Stalin insisted that the territories annexed by the Soviets in 1939 should remain in Soviet hands. This was particularly hard for Britain and France to accept as these countries entered the war for the sovereignty and integrity of Poland. The negotiations for territorial claims, as it happened often in the twentieth century, were developed around census figures and historical records. Stalin had to convince his western allies that the pre-war Eastern Poland was historically Ukrainian lands.

Another departure could be observed in the interpretation of the Pereiaslav Agreement. After 1937, the Pereiaslav Agreement of the seventeenth century and the following annexation was understood according to the 'lesser evil' formula. The formula argued that it was a lesser evil for Ukrainians to be annexed by Russia than by Turkey or Poland (Petrovs'kyi 1942a, 1942b, 1943a). During the war, however, this annexation agreement became a 'historical declaration of fraternity between the Russian and Ukrainian nations'.[19] The annexation of Ukraine by Russia (Russian: *prisoedinenie*, Ukrainian: *pryednannia*) was not only a 'lesser evil', but also a natural consequence of a fraternity. As part of this new interpretation, the Pereiaslav Agreement became *the* crucial point in Ukrainian history and Khmel'nyts'kyi became *the* most important figure in the history. Consequently, earlier works of Ukrainian history, including the 1943 volume, were criticized according to this new line. The aforementioned review of Enevych argued that the Ukrainian historians had made a 'serious mistake' in suggesting the lesser evil formula alone: 'Apart from this external reason, there were also domestic reasons, [such as] ethnographic, historical, cultural, and linguistic [factors], similar domestic habits [*pobutovoï*], and even the religious affinity of the Ukrainian nation with the Russian nation.' The correct interpretation was the following:

> Foreign invaders tore Ukraine away from Russia, but the union and friendship between the Ukrainian and Russian nations was preserved.... In the works written on Ukrainain history, it is insufficiently underlined that the accession of Ukraine to Russia [by the Pereiaslav] is not the beginning of the union of Ukrainian and Russian peoples. This is merely a political and juridical formulation of the existing union between two nations for the course of centuries [which was] artificially ruptured by foreign invaders.

In order to find a Ukrainian supporter for this view, Enevych referred to the work of Kostomarov, a nineteenth-century Ukrainian scholar and a federalist within the Russian Empire (Spogady pro Dvokh 1861).[20] Thus, the historical link between Russians and Ukrainians was no longer the solidarity of the toiling masses; it was instead an ethno-linguistic link. That is why the character of the Austrian rule in Galicia was different from the Russian rule in right-bank Ukraine, for the latter was not the rule of an alien force or an occupation.[21] This turn can be seen in Petrovs'kyi's works in the last months of 1943 and 1944 (Petrovs'kyi 1943b, 1944a). The lesser evil formula was gradually dropped and the Pereiaslav Agreement became an act that enabled the reuniting of two fraternal nations. At the same time, this interpretation moved the Ukrainian national history further from the Marxist guidelines towards romantic national narrative. The only acknowledged classes were the Polish landlords, and the only class struggle was between them and Ukrainian peasants. Yet, class divisions and their struggle within the Ukrainian and Russian nations were delicately removed. Each nation, as the Marxist critics would argue, was turned into a 'single stream' (*edinnyi potok*) without any internal divisions based on the relations of production.

While the meaning of the Pereiaslav transformed, the emphasis on Khmel'nyts'kyi, the leader of the Ukrainian side of the agreement, increased. From the beginning of the war, Khmel'nyts'kyi was celebrated as a national hero fighting for the independence and freedom of the Ukrainian nation against the foreign occupants. His class struggle for Cossacks and the peasant class diminished and disappeared (Huslystyi 1943). Although it was an odd number for an anniversary, on 8 August 1942, the Academy of Sciences of the Ukrainian SSR and the Union of the Soviet Writers of Ukraine organized meetings in Ufa to commemorate the 285th anniversary of Khmel'nyts'kyi's death (Santsevich and Komarenko 1986, 50; Petrovs'kyi 1944b). In the following year, propaganda around the image of Khmel'nyts'kyi was intensified. When the city of Pereiaslav was liberated from German occupation, the Soviet government renamed this hometown of Khmel'nyts'kyi and the place where the agreement of 1654 was signed as Pereiaslav-Khmel'nyts'kyi. It was Stalin who proposed this change. At the same time, when the liberation of the eastern regions of Ukraine began, Khrushchev proposed to Stalin the establishment of a military order of Bohdan Khmel'nyts'kyi. After gaining the approval of Stalin, Khrushchev and M. Bazhan, the eminent Ukrainian writer, worked on this project.[22] The image of the famous hetman was at the centre of the medal. Various sketches were examined by Khrushchev and then by Stalin.[23] The military order of Khmel'nyts'kyi was established on 10 October 1943. Another resolution of the Central Committee of the CPU on 29 October 1943 asked historians to organize talks on Khmel'nyts'kyi, publish brochures on this historical figure, and to print his portrait (Santsevich and Komarenko 1986, 50). Finally, when a competition for the national anthem of the Ukrainian SSR was organized in 1944, Khmel'nyts'kyi, as the primary figure in Soviet Ukrainian history, found his way into most of the proposed lyrics.[24] January 18 1944 was the 290th anniversary of the Pereiaslav Agreement. The renaming of the town of Pereiaslav and the establishment of a military order offered an ideal opportunity to increase the public awareness of this agreement. The Soviet regime officially celebrated the Pereiaslav Treaty for the first time in 1944, on Nikita Khrushchev's recommendations. In his letter to Stalin, Khrushchev requested approval for a grand celebration in Kharkiv, and pointed to the reason behind this anniversary celebration. According to Khrushchev, the celebration of this day would act as a propaganda response to the

German propaganda disseminated during their occupation of Ukraine, and to Ukrainian nationalist propaganda opposed to the union of Ukraine and Russia. Khrushchev added that the aim would be to underline the positive value of this agreement for the history of the Ukrainian and Russian nations. As Khrushchev noted at the end of his letter, this momentous day had never been celebrated in the Ukrainian SSR.[25] The image of Khmel'nyts'kyi as the defender of the fatherland and initiator of the Ukrainian annexation to Russia was so important that Soviet authorities censored the poems of another selectively constructed figure, Taras Shevchenko. When the collection of poems was published in 1950, eighteen verses that criticized Khmel'nyts'kyi and the Russian imperial order, including 'Iak by ty, Bohdane', 'Rozryta mohyla', 'Do Osnov'ianenka', and 'Chigirine' were removed from the tomes. Such a deification of an individual would only be expected to appear in a romantic national history and it was utterly distant from the Marxist understanding of history.

## Soviet national propaganda targeting Ukrainians

While historians continued to construct the national history, they also used for the wartime propaganda needs the narrative that they had constructed since 1937. Following the hasty retreat of the Red Army in 1941, Soviet propaganda in the Ukrainian territories, as in other German occupied lands, was poorly organized. Until the Battle of Moscow, the front line constantly moved eastwards as the German troops advanced. This created a chaotic situation. Soviet Radio transmission units were destroyed or broken, and messages from Moscow could not reach the occupied lands. The population in the occupied regions was exposed to an abundant amount of German propaganda material distributed by German planes. Despite these obstacles, the agitation-propaganda section of the CPU worked on propaganda campaigns. The propagandists and ideologists observed the German propaganda activities, studied their materials, and prepared responses. Eventually, along with the victories on the battlefields, Soviet Ukrainian political propaganda also gained the upper hand.[26]

During the period from 1941 to 1945, Soviet Ukrainian propaganda targeted three groups. The first was the Ukrainian population, which remained under German occupation until the complete removal of German forces from Ukraine in the summer of 1944. The Bolsheviks aimed to dissuade this population from serving the Germans in any capacity. In October 1942, Moscow decided to develop underground resistance to the German occupation and the formation of clandestine party organizations in the occupied Ukrainian territories was ordered (Kuzmin 1954, 34). Khrushchev, the first secretary of the CPU, received periodical reports from the NKVD Ukrainian SSR on the situation of the occupied territories. These reports included notes on the mood of the population.[27] Propaganda activities were organized according to these reports. The second group consisted of Ukrainians who were under Soviet rule, either the evacuees in Russia and Central Asia who participated in production at the home front or the Ukrainian Red Army soldiers who fought at the front lines. The Ukrainians came second after the Russian contingency in the Red Army. By the end of the war, the losses of the Ukrainian combatants in the Red Army uniforms reached to 1,377,400 (Krivosheev 2009, 52). The Ukrainian civil loss was much higher than this figure. The third target audience for propaganda was the population living in the newly annexed territories. Though they had experienced a Soviet period in between 1939 and 1940–1, it was short-lived. When the Red Army removed German occupation forces from these areas, the CPU started a lecture-propaganda series in L'viv, Ternopil', Rivne, northern Bukovina, and the Uzhhorod (Transcarpathia) regions. The Soviet propaganda had multiple aims in these territories: the ideological indoctrination of the locals; the constructing a historical unity of all these territories as part of the Ukrainian fatherland in the minds of the locals; and convincing them to distance themselves from the Ukrainian nationalist guerrilla organizations.[28]

The Soviet propaganda used historical figures and themes in the wartime propaganda targeting these three groups. The leading Ukrainian Bolshevik and ideologist Dmitro Manuïl's'kyi produced numerous propaganda brochures with a circulation of 100,000. As a prominent ideologue, he was also actively involved in different stages of constructing the national history of Ukraine. His propaganda texts were printed in high volumes and addressed both the contemporary conflict with the Nazis and historical episodes (Manuil'skii 1942, 1943, 1944).[29] When the Ukrainian authorities addressed Ukrainians in the occupied territories in a radio broadcast in September 1941, they called on the population to resist the Germans and emphasized that 'Each Ukrainian who is a descendant of brave and freedom-loving Zaporozhian Cossacks cries with pride: "It is better to die than to fall into this shameful slavery."'[30] The same use of history could be seen in a declaration issued by the CPU and the Soviet Ukrainian government. The Soviet leaders announced:

> The cursed enemy occupied part of our dear Ukraine by a perfidious attack. This cannot scare our mighty belligerent nation. The German mongrel-knights were hacked by the swords of the soldiers of Danylo Halyts'kyi, they were chopped by the sabres of the Cossacks of Bohdan Khmel'nyts'kyi.... We have always defeated the German bandits.[31]

Moreover, this declaration addressed Ukrainians for the first time as 'the Great Ukrainian nation'.[32] In fact, the 'greatness', which was always secured for Russians, was temporarily used in 1939, when the Red Army crossed the Polish border. A leaflet addressing the Ukrainians in the Polish Ukraine and signed by the commander of the Red Army, Semen Timoshenko, started with 'To the Workers and Peasants of Western Ukraine', and ended with the phrase 'Long live the great and free Ukrainian nation!' (Picheta 1940, 128–129). Extolling the greatness of Ukrainians returned during the Second World War, and appeared in some statements until 1944. This description can also be seen in the work of Ukrainian historians. For instance, Petrovs'kyi in his account of the Pereiaslav Agreement defined the event as the union of two *great*, consanguineous nations (*ob'ednannia dvokh velykykh iedynokrovnykh narodiv*) (Petrovs'kyi 1941, 3). K. Huslystyi in his essay on Khmel'nyts'kyi named the latter 'the great leader' of 'the great freedom-loving Ukrainian nation' (Huslystyi 1943). This emphasis can be seen in some official degrees after 1941. The resolution of the Central Committee of the CPU and the Soviet Ukrainian government on the renaming of Pereiaslav to Pereiaslav-Khmel'nyts'kyi reiterated in 1943 the 'greatness' of the Ukrainian nation. This was the place where 'the indissoluble union of the two fraternal and consanguineous peoples, the great Ukrainian nation and the great Russian nation'[33] was signed.

By April 1942, thirteen popular-historical texts published for propaganda purposes covered different periods of Ukrainian national history.[34] The historical narratives in these propaganda materials were anti-German, anti-Polish, and anti-Hungarian.[35] Historical publications aimed to explain 'the struggle of the Slavic nations against the German occupiers; and a thorough explanation of the struggle of the nations of the USSR and in particular of the Russians, Ukrainians, and Belorussians, against the Germans and other foreign occupants'. Two of the initial titles in August 1941 were 'National militia in 1612' and 'Partisan movement in the War of the Fatherland of 1812'.[36] According to the head of the Ukrainian Academy of Sciences, the German propaganda and publications in the occupied territories argued about the common interests of the Ukrainian and German nations and the antagonism between Ukrainians and Russians. The publications on the history and culture of Ukraine aimed to reply the German and Ukrainian nationalists' arguments.[37]

During the war, various Ukrainian historical figures were used for Soviet propaganda in Ukraine. While the champion of these figures was Bohdan Khmel'nyts'kyi, he was not alone in the Ukrainian pantheon. Chronologically, the first were the leaders of the Kyïvan Rus'. As the princes of the Kyïvan state were considered common ancestors of today's Russians, Ukrainians, and Belorussians, they could be used in both Russian and Ukrainian histories. Next came Danylo Halyts'kyi, the prince of Galicia and Volhynia in the twelfth century. Other figures included the Ukrainian Cossack hetmans and leaders, Petro Konashevych-Sahaidachnyi, Maksym Kryvonis, and Ivan Bohun. There were also booklets on the heroic deeds of Mykola Shchors and Vasyl' Bozhenko, the Red Cavalry leaders of the Russian Civil War in Ukraine. The biographies of Danylo Halyts'kyi, Petro Konashevych-Sahaidachnyi, Ivan Bohun, Bohdan Khmel'nyts'kyi, Semen Palii, Ustym Karmaliuk, Taras Shevchenko, and Ivan Franko were published in a series of popular-historical texts under the title 'Our Great Forefathers' (*Nashi Velyki Predky*) (Huslystyi 1942a, 1942b; Petrovs'kyi 1942a, 1942b; Diadychenko 1942; Kyryliuk 1942; Sherstiuk 1943).[38] The first pages of this series quoted from the Soviet government's declaration upon the first meeting of Ukrainian representatives following the German occupation, which stated, 'The freedom-loving Ukrainians, the descendants of the glorious fighters of the fatherland, Danylo Halyts'kyi and Sahaidachnyi, Bohdan Khmel'nyts'kyi and Bohun, Taras Shevchenko and Ivan Franko, Bozhenko and Mykola Shchors, will never become slaves of the Germans.' This list, akin to

Stalin's famous list of Russian historical figures, enumerated the figures of the Soviet Ukrainian national narrative.[39]

As fighting against the German army continued, Germanic–Slavic antagonism as a historical theme became part of Soviet historiography for both Ukraine and Russia. These narratives naturally denied any Norman (i.e. Germanic–Nordic) element in the foundation of the Kyïvan Rus'. They emphatically depicted the Kyïvan Rus' as a common state of all Eastern Slavs. These works traced the history of Germanic–Slavic antagonism and also accounted for the anti-Slavic and expansionist history that had been constructed in the nineteenth century (Iastrebov 1941, 10; Derzhavin 1942; Grekov 1942; Derzhavin 1943; Mavrodin 1944, 1945a; Needly 1944. For naming the Antes and Venedi as Russians, see Mavrodin 1945b). The German policy of '*Drang nach Osten*' was described as an anti-Slavic expansionist policy, which had been consistently pursued for centuries. The narrative retrojected this German expansionism, however, to a time before the Teutonic Knights. According to one of the essays in the collection, Germans had been enemies of all Slavs, including the forefathers of Ukrainians, since the eleventh century, when 'Germans' under the leadership of the Polish king occupied the Kyïvan Rus'. While the prince of Galicia–Volhynia was fighting against the Germans in order to protect the Eastern Slavic lands, Aleksandr Nevskii was fighting in the north for the same cause. Subsequently, the text described how this united eastern Slavdom transformed into a pan-Slavic opposition to the Germans with the inclusion of the Poles at the Battle of Grunwald in 1410. Other essays in this collection addressed subsequent confrontations on the western front of the Russian Empire, interpreting each as an aggression against both Russia and Ukraine (Borot'ba ukraïns'koho narodu proty 1942. The articles in this book were: Huslystyi 1942c; Los' 1942; Suprunenko 1942a, 1942b; Shul'ga 1942). The Ukrainian–German conflict was even founded in a description of Napoleon's march into the Russian Empire (Ukraïns'ki kozachi polky 1943).

## The free, united, and Soviet Ukraine

The armed struggle and ideological war continued between Ukrainian nationalists and the Soviet regime in the Ukrainian territories, which were re-taken from the Germans.[40] As Soviet forces moved westward into Ukraine, Khrushchev and other Ukrainian Communist Party leaders were kept well informed by the NKVD on the tactics and ideology of the nationalists.[41] In order to wage the ideological war, the Central Committee of the CPSU issued two resolutions on 27 September 1944 entitled 'On the Insufficiencies of Political Work among the Population of the Western Regions of the Ukrainian SSR' and 'On the Measures to assist Ukrainian SSR improving Mass-scale Political and Cultural Educational Work' (Kommunisticheskaia 1985, 524–531). In the following days, the CPU also issued a similar resolution emphasizing the shortcomings of political propaganda work in western Ukraine to combat Ukrainian nationalists. The resolution ordered that political propaganda meetings be organized in every single village, town, organization, and institution each month.[42] Newspapers and various other publications, as well as radio broadcasts, were ordered to concentrate on these propaganda efforts. Khrushchev, Manuïl's'kyi, Lytvyn, and other secretaries of the CPU organized the initial meetings in the regions and supervised the propaganda work.[43] When Khrushchev addressed Party workers in L'viv on the struggle against Ukrainian and Polish nationalists, he stressed:

> The most important and powerful weapon is ideological struggle; ideological-educational work with the masses ... we should not isolate ourselves. We must find a way to the masses. Is it possible to let the population be sympathetic to the OUN fighters [*ountsami*]? We have to know the slogans and programme of the OUN, so that we can deal with them fully armed.... That is why, comrades, we have to conduct educational work, offensive work.[44]

One of the easiest ways of 'finding a way to the masses' was constructing a Ukrainian national narrative which emphasized the historical brotherhood of Russia and Ukraine. Accordingly, the list of agitation-propaganda and political education materials, which was produced by the party, included the history of Ukraine and the joint struggle of the Russian and Ukrainian nations against foreign occupiers. These kinds of propaganda materials were already in circulation during the war such as 'L'viv – The Old Ukrainian City', 'The Centuries Old Struggle of the Slavs against German Agression', and 'Poltava'. Meanwhile, the obkoms of western Ukraine organized propaganda lectures on various subjects, including the history of Ukraine, and regional newspapers published articles on the subject as well.[45] Finally this argument of brotherhood was accompanied by a delicate campaign on religious unification under the Orthodox faith (Miner 2003, 163–202).

However, this Russian–Ukrainian brotherhood was not enough because this could also imply that the Soviet Union was a Russian state disguised under a red gown. There was also a Ukrainian national argument in finding a way to the masses. For the first time in history, the Soviet Army unified all the lands where Ukrainian speakers were in a majority. The Ukrainian Soviet history writing had to establish a historical background for this unification. Although various nationalist groups since the nineteenth century right up to Hrushevs'kyi had dreamed about or struggled for this ultimate goal, it was Khrushchev's and Manuïl's'kyi's right to boast of their achievement. At the first convention of the Supreme Soviet of the Ukrainian SSR after the end of the German occupation in March 1944, Khrushchev proudly pronounced on the unification of Ukraine after centuries-old anticipation. He asserted that the Soviet rule would not let the Polish émigré government in London take back historical Ukrainian lands, and the Polish–Ukrainian border would be established according to 'ethnographical lines' (Khrushchev 1944) by arguing that 'This was the dream of Bohdan Khmel'nyts'kyi, the courageous hetman of Ukraine, this is what Taras Shevchenko, the great democrat-revolutionary, fought for' (Manuïl's'kyi 1946,

7). Soviet propaganda materials also underlined this achievement. For example, in the appeal of the Soviet Ukrainian authorities to western Ukrainians, explaining the benefits of Soviet rule and calling on the OUN-UPA members to give up their armed struggle, one of the slogans at the end of the text was 'Long live the great Ukrainian nation, united in a single Ukrainian Soviet state'.[46]

In return, the political unification in 1944 asked the Soviet historiography to increase the emphasis on the historical or national unity of these regions that had actually been part of different imperial or national states for centuries. In fact, this demand can be traced back to 1939, when the Polish (Western) Ukraine was annexed by the Soviet Union. The description of Moscow in July 1940 clearly stated that in the modern history of Western Ukraine, 'It is very important to show social-cultural links between Western Ukrainian territories and Ukraine.'[47] The Soviet Ukrainian historiography provided the narrative necessary to present different parts of contemporary Ukraine (Transcarpathia, Galicia, Volhynia, Northern Bukovina, and the right and left banks of the Dnieper) as having a homogeneous culture and past dating back to the Kyïvan Rus'. Although these numerous territories had experienced various political rules and cultural influences for centuries, the national history aimed to provide a picture that presented them as linked to each other and unified by a Ukrainian national consciousness as well as cultural and ethnic homogeneity. In 1945 Petrovs'kyi published such historical accounts (Petrovs'kyi 1944a, 1945a, 1945b). He also put pressure on the historians in L'viv to write similar accounts which showed Western Ukraine, Bukovina, and the Carpathian Ukraine as intrinsic territories of Ukraine. These efforts of mobilizing Ukrainian scholars were closely supervised by Lytvyn and Khrushchev.[48] According to this interpretation of national history, the Soviet Union could be understood as the latest historical stage in Ukrainian history, in which national and class oppression was eliminated, and all Ukrainian lands were united. The Soviet Union did not represent an interruption in the national history, but rather the continuity of Ukrainian identity. From this point of view, it is no surprise that Ukrainian historians were criticized in 1944 for weakness in terms of 'showing the continuity of Ukrainian patriotic traditions and cultural heritage represented by Bolshevism'.[49]

The ideology of the regime that united the Ukrainian nation and fatherland was internationalist–Marxist. Both the Ukrainian and Russian Bolsheviks were after a socialist and united Ukraine. This fact brings us to the amalgamation of nation and class struggle in the past that was first developed before the war. This amalgamation in the constructed national past was continued during the war. Next to the Ukrainian national identity and its fraternity with the Russian nation, the internationalist class struggle was included to this narrative. Volhynia and Galicia, where class and national divisions overlapped, offered a fertile ground for this dual approach. For centuries, nearly all the landed gentry were Polish, while the peasants were Ukrainian. Consequently, the Soviet narrative emphasized the social and national oppression (*sotsialno i natsional'nyi gnet*) suffered by the Ukrainian nation for centuries (Petrovs'kyi 1944a). D. Manuïl's'kyi's comment at a meeting of Western Ukrainian teachers on 6 January 1945 provides a typical example of this approach. While explaining the advantages of the Soviet socialist system in Ukraine, he first provided historical examples of national oppression:

> For centuries the Ukrainian people defended themselves against those who encroached on their land. Brazen Teuton[ic Knight]s, greedy Hungarians, a conceited Polish gentry, arrogant Swedes, Tatar hordes, and Turkish Janissaries. Traitors and criminals like Hetman Mazepa helped them in their dark deeds.
> 
> (Manuïl's'kyi 1946, 7)

Then he moved to social oppression:

> It is well known that the major landowners were Russian and Polish. In right-bank Ukraine as well as in Galicia, there were Polish magnates possessing huge lands, such as Potots'ki, Sangushky, Radzyvilly, Branyts'ki, Sheptyts'ki, and others. Ukrainian peasants worked for these magnates for many years, and by taking lands from them, one of the essential foundations of national oppression was broken.... From whom were these factories and plants taken [in Ukraine during Soviet rule]? [They were taken] from capitalists. Not only from the Ukrainian capitalists; they were also taken from Russian capitalists, and from the capitalists of other countries – Germans, French, Belgians, and others.
> 
> (Manuïl's'kyi 1946, 3)

## Conclusions

The Soviet version of the Ukrainian national narrative was constructed after 1937. This was an anti-Polish narrative with the expectation of a war against a German–Polish assault against the USSR. The Galciian Prince Danylo Halyts'kyi, or the Cossack leader Bohdan Khmel'nyts'kyi, among other medieval figures, were incorporated into the national narrative and elevated to the national pantheon. The narrative was moved from a Marxist to a romantic national history with its idealized leaders and movements. The wartime propaganda used this national past, which had already been written since 1937, against the German occupants and the Ukrainian nationalists. At the same time, the Ukrainian Soviet historians continued to construct their national past and further romanticized and nationalized the past. The Second World War was not a temporary thaw in the construction of the past. On the contrary there was a steady and continuous effort pursued by both the local historians and the Ukrainian Bolsheviks to construct further a national history. Yet, the war conditions demanded that the historians accelerate this romantization and nationalization. The historians were criticized for not nationalizing the past thoroughly enough. If the wartime propaganda was a reason, then the second annexation of the western territories, the northern Bukovina, and Transcarpathian Rus' was another reason for the further nationalization. Only a national history could unite all these different territories under the rubric of fatherland. The Second World War had an unexpected impact on Ukraine. It accelerated the Ukrainization of the urban demography which had started in the 1930s. Now cities and towns were more Ukrainian than Polish and Jewish. The homogenization of demography was especially visible in multi-ethnic cities like L'viv and Odesa (Herlihy 1977). The reconstruction of war-torn towns after the war also changed the Ukrainian urban landscape and gave them a Ukrainian Soviet character (Tscherkes and Sawicki 2000; Ther and Czaplicka 2000). With its historical landscape in the minds and the tangible urban contemporary landscape, Ukraine became 'Ukraine' as never before. Yet, there is also another aspect of this nationalization. While the Marxist arguments in history writing evaporated further, the interpretation of the Pereiaslav Agreement turned from an agreement of the Cossack leading classes with the rulers of Muscovy into an agreement between the two fraternal nations, as if two nations had convened at the church of Pereiaslav and signed a partnership contract in 1654. Both the depiction of the Poles as eternal enemies of the national and the definition of the Russians as the immortal brothers of the nation in the constructed narrative were obvious national romantizations of the past, and they were political decisions based on international developments.

## Notes

1. RGANI, 52–1-133–15, October 8, 1943, Letter of Khrushchev to Dimitrov on the situation in the Western Ukraine.
2. The Germans were also involved in the war of propaganda. In wartime, memories were still fresh of forced collectivization, the Great Terror, and the annihilation of a generation of national political and cultural figures in Ukraine. German efforts to reveal mass graves of the NKVD victims aimed to increase this anti-Soviet and anti-Russian inclination among the Ukrainian population under occupation. They also promised Ukrainian peasants the free distribution of kolkhoz lands.
3. The planned Ukrainian history textbook for universities and higher institutions of education was a four-volume work. The Ukrainian textbook for schools was for the third and fourth grades. *TsDAHOU*, 1–23–91–50, April 4, 1942. The text of the short course for the third and fourth grade was ready for publication. See *TsDAHOU*, 1–23–436–34, May 5, 1943.
4. *TsDAHOU*, 1–70–46–104, February 9, 1943;
5. *TsDAHOU*, 1–70–48–8, April 23, 1942.
6. *TsDAHOU*, 1–70–46–104, February 9, 1943.
7. *TsDAHOU*, 1–70–46–99, January 14, 1943.
8. Kostiantyn Zakharovych Lytvyn (1907–1994) held a PhD in history. He was the head of the agitation-propaganda section of the CPU from September 1941 until 1951. See Litopys 2001, 605.
9. There are two files that contain the reviews: the first is *TsDAHOU*, 1–70–153 (first half of 1943), where the review of Bazhan can be found. The other one is *TsDAHOU*, 1–70–46, April 14, 1943, where the joint review of Lytvyn and Bazhan can be found.
10. *TsDAHOU*, 1–70–153–1 (first half of 1943).
11. *TsDAHOU*, 1–70–153–1/2 (first half of 1943); 1–70–46–146/149, April 14, 1943.
12. The first history textbook published during the war was *Narys istoriï Ukraïny* in 1942

(Huslystyi *et al.* 1942). The whole group consisted of eight historians. However, this work was considered to be a failed attempt.
13 The text also mentioned the Sclavini as another early Slavic tribe (Petrovs'kyi 1943a, 32–37).
14 *TsDAHOU*, 1–23–864–10/12, April 17, 1944.
15 *TsDAHOU*, 1–23–864–13/14, April 17, 1944.
16 *TsDAHOU*, 1–23–864–14/15, April 17, 1944.
17 Similarly, toponyms were Russified or Slavisized in the areas from which the Volga Germans and the Crimean Tatars were deported (Murray 2000). For a similar exercise in Turkey on changing toponyms see Öktem 2008.
18 *TsDAHOU*, 1–23–709–1/17, August 3, 1944.
19 For the summary of this new interpretation, see *TsDAHOU*, 1–70–151–18/39 (1943).
20 *TsDAHOU*, 1–23–864–18, April 17, 1944.
21 *TsDAHOU*, 1–23–864–15/16, April 17, 1944
22 *TsDAHOU*, 1–23–355–1, October 8, 1943; *TsDAHOU*, 1–23–328–1/4. The resolution of the Central Committee CPU and the Ukrainian Soviet Government was approved by the Presidium of the Supreme Soviet of the USSR on October 12, 1943.
23 One of the sketches contained the words 'for free Ukraine' (Ukrainian: *za vil'nu Ukraïnu*), but apparently this was considered a nationalist content lacking a Soviet dimension, and the final version did not bear any such phrase. *TsDAHOU*, 1–23–355–28/29, September 11, 1943.
24 For different proposed anthems, see *TsDAHOU*, 1–70–261–3 (April 1944); *TsDAHOU*, 1–70–261–7 (April 1944); *TsDAHOU*, 1–70–261–5 (April 1944); *TsDAHOU*, 1–70–262–16/17 (April 1944); *TsDAHOU*, 1–70–262–21 (April 1944).
25 *TsDAHOU*, 1–70–91–44 (autumn 1943).
26 The following documents may provide a picture of the Soviet Ukrainian propaganda work in the first stages of the war: *TsDAHOU*, 1–23–17–2, September 15, 1941; *TsDAHOU*, 1–23–17–11, October 17, 1941; *TsDAHOU*, 1–70–11–16/17, June 26, 1942.
27 For various examples of these NKVD Ukrainian SSR reports on the situation of the occupied territories in 1942, see the files *TsDAHOU*, 1–22–75–19/36, January 9, 1943; *TsDAHOU*, 1–23–124, for the reports in 1943, see *TsDAHOU*, 1–23–535.
28 For the agitation-propaganda works in this period of annexation between 1944 and 1945, see the following reports sent from regions to Khrushchev: *TsDAHOU*, 1–23–895–6/6ob, November 1944 (Chernihiv); 1–23–895–7/7ob, November 18, 1944 (Ochagovskii region); 1–23–895–20/25, November 15, 1944 (Ternopil'); 1–23–895–26–34, April 10, 1944 (Rovensk); 1–23–895–48–63, July 16, 1944 (Chernivets'ka region) (Ivlev and Iudenkov 1981).
29 D. Z. Manuil's'kyi was an important Ukrainian communist leader and an ideologue. He became a member of the Russian Social Denocrat Workers' Party (Bolsheviks) in 1907 and graduated from the Law Faculty of Sorbonne University in Paris in 1911. After the revolution in 1917, he returned to Russia. In 1921, he was the first secretary of the CPU, and became a member of the Central Committe CPSU in 1922. He worked at the Comintern from 1922 to 1942. Between 1942 and 1944, he worked at the General Political Administration of the Red Army. *TsDAHOU*, 1–70–95–29/30, (December 1944). For his biography by Soviet authors see Zav'ialov 1963; Suiarko 1979.
30 *TsDAHOU*, 1–23–17–28, September 15, 1941.
31 *TsDAHOU*, 1–23–17–11, October 17, 1941.
32 *TsDAHOU*, 1–23–17–11, October 17, 1941.
33 See the declaration mentioned above of the CPU and the Soviet Ukrainian government, *TsDAHOU*, 1–23–17–11, October 17, 1941; *TsDAHOU*, 1–23–328–2. The resolution of the Central Committee of the CPU and the Soviet Ukrainian government was approved by the Presidium of the Supreme Soviet of the USSR on October 12, 1943.

34 The works on Ukrainian history, which were published in 1942 and mentioned in the report of the Academy of Sciences of Ukrainian SSR included: K. Huslystyi, 'Borot'ba slov'ian proty nimets'kikh zaharbnikiv i rozhrom Tevtonichnogo ordena pid Hriunval'dom', 'Razhrom Ugors'kykh zaharonikiv na Ukrainy v XIII st.'; V. Diadichenko, 'Borot'ba ukrains'koho narodu proty shevds'kikh okupantiv 1708–9'; N. Tkachenko, 'T. Shevchenko proty voiovnichnoho Germizmu'; *TsDAHOU*, 1–23–91–46, April 4, 1942.

35 See the following texts for the activities and plans of the Institute of History at the Academy of Sciences of the Ukrainian SSR on producing a heroic past for the war efforts, and the correspondence between Petrovs'kyi, the head of this Insitute, and Lytvyn, the secretary for the agitation and propaganda of the CPU: *TsDAHOU*, 1–70–150–126/130 (1941); *TsDAHOU*, 1–70–46–1/12 (1942); *TsDAHOU*, 1–70–46–12/24 (1942); *TsDAHOU*, 1–70–48–5/12, April 23, 1942; *TsDAHOU*, 1–70–46–71/97 (autumn 1942); *TsDAHOU*, 1–70–46–99, January 14, 1943; *TsDAHOU*, 1–70–46–193/6, (the first half of 1943); *TsDAHOU*, 1–70–46–101/104, February 9, 1943; *TsDAHOU*, 1–70–121–3ob,4,7 (end of 1942); *TsDAHOU*, 1–70–151–4/5, May 19, 1943 (the list of anti-German historic events that Ukrainian historians used in their presentations); *TsDAHOU*, 1–70–151–6/9, May 19, 1943 (the list of anti-Polish historic events that Ukrainian historians used in their presentations); *TsDAHOU*, 1–70–151–10, May 19, 1943 (the list of anti-Hungarian historic events that Ukrainian historians used in their presentations).

36 Naukovyi arkhiv Preziydiï NANU, (P-251) – 1–92–19/21, August 22, 1941.

37 *TsDAHOU*, 1–23–91–49, April 4, 1942.

38 *TsDAHOU*, 1–23–864–9/10, April 17, 1944; *TsDAHOU*, 1–70–48–7, April 23, 1942. The list of biographies wase discussed at the meeting of the Institute of History and Archaeology in Ufa; NAIIU, 1–1–44–21, June 16, 1942.

39 Ivan Gonta, who organized an anti-Polish uprising in the eighteenth century, was also a national hero.

40 RGANI, 52–1–85–128/137, September 19, 1944. For the reports of the raikom and obkom secretaries in western Ukraine and the reports of the head of the NKGB Ukrainian SSR to Khrushchev on the activities of the Ukrainian nationalists and the armed struggle between the latter and the Soviet internal security forces in the region in 1944 and 1945, see *TsDAHOU*, 1–23–889–1/8, January 19, 1944; *TsDAHOU*, 1–23–889–18, June 21, 1944; *TsDAHOU*, 1–23–889–19/22 (end of July 1944); *TsDAHOU*, 1–23–889–32/36, June 6, 1944. *TsDAHOU*, 1–23–890–1/4, February 24, 1944; *TsDAHOU*, 1–23–890–5/12, February 1944; *TsDAHOU*, 1–23–890–13/18, March 31, 1944; *TsDAHOU*, 1–23–890–19/31, March 24, 1944; *TsDAHOU*, 1–23–890–32/40, April 14, 1944; *TsDAHOU*, 1–23–890–41/46 (not before April 15) 1944; *TsDAHOU*, 1–23–890–52/58, May 31, 1945; *TsDAHOU*, 1–23–890–66/72, September 8, 1944. There are more reports from the region on the armed and ideological war against the Ukrainian nationalists in 1944–5. See *TsDAHOU*, 1–23–890; *TsDAHOU*, 1–23–937–1/4, January 17, 1944 (the report of Khrushchev to Stalin on the activities of Ukrainian nationalists, after the former's investigative trip to western Ukraine); *TsDAHOU*, 1–70–67–38, April 27, 1944 (on the necessity of agitation-propaganda activities in the Western regions on the Kolkhoz issue). Also see *TsDAHOU* 1–16–25–72, July 15, 1943; *TsDAHOU*, 1–6–757–13/14, February 14, 1944; *TsDAHOU* 1–6–757–15/24, February 14, 1944.

41 See for example reports from the NKVD Ukrainian SSR and NKGB Ukrainian SSR to Khrushchev on the organization, history, and ideology of Ukrainian nationalists: *TsDAHOU*, 1–23–523–3/47, (after March) 1943; *TsDAHOU*, 1–23–523–47/58, April 30, 1943; *TsDAHOU*, 1–23–523–59/68, March 31, 1943; *TsDAHOU*, 1–23–523–69/72, May 24, 1943; *TsDAHOU*, 1–23–523–73/79, May 28, 1943; *TsDAHOU*, 1–23–523–84/92, June 14, 1943.

42 For another resolution on the political propaganda works in the Western Ukraine, see *TsDAHOU*, 1–6–819–20/28, July 9, 1945; a series of agitation and propaganda meet-

ings were organized after these warnings in 1944 and 1945. *TsDAHOU*, 1–23–895–6/6ob, November 1944 (Chernihiv); *TsDAHOU*, 1–23–895–7/7ob, November 18, 1944 (Ochagovskii region); *TsDAHOU*, 1–23–895–20/25, November 15, 1944 (Ternopil'); *TsDAHOU*, 1–23–895–26–34, April 10, 1944 (Rovensk); *TsDAHOU*, 1–23–895–48–63, July 16, 1944 (Chernivetsk); *TsDAHOU*, 1–23–1633–11/12, March 5, 1945 (L'viv); *TsDAHOU*, 1–23–1633–12/17a, February 26, 1945.
43 *TsDAHOU*, 1–6–778–121/174, October 7, 1944.
44 RGANI, 52–1–85–144, October 11, 1944.
45 *TsDAHOU*, 1–6–778–121/174, October 7, 1944.
46 *TsDAHOU*, 1–23–780–23 (1944). There were also lectures on Ukrainian literature, in particular on T. Shevchenko, I. Franko, L. Ukrainka, and M. Kotsiubyns'kyi.
47 Letter from Boris Grekov, the head of the Institute of History, Academy of Sciences of the USSR to M. Marchenko the Rector of the L'viv State University, *Arkhiv IU im. Krip'iakevycha NAN Ukraïny*, op. VI-f, No. G-4, ark. 84, July 13, 1940.
48 *TsDAHOU*, 1–70–394–1/5, January 18, 1945.
49 *TsDAHOU*, 1–23–864–24/26, April 17, 1944.

# Epilogue

During the war, as part of the emphasis on national aspects and unifying historical figures, the historians of Russia with nationalist tendencies gained a stronger voice. Yet, not everyone agreed with this Russocentric camp, including the co-editor of the Kazakh history, Anna Pankratova. She led some other Russian historians, who held an internationalist view, in a struggle against this rising Russocentric or Russian nationalist wave. Pankratova was a self-proclaimed watchdog for the purity of ideology and she kept the Marxist interpretations above temporary political and pragmatic turns. Pankratova wrote more than once to Stalin, Zhdanov, Malenkov, and Shcherbakov about these nationalist tendencies among Russian historians and asked for a meeting of historians with the Party leaders to discuss this issue.[1] As a result of her elaborate and alarming letters, a series of meetings of historians and party ideologists were organized by the Central Committee of the CPSU, with Malenkov chairing the first meeting on 29 May 1944. This was a preliminary meeting and Malenkov listed the issues that would be discussed in the following days.[2] The historians in Kyïv, Baku, and Almaty were aware of these discussions in Moscow; however, it was not yet clear if a change in the course of history writing was indeed occurring. Everyone waited for a resolution from the Central Committee. For two months, Zhdanov and Stalin (and at some point Shcherbakov and Mikoyan) worked on the resolution. After producing more than five drafts of the resolution, Stalin decided to halt the process and no resolution was issued.

While Zhdanov, Stalin, and Shcherbakov could not write up a resolution, the speeches and published articles of the party ideologists and propaganda chiefs in the following months put stronger emphasis on the Marxist interpretations. Starting with 1944, the party ideologists called for a Marxist interpretation of Russian history and criticized Tarle and other Russian historians. At the same time, the same party representatives attacked the narratives of the non-Russian nationalities by using the same Marxist arguments. The discussions started over the histories written in the republics of Mordovia, Mari, Tatarstan, and Kazakhstan and they were subjected to the close scrutiny of Moscow.

The political course that had been followed since 1937 increased the national consciousness among all titular nations. This course reached its maximum during the war. Although there was a strong continuity, the Communist Party officials in the republics refused to acknowledge it and began to position this policy of encouragement as if it was a temporary phenomenon for the wartime mobilization. This explanation was evident at a meeting of the directors and lecturers of departments of social sciences and humanities in the Azerbaijani SSR, the Armenian SSR, and the Georgian SSR in 1947. This meeting was prompted by criticisms on the Institute of History in Tbilisi and the textbook on the history of Georgia published in Tbilisi. When the participants started to question if the current line of historiography was correct or not, a high-ranking official from the CPA responded:

> [At] the time of the Patriotic War, we sometimes had to resort to means and methods of stimulation ... this was a stimulation against the enemy, [a stimulation] of hatred against the enemy. However, in that period we emphasized the historical veracity with regard to the martial traditions of our people, with regard to the patriotism of the people. That truth [of that time] has not ceased to be true now. The strength of our propaganda and agitation is that it has always been based on the Bolshevik truth. [At that time] it was right. At that time, that side bulged.[3]

In Ukraine, Lytvyn, the secretary in charge of the agitation-propaganda section of the CPU, speaking at the Ukrainian Writers Conference in August 1946, first enumerated the mistakes in the 1943 history. He then continued:

> Why did these comrades make these gross mistakes? Because they concluded from a wrong assumption that allegedly the party had changed its policy during the war. In the name of educating our nation in patriotism, many things were written about Aleksandr Nevskii, Suvorov, Kutuzov, and Bohdan Khmel'nyts'kyi. These followed the publication of several patriotic calls to the Ukrainian nation, in which great emphasis was placed on the historical heroic traditions of our nation. 'Kobzar' [by Shevchenko] was published in small numbers and distributed behind the enemy lines, as well as many leaflets in which the works of Shevchenko were used for purely propaganda purposes – some [comrades] made wrong conclusions out of these.[4]

There was also some 'bulge in the side' in the Kazakh narrative. The batyrs of various tribes or tribal unions were incorporated into the Kazakh national narrative long before the war. The wartime propaganda used and further popularized the history that had already been constructed before 1941. In addition, the wartime propaganda underlined two khans, Edyge and Kenesary Kasymov, in the list of national heroes. During the war, a propaganda letter, 'From the Kazakh Nation to the Kazakh Soldiers at the Front', was prepared by the agitation-propaganda sections of the CPK and Kazakh historians. The fact that Edyge had been included in this letter and other historical-propaganda materials became a hot topic at the conference of Kazakh historians in May 1946. When the moderate Kazakh historians were accused of making a 'mistake', Adil'gireev, one of the Kazakh historians, turned to the auditorium, where all the higher officials of the CPK were sitting, and said,

> You were sitting at the Central Committee [of the CPK]; you have to know [why Edyge was included].[5]

These were the early signs of a new series of discussions. Some of the party apparatchiks both in the centre and in the republics initialized a campaign of rewriting histories with the assistance of some of the local historians. This time, the narrative was pulled back from the national romantic aspects and the histories written since 1937 were attacked by increasingly orthodox Marxist interpretation. It is beyond the scope of this work but suffice it to mark that the discussions between the constructors of the national narratives since 1937 and their orthodox Marxist opponents in the republics continued until 1947 in Ukraine, and were prolonged till 1950 and 1951 in Azerbaijan and Kazakhstan respectively. Some aspects and elements that were incorporated into national narratives were retained, while others were jettisoned for the sake of 'ideological purity'. Yet, Soviet Russian national history writing neither experienced such prolonged discussions nor excluded figures or events that had been incorporated into the narrative. This difference paved the road to an unbalanced picture in the Soviet Union. While the Russian narrative remained closer to the national romantic definition of the past, other nationalities were contained by a Marxist critique. There were signs that Stalin may have had a hidden agenda of limiting other nationalities (Burdei 1991, 45), and this is traced back to 1944 (Brandenberger 2002, 187). Indeed, this was the agenda but the unbalanced picture did not become apparent until the late 1940s. While Zhdanovshchina was experienced by Moscow and Leningrad intellectuals as a crusade against liberalism and western influences in arts and literature, historians in the non-Russian republics experienced this period as an attack on their national histories and a purge against the historians who had meticulously constructed them since 1937.

The aims and factors that shaped national histories of non-Russian identities can only be revealed if they are examined beyond the comparison with the Russian case and moving towards an 'all-Union' context. Neither the rehabilitation of Russian nationality and Russian culture nor Russocentric history writing prevented the construction of national histories in the union-republics. Indeed, despite widely prevalent historical Russocentrism, the Soviet state vociferously argued at the time that every Soviet nation was a historical nation, and had to be clearly presented as such. The gradually emerging Russocentrism only influenced the formulation of 'fraternal' relations between Russians and other Soviet nations in these national histories. When the Pokrovskiian historiography was removed, national histories had to cover much more ground than relations with Russia, and ranged from an ethnogenesis narrative to historical figures, national heroes, historical enemies of the nation, and relations with neighbouring peoples other than the Russians. In fact, the whole period can be understood as an experiment in how to write a national history in the first socialist country. In a meeting with the Ukrainian historians and ideologists in 1947, Kaganovich confessed that Pokrovskii and his interpretation of the past was the only real history school that the Soviet Union had ever had.[6] The problem, which could not be definitely answered yet, was what to put down as a Marxist history. After the concept of Pokrovskii was declared as anti-Marxist, it was not always clear for the Party ideologists and Soviet historians how to conciliate the ideology, which defined the history of humanity as the history of classes and their struggles on the one hand, and a new emphasis on the titular nations of each union-republic with their unique pasts on the other. In Dovzhenko's *Ukraïna v ogni* the question Zaparozhian Lavrin poses to himself, just before the demise of his German villain, summarizes the dilemma: 'Have we been poor historians? Could not forgive each other? [Our] national pride did not shine in our books of class struggle?' (Dovzhenko 2010, 320)

If ideological concerns can constitute an important driver, then international relations should be seen as the other crucial driver. That is why, next to the 'all-Union' context, Soviet national history writing should also be seen in the context of international relations. The national histories of each republic were formulated in different ways, despite the one-party rule and one official ideology. This difference can be seen in various elements of the national narrative, such as the formulation of ethnogenesis, and the definition of national heroes and villains. If we compare the three cases, it becomes clear that Azerbaijani and Ukrainian narratives resembled romantic national histories more than the Kazakh case did. The reason behind this difference is that these histories were written under the influence of domestic, as well as international developments. In the 1930s, the fascist war threat, the urgency of the armaments drive, and a siege mentality were important inputs into the shaping of national narratives. The Azerbaijani national history and identity was constructed to reply Turkish and Iranian claims. This was a defensive attempt because after 1934 Soviet–Iranian and Soviet–Turkish relations gradually deteriorated. Azerbaijan turned from a red lighthouse, or an example for the Middle East, to a bulwark against a possible aggression with the Nazis' backing. The brotherhood between the Georgian–Armenian–Azerbaijani nations also aimed to create a defensive wall. The Ukrainian identity and history was also constructed to reply to an external threat. This threat was felt in the ideological form of German orientalism, which was elevated to the new heights by the Nazi regime. The mono-ethnic Slavic definition of Ukrainian national identity was constructed to answer this orientalism. The threat also was expected to embody itself as a German–Polish alliance against the Soviet Union. The brotherhood between the Ukrainian and Russian nations and the anti-Polish construction of Ukrainian history were again consequences of international relations. In the Kazakh case, however, the batyrs, the leaders of the anti-Russian uprisings in the nineteenth century, remained in the narrative. There was not an immediate urge for finding the ethnogenesis of the Kazakhs or promoting some Kazakh khans to write a defensive history against an anticipated enemy towards the USSR.

It is a repeated claim that Stalin had mobilized domestic support for the war in part by turning to Russian identity and Church. In fact, this statement stands as a generalization if we examine the war period. Yes, during Second World War, national histories were used to increase fighting spirit among the Red Army soldiers and production levels at the home front. But the Russian national identity and history was not the only one at the stage. While authorities in Moscow intensified a propaganda campaign decorated with the heroic past of the Russian nation, the local communist party officials ran a parallel propaganda campaign by using their national heroes and national-liberation struggles. Although national and religious sentiments were used in the union-republics, this did not mean that 1939 or 1941 was a turning point in the construction of national identities and histories. Historians did not write national narratives as a consequence of temporary concessions by the Bolsheviks when the latter were in a desperate situation and urged for the mobilization of the non-Russians. National narratives were already constructed long before the Second World War. During the war, the native historians utilized these ready narratives for the wartime propaganda efforts. At the same time, these national histories were constructed and disseminated further. The Party and state propaganda apparatus spread the narrative, which was constructed in the second half of the 1930s, to an unprecedented level. The wartime propaganda accelerated the homogenization of the past in the minds of individuals. Thus, the Second World War worked for the nation-building policies which were launched earlier on a greater scale. In this sense, there was a strong continuity. Yet, there was also a discontinuity. During the war, the Azerbaijani and Ukrainian narratives were altered in order to establish stronger links with the Southern (Iranian) Azerbaijan and Western (Polish) Ukraine respectively and to cement the territorial claims of Moscow. Although it is beyond the scope of this book, this switch was not limited to these two examples. The Georgian and Armenian narratives were also transformed between 1945 and 1947 from defending the Soviet borders to incorporating cross-border territories in Turkey in order to support Soviet territorial claims in those years.

The construction of national narratives sometimes faced intervention at the highest level from Moscow. Stalin's intervention in the Ukrainian and Azerbaijani cases or the commentaries and reports of the party ideologists at the agitation-propaganda section of the CPSU can be counted as such interventions. However, these interventions were rare and they could not cover every single aspect of these grand narratives. In nearly all cases, these interventions came when the political authorities wanted to secure history writing to support priorities in foreign policy. This tendency leads us back to the impact of the international political context on the construction and reconstruction of national histories. Although it was a powerful system, the Soviet state and leaders like Stalin were not the only factors that assigned the direction of these constructions. Rather, they reacted to certain developments instead of leading them. Regional geopolitical factors, developments in neighbouring countries, and foreign relations were dominant game setters.

Although the leading politicians and ideologists in Moscow declared some major principles, the national narratives, entailing enormous detail, had to be written by local apparatchiks and historians. The construction of national histories in the republics of Azerbaijan, Kazakhstan, and Ukraine was not merely a result of top-down communication from Moscow. The first secretaries, and the secretaries supervising agitation-propaganda departments, and ideologists in these departments of the republican communist parties were deeply involved in the process of writing national narratives. Nation-building and construction of national histories has been an elite project. The nation-building elites in other countries were eager to recruit the masses to their project but always jealously protected their right to define the particular nationalism they espoused. The indigenous Bolsheviks and scholars in each republic were not exceptions. They saw themselves as the vanguards of their nation, which was in the process of formation according to the best modernization and development project in the world. The generation of Stalin was born in the years after the turn of the century and came to prominence in the wake of the pre-war purges. Some of them were also promoted to the positions that became vacant thanks to the Great Terror. This generation, including historians and writers, remained active at the top of their institutions long after Stalin's death. The generation that received education and career opportunities in the 1920s and 1930s had similar ideals for the future and attitudes towards the pre-revolutionary period. For them, tsarism was an archaic order that only brought political oppression, economic exploitation, and national hatred upon them. This was a world of peasantry, nomadism and primitive economic production, illiteracy, blind and archaic traditions, religious faiths, and superstitions. The Soviet order was the elimination of all these evil aspects. They anticipated social justice and equality, fair working conditions, equal gender rights, industrialization, and urbanization. They were enthusiastic young Bolsheviks and their mission was to drag the whole country to Soviet modernity. Writing their national narratives was part of this bigger project.

The post-Soviet nation-builders in Azerbaijan, Ukraine, and Kazakhstan very often claim that they are recovering a past that was rejected by Soviet history writing. However, numerous elements of this national history had already been erected under Stalin. Such a claim of 'recovering' national histories and identities provides leverage to legitimize current regimes which are very often defined as corrupt, authoritarian, and malfunctioning. This claim for 'recovery' tells us less about the actual historical processes involved in the past and more about current social and political imperatives in these countries. In fact the Stalinist period is a crucial episode in the construction of national identities of these nations because the main theses in the national histories were established during this period. When these countries became independent in 1991, they already had a sufficient tradition of nationalizing the past, sufficient published literature, fundamental concepts to develop further, and indigenous experts. Consequently, we see the intermix of Soviet and post-Soviet modes of narratives and policies in Central Asia, the Caucasus, and Ukraine. The apparent success of the Soviet nation-building projects in the three cases has much to tell us about the failures of nation-building efforts elsewhere.

## Notes

1 RGASPI 5–6-224–84/87, May 12, 1944.
2 For Malenkov's speech and list see RGASPI 17–125–222–16/17, May 29, 1944. These meetings were held at the Central Committee CPSU on May 29, June 1 (Bushuev, Adzhemian, Pankratova, Nechkina); June 5 (Bakhrushin, Sidorov, Rubinshtein, Syromiatnikov, Mind); June 10 (Picheta, Efimov, Iakovlev, Gorodetskii, Grekov); June 22 (Bazilevich, Tarle, Tolstov, Genkina, Derzhavin, Pankratova); July 8 (Kovalev (a member of the directory of propaganda of the Central Committee of the CPSU), the historians Volgin, Volin, Amanzholov, Tarle, Grekov, Adzhemian, and Pankratova). Most of these archival materials were published in 1988 (Pis'ma 1988).
3 ARPIISPIHDA, 1–32–340–19/21, February 6, 1947.
4 *TsDAHOU*, 1–70–514–25, August 27, 1946.
5 UATEIA, 11–2–3–62; May 16, 1947.
6 *TsDAHOU* 1–70–753–171, April 29, 1947.

# Bibliography

## List of archives

AP RF: Arkhiv Prezidenta Rossiiskoi Federatsii (Archive of the President of the Russian Federation), Moscow, Russia.

Arkhiv IU im. Krip'iakevycha NAN Ukraïny: Arkhiv Instytutu Ukraïnoznavstva im. I. Kryp'iakevycha NAN Ukraïny. L'viv, Ukraine.

Arkhiv RAN: Arkhiv Rossiiskoi Akademii Nauk (The Archive of the Academy of Sciences of Russia). Moscow, Russia.

ARPİİSPİHDA: Azərbaycan Respublikası Prezidentinin İşlər İdarəsi Siyasi Partiyalar və İctimai Hərəkatlar Dövlət Arxivi (The Political Parties and Public Movements State Archive of the Executive Office of the President of the Republic of Azerbaijan). Baku, Azerbaijan.

GARF: Gosuarstvennyi arkhiv Rossiiskoi Federatsii (The State Archive of Russian Federation). Moscow, Russia.

HDA SBU: Haluzevyi derzhavnyi arkhiv Sluzhba bezpeki Ukraïny (The Branch State Archive of the Security Services of Ukraine). Kiev, Ukraine.

KROMM: Kazakstan Respublikasy Ortalyk Memlekettik Muragaty (The Central State Archive of the Republic of Kazakhstan). Almaty, Kazakhstan.

KRPM: Kazakstan Respublikasy Prezidentining Muraghaty (The Archives of the President of Kazakhstan). Almaty, Kazakhstan.

NAIIU: Naukovyi Arkhiv Instytutu Istoriï Ukraïny (The Scholarly Archive of the Institute of Ukrainian History of the National Academy of Sciences of Ukraine). Kiev, Ukraine.

Naukovyi arkhiv Prezydiï NAN Ukraïny (The Scholarly Archive of the Prezidium of the Ukrainian National Academy of Sciences). Kiev, Ukraine.

RGANI: Rossiskii Gosudarstvennyi Arkhiv Noveishei Istorii (The Russian State Archive of Contemporary History). Moscow, Russia.

RGASPI: Rossiiskii Gosudarstvennyi Arkhiv Sotsial'no-Politicheskoi Istorii (Russian State Archive of Socio-Political History). Moscow, Russia.

TsDAHOU: Tsentral'nyi Derzhavnyi Arkhiv Hromads'kykh Ob'ednan' Ukraïny (The Central State Archives of the Public Organizations of Ukraine). Moscow, Russia.

TsDAVOU: Tsentral'nyi Derzhavnyi Arkhiv Vyshchykh Orhaniv Vlady ta Upravlinnia Ukraïny (The Central State Archives of Supreme Bodies of Power and Government of Ukraine). Kiev, Ukraine.

UATEIA: Sh. Sh. Uəlikhanov Atyndağy Tarikh zhəne Etnologiia Institutynyng Arkhivy (The Archive of the Sh. Sh. Uelikahnov Institute of History and Etnography). Almaty, Kazakhstan.

# Primary and secondary sources

Abasov, M., Gritchenko, A., and Zeinalov, R. 1990. *Azerbaidzhan v gody Velikoi otechestvennoi Voiny*. Baku: Elm.

Abdi, K. 2001. Nationalism, Politics, and the Development of Archaeology in Iran. *American Journal of Archaeology* 105, no. 1: 51–76.

Abdykalykov, M. 1944. Amangel'dy i Narod. *Kazakhstanskaia Pravda*. June 18.

Abdykalykov, M. 1997. Istoriia pro to, kak delali Istoriiu. *Argumenty i Fakty Kazakhstana*. February 6.

Ablai. 1943. *Kazakhstanskaia Pravda*. October 17.

Aca, M. 2002. *Kazak Türklerinin Destanlari ve Destancilzk Gelenegi*, Konya: Komen.

Adambekov, B.K. 2001. Bor'ba Sovetskikh respublik za sozdanie voennoi ekonomiki v gody Velikoi Otechestvennoi voiny. In *Problemy istorii i etnologii Kazakhstana*, 132–139. Karagandy: Karaghandymemlekettik Universiteti.

Adler, N. 2005. The future of the Soviet past remains unpredictable: The resurrection of Stalinist symbols amidst the exhumation of mass graves. *Europe-Asia Studies* 57, no. 8: 1093–1119.

Afanasieva, I.N., ed. 1996. *Sovetskaia istoriografiia*. Moscow: RGGU.

Afra, General H. 1964. *Under Five Shahs*. London: John Murray.

Ahmad, F. 1993. *The Making of Modern Turkey*. London: Routledge.

Akiner, S. 1995. *The Formation of Kazakh Identity: From Tribe to Nation-State*. London: Royal Institute of International Affairs.

Aksenova, E.P. 2000. *Ocherki iz istorii otechestvennogo slavianovedeniia 1930-e gody*. Moscow: Institut slavianovedeniia.

Aksenova, E.P. and Vasil'ev, M.A. 1993 Problemy etnogonii slavianstva i ego vetvei v akademicheskikh diskussiiakh rubezha 1930–1940-kh godov. *Slavianovedenie*, no. 3: 42–66.

Akt istoricheskoi vazhnosti. 1939. *Bol'shevik*, no. 17: 6–11.

Aleksandrov, G. 1939. O khoziaistvennom, politicheskom i kul'turnom upadke pol'skogo gosudarstva. *Bol'shevik*, no. 17: 43–50.

Aleksandrov, G. 1941. Mif XX stoletiia. *Bol'shevik*, no. 13: 23–33.

Alekseeva, G.D. and Zheltova, G.I. 1977. *Stanovlenie i razvitie sovietskoi sistemty nauchno-Istoricheskikh ucherezhdenii (20–30-e gody)*. Tashkent: Izdatel'stvo FAN Uzbekskoi SSR.

Alekseeva, G.D. et al. 1997. *Istoricheskaia nauka Rossii v XX veke*. Moscow: Skriptoriy.

Allworth, E. 1990. *The Modern Uzbeks*, Stanford, CA: Hoover Institution Press, Stanford University.

Alpamys. 2004. *Kazakhstan: Natsional'naia entsiklopediia*. Vol. 1. Almaty: Kazak entsiklopediiasy.

Alpatov, V.M. 1991. *Istoriia odnogo mifa: Marr and marrizm*. Moscow: 'Nauka', Glav. red. vostochnoi lit-ry.

Altman, M. 1941. *Böyük rus sərkərdəsi Suvorov*, ed. İ. Hüseynov. Baku: Azərnəşr.

Altstadt, A.L. 1992. *The Azerbaijani Turks, Power and Identity under Russian Rule*. Stanford: CA: Hoover Institution Press, Stanford University.

Amanolahi, Sekandar. 2002. Reza Shah and the Lurs: The Impact of the Modern State on Luristan. *Iran and the Caucasus* 6, no. 1–2: 193–218.

Anderson, B. 2006. *Imagined Communities, Reflections on the Origin and Spread of Nationalism*. London: Verso.

Andriewsky, O. 2003. The Russian–Ukrainian Discourse and the Failure of the 'Little Russian Solution', 1782–1917. In *Culture, Nation and Identity: The Ukrainian-Russian Encounter (1600–1945)*, ed. A. Kappeler, Z.E. Kohut, F. Sysyn, and M. von Hagen, 182–214. Toronto: CIUSP.

Ansari, A.M. 2012. *The Politics of Nationalism in Modern Iran.* Cambridge: Cambridge University Press.

Antisovetskaia politika germanskogo fashizma i mezhdunarodnyi proletariat. 1933. *Bol'shevik* 11: 1–12.

Apollova N.G. 1948. *Prisoedinenie Kazakhstana k Rossii v 30-kh godakh XVIII veka.* Almaty: AN KazSSR.

Arakelian, B.N. 1941a. Armeniia v pervyi period arabskogo vladychestva i bor'ba armian za nezavisimost'. In *Nauchnyi sbornik, posviashchennyi 20-letiiu ustanovleniia Sovetskoi vlasti v Armenii*, 65–106. Erivan: n.a.

Arakelian, B.N. 1941b. Vosstanie armian protiv arabskogo iga v 703 godu. In *Izvestiia ArmFAN* [in Armenian], 5–6, no. 10–11: 55–62.

Araslı, H.M. 1942a. *Nizami və vətən.* Baku: EAAzF.

Araslı, H.M. 1942b. *Vətənpərvər qadınlar.* Baku: Azərnəşr.

Arat, Yeşim. 2010. Nation Building and Feminism in Early Republican Turkey. In *Turkey's Engagement with Modernity: Conflict and Change in the Twentieth Century*, ed. C. Kerslake, K. Öktem and P. Robins. Basingstoke: Palgrave Macmillan, in association with St Antony's College, Oxford.

Armstrong, J.A. 1990. *Ukrainian Nationalism.* Englewood, CO: Ukrainian Academic Press.

Artamonov, M. 1939a. Dostizheniia sovetskoi arkheologii. *Vestnik Drevnei Istorii*, no. 2: 122–129.

Artamonov, M.I. 1939b. Nekotorye voprosy drevnei istorii SSSR. *Vestnik Akademii nauk SSSR*, no. 4: 26–38.

Artamonov, M.I. 1950. *Proiskhozhdenie slavian.* Leningrad: B.i.

Artamonov, M.I. 1940. Pervobytnoe obshchestvo v svete noveishikh arkheologicheskikh issledovanii v SSSR. *Sovetskaia Nauka*, no. 4: 48–65.

Arutiunian, A. 1939. *Krest'ianskie dvizheniia v Armenii v pervoi chetverti XVII veka.* Erivan: Izd-vo ArmFAN.

Arvidsson, S. 2006. *Aryan Idols: Indo-European Mythology as Ideology and Science*, trans. Sonia Wichmann. Chicago and London: The University of Chicago Press.

Asfendiiarov, S. 1934. O Kazakskom epose. *Kazakhstanskaia Pravda.* August 5.

Asfendiiarov, S.D. 1993 [1935]. *Istoriia Kazakhstana.* Almaty: Kazak Universiteti.

Ashinin F.D. and Alpatov, V.M. 1994. *Delo Slavistov: 30-e gody.* Moscow: Nasledie.

Ashnin, F.D. and Alpatov, V.M. 1998. Delo professora B.V. Choban-Zade. *Vostok*, no. 5: 126.

Ashnin, F.D., Alpatov, V.M., and Nasilov, D.M. 2002. *Repressirovannaia tiurkologiia.* Moscow: Vost. Lit.

Aster, H. and Potichnyj, P.J. 1983. *Jewish Ukrainian Relations.* Oakville, Ontario: Mosaic Press.

Atabaki, T. 2000. *Azerbaijan, Ethnicity and the Struggle for Power in Iran.* London: I.B. Tauris.

Atabaki, T. 2002. Recasting and Recording Identities in the Caucasus. *Iran and the Caucasus* 6, no. 1–2: 219–236.

Atabaki, T. 2012. Recasting the Symbolic Identity of Babak Khorramdin. In *Iran Facing Others: Identity Boundries in a Historical Perspective*, ed. A. Amanat and F. Vejdani, 63–76. New York and Basingstoke: Palgrave Macmillan.

Atabaki, T. 2001. Recasting Oneself, Rejecting the Other: Pan-Turkism and Iranian Nationalism. In *Identity Politics in Central Asia and the Muslim World: Nationalism, Ethnicity and Labour in the Twentieth Century*, ed. Willem van Schendel and Erik J. Zürcher, 65–77. London and New York: I.B. Tauris.

Atabaki, T. 2006. Pan-Turkism and Iranian Nationalism. In *Iran and the First World War: Battleground of the Great Powers*, ed. Touraj Atabaki, 121–136. London: I.B. Tauris.

Atabaki, T. 2008. Ethnic Minorities, Regionalism and the Construction of New Histories in the Islamic Republic of Iran. In *Iran und iranisch geprägte Kulturen*, ed. M. Ritter, R. Kauz, and B. Hoffmann, 133–143. Wiesbaden: Dr. Ludwig Reichert Verlag.

Atabaki, T. 2009. Agency and Subjectivity in Iranian National Historiography. In *Iran in the 20th Century Historiography and Political Culture*, ed. Touraj Atabaki, 69–92. London: I.B. Tauris.

Atakishiev, A. 1989. *Istoriia Azerbaidzhanskogo Gosudarstvennogo Universiteta*. Baku: Izdat-vo Azerb. Universiteta.

Atatürk, M.K. 1995. *Nutuk*, ed. Bedi Yazıcı. Istanbul: n.a.

Atatürk, M.K. 1991. Basının Dikkate Alacağı Hususlar, March 4, 1920. *Atatürk'ün Tamim, Telgraf ve Beyannameleri*. Ankara: Atatürk Araştırma Merkezi, no. 4: 251–252.

Atatürk, M.K. 1997. Bakanlar Kurulu'nun Görev ve Yetkisini Belirten Kanun Teklifi Münasebetiyle [December 1, 1921]. In *Atatürk'ün Söylev ve Demeçleri*. Vol. 1. Ankara: Atatürk Araştırma Merkezi. 202–216.

Aubin, H. 1930. Der Deutsche Osten und das Deutsche Volk. *Deutsche Rundschau*, no. 56: 95–109.

Auerbakh, N.K. Gammerman, A.F., *et al.* 1935. *Paleolit SSSR: materialy po istorii dorodovogo obshchestva*. Moscow: OGIZ.

Avdiev, V., Mashkin, N., and Novitskii, G. 1940. Zhurnal po drevnei istorii no. 1–4 za 1939 god. *Bol'shevik*, no. 15–16: 105–112.

Axundov, Ə. 1942a. *Azərbaycan nağılları*. Baku: EAAzF.

Axundov, Ə. 1942b. *İsrafil Pəhlivan nağıl*. Baku: EAAzF.

Axundov Ə. and Rəhimov, S. 1941. *Qaçaq Nəbi*. Baku: Azərnəşr.

Aydoğan, Erdal. 2007. Kliment Yefromoviç Voroşilov'un Türkiye'yi Ziyareti ve Türkiye-Sovyet Rusya İlişkilerine Katkısı. *Ankara Üniversitesi Türk İnkilap Tarihi Enstitüsü Atatürk Yolu Dergisi*, no. 39: 337–357.

*Azerbaidzhanskaia Demokraticheskaia Respublika, Parlament, Stenograficheskie Otchety*. 1998. Baku: Izdatel'stvo Azerbaidzhan.

*Azerbaidzhanskii gosudarstvennyi universitet imeni Lenina: Pervoe desiatiletie 1919–1929*. 1930. Baku: Izdanie AGU.

Azərbaijan K(b)P Baki Komitetinin VII Plenumu. 1941. *Qommunist.* November 27.

*Azərbaycan Respublikası Naxçıvan Tarixi Atlası*. 2010. Baku: n.a.

*Azərbaycan Tarixi Atlası*. 2007. Baku: Bakı Kartoqrafıya Fabriki.

*Azərbaycan tarixi qısa oçerk: ən qədim zamanlardan XIX əsrə qədər*. 1943. Baku: EAAzF.

*Azərbaycan Tarixi: III–XIII əsrin I rübü yeddi cilddə. II cild*. 2007. Vol. 2. Baku: Elm.

*Azərbaycan Xalg Cumxuriyyəti (1918–1920), Parlament*. Vol. *1 and 2*. 1998. Baku: Azərbaycan nəşriyyatı.

*Azərbaycanda Sovet Hakimiyyəti Uğrunda Fəal Mubarizlər*. 1958. Baku: Azərbaycan Dölət Nəşriyyatı.

Baberowski, J. 1998. Stalinismus als imperiales Phänomen: Die islamischen Regionen der Sowjetunion 1920–1941. In *Stalinismus: Neue Forschungen und Konzepte*, ed. S. Plaggenborg, 113–150. Berlin: A. Spitz.

## Bibliography

Bagirov, G. 1936. O iafetichesko-tiurkskom iazykovom smeshenii. *Trudy Azerbaidzhanskogo filiala: seriya lingvistiki*, no. 31: 7–19.

Bagirov, M. 1934. O Rabote TsK AKP(b): Otchetnyi doklad XII s'ezdu AKP(b). Baku: Partizdat.

Bagirov, M. 1944. *Novye prava i novye zadachi azerbaidzhanskoi ssr: iz doklada na obshchebakinskom partiinom aktive18 fevralia 1944 goda.* Baku: Azerneshr.

Bagirov, M.D. 1938. Iz zakliuchitel'noi rechi sekretaria TsK KP(b)Azerbaijana tov. M.D. Bagirova na XIV s'ezde KP(b)Azerbaidzhana. *Bakinskii Rabochii.* June 16.

Bagirov, M.D. 1942. *Prevratim Kavkaz v Mogilu dlia Gitlerovtsev.* Baku: Azerneşr.

Baimurzin, A. 1940. Iz istorii zakhvata tsarizmom bol'shoi i srednei ord. *Izvestiia KazFAN: seriia istoricheskaia*, no. 1: 95–107.

Baku. 1891. *Entsiklopedicheskii Slovar'*, ed. I.E. Andreevskii, 2a: 771. St. Petersburg: F.A. Brokgauz i I.A. Efron.

Balashov, B.A. and Iurchenkov, V.A. 1994. *Istoriografiia otechestvennoi istorii (1917-nachalo 90-kh gg.)* Saransk: Izdatel'stvo Mordovsk. Univ-ta.

Banac, I., ed. 2003. *The Diary of Georgi Dimitrov: 1933–1949.* New Haven and London: Yale University Press.

Banani, A. 1961. *The Modernization of Iran 1921–1941.* Stanford, CA: Stanford University Press.

Baraboi, L. 1940. Kritika i bibliografiia. Retsenzii Istorii SSR. Petrovs'kyi M.N. Vyzvol'na viina ukraïns'koho narodu proty hnitu shliakhets'koï Pol'shchi I pryednannia Ukraïny do Rosiï. *Istorik-marksist*, no. 7: 137–140.

Barber J. and Harrison, M. 1995. *The Soviet Home Front, 1941–1945: social and economic history of the USSR in World War II.* London and New York: Longman.

Barfield, T.J. 1989. *The Perilous Frontier: Nomadic Empires and China.* Oxford: Basil Blackwell.

Barfield, T.J. 1993. *The Nomadic Alternative.* Englewood Cliffs. NJ: Prentice Hall.

Barsukov, E.Z. 1944. *Əli Ağa Şixlinski.* Baku: EAAzF.

Bartol'd, V.V. 1963a. Kratkii obzor istorii Azerbaidzhana. Sochineniia. Vol. 2/1, 775–783. Moscow: Izdatel'stvo Vostochnoi Literatury.

Bartol'd, V.V. 1963b. Mesto Prikaspiiskikh Oblastei v Istorii Musul'manskogo Mira. *Sochineniia.* Vol. 2(1): 651–774. Moscow: Izdatel'stvo Vostochnoi Literatury.

Bartol'd, V.V. 2002a. Tiurki (istoriko-etnograficheskii obzor). *Sochineniia.* Vol. 5, 576–595. Moscow: Nauka.

Bartol'd, V.V. 2002b. Dvenadtsat Lektsii istorii Turetskikh narodov Srrednei Azii. *Sochineniia.* Vol. 5, 19–194. Moscow: Nauka.

Bartol'd, V.V. 2002c. Istoriia Turetsko-Mongol'skikh narodov. *Sochineniia.* Vol. 5, 195–232. Moscow: Nauka.

Barushin, S. 1943. Ivan Grozyi. *Bol'shevik*, no. 13: 48–61.

Basarab, J. 1982. *Pereiaslav: A Historiographical Study.* Edmonton: CIUS, University of Alberta.

Batyrlar Destury. 1943. *Otandy Korghauda.* July 30.

*Batyrlar Zhyry.* 1939. Almaty: n.a.

Bayramlı, C. 2011. *Babək və Hürrəmilik Yalanlar və Gerçəklər.* Baku: Kitab Aləmi

Bayramov, A. 2006. *Səməd Vurğun: Milli və Ümumbəşəri.* Baku: Səda.

BBC News, 2005. Putin deplores collapse of USSR [online]. BBC News, 25 April. Available from: http://news.bbc.co.uk/1/hi/4480745.stm (accessed November 10, 2012).

Bekmakhanov, E. 2005. *Sobranie sochinenii v semi tomakh: Zhin' i deiatel'nost' uchenogo i istoriia Kazakhstana.* Vol. 1. Pavlodar: PGU.

Bekmakhanova E.B., *'Kazakhstan v 20–40-e gody 19 veka'. Stenogramma: Iuil' 1948 goda.* 2000. Almaty: Kenzhe Press.
Beliaeva, B.A. 1957. *Trudovoi geroizm rabochikh Azerbaidzhana v gody Velikoi Otechestvennoi Boiny (1941–1945).* Baku: Azneftizdat.
Belousov, S.N. 1937a. *Narysy z Istoriï Ukraïny, Kyïvs'ka Rus' i Feodal'ni Kniazivstva, (XII–XIIIct.).* Vol. 1 Kiev: Vyd-vo Akademiï nauk URSR.
Belousov, S.M. 1937b. Na istorychnomy fronti Ukraïny. *Komunist.* August 22.
Belousov, S.M. 1938. V Instytuti istoriï Ukraïny. *Visti.* October 11.
Belousov S.M. and Ogloblin, O.P. 1940. *Zakhidna Ukraïna: Zbirnyk.* Kiev: Vydavnytstvo Akademiï Nauk URSR.
Belousov, S.N., Petrovskii, N.N., Iastrebov, F.A., and Premysler, I.M. 1940a. *Bor'ba Ukrainskogo Naroda Protiv Panskoi Pol'shi.* Kiev: Gosudarstennoe Izdatel'stvo Politicheskoi Literatury pri SNK USSR.
Belousov, S.N., Petrovs'kyi, N.N., Iastrebov, F.A., and Premysler, I.M. 1940b. *Borot'ba Ukraïns'koho Narodu Proty Pans'koï Pol'shchi.* Kiev: Derzhavne Vydavnytstvo Politychnoï Literatury pry RNK URSR.
Belousov, S.M. *et al.* 1940. *Istoriia Ukraïny Korotkyi Kurs.* Kiev: Vyd-vo Akademiï nauk URSR.
Benningsen, A. and Lemercier-Quelquejay, C. 1961. *The Evolution of the Muslim Nationalities of the USSR and their Linguistic Problems.* London: Central Asian Research Centre.
Benningsen, A. and Lemercier-Quelquejay, C. 1967. *Islam in the Soviet Union.* London: Pall Mall Press.
Benvenuti F. 1995. A Stalinist Victim of Stalinism: 'Sergo' Ordzhonokidze. In *Soviet History, 1917–53: Essays in Honour of R.W. Davies*, ed. J. Cooper, M. Perrie, and E.A. Rees, 134–157. London: St. Martin's Press.
Beriia, L. 1934. Bol'sheviki zakavkaz'ia i bor'be za sotsialism. *Bol'shevik*, no. 11: 24–38.
Beriia, L. 1936a. *Pobeda Leninsko-Stalinskoi natsional'noi politiki.* Tbilisi: Zaria Vostoka.
Beriia, L. 1936b. *Novaia Konstitutsiia SSR i Zakavkazskaia Federatsiia.* Tbilisi: Zaria Vostoka.
Beriia, L. 1937. *Edinaia sem'ia narodov.* Tbilisi: Zaria Vostoka
Bernadiner, B. 1939. Rol narodnykh mass v istorii. *Pod znamenem marksizma*, no. 10.
Berr, H. 1927. Foreword. In *Ancient Persia and Iranian Civilization*, ed. C. Huart, ix–xix. London: Kegan Paul.
Bezugol'nyi, A. 2005. *Narody Kavkaza v Vooruzhennykh silakh SSSR v gody Velikoi Otechestvennoi voiny 1941–1945 gg.* Stuttgart: Ibidem.
Bialas W. and Rabinbach, A. 2007. *Nazi Germany and the Humanities.* Oxford: One World.
Biddiss M.D., ed. 1970a. *Gobineau: Selected Political Writings.* London: Cape.
Biddiss, M.D. 1970b. *Father of Racist Ideology: The Social and Political Thought of Count Gobineau.* London: Weidenfeld & Nicolson.
Bihl, W. 1994. Ukrainians in the Armed Forces of the Reich: the 14th *Waffen* Grenadier Division of the SS. In *German-Ukrainian Relations in Historical Perspective*, ed. H. Torke and J. Himka, 138–162. Edmonton: CIUSP.
Bilokin', S.I. 2002. Upravlinnia derzhavnym terorom. In *Politychnyi terror i teroryzm v Ukraïny: XIX–XXct. istorychni narysy*, 496–547. Kiev: Naukova Dumka.
Biz Zhenemiz! 1941. *Sotsialistik Kazakstan.* June 27.
Black, C.E., ed. 1962. *Rewriting Russian History.* New York: Vintage Books.

## 182  Bibliography

Blake R.P. and Frye, R.N.. 1949. History of the Nation of the Archers (The Mongols) by Grigor of Akanc. *Harvard Journal of Asiatic Studies* 12, no. 3–4: 269–399.
Blank, S. 1994. *The Sorcerer as Apprentice: Stalin as Commissar of Nationalities, 1917–1924.* Westport, CT and London: Greenwood.
Bochkarov, I.M., Ioannisani, A.Z. et al. 1931. *Uchebnik istorii klassovoi bor'by.* Moscow and Leningrad: OGIZ.
Bogenbai. 2004. *Kazakhstan: Natsional 'naia entsiklopediia,* Vol. 1. Almaty: Kazak entsiklopediiasy.
Bokeikhanov, A. 1923. *Materialy k istorii sultana Kenesary Kasymova: vospominaniia kara-kirgiza Kaligully Alibekova o poslednikh dnikah Kenesary.* Tashkent: n.a.
Bokeikhanov, A. 1996. *Istoricheskie sudby kirgizskogo naroda: izbrannoe.* Almaty: n.a.
Bolianovs'kyi, A. 2000. *Dyviziia 'Halychyna': Istoria.* L'viv: 'IU'.
Bor'ba protiv fashistskikh podzhigatelei voiny, za mir mezhdu narodami. 1938. *Bol'shevik*, no. 15: 1–10.
Boroboi, S. Ia. 1940. Natsional'no-osvoboditel'naia voina ukrainskogo naroda protiv pol'skogo vladychestva I evreiskoe naselenie Ukrainy. *Istoricheskie zapiski*, 81–124. Moscow: Izdatel'stvo akademii nauk SSSR.
*Borot'ba ukraïns'koho narodu proty nimets'kykh zaharbnykiv: Zbirka Stattei.* 1942. Ufa: Vydannia Akademiï Nauk URSR.
Bosworth, E.G. 1995. Browne and his 'A Year Amongst the Persians'. *Iran* 33: 115–122.
Bozdoğan, S. 2001. *Modernism and Nation Building: Turkish Architectural Culture in the Early Republic.* Seattle: University of Washington Press.
Braithwaite, R. 2007. *Moscow 1941: A city and its people at war.* London: Profile Books.
Brandenberger, D. 2002. *National Bolshevism.* Cambridge, MA: Harvard University Press.
Broekmeyer, Marius. 2004. *Stalin, the Russians, and their war: 1941–1945.* Trans. Rosalind Buck, 3–10. Madison: University of Wisconsin Press.
Browne, E.G. 1918. *Materials for the Study of the Bábí Religion.* Cambridge: Cambridge University Press.
Browne, E.G. 1902. A Literary History of Persia. London: T. Fisher Unwin.
Browne, E.G. 1910. Bab, Babis. In *Encyclopaedia of Religion and Ethics*, ed. James Hastings. Vol. 2: 299–308. New York: Charles Scribner's Sons.
Brubaker, R. 1994. Nationhood and the National Question in the Soviet Union and Post-Soviet Eurasia: An Institutionalist Account. *Theory and Society* 23, no. 1: 47–78, 49–52.
Brudny, Y.M. 1998. *Reinventing Russia: Russian Nationalism and the Soviet State, 1953–1991.* Cambridge, MA.: Harvard University Press.
Brüggemann, K. and Kasekamp, A. 2008. The Politics of History and the 'War of Momuments' in Estonia. *Nationalities Papers: The Journal of Nationalism and Ethnicity* 36, no. 3: 425–448.
Brunner, C. 2007. Geographical and Administrative Divisions: Settlements and Economy. In *The Cambridge History of Iran*, ed. E. Yarshater. Vol. 3(2): 747–777. Cambridge: Cambridge University Press.
Brzoza C. and Sowa, A.L. 2009. *Historia Polski 1918–1945.* Cracow: Wydawnictwo Literackie.
Budurowycz, B.B. 1963. *Polish–Soviet Relations 1932–1939.* New York and London: Columbia University Press.
Buell, R.L. 1939. *Poland: Key To Europe.* New York and London: A. Knopf.
Bugai, N. ed. 1992. *Iosif Stalin – Lavrentiiu Berii: 'Ikh nado deportirovat' …' Dokumenty, fakty, kommentarii.* Moscow: Druzhba narodov.

Bugai, N.F. 1995. *Soglasno Vashemu ukazaniiu.* Moscow: AIRO XX.
Bul'ba-Borovets, T. 1993. *Armiia bez derzhavy.* L'viv: Poklyk sumlinnia.
Buniatov Z. and Zeinalov R. 1990. *Ot Kavkza do Berlina.* Baku: Azernesher.
Burdei, G.D. 1991. *Istorik i Voina 1941–1945.* Saratov: Izdatel'stvo Saratovskogo Universiteta.
Burleigh, M. 1989. *Germany Turns Eastwards: A Study of Ostforschung in the Third Reich.* Cambridge: Cambridge University Press.
Bury, J.B. *et al.*, eds. 1926a. *The Cambridge Ancient History.* Vol. 2. Cambridge: Cambridge University Press.
Bury, J.B. *et al.*, eds. 1926b. *The Cambridge Ancient History.* Vol. 4. Cambridge: Cambridge University Press.
Bushkovich, P. 2003. What is Russia? Russian National Identity and the State, 1500–1917. In *Culture, Nation and Identity: The Ukrainian–Russian Encounter (1600–1945)*, ed. A. Kappeler, Z.E. Kohut, F. Sysyn, and M. von Hagen, 144–161. Toronto: CIUSP.
Bushuev, S.K. 1939. *Bor'ba gortsev za nezavisimost' pod rukovodstvom Shamilia.* Moscow and Leningrad: Izd-vo Akademii nauk SSSR.
Buzurbaev, G. 1941. Intelligentsia Kazakhstana v Dni Otechestvennoi Voiny. *Bolshevik Kazakhstana*, no. 10: 11–17.
Bykovskii, S.N. 1931. Iafeticheskii predok vostochnykh slavian – kimmeriitsy. IGAIMK. Vol. 8, issue 8–10.
Byzdyng Maidannyhg Batyry. 1943. *Otandy Korghauda.* February 21.
Cabbarlı, C. 2005. *Əsərləri: Dört cilddə.* Vol. 2. Baku: Şərq-Qərb.
Cağaptay, S. 2006. *Islam, secularism and nationalism in modern Turkey: who is a Turk?* London: Routledge.
Carrere d'Encausse, H. 1989. The National Republics Lose Their Independence. In *Central Asia: 120 Years of Russian Rule*, ed. Edward Allworth. Durham, NC and London: Duke University Press.
Carrere d'Encausse, H. 1992. *The Great Challenge.* New York: Holmes & Meier.
Carter, S. 1990. *Russian Nationalism: Yesterday, Today, Tomorrow.* London: Pinter.
Cecil, R. 1972. *The Myth of the Master Race: Alfred Rosenberg and Nazi Ideology.* London: T. Batsford.
Cəlal, Mir. 1942. *İsrafil.* Baku: Uşaqgəncnəşr.
Chaikovs'kyi, A.S. 1994. *Nevidoma viina: Partyzans'ky rukh v Ukraïni 1941–1944 rr.* Kiev: Ukraïna.
Cheburakov, N. 1941. Trudovoi geroizm sovetskogo naroda *Bol'shevik*, no. 15: 42–48.
Chehabi, H.E. 1999. From Revolutionary *Taṣnīf* to Patriotic *Surūd*: Music and Nation-Building in Pre-World War II Iran. *Iran*, 37: 143–154.
Chehabi, H.E. 1993. Staging the Emperor's New Clothes: Dress Codes and Nation-Building under Reza Shah. *Iranian Studies* 26, no. 3–4: 209–233.
Cherniak, E.B. 1969. *Zhandarmy istorii.* Moscow: Mezhdunarodnye otnosheniia.
Chlebowczyk, Jozef. 1980. *On Small and Young Nations in Europe.* Wroclaw: Zaklad Narodowy im. Ossolinskich.
Choban-Zade, B. 1926. O Blizkom rodstve Tiurskikh narechii. *Vsesoiuznyi Tiurkologicheskii S'ezd.* Baku: Bakinskii Rabochii.
Choban-Zade, B. 1936. Problema definitivnosti v tiurkskom iazyke. *Trudy Azerbaidzhanskogo Filiala: seriya lingvistiki*, 31: 21–34.
Chobanzade, B. and F. Agazade. 1929. *Turq grameri.* Baku: Azerneşr.
Christensen, A. 1925. *Le Regne du Roi Kawadh I et le communisme* Mazdakite. Copenhagen: Host & Son.

Chuloshnikov, A.P. 1924. *Ocherki po istorii Kazakh-Kirgizskogo naroda v sviazi s obshchimi istoricheskimi sud'bami drugikh tiurkskikh plemen: chast pervaia drevnee vremia i srednie veka*. Orenburg: Kirgizskoe gosudarstvennoe izdatel'stvo.

Clawson, P. 1993. Knitting Iran Together: The Land Transport Revolution, 1920–1940. *Iranian Studies* 26, nos. 3–4: 235–250.

Cleaves, F.W. 1949. The Mongolian Names and Terms in the History of the Nation of the Archers by Grigor of Akanc. *Harvard Journal of Asiatic Studies* 12, nos. 3–4: 400–443.

Connor, W. 1984. *The National Question in Marxist-Leninist Theory and Strategy*. Princeton, NJ: Princeton University Press.

Connor, W. 1992. The Soviet Prototype. In *The Soviet Nationality Reader: The Disintegration in Context*, ed. R. Denber. Boulder, CO and Oxford: Westview.

Conquest, R. 1970. *The Nation Killers: The Soviet Deportation of Nationalities*. London: Macmillan.

Conquest. R., ed. 1967. *The Politics of Ideas in the USSR*. London: The Bodley Head.

Cottam, R.W. 1979. *Nationalism in Iran*. Pittsburgh; London: University of Pittsburgh Press.

Crone, P. 1991. Kavad's Heresy and Mazdak's Revolt. *Iran* 29: 21–42.

Cronin, S. 2003. *The Making of Modern Iran, State and society under Riza Shah*. London: Routledge.

Cronin, S. 1999. The Politics of Radicalism within the Iranian Army: The Jahansuz Group of 1939. *Iranian Studies* 32, no. 1: 9.

Curta, F. 2001. *The Making of the Slavs: History and Archaeology of the Lower Danube Region, c.500–700*. Cambridge: Cambridge University Press.

Czaplicka, M.A. 1920. Slavs. In *Encyclopedia of Religion and Ethics*, ed. J. Hastings, 11: 587–595. New York: Charles Scribner's Sons.

Dadaşzadə, M.A. 1942. *Qəhrəmanlar bədii kino-ssenarilər*. Baku: Uşaqgəncnəşr.

Dadaşzadə, M.A. 1945. *Vətən səsi*. Baku: Azərnəşr.

Dadaşzadə, M.A. ed. 1941a. *Azərbaycan ədəbiyyatında xalq qəhrəmanları məqalələr*. Baku: EAAzF.

Dadaşzadə, M.A., ed. 1941b. *Vətən nəğmələri*. Baku: Uşaqgəncnəşr.

Dakhshleiger, G.F. 1969. *Istoriografiia sovetskogo Kazakhstana*. Almaty: Nauka

Dandamayev, M. and I. Medvedskaya. 2006. Media. Encyclopaedia Iranica, online edition, 15 August 2006, available at www.iranicaonline.org/articles/media.

Danylenko, V.M., Kas'ianov, H.V., and Kul'chyts'kyi, S.V. 1991. *Stalinizm na ukraïni: 20–30-ti roky*. Kiev: Lybid'.

Darabadi, P. 2008. The Caucasus and the Caspian in the Great Geostrategic Game on the Eve of and During World War II (Geohistorical Essay). In *The Caucasus and Globalization*, no. (2)1: 133–152.

Daryaee, T. 2009. *Sasanian Persia, The Rise and Fall of an Empire*. London: Tauris.

Das Judentum in Geschichte und Gegenwart. 1930. *Encyclopaedia Judaica*. Vol. 5, col. 503. Berlin: Eschkol.

Dashinskii, S. 1934. O proshloi i budushchei imperialisticheskoi voine. *Bol'shevik*, no. 13–14: 110–124.

Debicki, R. 1962. *Foreign Policy of Poland 1919–1939*. London and Dunmow: Pall Mall Press.

Deborin A.M., ed. 1936. *Voprosy istorii doklassovogo obshchestva: sbornik statei k piatidesiatiletiiu knigi Fr. Engel'sa 'Proiskhozhdenie sem'i, chastnoi sobstvennosti i gosudarstva*. Moscow and Leningrad: Izdat-vo Nauk Akad. Nauk SSSR.

Degitaeva, L.D. 1998. *Politicheskie represii v Kazakhstane v 1937–38gg. Sbornik dokumentov.* Almaty: Kazakhstan.

Dekada. 1938. *Bakinskii Rabochii.* April 18.

Dekada azerbaidzhanskogo iskustva. 1938. *Bakinskii Rabochii.* April 5.

Deletant, D. and Hanak, H., eds. 1988. *Historians as Nation-Builders, Central and South-Eastern Europe.* London: Macmillan Press.

Dengel', F. 1937. Niunbergskie zaklinaniia i fashistskaia deistvitel'nost. *Bol'shevik,* no. 19: 82–90.

Denis, M.E. 1905. L'Europe Orientale: Slaves, Lithuaniens, Hongrois: Depuis les origins jusqu'à la fin du XI͌ siècle. In *Historie Générale du IV ͤ Siècle a nos jours,* eds. Alfred Rambaud and Ernest Lavisse 1: 688–704. 12 vols. Paris: Librairie Armand Colin.

Derzhavin N. and Konstantinov F. 1943. Slaviane. *Sputnik agitator,* no. 17: 45–47.

Derzhavin N.S. 1939. Ob etnogeneze drevneishikh narodov dneprovsko-dunaiskogo basseina. *Vestnik Drevnei Istorii,* no. 1: 279–289.

Derzhavin, N.S. 1942. *Fashizm – zleishii vrag Slavianstva.* Kazan': Izd-vo Akad. Nauk SSSR.

Derzhavin, N.S. 1943. *Vekovaia bor'ba slavian s nemetskimi zakhvatchikami.* Moscow: Izdanie vseslavianskogo komiteta.

Derzhavin, N.S. 1944. *Proiskhozhdenie russkogo naroda: velikorusskogo, ukrainskogo, belorusskogo.* Moscow: Sov. Nauka.

Diadychenko. 1942. *Semen Palii.* Saratov: Ukrvydav pry TsK KPbU.

Diakonoff I.M., 1985. Media. In *The Cambridge History of Iran,* ed. I. Gershevitch, 36–148. Vol. 2 Cambridge: Cambridge University Press.

Diaz-Andreu M. and Champion, T., eds. 1996. *Nationalism and Archaeology in Europe.* London: UCL Press.

Dimitrov, G. 1939. Report by Comrade Dimitrov: The Fascist Offensive and the Tasks of the Communist International in the Fight for the Unity of the Working Class Against Fascism. *VII Congress of the Communist International: Abridged Stenographic Report of Proceedings,* 124–193. Moscow: Foreign Languages Publishing House.

Dolukhanov, P.M. 1996. *The Early Slavs: Eastern Europe from the Initial Settlement to the Kievan Rus.* London: Longman.

Doroshenko, D. 1942. *Istoriia Ukraïny z maliunkamy dlia shkoly i rodyny.* Cracow and L'viv: n.a.

Dovzhenko, O. 2010. *Ukraïna v ohni.* Kharkiv: Folio.

*Drevnetiurkskii slovar '.* 1969. Leningrad: Nauka.

Dreyfus, H. 1909. *Babismus und Behaismus.* Frankfurt a. M: Neuer Frankfurter Verlag.

Druzhinin N.M., 1990. *Izbrannye trudy vospominaniia mysli opyt istorika.* Moscow: Nauka.

Dubrovskii, A.M. 2005. *Istorik i vlast: istoricheskaia nauka v SSSR i kontseptsiia istorii feodal'noi Rossii v kontekste politiki i ideologii (1930–1950-e gg.).* Briansk: Izdatel'stvo Brianskogo gosudarstvennogo universiteta im. akad. I.G. Petrovskogo.

Dubrovsky, A.M. 1998. 'The People Need a Tsar': The Emergence of National Bolshevism as Stalinist Ideology, 1931–1941. *Europe-Asia Studies* 50, no. 5: 873–892.

Duchinski, F.H. [Duchiński F.H.]. 1864. Peuples Aryâs et Tourans, agriculteurs et nomades. Nécéssité des réformes dans l'exposition de l'histoire des peuples Aryâs-Européens et Tourans, particulièrement des Slaves et des Moscovites. Paris: Friedrich Klincksieck.

Duchinski, M.F. [Duchiński F.H.]. 1855. *La Moscovie et la Pologne: Extrait du Journal de Constantinople*: n.a.

## 186  Bibliography

Dulatov, M. 1994. *Shygarmalary*. Almaty: Zhazushy.

Dva Primera: Beket. 1942. *Kazakhstanskaia Pravda.* February 12.

Dvadtsatipiatiletie pervoi mirovoi imperialisticheskoi voiny. 1939. *Bol'shevik*, no. 13: 1–10.

Dvorkin, I. 1933. *Ekonomicheskaia programma germanskogo natsional-sotsializma*. Moscow: Partizdat.

Dvornik, F. 1956. *The Slavs: Their Early History and Civilization*. Boston: American Academy of Arts and Sciences.

Dzhafarzade, I., Klimov A.A., and Iampol'skii Z.I., eds. 1939. *Istoriia Azerbaidzhanskoi SSR uchebnik dlia 8 i 9 klassov*. Baku: Izdanie AzFAN.

Dzhanpoladian, R.M. 1943. *Smbat Khosrov - Shum Bagratuni*. Erivan: ArFAN.

Edilkhanova, S.A. 2005. *Kazakhsko-dzhungarskie vzaimootnosheniia v XVII–XVIII vekakh*. Almaty: Daik-Press.

Efimenko, P.P. 1934. *Dorodovoe obshchestvo: ocherki po istorii pervobytno-kommunisticheskogo obshchestva*. Moscow and Leningrad: Gos. Soz-econ. Izd-vo.

Efimenko, P.P. 1938. *Pervobytnoe opbshchestvo: Ocherki po istorii Paleoliticheskogo vremeni*. Leningrad: Gosud. Sotsial'-no-ekonomicheskoe izdatel'stvo.

Egorov, G. 1939. *Zapadnaia Belorussiia.* Moscow: Gos. izd-vo polit. lit-ry.

Ehlers, E. and Floor, W. 1993. Urban Change in Iran 1920–1941. *Iranian Studies* 26, no. 3–4: 251–275.

Əhmədov, Ramiz. 2004. *Mir Cəfər Bağırov*. Baku: Nurlan

Eissenstat, B.W. 1969. M.N. Pokrovsky and Soviet Historiography: Some Reconsiderations. *Slavic Review* 28, no. 4: 604–618.

Engels, F. 1972. *The Origin of the Family, Private Property and the State*. New York: Pathfinder Press.

Engels, F. 1987. Anti-Dühring 1877, Part III: Socialism, Theoretical. *Marx and Engels Collected Works* xxv. 50 vols. London: Lawrence & Wishart.

Enteen, G.M. 1978. *The Soviet Scholar-Bureaucrat, M.N. Pokrovskii and the Society of Marxist Historians.* University Park: Pennsylvania State University Press.

Eremian, S.T. 1944. *Amirspasalar Zakhariia Dolgorukii*. Erivan: n.a.

Erickson, A.K. 1960. E.V. Tarle: The Career of a Historian under the Soviet Regime. *American Slavic and East European Review*, 2: 202–216.

Eriksen, T.H. 2002. *Ethnicity and Nationalism*. London: Pluto.

Er-Kabanbai. 2005. *Kazakhstan: Natsional 'naia entsiklopediia*. Vol. 2. Almaty: Kazak entsiklopediiasy.

Erofeeva, I.V. 2007. Sobytiiai liudi kazakhskoi stepi (epokha pozdnego srednevek'ia i novogo vremeni) Kak ob'ekt istoricheskoi remistifikatsii. In *Nauchnoe znanie i mifotvorchestvo v sovremennoi istoriografii Kazakhstana*, eds. N.E. Masanov, Z.B. Abylkhozhin, and I.V. Erofeeva, 132–224. Almaty: Daik-Press.

Ettinger, S. 2007. Chmielnicki (Khmelnitski), Bogdan. *Encyclopaedia Judaica*. Second edition. Vol. 4: 654–656. London: Macmillan Refence USA.

Fadeev, A. 1941. Edinenie slavianskikh narodov v bor'be protiv gitlerizma. *Bol'shevik*, no. 15: 15–21.

Faghoory, M.H. 1993. The Impact of Modernization on the Ulama in Iran, 1925–1941. *Iranian Studies* 26, no. 3–4: 277–312.

Fasmer, M. [Max Vasmer]. 1986. *Etimologicheskii slovar' russkogo iazyka*. Vol. 1. Moscow: Progress.

Fathi, Asghar. 1986. Kasravi's Views on Writers and Journalists: A Study in the Sociology of Modernization. *Iranian Studies* 19, no. 2: 172.

Fawcett, L. 1992. *Iran and the Cold War: The Azerbaijan Crisis of 1946*. Cambridge: Cambridge University Press.
Fazlallakh, Rashid ad-Din. 1987. *Oguz-Name*. Baku: Elm.
Fisher, S.N. and Ochseneald, W. 1997. *The Middle East: A History*. Vol. 2. New York: McGraw-Hill.
Fitzpatrick, S. 2000. *Everyday Stalinism: Ordinary Life in Extraordinary Times: Soviet Russia in the 1930s*. Oxford: Oxford University Press.
Flügel, G. 1869. Bâbek, seine Abstammung und erstes Auftreten. *Zeitschriften der Deutschen Morgenländischen Gesellschaft* 23: 531–543.
Fonberg, L. and Liubchenko, V. 2005. *Narysy z istoriï ta kul'tury evreïv Ukraïny*. Kiev: Dukh i Litera.
Formozov, A.A. 1993. Arkheologiia I ideologiia (20–30-e gody). *Voprosy Filosofii* 2: 70–82.
Formozov, A.A. 2004. *Russkie arkheologi v period totalitarizma*. Moscow: Znak.
Fridliand, Ts. 1934. Podzhigateli Voiny. *Bor'ba klassov* 9: 91–92.
Frye, R.N. 1983. *The History of Ancient Iran*. Munich: C.H. Beck'sche Verlagsbuchhandlung.
Gaisinovich, A. 1937. *Pugachev*. Moscow: izd. tip. i zink. Zhurn-gaz ob'edinenia.
Gal'ianov, V. 1938. Kuda idet Pol'sha. *Bol'shevik*, no. 8: 61–68.
Gal'ianov, V. 1939. Mezhdunarodnaia obstanovka vtoroi imperialisticheskoi voiny. *Bol'shevik*, no. 4: 49–65.
Galiev, V.Z. 1998. *Khan Dzhangir o Orbulakskaia bitva*. Almaty: Ghylym.
Galuzo, P. (1928) 'Kolonial'naia politika tsarskogo pravitel'stva v Srednei Azii', *Istorik Marksist*, no. 9: 128–133.
Galuzo, P. 1929. *Turkestan-koloniia*. Moscow: Izdanie Kommunisticheskogo Universiteta Trudiashchikhsia Vostoka imeni I.V. Stalina.
Ganichev, V. 1995. Oni vyigrali voinu ... a vy? *Nash Sovremennik* 5: 113–128.
Garlinski, J. (1992) 'The Polish–Ukrainian Agreement 1920', in *The Reconstruction of Poland, 1914–23*, P. Latawski, 55–70. London: Macmillan.
Garthoff. R.L. 1954. *How Russia Makes War: Soviet Military Doctrine*. London: George Allen & Unwin Ltd.
Gasanly, D. (Cemil Hasanli). 2008. *SSSR–Turtsiia: ot neitraliteta k kholodnoi voine (1939–1953)*. Moscow: Zentr Propagandy.
*Gazi Mustafa Kemal Atatürk'ün 1923 Eskişehir-İzmit Konuşmaları*. 1996. Ed. A. Inan. Ankara: TTK.
Geary, P.J. 2002. *The Myth of Nations, The Medieval Origins of Europe*. Oxford: Princeton University Press.
Geiden, K. 1935. *Istoriia germanskogo fashizma*. Moscow: Sotsekgiz.
Geins, A. 2007. *Sobranie literaturnykh trudov*. Astana: Altyn kitap.
Genkina, E. 1943. Lenin o bratstve i druzhbe narodov SSSR. *Bol'shevik* no. 1: 35–45.
Geroi-Batyry Kazakhskogo Naroda. 1943. *Kazakhstanskaia Pravda*. October 17.
*Geroicheskoe proshloe russkogo naroda: Sokrashchennye i pererabotannye stenogrammy lektsii, prochitannykh na sbore frontovykh agitatorov*. 1943. Moscow: Voenizdaat.
Gobineau A. 2003. From the Essay on the Inequality of Human Races. In *Racism a Global Reader*, ed. K. Reilly, S. Kaufman, and A. Bodino. Armonk, NY: M.E. Sharpe.
Gofman, K. 1938. Ekonomicheskaia podgotovka germanskogo fashizma k voine. *Bol'shevik*, no. 8: 69–76.
Gogun, A. and A. Kentii. 2006. *Krasnye partizany Ukainy 1941–1944*. Kiev: Ukrainskii izdatel'skii soiuz.

## 188  Bibliography

Gol'dshtein, I. 1939. *Kak pol'skie pany ugnetali krestian*. Moscow: Gos. Izd-vo polit. litry.
Golden, P.B. 1998. *Nomads and Sedentary Societies in Medieval Eurasia*. Washington DC: American Historical Association.
Golden, P.B. 2009. Migrations, ethno-genesis. In *The Cambridge History of Inner Asia: The Chinggisid Age*, ed. N. Di Cosmo, A.J. Frank, and P.B. Golden, 109–119. Cambridge: Cambridge University Press.
Golden, P.B. 1992. *An Introduction to the History of the Turkic Peoples: Turcologica 9*: 283–308. Wiesbaden : Otto Harrassowitz.
Goodhart, A.L. 1920. *Poland and the Minority Races*. London and New York: G. Allen and Unwin.
Gorianov, B.T. 1939. Slavianskie poseleniia VI v. i ikh obshchestvennyi stroi. *Vestnik Drevnei Istorii*, no. 1: 308–318.
Gorlanov O.A. and Roginskii, A.B. 1997. Ob arestakh v zapadnykh oblastiakh Belorussii I Ukrainy. In *Repressii protiv poliakov i pol'skikh grazhdan*, ed. L.S. Eremina, 77–113. Moscow: Zven'ia.
Gorodtsov, V.A. 1901. Russkaia doistoricheskaia keramika. *Trudy 11-ogo Arkheologicheskogo s'ezda v Kieve*. Vol. 1: 577–672. Moscow: Tipografiia G. Lissnera i A. Geshelia.
Gorodtsov, V.A. 1908. *Pervobytnaia arkheologiia*. Moscow: Mosk. arkheol. in-t.
Gratsianskii, N.P. 1938. Nemetskaia agressiia v Pribaltike v XIII-XV vekakh. *Istorik-Marksist*, no. 6 (70): 87–111.
Grechko, A.A., *et al.* 1974. *Istoriia vtoroi mirovoi voiny, 1939–1945*. Vol. 3. Moscow: Voennoe izdatel'stvo Minoborony SSSR.
Grekov, B.D. 1936. *Feodal'nye otnosheniia v kievskom gosudarstve*. Moscow: Izdatel'stvo ANSSSR.
Grekov, B.D. 1937. Itogi izucheniia istorii SSSR za dvatsat' let. *Izvestiia AN SSSR. Otdel' obshch. Nauk*, no. 5: 1101–1113.
Grekov, B.D. 1939. *Protiv istoricheskoi kontseptsii M. N. Pokrovskogo: sbornik statei*. Vol. 1. Moscow and Leningrad: Izd-vo Akademii nauk SSSR.
Grekov, B.D. 1940. *Protiv antimarksistskoi kontseptsii M. N. Pokrovskogo: sbornik statei*. Vol 2. Moscow and Leningrad: Izd-vo Akademii nauk SSSR.
Grekov, B.D. 1942. *Bor'ba Rusi za sozdanie svoego gosudarstva*. Moscow and Leningrad: Izd-vo Akad. Nauk SSSR.
Grekov, B.D. 1945. Obrazovanie russkogo gosudarstva. *Bol'shevik*, no. 11–12: 25–34.
Grenoble, L.A. 2003. *Language Policy in the Soviet Union*. Dordrecht, Boston, and London: Kluwer Academic Publishers.
Grigor, T. 2004. Recultivating 'good taste': The early Pahlavi modernists and their society for national heritage. *Iranian Studies* 37, no. 1: 17–45.
Grigorian, F. 1946. *Smbat I Bagratuni*. Erivan: n.a.
GUBAIDULLIN Gaziz (Aziz) Salikhovich (pseudonym: G. Gaziz) (1887–1938). http://memory.pvost.org/pages/gubajdullings.html (accessed November 7, 2009).
Gubaidullin Gaziz Salikhovich. http://lists.memo.ru/index4.htm (accessed November 8, 2009).
Gubaidullin, S.G. 1926. Razvitie istoricheskoi literatury u Tiurko-tatarskikh narodov. *Vsesoiuznyi Tiurkologicheskii S'ezd*. Baku: Bakinskii Rabochii.
Gubaidullin, S.G. 1994 [1924]. *Istoriia tatar*. Moscow: Moskovskii Litsei.
Gubaidullin, G. 1997. Ia sredi tovarishchei schitalsia khoroshim disputantom. *Gasyrlar Avazy* 1–2: 120–122.

Guidi, M. Mazdak. *Encyclopaedia of Islam*. 2nd edn. ed. P. Bearman, T. Bianquis, C.E. Bosworth, E. van Donzel, and W.P. Heinrichs. In Brill Online. Oxford University libraries, www.brillonline.nl/subscriber/entry?entry=islam_SIM-5091 (accessed September 10, 2011).

Gur'ianov, A.E. 1997. Pol'skie spetspereselentsy v SSSR v 1940–1941 gg. In *Repressii protiv poliakov i pol'skikh grazhdan*, ed. L.S. Eremina, 114–136. Moscow: Zven'ia.

Gurevich, F. 1936. Srednevekovaia nemetskaia imperiia v fashistskoi istoriografii. *Bor'ba klassov* 10: 92–102.

Gurevich, L. 1992. *Totalitarizm protiv intelligentsia*. Almaty: Karavan.

Hanover, N. 1950. *Abyss of Despair (Yeven Metzulah): The Famous 17th Century Chronicle Depicting Jewish Life in Russia and Poland during the Chmielnicki Massacres of 1648–1649*. New York: Bloch.

Härke, H. 1998. Archaeologists and Migrations. *Current Anthropology* 39, 1: 19–45, 23.

Harley, J.H. 1939. *The Authentic Biography of Colonel Beck: Based on the Polish by Conrad Wrzos*. London: Hutchinson & Co.

Harris, G.S. 1995. The Russian Federation and Turkey. In *Regional Power Rivalries in the New Eurasia: Russia, Turkey and Iran*, ed. Alvin Z. Rubinstein and Oles M. Smolansky, 3–6. Armonk, NY: M.E. Sharpe.

Harrison, M. 1985. *Soviet Planning in Peace and War 1938–1945*. Cambridge: Cambridge University Press.

Harrison, M. 1996. *Accounting for War: Soviet production, employment, and the defense burden, 1940–45*. Cambridge: Cambridge University Press.

Harrison, M. and R.W. Davies, 1997. The Soviet Military-Economic Effort during the Second Five-Year Plan (1933–1937). *Europe-Asia Studies*, no. 49 (3): 369–406.

Hasanli, J. 2006. *At the Dawn of the Cold War, The Soviet–American Crisis over Iranian Azerbaijan, 1941–1946*. Oxford: Rowman & Littlefield.

Hayit, B. 1963. *Some Problems of Modern Turkistan History: An Analysis of Soviet Attacks on the Alleged Falsifiers of the History of Turkistan*. Dusseldorf: East European Research Institute.

Heer, N. 1973. *Politics and History in the Soviet Union*. Cambridge, MA: MIT Press.

Herlihy, P. 1977. The Ethnic Composition of the City of Odessa in the Ninteenth Century. *Harvard Ukrainian Studies* 1, no. 1: 53–78.

Hertz, F. 1928. *Race and Civilization*. London: Macmillan.

Himka, J-P. 2006. The Basic Historical Identity Formation in Ukraine: A Typology. *Harvard Ukrainian Studies* 28, no. 1–4: 483–500.

Hirsch, F. 2002. Race without the Practice of Racial Polities. *Slavic Review* 61, no. 1: 30–43.

Hirsch, Francine, 2005. *Empire of Nations: Ethnographic Knowledge and the Making of the Soviet Union*. Ithaca, NY: Cornell University Press.

Hirsch, Francine. 2000. Towards an Empire of Nations: Border-Making and the Formation of 'Soviet' National Identities. *The Russian Review* 59, no. 2: 201–226.

Hoffmann, D.L. 2000. The Soviet Empire: Colonial Practices and Socialist Ideology. *Russian Review* 59, 2: vi–viii.

Hoffmann-Kutschke, A.F. 1925. *Die Wahrheit über Kyros, Dareias und Zoroastres, Beiträge zur Erforschung der älteren arischen*. Stuttgart: W. Kohlhammer.

Hosking, G. 1997. *Russia: People and Empire 1552–1917*. Cambridge, MA.: Harvard University Press.

Hosking, G. 1998. Empire and Nation-Building in Late Imperial Russia. In *Russian Nationalism Past and Present*, eds. Geoffrey Hosking and Robert Service, 19–34. London: Macmillan.

Hosking, G. 2002. The Second World War and Russian National Consciousness. *Past and Present* 175, no. 1: 162–187.
Hrushevs'kyi [Hrushevsky], M. 1898. Anty: Uryvok z istoryï Ukraïny-Rusy. *Zapysky Naukovoho tovarystva imeny Shevchenka*, no. 21: 1–16 (own pagination).
Hrushevs'kyi [Hrushevsky], M. 1904. Biblïografiia. *Zapysky Naukovoho tovarystva imeny Shevchenka* no. 60: 7–9 (own pagination).
Hrushevs'kyi, M. 1911. Novi konstruktsiï pochatkiv slovians'koho i ukraïns'ko-rus'koho zhytia. *Zapysky Naukovoho tovarystva imeny Shevchenko*, no. 103: 5–27.
Hrushevsky, M. 2002. The Cossack Age, 1626–1650. In *History of Ukraine-Rus'* 8, ed. F.E. Sysyn and M. Yurkevich, 516–519. Edmonton: CIUSP.
Hrushevsky, M. 2005. *History of Ukraine-Rus'*. Vol. 1. Edmonton: CIUSP.
Huart, C. 1927. *Ancient Persia and Iranian Civilization*. London and New York: Kegan Paul, Alfred A. Knopf.
Hunczak, T., ed. 1977. *The Ukraine, 1917–1921: A Study in Revolution*. Cambridge, MA.: Harvard Ukrainian Research Institute.
Huseinov, H. 1941. SSRi Elimler Akademiiasy Azerbaijan Filialy Veten Muharibesi Kunlerinde. *Qommunist*. October 25.
Hüseynov, İ. 1941a. *Slavyan xalqlarının vahid cəbhəsi*. Baku: EAAzF.
Hüseynov, H. ed. 1941b. *Qəhrəman Moskva! Əziz Moskva!* Baku: EAAzF.
Hüseynov, İ. ed. 1942. *Azərbaycanın şanlı oğulları*. Vol. 1. Baku: Azərnəşr
Hüseynov, İ. 1943. *İsmayıl Səfəvi*. Baku: EAAzF.
Hüseynov İ. ed. 1945. *Azərbaycanın şanlı oğulları*. Vol. 3. Baku: Azərnəşr.
Huslystyi, K. 1939. *Ukraïns'ki Zemli pid Vladoiu Lytvy, Zakhoplennia Ïkh Pol'shcheiu*. Kiev: Gosudarstennoe Izdatel'stvo Politicheskoi Literatury pri SNK USSR.
Huslystyi, K. 1942a. *Danylo Halyts'kyi*. Saratov: Ukrvydav pry TsK KPbU.
Huslystyi, K. 1942b. *Petro Konashevych-Sagaidachnyi*. Saratov: Ukrvydav pry TsK KPbU
Huslystyi, K. 1942c. Borot'ba ukraïns'koho narodu proty nimets'kykh zaharbnykiv u XIII-XV st.st. In *Borot'ba ukraïns'koho narodu proty nimets'kykh zaharbnykiv: Zbirka Stattei*, 5–11. Ufa: Vydannia Akademiï Nauk URSR.
Huslystyi, K. 1943. Velikii syn ukrainskogo naroda Bogdan Khmel'nitskii. *Sputnik Agitatora*, no. 22: 40–42.
Huslystyi, K.G. 1945. *Heroïchne mynule Kyeva: stenohrama publichnoï lektsiï kandydata istorychnykh nauk K.H.Huslystogo, shcho prochytana 29 Bereznia 1945 roku v zali Derzh. Filarmoniï v Kyevi*. Kiev: Lektsiine biuro upravlinnia v spravakh vyshchoï shkoly pry RNK URSR.
Huslystyi, K.G., Slavin, L., and Iastrebov, F.A. 1942. *Narys istoriï Ukraïny*. Ufa: Vyd-vo AN URSR.
Iakovlev, A.I. 1943. *Khlopstvo i kholopy v Moskovskom gosudarstve XVII v. Po arkhivnym dokumentam Kholop'ego i Posol'skogo prikazov, Oruzheinoi palaty i Razriada. Tom 1*. Moscow: Akademiia nauk SSSR.
Iakunin A., and V. Shakhmatov. 1940. Vosstaniia v Kazakhstane v 50 godakh XIX v. *Izvestiia KazFAN: seriia istoricheskaia* 1: 63–94.
Iampol'skii, Z.I. 1941. *Vosstanie Babaka, kratkii ocherk*. Baku: Izdatel'stvo AzFAN.
Iaroslavskii, E. 1939. Nevypolnennye zadachi istoricheskogo fronta. *Istorik-marksist*, no. 4: 3–11.
Iaroslavskii, E. 1941. Bor'ba slavianskikh narodov protiv germanskogo fashizma. *Bol'shevik*, no. 13: 10–22.
Iastrebov, F.O. 1941. *Kyïvs'ka Rus'*. Kiev: Politvydav pry TsK KP(b)U.

Iavors'kyi, M. 1926. *Korotka istoriia Ukraïny*. Kharkiv. Derzhavne vydavnytstvo Ukraïny.
Iavors'kyi, M. 1927. *Narysy z istoriï revoliutsiinoï borot'by na Ukraïni*. Vol. 1. Kharkiv: n.a.
Iavors'kyi, M. 1928. *Istoriia Ukraïny*. Kharkiv: Derzhavne vydavnytstvo Ukraïny.
Ibragimov, S.D. 1975. *General Ali Aga Shikhlinskii (Zhizn' I deiatel'nost')*. Baku: Azgosizdat.
Ibrahimbeili, K.M. 1977. *Krakh 'Edelweisa' i Blizhnyi Vostok*. Moscow: Nauka.
İbrahimov, Z. 1942. *Nemes aqressiyasına qarşı rus xalqının qəhrəman mübarizəsi tarixindən*. Baku: Azərnəşr.
İbrahimov, Z. 1944. *Babək*. Baku: Azərnəşr.
İbrahimov, Z. 1944. *Böyük döstluq*, Baku: Azərnəşr.
Ilichev, L. 1938. K Voprosu o roli lichnosti v istorii' G.V. Plekhanova. *Bolshevik*, no. 13: 87–96.
Illeritskii, V.E. and Kudriavtsev, I.A. 1971. *Istoriografiia istorii SSSR*. Moscow: Vysshaia shkola.
Ilnytzkyj, O.S. 2003. Modeling Culture in the Empire: Ukrainian Modernism and the Death of the All-Russian Idea. In *Culture, Nation and Identity: The Ukrainian-Russian Encounter (1600–1945)*, ed. A. Kappeler, Z.E. Kohut, F. Sysyn, and M. von Hagen, 298–324. Toronto: CIUSP.
Ilovaiskii, D.I. 1876–1899. *Istoriia Rossii*ю 4 vols. Moscow: Tip. Gracheva.
Iovchuk, M. 1941. Velikie traditsii russkogo patriotizma. *Bol'shevik*, no. 11–13: 42–48.
Isakov, P. 1937. O Natsional'noi konsolidatsii Kazakhskogo naroda. *Bol'shevik Kazakhstana*, no. 5: 68–78.
Isatai i Makhambet. 1943. *Kazakhstanskaia Pravda*. 20 October 20.
Ismailov, Eldar. 2003. *Vlast' i Narod, Poslevoennyi Stalinizm v Azerbaidzhane*. Baku: Adil'ogly.
*Istoriia Azerbaidzhana kratkii ocherk*. 1941. Baku: Izdatel'stvo AzFAN.
*Istoriia Azerbaidzhana: chast' 1: uchebnoe posobie dlia srednikh shkol*. 1946. Baku: Izdatel'stvo AN Azerbaidzhanskoi SSR.
*Istoriia Velikoi Otechestvennoi voiny Sovietskogo Soiuza 1941–1945*. 1961. Vol. 2. Moscow: Voennoe izdatel'stvo.
Iudin, P. 1939. Marksistkoe uchenie o roli lichnosti v istorii. *Pod znamenem marksizma*, no. 5.
Iudin, P. 1941a. Germanskii fashizm - liutnyi vrag slavianskikh narodov v bor'be protiv gitlerizma. *Bol'shevik*, no. 15: 35–41.
Iudin, P. 1941b. Razdavit' fashistskuiu gadinu!, *Bol'shevik*, no. 11–12: 22–31.
Iurkova, O.V. 2001. *Dokumenty pro stvorennia i pershi roky diial'nosti Instytutu istoriï Ukraïny AN URSR*. Kiev: Instytut istoriï Ukraïny.
Iusian, M.G. 1943. *David-Bek*. Erivan: n.a.
Iusova, N. 2006. Stanovlennia radians'koï etnohenetyky (v svitli hlotohonichnoï teoriï M. Marra. *Problemy istoriï Ukraïny: fakty, sudzhennia, poshunky*, no. 15: 168–189. Kiev: Instytut istoriï Ukraïny NAN.
Iusova, N. 2007. Persha narada z pytan' etnogenezu I stvorennia spetsial'noï komisiï z problematyky pokhodzhennia narodiv u konteksti aktualizatsiï etnogenetychnykh doslidzhen' v SRSR (kinets' 1930-kh rr.). *Problemy istoriï Ukraïny: fakty, sudzhennia, poshuky*, no. 16: 356–369.
Iusova, N.M. 2000. Geneza kontseptu 'davn'orus'ka narodnist'' u radians'kii istorychnii nautsi. *Ukraïns'kyi istorychnyi zhurnal*, no. 6: 35–64.

Iusova, N. 2005. *Henezys kontseptsii davn'orus'koï narodnosti v istorychnii nautsi srsr (1930-ti - persha polovyna 1940-kh rr.).* Vinnytsa: Konsol'.

Ivanov, L. 1936. *Morskoe sopernichestvo imerialisticheskikh derzhav.* Moscow: Sotsekgiz.

Ivanov, M.C. 1939. *Babidskie Vosstaniia v Irane (1848–1852).* Moscow and Leningrad: Izdatel'stvo Akademii Nauk SSSR.

Ivlev I.A. and A.F. Iudenkov. 1981. *Oruzhiem kontrpropagandy: sovetskaia propaganda sredi naseleniia okkupirovannoi territorii sssr. 1941–1944gg.* Moscow: Mysl'.

Iz Rezoliutsii Politsekretariata IKKI o Polozhenii v Pol'she i Zadachakh Kompartii Pol'shi. 1998. In *Komintern i Idea Mirovoi Revoliutsii*, 765–768. Moscow: Nauka

Jackson Jr, G.D. 1960. *Comintern and Peasant in Eastern Europe 1919–1930.* New York and London: Columbia University.

Jordanes. 1960. *The Gothic History of Jordanes [De Origine Actibusque Getarum or Getica]*, intro by C.C. Mierow. Cambridge: Speculum Historiale.

Jowitt, K. 1993. *New World Disorder: The Leninist Extinction.* Berkeley: University of California Press.

Justi, F. 1879. *Geschichte des alten* Persiens. Berlin: G. Grote.

K izucheniiu istorii: Sbornik. 1937. Moscow: Partizdat.

Kabanbai Kozhakuly. 2005. *Kazakhstan: Natsional 'naia entsiklopediia* 3. Almaty: Kazak entsiklopediiasy.

Kabulov, I. 1936. Za Marksistskuiu istoricheskuiu nauku. *Bol'shevik Kazakhstana*, no. 3: 47–52.

Kabulov. 1934. Marksistsko-leninstuiu kritika kazakskoi literatury. *Kazakhstanskaia Pravda.* August 9.

Kadyrbaev, A.S. 1993. *Ocherki istorii srednevekovykh Uigurov, Dzhalairov, Naimanov i Kireitov.* Almaty: Rauan.

Kagarov, E. 1937. *Perezhitki pervobytnogo kommunizma v obshchestvennom stroe drevnikh grekov i nemtsev.* Leningrad and Moscow: Izd-vo Nauk Akademii nauk SSSR.

Kaidanov, I. 1832. *Nachertanie istorii gosudarstva Rossiiskago.* St. Petersburg: tip. Med. dep. M-va vn.del.

Kalinin, M. 1941. Otechestvennaia voina sovetskogo naroda protiv nemetskikh zakhvatchikov. *Bol'shevik*, no. 24: 7–22.

Kalinin, M. 1943a. Edinaia boevaia sem'ia. *Sputnik agitator*, no. 15–16: 7–10.

Kalinin, M. 1943b. O partiino-massovoi rabote. Moscow: Gozpolitizdat.

Kamenetsky, I. 1956. *Hitler's Occupation of Ukraine (1941–44): A Study of Totalitarian Imperialism.* Milvaukee, WI: The Marquette University Press.

Kammari, M. 1940. O proletarskom internatsionalizme i sovetskom patriotizme. *Bol'shevik*, no. 15–16: 28–42.

Kamp, M. 2006. *The New Woman in Uzbekistan: Islam, Modernity, and Unveiling under Communism.* Seattle, WA: University of Washington Press.

Kandiyoti, D. 2002. Post-Colonialism Compared: Potentials and Limitations in the Middle East and Central Asia. *International Journal of Middle East Studies* 34 (2): 279–297.

Kandiyoti, D. 2006. The Politics of Gender and the Soviet Paradox: Neither Colonized, nor Modern. *Central Asian Survey* 26 (4): 601–623.

Kapaeva, A.T. 2004. *Kul'tura i politika (Gosudarstennaia Politika v oblastikul'tury v Kazakhstanevovtoroipolovine 1940-kh–1991gg.).* Almaty: Atamura.

Kaplan, V. 2009. The Vicissitudes of Socialism in Russian History Textbooks. *History and Memory* 21 (2), 83–109.

Kappeler, A. 2009. From an Ethnonational to a Multiethnic to a Transnational Ukrainian History. In *A Laboratory of Transnational History: Ukraine and Recent Ukrainian Historiography*, ed. G. Kasianov and P. Ther, 51–80. Budapest: Central European University Press.

Karaganda gotovitsia k vyboram. (1937) *Pravda*, September 26.

Karamzin, N.M. 1833–1835. *Istoriia gosudarstva Rossiiskago*, 12 vols. St Petersburg: V Tip. vdovy Pliushar s synom.

Karasai Batyr. 2004. *Kazakhstan: Natsional 'naia entsiklopediia*. Vol. 3. Almaty: Kazak entsiklopediiasy.

Karpinskii, V. 1943. V chem velikaia sila sovetskogo patriotizma. *Sputnik agitator*, no. 5: 5–10.

Karpovich, M. 1943. Klyuchevski and Recent Trends in Russian Historiography. *Slavonic and East European Review* 2, no. 2: 31–39.

Kas'ianov, H.V. and Danylenko, V.M. 1991. *Stalinizm i ukraïns'ka intelihentsiia (20–30-i roky)*. Kiev: Naukova Dumka.

Kasenov, E.V. 2006. Vek kazakhsko-dzhungarskogo protivostoianiia. Pavlodar: Eko.

Kashani-Sabet, F. 1999. *Frontier Fictions, Shaping the Iranian Nation, 1804–1946*. Princeton and Chichester: Princeton University Press.

Kasianov, G. 2009. 'Nationalized' History: Past Continuous, Present Perfect, Future.... In *A Laboratory of Transnational History: Ukraine and Recent Ukrainian Historiography*, ed. G. Kasianov and P. Ther, 7–23. Budapest: Central European University Press.

Katouzian, H. 1979. Nationalist Trends in Iran, 1921–1926. *International Journal of Middle East Studies* 10, no. 4: 533–551.

Katouzian, H. 2009. *The Persians Ancient, Mediaeval and Modern Iran*. New Haven: Yale University Press.

Kazachenko, A. 1937. Zamechatel'nyi istoricheskii urok. *Istoricheskii zhurnal*, no. 3–4.

Kazak khalkynyng zhauyngerlik desturi. 1941. *Sotsialistik Kazakstan*. October 12.

Kazakhsko-Zhongarskie voiny. 2004. *Kazakhstan: Natsional 'naia entsiklopediia*. Vol. 3. Almaty: Kazak entsiklopediiasy.

*Kazakhstan v pervyi god Otechestvennoi voiny protiv nemetsko-fashistskikh zakhvatchikov: Sbornik dokumentov*, 1943. Almaty: KazOGIZ.

Kazakstanda. 1943. *Otandy Korghauda*. October 20.

Kazaktar. 1942. *Otandy Korghauda*. November 18.

Kazem-Bek, Aleksandr. 1865. *Bab i Babidy: religiozno-politicheskiia smuty v Persii v 1844–1852 godakh*. St. Petersburg: V Tip V.N. Maikova.

Kaziev M. (M. Qazıyev). 1942b. *Azərbaycanda vətəndaş müharibəsi qəhrəmanları*. Baku: Azərnəşr.

Kaziev, M. 1942a. *Iz istorii bor'by azerbaidzhanskogo naroda protiv inozemnykh zakhvatchikov*. Baku: Azerneshr.

Keddie, N.R. 1980. Religion and Irreligion in Early Iranian Nationalism. In *Iran Religion, Politics and Society: Collected Essays*, ed. N.R. Keddie, 13–52. London: Frank Class.

Keep, J., ed. 1964. *Contemporary History in the Soviet Mirror*. London: Allen and Unwin.

Kenesary Kasymov. 1943. *Kazakhstanskaia Pravda*. October 26.

Kentii, A. 2008. *Zbroinyi chyn Ukraïns'kykh natsionalistiv 1920–1956*. Vol. 2. Kiev: Derzhavnyi komitet arkhiviv Ukraïny.

Kenzhebaev, B. 1943. Povest' o kazakhskoi muzyke. *Kazakhstanskaia Pravda*. November 13.

Kerimova, T. 2005. *Iz Istorii Natsional'noi Akademii Nauk Azerbaidzhana*. Baku: Taxsil.

## 194  Bibliography

Khalid, A. 1999. The Emergence of a Modern Central Asian Historical Consciousness. In *Historiography of Imperial Russia: The Profession and Writing History in a Multinational State*, ed. T. Sanders, 433–452. London and New York: M.E. Sharpe.

Khalid, A. 2006. Backwardness and the Quest for Civilization: Early Soviet Central Asia in Comparative Perspective. *Slavic Review* 65 (2): 231–251.

Khanlari, P.N. 1967. *Tarikh-e Iran. For the 6th Grade*. Tehran: Sherkat Sahabi Tab' va Nashr Ketab-hay Darsi Iran.

Khaustov, V.N. 1997. Iz predystorii massovykh repressii protiv poliakov Seredina 1930-kh gg. In *Repressii protiv poliakov i pol'skikh grazhdan*, ed. L.S. Eremina, 10–21. Moscow: Zven'ia.

Khersonets, I.M. 1986. At the Turning Point. In *Political Thought of the Ukrainian Underground 1943–1951*, ed. P.J. Potichnyj and Y. Shtendera, 229–242. Edmonton: CIUS.

Khineyko, I. (2005) Fostering National Identity in Ukraine: Regional Differences in the Attitude to National Symbols. *Journal of Ukranian Studies* 30, no. 2: 85–104.

Khlevniuk, O. (2000) The Reasons for the 'Great Terror': the Foreign-Political Aspect. In *Russia in the Age of Wars 1914–1945*, ed. S. Pons and A. Romano, 159–169, Milan: Feltrinelli.

Khlevnyuk, O. (1995) The Objectives of the Great Terror, 1937–1938. In *Soviet History, 1917–1953*, ed. J. Cooper, M. Perrie, and E.A. Rees, 158–176, London: Macmillan.

Khlevov, A.A. (1997) *Normanskaia problema v otechestvennoi istoricheskoi nauke*, St. Petersburg: Izdatel'stvo s.-Petersburgskogo universiteta.

Khronika. (1937) *Istorik-marksist*, no. 5: 266.

Khronika. (1939) *Istorik-Marksist*, no. 3: 213.

Khrushchev, N. 1944. Osvobozhdenie ukrainkikh zemel' ot nemetskikh zakhvatchikov i ocherednye zadachi vosstanovleniia narodnogo khoziaistva Sovetskoi Ukrainy: Doklad Predsedatelia Soveta Narodnykh Komissarov Ukrainskoi SSR tov. N.S. Khrushcheva na VI sessii Verkhovnogo Soveta USSR 1 marta 1944 goda v gorode Kieve. *Bol'shevik*, no. 6: 7–35.

Khrushchev, N. 2004. *Memoirs of Nikita Khrushchev: Commissar (1918–1945)*. Vol. 1. Philadelphia: Pennsylvania State University.

Khuluflu, V. 1930. *Seljuq Dövletinin Daxili Quruluşuna Dair*. Baku: n.a.

Kian, Azadeh and Riaux, Gilles. 2009. Crafting Iranian Nationalism: Intersectionality of Aryanism, Westernizm and Islamism. In *Nations and their Histories: Constructions and Representations*, ed. S. Carvalho and F. Gemenne, 189–203. London: Palgrave Macmillan.

Kikodze, G. 1945. *Iraklii Vtoroi: monografiia*. Tbilisi: Zaria Vostoka.

Kino, T. 1941. *Sotsialistik Kazakstan*. December 3.

Kirschbaum, J.M. 1962. Pavel Josef Šafárik and His Contribution to Slavic Studies. *Slavistica*, no. 43: 7, 19. Winnipeg.

Kirschenbaum, L.A. 2006. *The Legacy of the Siege of Leningrad, 1941–1995: Myth, Memories, and Monuments*. Cambridge: Cambridge University Press.

Klier, J. and Lambroza, S., eds. 1992. *Pogroms: Anti-Jewish Violence in Modern Jewish History*. Cambridge: Cambridge University Press.

Knorin V., ed. 1934. *Kratkaia istoriia VKP(b)*. Moscow: Partiinoe izdatel'stvo.

Knorin, V. 1933. Fashizm, Sotsial-demokratiia, kommunisty. *Bol'shevik*, no. 24: 25–45.

Kobylyanskiy, I. 2003. Memories of War, Part 2: On the railroads, the battle on the outskirts of Vishnyovy hamlet, mysterious are the ways of the Lord, fear, and about blocking detachments. *Journal of Slavic Military Studies* 16 (4): 147–156.

Kohl, P.L. 1998. Nationaism and Archaeology: On the Constructions of Nations and the Reconstructions of the Remote Past. *Annual Review of Anthropology* 27: 223–246.
Kohl P.L. and Fawcett C., eds. 1995. *Nationalism, Politics and the Practice of Archaeology.* Cambridge: Cambridge University Press.
Kohl, P.L., Kozelsky, M., and Ben-Yehuda, N., eds. 2007. *Selective Remembrance, Archaeology in the Construction, Commemoration, and Consecration of National Pasts.* Chicago: University of Chicago Press.
Kohut, Z.E. 1998. The image of Jews in Ukraine's Intellectual Tradition: The Role of 'Istoriia Rusov'. *Harvard Ukrainian Studies* 22: 343–358.
Kohut, Z.E. 1999. The development of a Ukrainian National Historiography in Imperial Russia. In *Historiography of Imperial Russia: The Profession and Writing History in a Multinational State*, ed. T. Sanders, 453–478. London, New York: M.E. Sharpe.
Kolonitskii, B. 2009. Russian Historiography of the 1917 Revolution New Challenges to Old Paradigms? *History and Memory* 21 (2): 34–59.
Komkov, G.D. 1983. *Na ideologicheskom fronte Velikoi otechestvennoi... .* Moscow: Nauka.
*Kommunisticheskii International: Kratkii Istoricheskii Ocherk.* 1969. Moscow: Izdatel'stvo Politicheskoi Literatury.
*Komu my idem pomoch'.* 1939. Moscow: Voenizdat.
Kongress edinstva mirovgo rabochego klassa. 1935. *Bol'shevik*, no. 16: 1–9.
Koniskii, G [Konys'kyi, H]. 1846. *Istoriia Rusov ili Maloi Rosii.* Moscow: Universitetskaia tipografiia.
Konshin, N. 2007. *Trudy po kazakhskoi etnografii.* Astana: Altyn kitap.
Konstantinov, F. 1938. O Marksistkom ponimanii roli lichnosti v istorii. *Bolshevik*, no. 10–11: 29–51.
Konstantinov, F. 1939. Rol idei v obshchestvennom razvitii. *Pod znamenem marksizma*, no. 10.
Korniichuk, O. 1988. *Encyclopaedia of Ukraine.* Vol. 2, 611–612. Toronto: University of Toronto Press.
Korobkov, N. 1944. 'Russkie voenno-morskie traditisii', *Bol'shevik*, no. 5: 50–64.
Korolev, St. 1990. Pravoslavie I Velikaka otechestvennaia voina v 1941–1945 godakh. *Molodaia Gvardiia* 5: 204–208.
Kossina, G. 1932. *Germanische Kultur im ersten Jahrhundert nach Christus.* Vol. 1. Leibzig: Ferlag von Curt Kabitzsch.
Kossinna, G. 1919. *Das Weichselland, ein uralter Heimatboden der Germanen.* Danzig: Kafemann.
Kostiuk, H. 1960. *Stalinist Rule in the Ukraine: A Study of the Decade of Mass Terror.* London: Stevens & Sons.
Kotkin, S. 2001. Modern Times: The Soviet Union and the Interwar Conjuncture. *Kritika* 2 (1): 111–164.
Kovalevskii, P.I. 1914. Kavkaz. Narody Kavkaza 1. St. Petersburg: tip. M.I. Akinfieva
Kozybaev, I.M. 1992. Istoricheskaia nauka Kazakhstana (40–80e gody XX veka). Almaty: KazakUniversiteti
Kozybaev, M.K. 1991. *Istoriia i sovremennost'.* Almaty: Gylym.
Kozybaev, M.K. 2006 [1998]. Kazakhskie istochniki po istorii XVIII-nachala XX vv. In *Problemy Metodologii, Istoriografii i istochnikoveddeniia istorii Kazakhstana: izbrannye Trudy*, ed. M.K. Kozybaev, 120–145. Almaty: Ghylym.
Krainov, P. 1939. Dni radosti i schast'ia osvobozhdennykh narodov. *Sputnik agitator*, no. 21: 31–35.

## Bibliography

Krasovskii, M.I. 2007. *Obraz zhizni kazakhov stepnykh okrugov*. Astana: Altyn kitab.
*Kratkii kurs istorii VKP(b)(1938)*. 1938. Moscow: Ogiz.
*Kratkii otchet o rabote Akademii v 1935*. 1936. Leningrad: Izd. Oblono.
Krawchenko, B. 1990. National Memory in Ukraine: The Role of the Blue and Yellow Flag. *Journal of Ukrainian Studies* 15, no. 1: 2–21.
Krivosheev, G.F. 1997. *Soviet Casualties and Combat Losses in the Twentieth Century*. London: Greenhill Books.
Krivosheev, G.F., ed. 2009. *Velikaia otechestvennaia bez grifa sekretnosti: Kniga poter'*. Moscow: Veche.
Kroviakov, N. 1941. *Shamil': ocherk iz istorii bor'by narodov Kavkaza za nezavisimost'*. Groznyi: Chechinggosizdat.
Krüger, P. 2003. The European East and Weimar Germany. In *Germany and the European East in the Twentieth Century*, ed. E. Mühle, 7–28. Oxford and New York: Berg.
Kubijovyč, V., and Markus, V. 1988. Jews. *Encyclopaedia of Ukraine* 2: 385–393. Toronto: University of Toronto Press.
Kuchabsky, V. 2009. *Western Ukraine in Conflict with Poland and Bolshevism, 1918–1923*. Edmonton, Toronto: CIUSP.
Kunik, A. 1903. *Izvestiia al-Bekri i drugikh avtorov o Rusi i slavianakh razyskaniia A. Kunika*. St. Petersburg: Tipografiia Imperatorskoi Akademii nauk.
Kunik, A. 1878. O vremeni, v kotorom zhil izrail'tianin Ibragim ibn-Iakub. In *Izvestiia al-Bekri i drugikh avtorov o Rusi i slavianakh*, ed. V.R. Rozen, 65–117. St. Petersburg: Tip. Imp. akademīi nauk.
Kunik, E. 1844. *Die Berufung der Schwedischen Rodsen durch die Finnen und Slawen: eine Vorarbeit zur Entstehungsgeschichte des Russischen States*. 2 vol. St. Petersburg: Druckerei der kaiserlichen academie der w-issenschaften.
Kurmangali K.S., ed. 2001. *Obychai i obriady kazakhov v proshlom i nastoiashchem*. Almaty: Ghylym.
Kushner, P. 1927. Nuzhno li izuchat obshchestvennye formy. *Istorik-Marksist*, no. 6: 206–214.
Kuusinen, O. 1933. Fashizm, opasnost' voiny i zadachi kommunisticheskikh partii: doklad na XIII plenume IKKI. *Bol'shevik*, no. 24: 11–24.
Kuusinen, O. 1934a. Fashizm, opasnost' voiny i zadachi kommunisticheskih partii. *Bol'shevik*, no. 2: 42–61.
Kuusinen, O. 1934b. Fashizm, opasnos't voiny i zadachi kompartii (okonchanie). Bol'shevik, no. 3–4: 81–86.
Kuusinen, O. 1935. Molodezh' i bor'ba protiv fashizma i boennoi opasnosti. *Bol'shevik*, no. 16: 10–22.
Kuzmin, N.F. 1954. *Kommunisticheskaia partiia-vdokhnovitel i organizator borby ukrainskogo naroda za sozdanie i ukreplenie ukrainskogo sovetskogo gosudarstva*. Moscow: Znanie.
Kyryliuk, E. 1942. *Ivan Franko*. Saratov: Ukrvydav pry TsK KPbU.
L'vova, A. 1938. Pol'skii fashizm na sluzhbe u Gitlera. *Sputnik Agitatora*, no. 8: 31–32.
Landau, J.M. 1995. *PanTurkism from Irredentism to Cooperation*. London: Hurst & Company.
Lavrent'ev, V. 1930. *Kapitalizm v Turkestane, burzhuaznaia kolonizatsiia Srednei Azii*. Leningrad: Izdatel'stvo Kommunisticheskoi Akademii.
Lebedev, V., Bushuev, S., and Genkina, E. 1941. Tsennoe posobie po istorii SSSR. *Bol'shevik*, no. 2: 85–96.

Bibliography 197

Lenczowski, G. 1949. *Russia and the West in Iran, 1918–1948: A Study in Big Power Rivalry.* Ithaca, NY: Cornell University Press.

*Lenins'ka teoretychna spadshchyna v ukraïns'kii radians'kii istoriografii.* 1969. Kiev: Naukova Dumka.

Lənkəranlı, Z. [Iampol'skii]. 1943a. *Babək.* Baku: EAAzF.

Lənkəranlı, Z. [Iampol'skii]. 1943b. *Azərbaycanlıların Roma işğalçılarına qarşı mübarizəsi.* Baku: EAAzF.

Leonidov, N. 1941. Kogda i kak russkii narod bil germanskikh zakhvatchikov. *Bol'shevik*, no. 11–12: 84–96.

Leont'ev A. and N. Mikhailov, eds. 1938. *RSFSR.* Moscow: Gosudarstvennoe politicheskoi literatury.

Levi, G. 1936. *Germanskie monopolii.* Moscow: Sotsekgiz.

Levin, Ş. 1941. *Brusilov hücumu*, ed. Orucov. Baku: EAAzF.

Levine, I.D. 2004. [1919]. Armenia Resurrected. *The International Journal of Kurdish Studies* 18, no. 1/2: 81–89.

Lewis, Bernard. 2002. *The Emergence of Modern Turkey.* New York and Oxford: Oxford University Press.

Lewshin, A. 2007. *Opisanie ord i stepei kazakhov.* Astana: Altyn kitap.

Lichnye Arkhivnye Fondy v Gosudarstvennykh Khranilishchakh SSSR. www.rusarchives.ru/guide/lf_ussr/zem_zjak.shtml (accessed November 6, 2009).

Lieven, D. 1995. The Russian Empire and the Soviet Union as Imperial Polities. *Journal of Contemporary History* 30, no. 4: 607–635.

Lieven, D. 2003. *Empire: The Russian Empire and Its Rivals.* London: Pimlico.

Lih, T.L., Naumov, O.V., and Khlevkiuk, O.V. 1995. *Stalin's Letters to Molotov 1925–1936.* New Haven and London: Yale University Press.

Likhomanov, M.I. 1974. Razmeshchenie i ispol'zovanie evakuirovannogo naseleniia v vostochnykh raionakh. In *Sovetskii tyl v Velikoi Otechestvennoi Voine, Trudovoi podvig naroda*, ed. P.N. Pospelov, 181–191. Vol. 2. Moscow: Mysl'.

Lindner, R. 1999. Forum: New directions in Belarusian studies besieged past: National and court historians of Lukashenka's Belarus. *Nationalities Papers: The Journal of Nationalism and Ethnicity* 27 (4): 631–647.

Lipets, R. 1984. *Obrazy batyra i ego konia v tiurko-mongol'skom epose.* Moscow: Nauka.

Literatura germanskikh fashistov pered prikhodom ikh k vlasti. 1933. *Bol'shevik* 14: 77–93.

*Litopys UPA Nova seriia: Borot'ba proty UPA i natsionalistichnoho pidpillia: direktyvni dokumenty TsK Kompartiï Ukraïny 1943–1959.* 2001. Vol. 3.

Litvinov. M. 1938. *Protiv agressii.* Moscow: Gospolitizdat.

Liubimov, N.N. 1938. *Finansy fashistskikh gosudarstv.* Gosfinizdat.

Liulevicius, V.G. 2009. *The German Myth of the East: 1800 to the Present.* Oxford: Oxford University Press.

Logutov, N.A. 2007. Ocherk rodovogo byta kazakhov i razpredelenie osnovnykh kazakhskikh rodov na teritorii byv. Semipalatinskoi gubernii. In *Trudy Semipalatinskogo kraevedov kontsa XIX – nachala XX v*, 171–202. Astana: Altyn kitap.

Los', F. 1942. Uchast' ukraïntsiv u borot'bi Rosiï proty Prusiï za Semyrichnï viiny. In *Borot'ba ukraïns'koho narodu proty nimets'kykh zaharbnykiv: Zbirka Stattei*, 12–8. Ufa: Vydannia Akademiï Nauk URSR.

Lozytskyi, V.C. 2005. *Politbiuro TsK Kompartiï Ukraïny: istoriia, osoby, stosunky (1918–1991).* Kiev: Heneza.

Luckyj, G.S.N. 1956. *Literary Politics in the Soviet Ukraine, 1917–1934*. New York: Columbia University Press.

Lypyns'kyi, V. 1954 [1920]. *Ukraïna na Perelomi 1657–1659*. New York: Bulava.

Lystivky partiinoho pidpillia i partyzanskykh zahoniv Ukraïny u roky Velikoi Vitchyznianoi viiny. 1969. Kiev: n.a.

Lytvyn, V.M. *et al.* 2007. *Ukraïna: politychna istoriia XX-pochatok XXI st.* Kiev: Parlaments'ke vydavnytstvo.

Mace, J.E. 1983. *Communism and the Dilemmas of National Liberation: National Communism in Soviet Ukraine, 1919–1933*. Cambridge, MA: Harvard Ukrainian Research Institute.

Mackiewicz, S. 1944. *Colonel Beck and His Policy*. London: Eyre and Spottiswoode.

Mad'iar, L. 1933. Fashizm i opasnost' voiny. *Bol'shevik*, no. 9: 20–32.

Magocsi, P.R. 1996. *A History of Ukraine*. Toronto: University of Toronto Press.

Magomedov, R. 1939. *Bor'ba gortsev za nezavisimost' pod rukovodstvom Shamilia*. Makhachkala: Daggiz.

Magomedov, R. 1940a. *Shamil'*. Makhachkala: Dagestanskoe gosudarstvennoe izdatel'stvo.

Magomedov, R. 1940b. *Dagestan v period tsarskogo zavoevaniia*. Makhachkala: Dagestanskoe gosudarstvennoe izdatel'stvo.

Magomedov, R. 1940c. *Vosstanie gortsev Dagestana v 1877g*. Makhachkala: Dagestanskoe gosudarstvennoe izdatel'stvo.

Maksymovych, M.A. 1876. *Sobranie sochinenii: otdel' istoricheskii*. Vol. 1. Kiev: n.a.

Mamedova, N.M. *et al.* 2010. Sovetskii Soiuz i Iran (1933–1945). In *SSSR i Strany Vostoka Nakanune i v Gody Vtoroi Mirovoi Voiny*, ed. V.V. Naumkin. Moscow: Institut vostokovedeniia RAN.

Mammadkhanly Anvar. 1382 [2003–2004]. Babak. Tehran: Andishe.

Mamulia, G.G. 2011. *Gruzinskii legion vermakhta*. Moscow: Veche.

Manuil'skii, D. 1935a. Itogi VII kongressa Kommunistichskogo Internatsionala. *Bol'shevik*, no. 18: 27–41.

Manuil'skii, D. 1935b. Itogi VII kongressa Kommunisticheskogo Internatsionala. *Bol'shevik*, no. 19: 7–24.

Manuil'skii, D. 1937. O kapitalisticheskom okruzhenii SSSR. *Bol'shevik*, no. 9: 25–34.

Manuil'skii, D.Z. 1942. *Sudba Nashei Pobedy v Vashikh Rukakh, Tovarishchi Krasnoarmeitsy i Komandiry*. N.a.

Manuil'skii, D.Z. 1943. *Gitlerovskaia Tiurma Narodov*. Moscow: OGIZ, Gospolitizdat.

Manuil'skii, D. 1944. Dukh velikogo Lenina vdokhnovlaet nas v bor'be s nemetsko-fashistskimi zakhvatchikami. *Bol'shevik*, no. 1: 20–31.

Manuil's'kyi, D.Z. 1944. *Narod-Geroi, Narod-Voin*. Kiev: Ukraïns'ke derzhavne vydavnitstvo.

Manuïl's'kyi, D. 1946. *Ukraïns'ko-nimets'ki natsionalisty na sluzhby u fashists'koï nimechchyny: dopovid' 6-go sichnia 1945 roku na naradi uchyteliv zakhidnykh oblastei Ukraïny*. Ukraïns'ke derzhavne vydavnitstvo.

Mar'iamov, G.B. 1992. *Kremlevskii tsenzor: Stalin smotrit kino*. Moscow: Konfiderazia souza kinematogrofistov 'Kinozentr'.

Marashi, A. 2008. *Nationalizing Iran, Culture, Power, and the State, 1870–1940*. Seattle: University of Washington Press.

Marchenko M. 1938c. Istorychnyi urok pol's'kii shliakhti. *Komunist*. June 28.

Marchenko, M. 1938a. Vyzvol'na viina ukraïns'koho narodu v 1648–1654 rr. *Komsomol's'kyi propahandyst*, no. 10.

Marchenko, M. 1938b. Pol's'ki pany – odvichni vorogy Lytvy. *Komunist.* April 5.
Marchenko, M. 1939a. Z geroïchnoho mynuloho Ukraïny: Ivan Bohun. *Proletars'ka Pravda.* January 28.
Marchenko, M. 1939b. Zapadnaia Ukraina – zemlia ukrainskikh rabochikh i krest'ian. *Krasnaia Armiia.* September 18.
Marchenko, M. 1940. Do pytannia rozvytku feodal'nykh vidnosyn na Ukraïni v rr. 1650–1660. *Zapysky istorychnogo ta filologichnogo fakul'tetiv: L'vivs'kyi derzhavnyi universytet im. I. Franka* 1: 25–39.
Marchenko, M. 1941. *Borot'ba Rosiïi Pol'shchi za Ukraïny (1654–1664 rr.).* Kiev: Vydavnytstvo akademiï nauk URSR.
Markwick, R.D. 2001. *Rewriting History in Soviet Russia: The Politics of Revisionist Historiography, 1956–1974.* Basingstoke: Palgrave.
Marr, N. 1933. Izbrannye raboty. 5 vols. Leningrad: Gosudarstvennoe sotsial'no-ėkonomicheskoe izdatel'stvo.
Marr, N.I., ed. 1934. *Karl Marks i problemy istorii dokapitalisticheskikh formatsii: sbornik k piatidesiatiletniiu so dnia smerti Karla Marksa.* Moscow and Leningrad: Gos. soz-econom. Izdat-vo.
Martin, T. 1998. The Origins of Soviet Ethnic Cleansing. *The Journal of Modern History* 70, no. 4: 813–861.
Martin, T. 2000. Modernization or neo-traditionalism? Ascribed Nationality and Soviet Primordialism. In *Stalinism: New Directions*, ed. S. Fitzpatrick, 348–367. London: Routledge.
Martin, T. 2001. *An Affirmative Action Empire: Nations and Nationalisms in the Soviet Union, 1923–1939.* Ithaca, NY: Cornell University Press.
Marx, K. 1986. 'Revelations of the Diplomatic History of the 18th Century'. In K. Marx and F. Engels, *Collected Works*, 25–96. London: Lawrence & Wishart.
Masanov, E.A. 2007a. *Ocherk istorii etnograficheskogo izucheniia kazakhskogo naroda v SSSR.* Astana: Altyn kitap.
Masanov, N.E. 2007b. *Mifologizatsiia problem etnogeneza kazakhskogo naroda i kazakhskoi nomadnoi kul'tury. In Nauchnoe znanie*, ed. Masanov, Abylkhozhin, and Erofeeva, 52–131.
Materialy fevral'sko-martovskogo (1937g.) Plenuma TsK VKP(b). 1994. *Voprosy Istorii*, no. 1: 26.
*Materialy po istorii Kazakhskoi SSR (1785–1828 gg.).* 1940. Moscow and Leningrad: AN SSSR.
Matorin, N.M., ed. 1932. *Pervobytnoe obshchestvo: sbornik statei.* Moscow: Zhurn.
Matthee, Rudi. 1993. Transforming Dangerous Nomads into Useful Artisans, Technicians, Agriculturists: Education in the Reza Shah Period. *Iranian Studies* 26, no. 3–4: 313–336.
Mavrodin, V.V. 1944. *Bor'ba russkogo naroda za Nevskie berega.* Leningrad: OGIZ
Mavrodin, V.V. 1945a. *Obrazovanie Drevnerusskogo gosudarstva.* Leningrad: Izd-vo. Leningradskogo gos. ordena Lenina universiteta
Mavrodin, V.V. 1945b. *Narodnye dvizheniia protiv inozemnykh zakhvatchikov v drevnei Rusi.* Leningrad: Gospolitizdat.
Mawdsley, E. 2007. *Thunder in the East: The Nazi-Soviet War, 1941–45*, London: Hodder.
Mazhitov, S.F., 2005. *Istorik Ermukhan Bekmakahnov.* Astana: Foliant.
Mazour, A.G. 1971. *The Writing of History in the Soviet Union.* Stanford, CA: Hoover Institution Press.

Mazour, A.G. and Bateman, H.E. 1952. Recent Conflicts in Soviet Historiography. *The Journal of Modern History* 24, no. 1: 56–68.
Meindorf, E.K. 2007. Puteshestvie iz Orenburga v Bukharu. In *Etnografiia kazakhov v zapiskakh rossiiskikh puteshestvennikov nachala XIX v.*, 157–235. Astana: Altyn kitap.
Mel'nychuk O.S., ed. 1982. *Etymolohichnyi slovnyk ukrai'ns'koi' movy.* Kiev: Naukova Dumka.
Məmmədov, A. 2007b. *Baş Tutmamış Çevriliş.* Baku: El-Alians
Məmmədov, F. 2007a. *Mir Cəfər Abbasoğlu Bağırov (tərcümeyi-hala dair ştrixlər, yaxud tarixin həqiqəti- həqiqətin tarixi).* Baku: Nurlan.
Məmmədov, F. 2008. *Mir Cəfər Bağırov: Xruşşovun Qərəzli və Sifarişli Bakı Divanxanası.* Baku: Şəms.
Merzon, I. 1935. Kak pokazyvat istoricheskikh deyatelei v shkolnom prepodavanii istorii. *Borba Klassov*, no. 5: 53–59.
Mess, B. 2008. *The Science of the Swastika.* Budapest: Central European University Press.
Mezhrespublikanskoe soveshchanie po propaganda i agitatsii v Tashkente. 1943. *Sputnik agitator*, no. 3–4: 38–40.
Michaels, P.A. 2000. Medical Propaganda and Cultural Revolution in Soviet Kazakhstan, 1928–41. *Russian Review* 59, no. 2: 159–178.
Michaels, Paula, 2003. *Curative Powers: Medicine and Empire in Stalin's Central Asia.* Pittsburgh, PA: University of Pittsburgh Press.
Mikhailov M. and Orlov, E. 1940. Istoricheskaia spravedlivost' vosstanovlena. *Bol'shevik*, no. 11–12: 91–97.
Miller, A. 2003. *The Ukrainian Question: The Russian Empire and Nationalsim in the Nineteenth Century.* Budapest: Central European University Press.
Miller, A. 2008. *The Romanov Empire and Nationalism.* Budapest: Central European University Press.
Min, D. 1939. *Zapadnaia Ukraina.* Moscow: Gos. izd-vo polit. lit-ry.
Minaev, V. 1941. Konets gitlerovskoi agentury v Irane. *Bol'shevik*, no. 22: 38–48.
Miner, S.M. 2003. *Stalin's Holy War: Religion, Nationalism, and Alliance Politics, 1941–1945.* Chapel Hill and London: The University of North Carolina Press.
Minns, E.H. 1913. *Scythians and Greeks.* Cambridge: Cambridge University Press.
Mishulin, A.V. 1939. Drevnie slaviane i sud'by Vostochnorimskoi imperii. *Vestnik Drevnei Istorii*, no. 1: 290–307.
Mitchell, C.P. 2009. *The Practice of Politics in Safarid Iran: Power, Religion and Rhetoric.* London: I.B. Tauris.
Molotov, V. 1941. Vystuplenie po radio Zamestitelia Predsedatelia Soveta Narodnykh Komissarov Soiuza SSR i Narodnogo Komissara Inostrannykh Del. tov. V.M. Molotova 22 iiunia 1941 goda. *Pravda.* July 23.
Molotov, V. 1939a. Rech' po radio Predsedatelia Soveta Narodykh Komissarov SSSR tov. V.M. Molotov, 17 sentiabria 1939 goda. *Bol'shevik*, no. 17: 1–3.
Molotov, V. 1939b. Nota pravitel'stva SSSR, vruchennaia pol'skomu poslu v Moskve utrom 17 sentiabria 1939 goda. *Bol'shevik*, no. 17: 4–5.
Molotov, V.M. 1936. Rech' tov. V. M. Molotova na prieme delegatsii trudiashchikhsiia Sovetskoi Armenii, 30 Dekabria 1935 goda. *Pravda.* January 6.
Molotov, V.M. 1938. 21-aia godovshchina Oktiabrskoi revoliutsii: doklad na torzhestvennom zasedanii moskovskogo soveta 6-go niabria 1938g. *Bol'shevik*, no. 21–22: 25–37.
Momen, M., ed. 1981. *The Bábí and Bahá'í Religions 1844–1944: Some Contemporary Western Accounts.* Oxford: George Roland.

Momen, M. 1987. *Selections from the Writings of E G. Browne on the Bábí and Bahá'í Religions.* Oxford: George Roland.

Motyl, A. 1980. *The Turn to the Right: The Ideological Origins and Development of Ukrainian Nationalism, 1919–1929.* New York: Distributed by Columbia University Press.

Motyl, A.J. 1992. From Imperial Decay to Imperial Collapse: The Fall of the Soviet Empire in Comparative Perspective. In *Nationalism and Empire: The Habsburg Empire and the Soviet Union*, ed. R.L. Rudolph and D.F. Good, 15–43. New York: St Martin's Press in association with the Center for Austrian Studies, University of Minnesota.

Mühle, E. 2003. The European East on the Mental Map of German *Ostforschung*. In *Germany and the European East in the Twentieth Century*, ed. E. Mühle, 107–130. Oxford and New York: Berg.

Mukanov, M.S. 1991. *Etnicheskaia territoriia kazakhov v XVIII nachale XX vekov.* Almaty: Kazakhstan.

Müller, M.G. 2003. Poland and Germany from Interwar Period through to Time of Détente. In *Germany and the European East in the Twentieth Century*, ed. E. Mühle, 91–106. Oxford and New York: Berg.

Muradian, G.B. 1943. *Vardan Mamikonian.* Erivan: n.a.

Murray, J. 2000. *Politics and Place Names: Changing Names in the Late Soviet Period.* Birmingham: Department of Russian, University of Birmingham.

Na osvobozhdennoi zemle (Po materialam tsentral'nykh gazet). 1939. *Sputnik agitator*, no. 19: 26–30.

Na sessii OON AN SSSR (oktiabr' 1938 g.). 1938. *Vestnik drevnei istorii*, no. 4: 259–265.

Nadav, M. 1984. The Jewish Commuity of Nemyriv in 1648: Their Massacre and Loyalty Oath to Cossacks, *Harvard Ukrainian Studies* 8, no. 3/4: 376–395.

Nafisi, S. 1333 [1954]. *Babak Khurram'din.* Tehran: Chap Tabish.

Nağıyev, H., Verdiyeva, H. 2007. *Azərbaycan Tarixi (e. ə. IX-e. XII əsrləri).* Baku, n.a.

Najimi, N. 1368 [1989–1990]. *Babak-i Khurram'din.* Tehran: Adib.

Nash, G. 2009. Introduction. In *Comte de Gobineau and Orientalism: Selected eastern writing*, ed. G. Nash, 1–20. London: Routledge.

Natisk fashistskikh agressorov i bor'ba SSSR za mir. 1938. *Bol'shevik*, no. 7: 1–6.

*Nauka o rasakh i rasizm.* 1938. Moscow: Izd-vo Akademii nauk SSSR.

Nauryzbai. 2004. *Kazakhstan: Natsional'naia entsiklopediia.* Vol. 4. Almaty: Kazak entsiklopediiasy.

Nazarov, F. 2007. Zapiski o nekotorykh narodakh i zemliakh srednei chasti azii. In *Etnografiia kazakhov v zapiskakh rossiiskikh puteshestvennikov nachala XIX v.*, 85–155. Astana: Altyn kitap.

Needly, Z.R. 1944. *Vekovaia bor'ba zapadnykh i Iuzhnykh slavian protiv germanskoi agressii.* Moscow: OGIZ.

Nefisi, S. [Sa'id Nafisi]. 1998. [1954] *Babak.* Istanbul: Berfin.

Nekrich, A.M. 1963. *Vneshnaia politika Anglii, 1939–1941.* Moscow: Izdatel'stvo akademii nauk SSSR.

Neretina, S.S. 1990. Smena istoricheskikh paradigm v SSSR (1920–1930gg.). In *Nauka i vlast*, ed. A.P. Ogurtsov and B.G. Iudin, 32–35. Moscow: Izdatel'stvo AN SSR.

Niederle, L. 1912. Najdawniejsze Siedziby Słowian. In *Początki Kultury Słowiańskie*, ed. A. Brückner, L. Niederle, and K. Kadlec, 1–17. Cracow: Nakładem Akademii Umiejętności.

## 202  Bibliography

Nöldeke, T. 1879a. Orientalischer Socialismus. *Deutsche Rundschau* 18, no. 5: 284–291.

Nöldeke, T. 1879b. *Geschichte der Perser und Araber zur Zeit der Sasaniden aus der arabischen Chronik des Tabari.* Leyden: Brill.

Northrop, D. 2000. Languages of Loyalty: Gender, Politics, and Party Supervision in Uzbekistan, 1927–41. *Russian Review* 59, no. 2: 179–200.

Northrop, D. 2004. *Veiled Empire: Gender and Power in Stalinist Central Asia.* Ithaca, NY: Cornell University Press.

Nove, A. 1967. *Soviet Middle East: a model for a development?* London: Allen & Unwin.

O panslavizme (Istoricheskaia spravka). 1940. *Bol'shevik*, no. 10: 85–89.

O vreditel'stve v oblasti arkheologii i o likvitadtsii ego posledstvii. 1937. *Sovietskaia Arkheologiia*, no. 3: v–x.

Ob itogakh diskusii o periodizatsii istorii SSSR. 1951. *Voprosy Istorii*, no. 3: 53–60.

Obrashchenie uchastnikov Vseslavianskogo mitinga, sostoiavshegosia 10–11 avgusta v Moskve. 1941. *Bol'shevik*, no. 15: 3–4.

*Ocherki istorii istoricheskoi nauki v SSSR. 1966.* 5 vols. Moscow: Izd-vo Akademii nauk SSSR.

*Ocherki istorii istoricheskoi nauki v SSSR. 1985.* 5 vols. Moscow: Izd-vo Akademii nauk SSSR.

Odarchenko, P. 1994. *Taras Shevchenko i Ukraïnska literatura.* Kiev: Smoloskyp.

Ohloblyn, O.P. 1939. *Ukraïna v chasy Petra I.* Kiev: Vydavnytstvo Akademiï Nauk URSR.

Öktem, K. 2008. The Nation's Imprint: Demographic Engineering and the Change of Toponymes. In *Republican Turkey. European Journal of Turkish Studies* [Online] 7. http://ejts.revues.org/index2243.html. (accessed September 12, 2011).

Olcott, M.B., 1995. *The Kazakhs.* Stanford, CA: Hoover Institution Press.

Önen, N. 2005. *İki Turan, Macaristan ve Türkiye'de Turancılık.* İstanbul: İletişim Yayınları.

Orlov, A.S. 1945. *Kazakhskii geroicheskii epos.* Moscow and Leningrad: Izdatel'stvo Akademii Nauk SSSR.

Orucov, Q. 1984. *Azərbaycan Qafqaz döyüşlərində.* Baku: Azərnəşr.

Osipov, K. 1939. *Bogdan Kmel'nitskii.* Moscow: Molodaia Gvardiia.

Osipov, K. 1942. *Prussiya ilə yeddiillik müharibə və Berlinin alınması.* Baku: Azərnəşr.

Otan Soghysynyng Batyry. 1942. *Otandy Korghauda.* November 6.

Otegen. 2004. *Kazakhstan: Natsional'naia entsiklopediia.* Vol. 3. Almaty: Kazak entsiklopediiasy.

Otvety na voprosy chitatelei: 1. Natsia i narodnost'. 1940. *Bol'shevik*, no. 13: 55–62.

Palmer, E.H. 1867. *Oriental Mysticism: A Treatise on the Sufiistic and Unitarian Theosophy of the Persians.* Cambridge: Deighton, Bell, and Co.

Pan'kivs'kyi, K. 1983. *Roky nimets'koï okupatsiï 1941–1944.* New York: Zhyttia I Misli.

Pankratova A.M. ed. 1940. *Istoriia SSSR: Uchebnik dlia 8, 9 i 10-kh klassov srednei shkoly.* Moscow: Uzhpedgiz.

Pankratova, A. 1942. Sovetskaia istoricheskaia nauka za 25 let i zadachi istorikov v usloviiakh velikoi otechestvennoi voiny. In *Dvadtsat' piat' let istoricheskoi nauki v SSSR*, ed. V. Volgin, E.V. Tarle, and A.M. Pankratova, 3–40. Moscow: Izdatel'stvo akademii nauk Soiuza SSR.

Pankratova, A. and Abdykalykov M., ed. 1943. *Istoriia Kazakhskoi SSR.* Almaty: KazOGIZ.

Parsinejad, Iraj. 2003. *A History of Literary Criticism in Iran (1866–1951): Literary*

*Criticism in the Works of Englightened Thinkers of Iran: Akhundzade, Kermani, Malkom, Talebof, Maraghe'i, Kasravi and Hedayat.* Bethesda, MD: Ibex.

*Partiino-politicheskaia rabota v Sovetskikh voorushennykh silakh v gody Velikoi otechestvennoi voiny 1941–1945: Kratkii istoricheskii obzor.* 1963. Moscow: Voennoe izdatel'stvo Ministerstva oborony SSSR.

Paşayev, M.C., ed. 1941. *Vətən haqqında xalq şeirləri.* Baku: EAAzF.

Pashaev, A. 1996. Gaziz Gubaidullin kak vidnyi istorik-arkhivist. *Gasyrlar Avazy,* no. 1–2: 181–185.

Pashaev, A.A., ed. 2006. *Zaqafqaziya Seyminin Müsəlman Fraksiyası və Azərbaycan Milli Şurası İclaslarının Protokolları 1918-ci İl: Protokoly zasedanii musul'manskikh fraktsii zakavkazskogo seima i Azerbaidzhanskogo natsional'nogo soveta 1918g.* Baku: Adiloğlu.

Passek, T. 1938. Issledovaniia Tripol'skoi Kul'tury v USSR za 20 let. In *Vestnik Drevnei Istorii,* no. 1: 261–278.

Passek, T. and Bezvenglinskii, B. 1939. Novye otkrytiia Tripol'skoi arkhaeologicheskoi ekspeditsii v 1939 g. *Vestnik Drevnei Istorii,* no. 4: 186–192.

Pavlenko, P. 1941a. Slava otvazhnym geroiam, *Bol'shevik,* no. 11–12: 18–21.

Pavlenko, P.1941b. Boevaia druzhba sovetskikh narodov *Bol'shevik,* no. 11–13: 34–36.

Peisker, J. 1905. *Die älteren Beziehungen der Slaven zu Turkotataren und Germanen und ihre sozialgeschichtliche Bedeutung.* Berlin: W Kohlhammer

Peisker, J. 1910. *Neue Grundlagen zur Slavischen Altertumskunde.* Stuttgart and Berlin: n.a.

Peisker, J. 1913. The Expansion of the Slavs. In *The Cambridge Medieval History* 2: 418–458. Cambridge: Cambridge University Press.

Pelech, O. 1993. The State and the Ukrainian Triumvirate in the Russian Empire 1831–47. In *Ukrainian Past, Ukrainian Present,* ed. Bohdan Krawchenko, 1–17. London: Macmillan.

Pelenski, J. 1990. The Cossack Insurrection in Jewish-Ukrainian Relations. In *Ukrainian-Jewish Relations in Historical Perspective,* ed. Peter J. Potichnyj and Howard Aster, 31–42. Edmonton: CIUS.

Pervukhin, M.G. 1974. 'Perebazirovanie promyshlennosti'. In *Sovetskii tyl: v velikoi otechestvennoi voine,* ed. P.N. Pospelov, 10–30. Vol. 2. Moscow: Mysl.

Petrov N.V. and Roginskii, A.B. 1997. Polskaia operatsiia" NKVD 1937–1938 gg. In *Repressii protiv poliakov i pol'skikh grazhdan,* ed. L.S. Eremina, 22–43. Moscow: Zven'ia.

P[etrovs']kyi, M. 1938. Z istorii vyzvol'noï borot'by ukraïns'koho narodu proty shliakhets'koï Pol'shchi. *Bil'shovyk Ukraïny,* no. 8: 73–84.

Petrovs'kyi, M. 1941. *Byzvol'na Viina Ukraïns'kogo Narodu Proty Gnitu Shliakhets'koï Pol'shchi i Pryednannia Ukraïny do Rosiï (1648–1654 rr.).* N.a.: Politvydav pry TsK KP(b)U.

Petrovs'kyi, M. 1942a. *Ivan Bohun.* Saratov: Ukrvydav pry TsK KPbU.

Petrovs'kyi, M. 1942b. *Bohdan Khmel'nyts'kyi.* Saratov: Ukrvydav pry TsK KPbU.

Petrovs'kyi, M. 1945a. *Zakhidna Ukraïna (istorychna Dovidna).* Kiev: Ukraïns'ke derzhavne vydavnitstvo.

Petrovs'kyi, M. 1945b. *Bukovyna: Istorychna dovidka.* Kiev: Ukraïns'ke derzhavne vydavnitstvo.

Petrovs'kyi, M.N. 1944b. Bohdan Khmel'nyts'kyi: do 285-littia z dnya smerti. *Visti,* no. 1–2: 20–29.

Petrovs'kyi, M.N. 1939. *Narysy z Istoriï Ukraïny, Vypusk IV: Vyzvol'na Viina*

## 204  Bibliography

*Ukraïns'kogo Narodu Proty Gnitu Shliakhets'koï Pol'shchi I Pryednannia Ukraïny do Rosïi.* Kiev: Vydavnytsvo Akademiï Nauk URSR.
Petrovs'kyi, M.N. 1943b. *Nezlamnyi dukh velikogo Ukraïns'kogo narodu.* Kharkiv: Ukraïns'ke derzhavne vydavnitstvo.
Petrovs'kyi, M.N., ed. 1943a. *Istoriia Ukraïny.* Ufa: Vyd-vo AN URSR.
Petrovskii N. [M. Petrovs'kyi]. 1944a. Vossoedinenie ukrainskogo naroda v edinom ukrainskom sovetskom gosudarstve. *Bol'shevik*, no. 1: 42–55.
Petrovskii, N.N. 1939. *Voennoe Proshloe Ukrainskogo Naroda.* Moscow: Gos. voennoe izd-vo.
Petruşevski, İ.P. 1943. *Azərbaycan xalqının XIII-XIV əsrlərdəki qəhrəmanlıq mübarizəsindən.* Baku: EAAz.
Petrushevskii, I.P. 1942. *Velikii patriot shirvanshakh Ibragim.* Baku: Izdatel'stvo AzFan.
Petrushevskii, I.P. 1941. *Iz geroicheskoi bor'by azerbaidzhanskogo naroda v XIII-XIV vekakh.* Baku: Izdatel'stvo AzFAN.
Phelps, Myron H. 1912. *Life and Teachings of Abbas Effendi: a study of the religion of the Babis, or Beha'is founded by the Persian Bab and by his successors, Beha Ullah and Abbas Effendi.* New York: Putnam.
Piaskovskii, A., 1943. Istoriia Kazakhskoi SSR. *Pravda.* July 10.
Picheta, V. 1940. *Osnovnye Momenty Istoricheskogo Razvitiia Zapadnoi Ukrainy i Zapadnoi Belorussii.* Moscow: Gosudarstvennoe Sotsial'no-Ekonomicheskoe Izdatel'stvo.
Picheta, V. and Krut', V. 1941. Kritika i Bibliografiia: Kriticheskie Stat'i i Obzory: 'Istoriia Ukraïny' Korotyi kurs. *Istorik-Marksist* 6: 103–110.
Pigarev, K. 1943. *Soldat-polkovodets: Ocerhki o Suvorove* Moscow: Goslitizdat.
Pipes, R. 1997. *The Formation of the Soviet Union: Communism and Nationalism 1917–1923.* Cambridge, MA: Harvard University Press.
Pis'ma Anny Mikhailovny Pankratovoi. 1988. *Voprosy istorii*, no. 11: 54–79.
Pisarevski, Q.Q. 1941. *1809-cu ildə rus ordusunun buzlar üzəri ilə səfəri*, ed. İ. Hüseynov. Baku: EAAzF.
Plokhy, S. 1992. The Symbol of Little Russia: The Pokrova Icon and Early Modern Ukrainian Political Ideology. *Journal of Ukrainian Studies* 17, no. 1–2: 171–188.
Plokhy, S. 2001. *The Cossacks and Religion in Early Modern Ukraine* Oxford: Oxford Unviersity Press.
Plokhy, S. 2005a. *Unmaking of Imperial Russia: Mykhailo Hrushevsky and the Writing of Ukrainian History.* Toronto: University of Toronto Press.
Plokhy, S. 2005b. Bourgeois Revolution or Peasant War? Early Soviet Debates on the History of the Khmelnytsky Uprising. In *Synopsis: A Collection of Essays in Honour of Zenon E. Kohut*, ed. S. Plokhy and F.E. Sysyn, 345–370. Edmonton and Toronto: CIUSP.
Plokhy, S. 2005c. Writing the *History* in the USSR. In *History of Ukraine-Rus'*, M. Hrushevsky, bk. 1: xxix–lxiv. Vol. 9. Toronto: Edmonton: CIUSP.
Plokhy, S. 2006. *The Origins of the Slavic Nations: Premodern Identities in Russia, Ukraine and Belarus.* Cambridge: Cambridge University Press.
Plokhy, S. 2008a. *Ukraine and Russia: Representations of the Past.* Toronto: University of Toronto Press.
Plokhy, S. 2008b. Introduction: Renegotiating the Pereiaslav Agreement. In *History of Ukraine-Rus'*, ed. M. Hrushevsky, bk 2/1: xxvii–lv. Vol. 9. Toronto: Edmonton: CIUSP.
Plokhy, S. 2011. The Call of Blood: Government propaganda and public response to the Soviet entry into World War II. *Cahiers du Monde russe* 52, no. 2–3: 293–319.

Plokhy, S. 2012. *The Cossack Myth: History and Nationhood in the Age of Empires*. Cambridge: Cambridge University Press.
Podorozhnyi, M.E. 1940. *Vyzvol'na Viina Ukraïns'kogo Narodu (1648–1654 rr.)*. Kiev: Derzhavne Vydavnytstvo Politychnoï Literatury pry RNK URSR.
Pogodin, A. 1901. *Iz istorii slavianskikh peredvizhenii*. St Petersburg: A.P. Lopukhina.
Pokrovskii, M. 1933a. *Russkaia istoriia v samom szhatom ocherke*. Moscow: Partinoe izd-vo.
Pokrovskii, M.N. 1933b. *Istoricheskaia nauka i borba klassov*. Moscow and Leningrad: Gosudarstvennoe Sotsial'no-Ekonomicheskoe Izdatel'stvo.
Pokrovskii, M.N. 1970. Prison of Nations. In *Russia in World History*, ed. M.N. Pokrovskii, 108–116. Ann Arbor: University of Michigan Press.
Pokrovskii, M.N. 1966. *Izbrannye proizvedeniia v chetyrekh knigakh*. Vol. 1. Moscow: Mysl'.
Pokrovskii, M.N. 1967. *Izbrannye proizvedeniia v chetyrekh knigakh*. Vol. 3. Moscow: Mysl'.
*Poland and Ukraine in the 1930s and 1940s: Documents from the Archives of the Secret Services*. 2012. Łódź, Warsaw, Kiev: The Institute of National Remembrance – Commission of the Prosecution of Crimes against the Polish Nation, The Security Service of Ukraine Branch State Archives, Institute of Political and Ethno-National Studies at the National Academy of Sciences of Ukraine.
Polonsky, A. 1972. *Politics in Independent Poland 1921–1939*. Oxford: Clarendon Press.
Popson, N. 2001. The Ukrainian history textbook: Introducing children to the 'Ukrainian nation'. *Nationalities Papers: The Journal of Nationalism and Ethnicity* 29 (2): 325–350.
Pospelov, M.S. and Burnashev, T.S. 2007. Poezdka Pospelova i Burnasheva v Tashkent v 1800 godu. In *Etnografiia kazakhov v zapiskakh rossiiskikh puteshestvennikov nachala XIX v.*, 7–83. Astana: Altyn kitap.
Poulton, H. 1997. *Top Hat, Grey Wolf and Crescent, Turkish Nationalism and the Turkish Republic*. London: Hurst.
Powell, A. 1951. The Nationalist Trend in Soviet Historiography. *Soviet Studies* 2, no. 4: 372–377.
*Prepodavanie istorii v usloviiakh Velikoi Otechestvennoi Voiny: Metodologicheskoe posobie dlia uchitelei srednyk hshkol KazSSR*. 1942. Almaty: AzFAN.
Price, M.P. 1918. *War and Revolution in Asiatic Russia*. London: George Allen & Unwin.
*Prikazy narodnogo komissara oborony SSSR. 1937–21 iiunia 1941g*. 1994. Vol. 13. Moscow: Terra.
Pritsak, O. 1976. *The Origin of Rus': An Inaugural Lecture, October 24, 1975*. Cambridge, MA.
*Protiv fashistskikh podzhigatelei voiny*. 1937. Moscow and Leningrad: Leningr. obl. izd-vo.
*Protiv fashistskoi fal'sifikatsii istorii: sbornik statei*. 1939. Moscow and Leningrad: B i Izd-vo Akad. Nauk SSSR.
Proty Burzhuaznykh Natsionalistiv. 1937. *Komunist*. October 5.
Prymak T.M. 2001. Dmytro Doroshenko: A Ukrainian Émigré Historian of the Interwar Period. *Harvard Ukrainian Studies* 25: 31–56.
Prymak, T.M. 1981. Mykhailo Hrushevsky: Populist or Statist? *Journal of Ukrainian Studies* 6, no. 1: 65–78.
Pyskir, M.S. 2001. *Thousands of Roads: A Memoir of a Young Woman's Life in the Ukrainian Underground During and After World War II*. London and Jefferson, NC: McFarland & Co.

Qaraqızı, Ulduzə. 2003. *Babək: Milli kinonun monumental filmi. Ekspress qəzeti.* July 3.
Qorodetski, Y. 1941. *1918-ci ildə Ukraynada Qerman işğalçılarına qarşı vətən müharibəsi*, ed. Orucov. Baku: EAAzF.
Qurban, T. 2006. *Düşmənlərindən Güclü Şəxsiyyet.* Baku: Şirvannşər
Radek, K. 1933. Novyi etap fashizatsii Germanii. *Bol'shevik*, no. 3: 39–57.
Radek, K. 1936. Sovietskii patriotizm. *Pravda.* May 1.
Radetskii, E. 1939. Na mezhdunarodnye temy: Razval pansko Pol'shi. *Sputnik agitatora* 19: 36–38.
Radlov, V.V. 2007a. 'Tiurkskie stepnye kochevniki (Iz Sibiri)'.In *Tiurkskie stepnye kochevniki*, V.V. Radlov, 5–180. Astana: Altyn kitap.
Rady, M. 1999. The German Settlement in Central and Eastern Europe during the High Middle Ages. In *The German Lands and Eastern Europe*, ed. R. Bartlett and K. Schönwälder, 11–47. London: Macmillan.
Rahim, M. 1942. *Vətən sevgisi.* Baku: Azərnəşr.
Rahim, M. 1946. *Ölməz qəhrəman.* Baku: Uşaqgəncnəşr.
Ramazani, R.K. 1966. *The Foreign Policy of Iran: A Developing Nation in World Affairs 1500–1941.* Charlottesville, VA: University Press of Virginia.
Rambaud, A. 1878. *Historie de la Russie.* Paris: Hachette.
Rambaud, A. 1898. *Russia.* 2 vols. New York: Peter Fenelon Collier.
Ravdonikas, V.I. 1931. Za Marksistskuiu istoriiu material'noi kul'tury. IGAIMK 8, issue 3–4.
Ravdonikas, V.I. 1932. Peshchernye goroda Kryma i gotskaia problema v sviazi so stadial'nym razvitiem severnogo prichernomor'ia. GAIMK 12: 5–106.
Rawlinson, G. (1871) *The Five Great Monarchies of the Ancient Eastern World; History, Geography, and Antiquities of Chaldea, Assyria, Babylon, Media, and Persia, Collected and Illustrated frrom Ancient and Modern Sources. Second Edition.* Vol. 2. New York: Scribner, Welford, and Co.
Rawlinson, G. (1873) *The Sixth Great Oriental Monarch; or the Geography, History, and Antiquities of Parthia, Collected and Illustrated from Ancient and Modern Sources.* London: Longmans, Green, and Co.
Rawlinson, G. (1876) *The Seventh Great Oriental Monarch or the Geography, History, and Antiquities of the Sassanian or New Persian Empire, Collected and Illustrated from Ancient and Modern Sources.* London: Longmans, Green, and Co.
Rawlinson, G. (1878) *The Origins of Nations: In Two Parts: On Early Civilizations. On Ethnic Affinities, etc.* London: The Religious Tract Society.
Rəhimov, S. and Hüseynov İ., eds. 1944. *Azərbaycanın şanlı oğulları.* Vol. 3. Baku: Izdate'stvo AzFAN.
Reich, K. (2000) *Singing the Past.* Ithaca and London: Cornell University Press.
Rezoliutsii 1-go Vsesoiuznogo tiurkologicheskogo s'ezda. 1926. In *Pervyi vsesoiuznyi tiurkologicheskii s 'ezd*, 401–408. Baku: Bakinskii Rabochii.
Rezun, M. (1981) *The Soviet Union and Iran: Soviet Policy in Iran from the Beginnings of the Pahlavi Dynasty until the Soviet Invasion in 1941.* Geneva: Sijthoff & Noordhoff International; Institut Universitaire de Hautes Etudes Internationales.
Riazanov, A.F. (1927) *Vosstaniia Isataia Taimanova (1836–1838).* Kzyl-Orda: lzdatel'stvo Obshchestva Izucheniia Kazakhstana.
Riazanov, A.F. (1928) *Sorok let bor'by zanatsional 'nuiu nezavisiomost' kazakskogo naroda (1797–1 838g.*, Kzyl-Orda: lzdatel'stvo Obshchestva Izucheniia Kazakhstana.
Ridgeon, L. (2004) Ahmad Kasravi's Criticisms of Edward Granville Browne, *Iran* 42: 219–233.

Rikhter, M. (1935) Voennaia politika Gitlera i zadachi germanskoi kompartii, *Bol'shevik* 8: 34–50.

Rives, J.B. (1999) Introduction. In *Germania*, C. Tacitus, 1–76, Oxford: Clarendon.

Ro'i, Y. (2009) The Transformation of Historiography on the 'Punished Peoples', *History and Memory* 21 (2): 150–176.

Roberts, G. (2000) The Fascist War Threat and Soviet Poltics in the 1930s. In *Russia in the Age of Wars 1914–1945*, ed. S. Pons and A. Romano, 147–158, Milan: Feltrinelli.

Roberts, H.L. 1953. The Diplomacy of Colonel Beck. In *The Diplomats 1919–1939*, 579–614. Princeton, NJ: Princeton University Press.

Rodgers, P.W., 2007. 'Compliance or contradiction'? Teaching 'History' in the 'New' Ukraine. A view from Ukraine's Eastern Borderlands. *Europe-Asia Studies* 59 (3): 503–519.

Roemer, H. 1912. *Die Babi-Beha'i: die jüngste mohammedanische sekte.* Potsdam: Verlag der Deutschen orientalism.

Rogger, H. 1960. *National Consciousness in Eighteenth-Century Russia.* Cambridge, MA: Harvard University Press.

Roos, H. 1966. *A History of Modern Poland.* London: Eyre & Spottiswoode.

Rosdolsky, R. 1986. *Engels and the 'Nonhistoric' Peoples: the National Question in the Revolution of 1848.* Glasgow: Critique Books.

Rostovtzeff, M. 1922. *Iranians and Greeks in South Russia.* Oxford: Clarendon Press.

Roszkowski, W. 2006. *Historia Polski 1914–2005.* Warsaw: Wydawnictwo Naukowe PWN.

Roy, O. 2000. *The New Central Asia: The Creation of Nations.* London: I.B. Tauris.

Rozhin, P. 1943. Ob agitatsii na rodnom iazyke. *Sputnik Agitatora* 21: 45–46.

*Rozvytok istorychnoï nauky na Ukraïni za roky Radians'koï vlady.* 1973. Kiev: Naukova Dumka.

*Rozvytok nauky v Ukraïns'kii RSR za 40 rokiv.* 1957. Kiev: Vid-vo AN URSR.

Rubinshtein, A.Z. 1982. *Soviet Policy Towards Turkey, Iran and Afghanistan: The Dynamics of Influence.* New York: Praeger.

Rubl'ov, O.C. 1996. Malovidomi storinky biografiï ukraïns'kogo istoryka. *Ukraïns'kyi istorychnyi zhurnal*, no. 1: 106–129.

Rudnytsky, I.L. 1987b. Franciszek Duchiński and his impact on Ukrainian political thought. In *Essays in Modern Ukrainian History by I.L Rudnytsky*, ed. P.L. Rudnytsky, 187–201. Edmonton: CIUS, University of Alberta.

Rudnytsky, Ivan L. 1987a. Observations on the Problem of 'Historical' and 'Non-Historical' Nations. In *Essays in Modern Ukrainian History*, ed. Peter L. Rudnytsky, 37–48. Edmonton: University of Alberta.

Russell, J.R. 2005. Early Armenian Civilization. In. *The Armenians: Past and Present in the Making of National Identity*, ed. E. Herzig and M. Kurkchiyan, 23–40. London and New York: Routledge Curzon.

Russell, J.R. 1997. The Formation of the Armenian Nation. In *The Armenian People from Ancient to Modern Times volume 1: The Dynastic Periods: From Antiquity to the Fourteenth Century*, ed. R.G. Hovannisian, 19–36. Basingstoke and London: Macmillan.

Rüstəm, S. 2005. Seçilmiş əsərləri: Üç cilddə. Vol. 2. Baku: Şərq-Qərb.

Rybakov, B.A. 1939. Anty i Kievskaia Rus'. *Vestnik drevnoi istorii*, no. 1: 319–337.

Rykov, P.S. 1936. *Ocherki po istorii Nizhnego Povolzh'ia.* Saratov: Sarat. Kraev. Izd-vo.

Rza, R. 1942. *Vətən.* Baku: Azərnəşr.

S kremlevskoi tribuny: Vyderzhki iz rechei proiznesenykh na vneocherednoi piatoi sessii Verkhovnogo Soveta SSSR. 1939. *Sputnik agitator* 21: 27–30.

Sabol, S. 2003a. Kazak Resistance to Russian Colonization: Interpreting the Kenesary Kasymov Revolt, 1837–1847. *Central Asian Survey*, no. 22, vol. 2/3: 231–252.
Sabol, S. 2003b. *Russian Colonization and the Genesis of Kazakh National Consciousness.* New York: Palgrave Macmillan.
Safamanesh, K. 2009. Architectural Historiography 1921–42. In *Iran in the 20th Century Historiography and Political Culture*, ed. T. Atabaki, 121–154. London: I.B. Tauris.
Said, E. 1991. *Orientalism*. London: Penguin.
Santsevich, A.V. and Komarenko, N.V. 1986. *Razvitie istoricheskoi nauki v Akademii nauk Ukrainskoi SSR 1936–1986 gg*.Kiev: Naukova Dumka
Sarghozhaev, N. 1998. *Bölek Batyr: Tarikhi-tanymdyk khikaiattar.* Almaty: Rauan.
Saunders, D.B. 1982. Historians and Concepts of Nationality in Early Nineteenth-Century Russia. *The Slavonic and East European Review* 60, no. 1: 44–62.
Savushkin, L.M. 1990. *Ideologiia sovetskogo tyla: problem i protivorechiia. 1941–1945gg.* Voronezh: Izdadel'stvo Voronezhskogo Universiteta.
Schlesinger, R. 1950a. Recent Soviet Historiography I. *Soviet Studies* 1, no. 4: 293–312.
Schlesinger, R. 1950b. Recent Soviet Historiography II. *Soviet Studies* 2, no. 1: 3–21.
Schlesinger, R. 1950c. Recent Soviet Historiography III. *Soviet Studies* 2, no. 2: 138–162.
Schlesinger, R. 1951a. Recent Soviet Historiography IV. *Soviet Studies* 2, no. 3: 265–288.
Schlesinger, R. 1951b. Note on Recent Soviet Historiography, Part IV. *Soviet Studies* 3, no. 1: 64.
Schlesinger, R. 1952. Recent Discussions on the Periodization of History. *Soviet Studies* 4, no. 2: 152–169.
Schniemann, T. 1886. *Russland, Polen und Livland bis ins 17. Jahrhundret.* 2 vols. Berlin: G. Grote.
Scott, J.C. 1998. *Seeing Like a State: How Certain Schemes to Improve the Human Condition Have Failed.* New Haven.: Yale University Press.
Sel'vinskii, I. 1946. *Babek; Tragediia*.Moscow: Sovetskii pisatel'.
Sela, R. 2011. *The Legendary Biographies of Tamerlane: Islam and Heroic Apocrypha in Central Asia*, Cambridge: Cambridge University Press.
Serhiichuk, V. 2000. *Radians'kyi partyzany proty OUN-UPA.* Kiev: Ukraïns'ka Vydavnycha Spilka.
Serhiichuk, V. 2003. *Poliaky na Volyni u roky Drugoï svitovoïviiny: Dokumenty z ukraïns'kykh arkhiviv i pol's'ki publikatsiï.* Kiev: Ukraïns'ka Vydavnycha Spilka.
Şərifli, M. 1944. *Azərbaycan xalqının monqol istilaçılarına qarşı mübarizəsi tarixindən.* Baku: EAAzF.
Sevortian, E.V. 1978. *Etimologicheskii slovar tiurkskikh iazykov: obshchetiurkskie i mezhtiurkskie osnovy na bukvu 'B'.* Moscow: Nauka.
Shaiakhmetov, Zh. 1941a. Kazakhskii narod aktivnyi uchastnik Velikoiotechestvennoi voiny. *Bolshevik Kazakhstana*. September 10.
Shaiakhmetov, Zh. 1941b. Kazak khalky. *Sotsialistik Kazakstan*. September 14.
Shaiakhmetov, Zh. 1942. *Dadim Krasnoi armii, strane bol'she miasa, masla, shersti.* Almaty: KazOGIZ.
Shakhai, D. 1986. Our Tactics with Regard to the Russian People. In *Political Thought of the Ukrainian Underground 1943–1951*, ed. P.J. Potichnyj and Y. Shtendera, 283–318. Edmonton: CIUS.
Shakhmatov, V. 1940. Zemel'nye otnosheniia vo vnutrennei (bukeevskoi) orde v nachale XIX v. *Izvestiia KazFAN: seriia istoricheskaia* 1: 31–61.
Shaldzhian, S.A. 1941. Delmiki i ikh pokhody v Armeniiu. *Izvestiia ArmFAN* 5–6 /10–11: 107–115.

Shaldzhian, S.A. 1942. Armianskie strelki. *IzvestiiaArmFAN* 1–2/15–16: 31–33.
Shapoval, I. 1990. *M.S. Khrushchev na Ukraïni*. Kiev: Tovarystvo Znannia.
Shapoval, I. 1993. *Ukraïna 20–50-kh rokiv: storinky nenapysanoï istoriï*. Kiev: Naukova Dumka.
Shapoval, Y. 2003. The GPU-NKVD as an Instrument of Counter-Ukrainization in the 1920s and 1930s. In *Culture, Nation and Identity: The Ukrainian-Russian Encounter (1600–1945)*, ed. A. Kappeler, Z.E. Kohut, F. Sysyn, and M. von Hagen, 325–343. Toronto: CIUSP.
Sharif, A.A. 1976. Suleiman Rustam. *Bol'shaia Sovetskaia Entsiklopediia*. Vol. 25. Moscow: Sovetskaia Entsiklopediia.
Sharova, A.V. 2004. Malen'kie radosti bol'shogo terrora: pervye gody Instituta istorii AN SSSR. *Odissei: Chelovek v istorii*, 318–350. Moscow: Nauka.
Shaw I. and Jameson, R. 1999. *A Dictionary of Archaeology*. Oxford: Blackwell.
Shcherbakov, A. 1941. Gitler obmanyvaet nemetskii narod. *Bol'shevik*, no. 21: 11–12.
Shcherbakov, A. 1944. Pod znamenem Lenina-Stalina sovetskii narod idet k pobede. *Bol'shevik*, no. 1: 11–20.
Shelukhin, S. 1929. *Zvidkilia pokhodyt' Rus': Teoriia Kel'ts'koho pokhodzhennia Kyïvs'koï Rusy z Frantsiï*. Prague: n.a.
Sherstiuk, F. 1943. *Ustym Karmaliuk*. Moscow: Ukrizdat.
Shestakov A.V., ed. 1938. *Istoriia SSSR kratkii kurs*. Moscow: Gosudarstvennoe uchebno-pedagogicheskoe izdatel'stvo.
Shestakov, A.1937. Osnovnye problemy uchebnika Kratkii kurs istorii SSSR. *Istorik-marksist* 3: 85–98.
Shevchenko, T.H. 1939. *Vybrani Tvory: u poriadkuvannia, vstupna stattia i komentari akademika O.I. Bilets'kogo*. Kiev: Vydavnytstvo dytiachoï literatury.
Shigabdinov, R. 2002. Uzbekskii period nauchnoi deiatel'nosti professora Gaziza Gubaidullina. *Gasyrlar Avazy*, 1–2.
Shkandrij, M. 1992. *Modernists, Marxists, and the Nation: The Ukrainian Literary Discussion of the 1920s*. Edmonton: CIUS.
Shklovsky, V. and Sheldon, R. 1968. The End of the Caucasian Front. *Russian Review* 27, no. 1: 17–68.
Shmidt, O. *et al.* 1926. Azerbaidzhanskaia SSR. *Bol'shaia Sovetskaia entsiklopediia*. Vol. 1, col. 659. Moscow: Bol'shaia Sovetskaia entsiklopediia.
Shmidt, O. *et al.* 1935. Khmel'nitskii. *Bol'shaia Sovetskaia entsiklopediia* 59: col. 816–817. Moscow: Bol'shaia Sovetskaia entsiklopediia.
Shmidt O. *et al.* 1937. Kazakhskaia SSR. *Bol'shaia sovetskaia entsiklopediia*, xxxi, col. 588–591. Vol. 31, Moscow: Sovetskaia Entsiklopediia.
Shnirel'man, V.A. 1993. Zlokliucheniia odnoi nauki: etnogeneticheskie issledovaniia i stalinskaia natsional'naia politika. *Etnograficheskoe obozrenie*, no. 3: 42–66.
Shnirelman, V.A. 1995. From Internationalism to Nationalism: Forgotten Pages of Soviet Archaeology in the 1930s and 1940s. In *Nationalism, Politics and the Practice of Archaeology*, eds P.L. Kohl and C. Fawcett, 120–138. Cambridge: Cambridge University Press.
Shnirelman, V.A. 1996a. *Who Gets the Past? Competition for Ancestors among Non-Russian Intellectuals in Russia*. Washington DC, Baltimore and London: Johns Hopkins University Press.
Shnirelman, V.A. 1996b. The Faces of Nationalist Archaeology in Russia. In *Nationalism and Archaeology in Europe*, ed. M. Diaz-Andreu and T. Champion, 218–242. London: UCL Press.

## 210  Bibliography

Shostakovich, 1995. *Testimony: The Memories of Dmitri Shostakovich*, ed. Solomon Volkov. New York: Limelight.

Shteppa, K. 1962. *Russian Historians and the Soviet State*. New Brunswick, NJ: Rutgers University Press.

Shul'ga, Z. 1942. Borot'ba ukraïns'koho selianstva proty nimets'ko-fashists'kykh okupantiv. In *Borot'ba ukraïns'koho narodu proty nimets'kykh zaharbnykiv: Zbirka Stattei*, 37–48. Ufa: Vydannia Akademiï Nauk URSR.

Shunkov, V. 1941. Institut istorii Akademii nauk SSSR v 1940 godu. *Istorik-Marksist*, no. 3: 155.

Simon, G. 1991. *Nationalism and Policy Toward the Nationalities in the Soviet Union: From Totalitarian Dictatorship to Post-Stalinist Society*. Boulder, CO and Oxford: Westview.

Simonov, N.S. 1996. *Voenno-promyshlennyi kompleks SSSR v 1920–1950-e gody: tempy ekonomicheskogo rosta, struktura, organizatsiia proizvodstva i upravlenie*. Moscow: Rosspen.

Siov, S.G., 2001. *Intelligentsiia i Vlast' v Sovietskom Obshchestve v 1946–1964 gg.* [volume 1] *Pozdnii Stalinizm (1946-Mart 1953gg.)*. Omsk: SIbbADI.

Şıxlinski, Ə. İ. 1944. *Xatirələrim*, preface E.Z. Barsukov. Baku: EAAzF.

Şıxlinski, Ə. 1926. *Ruscadan türkcəyə qısa döyüş sözlüyü [Mətn]: təlimnamə və nizamnamələri, elmi hərbi kitabları ruscadan türkcəyə çevirmək üçün yardımlıq*. Baku: Azərb. Hərbi.

Sizov, S.G. 2001. *Intelligentsiia i vlast' v Sovietskom obshchestve v 1 94 6–1 964gg. Pozdnii stalinizm (1946-Mart 1953gg.)*. Omsk: Sibadi.

Skrynnikova, T. 1997. *Kharizma i vlast ' v epokhu chingis-khana*. Moscow: RAN.

Slater, W. 1998. Russia's imagined history: Visions of the Soviet past and the new 'Russian idea'. *Journal of Communist Studies and Transition Politics* 14 (4): 69–86.

Slezkine, Y. 1994. The USSR as a Communal Apartment, or How A Socialist State Promoted Ethnic Particularism. *Slavic Review* 53, no. 2: 414–452.

Slezkine, Y. 1996. N.Ia. Marr and the National Origins of Soviet Ethnogenetics. *Slavik Review* 55, no. 4: 826–862.

Slezkine, Y. 2000. Imperialism as the Highest Stage of Socialism. *Russian Review* 59, no. 2: 227–234.

Smith, K.E. 2002. *Mythmaking in the New Russia: Politics and Memory during the Yeltsin Era*. London: Cornell University Press.

Smolii, V.A. 1996. U leshchatakh totalitarirayzmu: pershe dvadtsiatirichchia Instytutu istoriï NAN Ukraïni (1936–1956rr.) Kiev: Institute istoriï NAN Ukraïni.

Smolii, A., ed. 2006. *Natsional'na akademiia nauk Ukraïny: Instytut istoriï Ukraïny, NAN Ukraïny*. Kiev: Instytut istoriï Ukraïny.

Sokolov, O.D. 1966. Razvitie istoricheskikh vzgliadov M.N. Pokrovskogo. In *Izbrannye proizvedeniia v chetyrekh knigakh*, M.N. Pokrovskii, 5–71, 66. Vol. 1. Moscow: Mysl'.

Sokolova, A. 1934. O perepodavanii istorii v fashistskoi Germanii. *Bor'ba klassov* 5–6: 63–76.

Solovev, S.M. 1893–95. *Istoriia Rossii s drevneishikh vremen*, 6 vols. St. Petersburg: tip tov-va Obtshst.Pol'za.

Solovnikov, A. 1944. Za vysokuiu ideinost' sovetskogo iskusstva. *Bol'shevik*, no. 19–20: 52–64.

Sonov, I. 1938. Polozhenie nardnykh mass v Pol'she. *Sputnik Agitatora*, no. 10: 31–33.

Sourdel, D. Babak. *Encyclopaedia of Islam*. 2nd edn, ed. P. Bearman, Th. Bianquis, C.E. Bosworth, E. van Donzel, and W.P. Heinrichs. In Brill Online. Oxford University

libraries, www.brillonline.nl/subscriber/entry?entry=islam_SIM-0979 (accessed September 10, 2011).
*Sovetskaia ekonomika v period Velikoi otechestvennoi voiny 1941–1945 gg.* 1970. Moscow: Nauka.
*Sovremennye mezhdunarodnye otnosheniia i vneshnaia politika Sovetskogo Soiuza.* 1974. Moscow: Mysl'.
Spitsyn, A.A. 1898/9. Rasselenie drevne-russkikh plemen po arkheologicheskim dannym. *Zhurnal Ministerstva prosvesheniia*, 301–340.
Spogady pro Dvokh Maliariv. 1861. *Osnova.*
Spravochnik agitatora: Bor'ba ukrainskogo i belorusskogo narodov protiv panskoi Pol'shi. 1939a. *Sputnik agitator* 19: 31–33.
Spravochnik agitatora: Zapadnaia Ukraina i Zapadnaia Belorussiia. 1939b. *Sputnik agitatora* 18: 36–39.
Srym Datov. 1943. *Kazakhstanskaia Pravda.* October 19.
Stalin, I.V. 1941a. Vystuplenie po radio Predzedatelia Gosudarstvennogo Komiteta Oborony I.V. Stalina 3 iiulia 1941 goda. *Bol'shevik*, no. 11–12: 1–5.
Stalin, I.V. 1941b. Doklad Predsedatelia Gosudarstennogo Komiteta Oborny tovorhishcha I.V. Stalina, na torzhestvennom zasedanii moskovskogo soveta deputatov trudiashchikhsia s partiinymi i obshchestvennymi organizatsiiami g. moskvy 6 noiabria 1941 goda. *Bol'shevik*, no. 23: 1–9.
Stalin, I.V. 1941c. Rech' Predsedatelia Gosudarstvennogo Komiteta Oborony i Narodnogo Komissara Oborony tovarishcha I.V. Stalina na parade krasnoi armii 7 noiabria 1941g. na krasnoi ploshchadi v moskve, *Bol'shevik*, no. 23: 10–11.
Stalin, I.V. 1953b. O Velikoi Otechestvennoi voine Sovetskogo Soiuza. Moscow: Gospolitizdat.
Stalin, J. 1937. Zakliuchitel'noe Slovo Tovarishcha Stalina na Plenume TsK VKP(b) 5 Marta 1937. *Istoricheskii Zhurnal*, no. 3: 18–27.
Stalin, J.V. 1934. *Marksizm i natsional'no-kolonial'nyi vopros.* Moscow: Partizdat.
Stalin, J.V. 1953a. The Immediate Tasks of Communism in Georgia and Transcaucasia [July 6, 1921]. *Works*, 90–102. Vol. 5. Moscow: Foreign Languages Publishing House.
Stalin, J.V. 1954a. Report to the Seventeenth Party Congres on the Work of the Central Committee of the CPSU(B), January 26, 1934. *Works.* Vol. 13. Moscow: Foreign Languages Pub. House.
Stavrovskii, A.I., ed. 1920. *Adres'-Kalendar' Azerbaidzhanskoi Respubliki na 1920-i g.* Baku: Pravitel'stvennaiia tipografiia Azerbaidzhan.
Steblin-Kamenskaia, M.I. 1942. K Istorii Vosstaniia Sultana Kenesary Kasymova. *Istoricheskie Zapiski*, no. 13: 234–255.
Strumins'kyj, Bohdan. 1979–1980. Were the Antes Eastern Slavs. *Harvard Ukrainian Stuides* 3–4: 786–796.
Suiarko, L.O. 1979. *Dimtro Zakharovich Manuïl'skyi.* Kiev: Naukova Dumka.
Şükürzadə, Ə. 1943a. *Fətəli xan.* Baku: EAAzF.
Şükürzadə, Ə. 1943b. *Qacar işğalçılarına qarşı mübarizə tariximizdən.* Baku: EAAzF.
Sulti, R. 1998. *Edigey Destanı.* Ankara: Türksoy.
Sumbatzade, A.S. 1987. *Azerbaidzhanskaia istoriographiia XIX-XX vekov.* Baku: Elm.
Suny, R.G. 1993. *The Revenge of the Past, Nationalism, Revolution and the Collapse of the Soviet Union.* Stanford, CA: Stanford University Press.
Suny, R.G. 1995. Ambiguous Categories: States, Empires and Nations. *Post-Soviet Affairs* 11, 2: 185–196.

Suny, R. 2001. Constructing Primordialism: Old Histories for New Nations. *The Journal of Modern History* 73, no. 4: 862–896.
Suprunenko, M. 1942a. Krakh nimets'koï okupatsiï na Ukraïni z 1918 r. In *Borot'ba ukraïns'koho narodu proty nimets'kykh zaharbnykiv: Zbirka Stattei*, 19–28. Ufa: Vydannia Akademiï Nauk URSR.
Suprunenko, M. 1942b. Ukraïna naperedodni v vitchyznianii viini proty nimets'kofashysts'kykh zaharbnykiv. In *Borot'ba ukraïns'koho narodu proty nimets'kykh zaharbnykiv: Zbirka Stattei*, 29–36. Ufa: Vydannia Akademiï Nauk URSR.
*Svod statisticheskikh dannykh o naselenii Zakavkazskogo Kraia izvlechennykh iz Posemeinykh spiskov 1886 goda*. 1893. Tbilisi: n.a.
Svod znanii o evreistve i ego kul'ture v proshlom i nastoiashchem. 1913. *Evreiskaia Entsiklopediia* 15: 646. St. Petersburg: n.a
Swietochowski, T. and Collins, B.C. 1999. *Historical Dictionary of Azerbaijan*. Lanham, MD and London: Scarecrow Press.
Swietochowski, T. 1993. Russia's Transcaucasian Policies and Azerbaijan: Ethnic Conflict and Regional Unity. In *In a Collapsing Empire*, ed. Marco Buttino, 191–192. Milan: Feltrinelli.
Swietochowski, T. 1994. Azerbaijan's Triangular Relationship: The Land Between Russia, Turkey and Iran. In *The New Geopolitics of Central Asia*, ed. Ali Banuazizi and Myron Weiner, 118–135. London: Tauris.
Swietochowski, T. 1995. *Russia and Azerbaijan: A Borderland in Transition*. New York: Columbia University Press.
Sysoev, V.M. 1925. *Kratkii ocherk istorii Azerbaidzhana [Severnogo]*. Baku: 2-ia Gostipografiia.
Sysyn, F.E. 2000. Grappling with the Hero: Hrushevs'kyi Confronts Khmel'nyts'kyi. In *Cultures and Nations of Central and Eastern Europe: Essays in Honor of Roman Szporluk*, ed. Z. Gitelman, L. Hajda *et al*, 589–610. Cambridge, MA: Ukrainian Research Institute, Harvard University.
Sysyn, F.E. 2001. *Mykhailo Hrushevsky*. Saskatoon: Heritage Press.
Sysyn, F.E. 2002. Introduction: Assessing the 'Crucial Epoch': From the Cossack Revolts to the Khmelnytsky Uprising at Its Height. In *History of Ukraine-Rus'*, ed. M. Hrushevsky, xxxi–lxx. Vol. 8. Toronto, Edmonton: CIUSP.
Sysyn, F.E. 1990. The Jewish Factor in the Khmelnytsky Uprising. In *Ukrainian-Jewish Relations in Historical Perspective*, ed. P.J. Potichnyj and H. Aster, 43–54. Edmonton: CIUS.
Sysyn, F. 1999. Introduction to Mykhailo Hrushevsky's *History of Ukraine-Rus'*. In *Historiography of Imperial Russia: The Profession and Writing History in a Multinational State*, ed. T. Sanders, 344–372. London and New York: M.E. Sharpe.
Szelągowski, A. 1920. *Obrazy z dziejów Polski*. Warsaw: Instytut wydawniczy 'Bibljoteka polska'.
Szporluk, R. 1970. Introduction. In *Russia in World History: Selected Essays*, ed. M.N. Pokrovskii, 1–46. Ann Arbor: University of Michigan Press.
Szporluk, R. 1992. Polish–Ukrainian Relations in 1918: Notes for Discussion. In *The Reconstruction of Poland, 1914–23*, P. Latawski, 41–54. London: Macmillan.
Szporluk, R. 1997. The Fall of the Tsarist Empire and the USSR: The Russian Question and Imperial Overextension. In *The End of Empire? The Transformation of the USSR in Comparative Perspective*, ed. K. Dawisha and B. Parrott, 65–93. Armonk, NY: M.E. Sharpe.
Szporluk, R. 2006. Lenin, 'Great Russia', and Ukraine. *Harvard Ukrainian Studies* 28, no. 1–4: 611–626.

Tacitus. 1999. *Germania.* Oxford: Clarendon Press.
Tahirova, F. 2010. *Şostakoviç ve Türkiye.* Istanbul: Pan.
Talibzadah, M. 1381 [2002–2003]. *Babak Sardar-i sar-i dar.* Tehran: Asman-i AbiNashr-i Markaz.
Tapper, R. 1966. Black Sheep, White Sheep and Red-Heads: A Historial Sketch of the Shahsavan of Azarbaijan. *Iran* 4: 61–84.
Tarakanov, N. 1943. O liubvi russkogo naroda k svoemu otechestvu. *Sputnik agitator,* no. 13: 9–13.
Tarle, E. 1941a. O Krymskoi voine. Bol'shevik, no: 6: 46–64.
Tarle, E. 1941b. Nachalo kontsa. *Bol'shevik,* no. 11–12: 32–38.
Tarle, E. 1941c. *1812-ci il vətən müharibəsi və Napoleon imperiyasının darmadağın edilməsi,* trans. Ə.H. Orucov. Baku: EAAzF.
Tarle, E.V. 1937. Fashistskoe falsifikatory istorii. *Vestnik znaniia,* no. 7–8: 2–7.
Taşçiyan, L.P. 1941. *Dimitri Donskoy.* Baku: EAAzF.
Tavakoli-Targhi, M. 2009. Historiography and Crafting Iranian National Identity. In *Iran in the 20th Century: Historiography and Political Culture,* ed. T. Atabaki. London and New York: I.B. Tauris.
Təhmasib, M. 1941. *Azərbaycan xalqının qəhrəmanlıq eposu parçalar.* Baku: EAAzF.
Təhmasib, M. 1942. *Azərbaycan xalqının qəhrəman oğulları.* Baku: EAAzF.
Təhmasib, M. 1943a. *Bayatılar.* Baku: EAAzF.
Təhmasib, M., ed. 1943b. *Dədə Qorqud dastandan parçalar.* Baku: EAAzF.
Təhmasib, M., ed. 1943c. *Koroğlu qoşmaları parçalar.* Baku: EAAzF.
Təhmasib, M.H and Araslı, M.H., eds. 1941. *Azərbaycan nağılları.* Baku: EAAzF.
Tel'vak, V. 2008. *Tvorcha spadshchyna mykhaila hrushevs'kogo v otsinkakh suchasnykiv (kinets' XIX – 30-ti roky XX stolittiia).* Kiev: Drogovych.
Ter-Qriqoryan, T.İ. 1942. *Artsaxın ərəb işğalçılarına qarşı mübarizəsi.* Baku: EAAzF.
Ther, P. and Czaplicka, J. 2000. War versus Peace: Interethnic Relations in Lviv during the First Half of the Twentieth Century. *Harvard Ukrainian Studies* 24: 251–284.
Tikhomirov, M. 1939. Zapadnaia Ukraina i Zapadnaia Belorussiia. *Bol'shevik,* no. 17: 58–66.
Tillett, L.R. 1969. *The Great Friendship: Soviet Historians on the Non-Russian Nationalities.* Chapel Hill, NC: University of North Carolina Press.
Tillett, L.R. 1961. Shamil and Muridsm in Recent Soviet Historiography. *American Slavic and East European Review* 20, no. 2: 253–269.
Tishkov, V. 1997. *Ethnicity, Nationalism and Conflict in and after the Soviet Union.* London: Sage.
Todorova, M. and Gille, Z., eds, 2010. *Post-Communist Nostalgia.* Oxford: Bergham Books.
Togan, Z.V. 1942–47. Özbek Hanlarının Kazak ve Astarkhanlı Şubeleri. In *Bugünkü Türkili (Türkistan) ve Yakın Tarihi, cilt 1, Batı ve Kuzey Türkistan.* Istanbul: Arkadaş İbrahim Horoz ve Güven Basımevleri.
Tokenov, A.S. (1993) 'Sandzhar Dzhafafarovich Asfendiiarov i ego 'Istoriia Kazakhstana' (s drevneishikh vremen)', in *Istoriia Kazakhstana,* S.D. Asfendiiarov, 3–11, Almaty: Kazak Universiteti.
Tolochko, A.P. 2012. Spor o nasledii kievskoi rusi v sredine XIX veka: Maksimovich vs Pogodin. In *Istoricheskaia kul'tura imperatorskoi Rossii: formirovanie predstavlenii o proshlom,* ed. A.N. Dmitriev, 92–112. Moscow: Publishing House of the Higher School of Economics.
Tolybekov, S., 1944. VII sessiia Verkhovnogo Soveta Kazakhskoi SSR I-go sozyva: Prenniia po dokladu o Gosudarstvennom biudzhete Kazakhskoi SSR na 1944 god:

## 214 Bibliography

Rech' nachal'nika Upravleniia po delam iskusstv pri Sovnarkome Kazakhskoi SSR tov. Tolybekova. *Kazakhstanskaia Pravda*. April 18.

Tolz, V. (2001) *Russia*, London: Arnold.

Tomara, M. 1936. *Babek, zhizn' zamechatel'nykh liudei*. Moscow: izd I tip, i zink. Zhurn. gaz. ob'edinenia.

Tomsinskii, S.G. 1925. Rol' rabochikh v Pugachevskom vostanii. *Krasnaia Nov'* 2: 170–191.

Tomsinskii, S.G. 1927. O kharaktere pugachevshiny. *Istorik Marksist* 6: 48–78.

Tomsinskii, S.G. 1932. *Krest'ianskoe dvizhenie v feodal 'no-krepostnoi Rossii*. Leningrad and Moscow: Gosudarstvennoe Sotsial'no-Ekonomicheskoe İzdatel'stvo.

Tomsinskii, S.G. 1934a. *Ocherki istorii feodal'no-krepostnoi Rosii* 5. Moscow and Leningrad: Gosudarstvennoe Sotsial'no-Ekonomicheskoe Izdatel'stvo.

Tomsinskii, S.G. 1934b. *Ocherki Istorii feodal'no-krepostnoi Rossii, chast' 1, Krest'ianskie voiny v epokhu obrazovaniia Imperii*. Moscow and Leningrad: Gosudarstvennoe Sotsial'no-Ekonomicheskoe Izdatel'stvo.

Toynbee, A.J. 1916. *British View of the Ukrainian Question*. New York: Ukrainian Federation of USA.

Trapper, R., ed. 1983. *The Conflict of Tribe and State in Iran and Afghanistan*. New York: St Martin's Press.

Tret'iakov, P.N. 1941. K istorii plemen Verkhnego Povolzh'ia v I tysiacheletii n. e. *Materialy i issledovaniia po arkheologii SSSR 5: 90–97*. Leningrad: Izdatel'stvo Akademii Nauk SSSR.

Tret'iakov, P.N. 1939. *Arkheologicheskie pamiatniki vostochnoslavianskikh plemen v sviazi s problemoi etnogeneza. Kratkie soobshcheniia IIMK 2: 3–5*. Leningrad: Izdatel'stvo Akademii Nauk SSSR.

Tret'iakov, P.N. 1940. *Nekotorye voprosy etnogonii vostochnogo slavianstva. Kratkoe soobshchenia IIMK* 5: 10–17. Leningrad: Izdatel'stvo Akademii Nauk SSSR.

Tret'iakov, P.N. 1948. *Vostochnoslavianskie plemena*. Moscow and Leningrad: Izdatel'stvo Akademii Nauk SSSR.

Trofimuk, A. 1939. Vtoroe Baku. *Bol'shevik*, no. 19: 65–77.

*Trudy Pervoi vsesoiuznoi konferentsii istorikov marksistov*. Vol. 1. 1930a. Moscow: Izdatel'stvo Kommunisticheskoi Akademii.

*Trudy Pervoi vsesoiuznoi konferentsii istorikov marksistov*. Vol. 2. 1930b. Moscow: Izdatel'stvo Kommunisticheskoi Akademii.

Tscherkes, B. and Sawicki, N. 2000. Stalinist Visions for the Urban Transformation of Lviv, 1939–1955, *Harvard Ukrainian Studies* 24: 205–222.

Tul'skii, N. 1938. Vooruzhennye sily germanskogo fashizma. *Sputnik Agitatora*, no. 8: 37–38.

Tynyshpaev, M. 1997 [1925]. *Istoriia kazakhskogo naroda*. Almaty: Kazak Universiteti.

Udal'tsov, A.D., ed. 1937. *Drevnie germantsy: sbornik dokumentov*. Moscow: Gosudarstvennoe sotsial'no-ekonomicheskoe izdatel'stvo.

Ukrainkikh zemel' ot nemetskikh zakhvatchikov i ocherednye zadachi vosstanovleniia narodnogo khoziaistva Sovetskoi Ukrainy: Doklad Predsedatelia Soveta Narodnykh Komissarov Ukrainskoi SSR tov. N.S. Khrushcheva na VI sessii Verkhovnogo Soveta USSR 1 marta 1944 goda v gorode Kieve. *Bol'shevik*, no. 6: 7–35.

*Ukraïns'ki kozachi polky i ukraïns'ke opolchennia u vitchyznianii viini 1812 roku*. 1943. N.a.

Ul'brikht, V. 1938. Bor'ba protiv voennoi politiki Gitlera i Germanii. *Bol'shevik*, no. 9: 65–78.

Uldricks, T.J., 2009. War, Politics and Memory Russian Historians Reevaluate the Origins of World War II. *History and Memory* 21 (2): 60–82.
Ul'ianov, N. 2004. *Ukrainskii separatism. Ideologicheskie istoki samostiinosti*. Moscow: Eksmo.
Ul'ianov, N. 2007. *Proiskhozhdenie ukrainskogo separatizma*. Moscow: Grifon.
Undasynov, N., 1944. VII sessiia Verkhovnogo Soveta Kazakhskoi SSR I-go sozyva. *Kazakhstanskaia Pravda*. April 14.
Ustinkin S. 1941. Germanskii stal'noi trest. Moscow: Gospolitizdat.
Ustrialov, N.G. 1839–41. *Russkaia istoriia*, 5 vols. St. Petersburg: n.a
Valikhanov, C. 1984. Istoricheskie predaniia o batyrakh XVIII v. In *Sobranie sochinenii v piati tomakh*, ed. C. Valikhanov, 216–222. Vol. 1. Almaty: Glavnaia redaktsiia KSE.
Vamberi, A. 2007. *Puteshestvie po Srednei Azii*. Astana: Altyn kitap.
Vanag N. and S. Tomsinskii, 1928. *Ekonomicheskoe razvitie Rossii: epokha promyshlennogo kapitalisma*. Moscow and Leningrad: Gos. izd-vo.
van der Leeuw, C. 2000. *Azerbaijan a Quest for Identity, A Short history*. New York: St Martin's Press.
Van Horn Melton, J. 1994. From Folk History to Structural History: Otto Brunner (1898–1982) and the Radical-Conservative Roots of German Social History. In *Paths of Continuity: Central European Historiography from the 1930s to the 1950s*, eds. H. Lehmann and J. van Horn Melton, 263–292. Cambridge: Cambridge University Press.
Varga, E. 1939. Kapitalizm nakanune pervoi i vtoroi imperialisticheskikh voin. *Bol'shevik*, no. 13: 11–22.
Varga, E. 1940. Pechal'nye itogi rumynskogo gospodstva v Bessarabii. *Bol'shevik*, no. 15–16: 43–58.
Varga, E. 1941. Sotsial'naia demagogiia gitlerizma *Bol'shevik*, no. 22: 13–30.
Varga, E. Gekkert, F., and Khmel'nitskii E., eds. 1934. *Germanskii fashizm u vlasti*. Moscow: Sotsekgiz.
Vasary, I. 2009. The Jochid Realm: The Western Steppe and Eastern Europe. In *The Cambridge History of Inner Asia: The Chinggisid Age*, eds. N. Di Cosmo, A.J. Frank, and P.B. Golden, 67–88. Cambridge: Cambridge University Press.
Vasetskii G., 1941. Nesokrushimoe edinstvo velikogo sovetskogo naroda. *Bol'shevik*, no. 14: 35–41.
Vasil'ev, N. 1941. Fashistskii 'novyi pariadok' na Balkanakh. *Bol'shevik*, no. 21: 27–33.
Vasil'kov I.V. and Sorokina, M.I., CHOBAN-ZADE Bekir (Vekir) Vagapovich (Bekirbei, Bekir Vaan, Vagap-ogly) (1893–1937). http://memory.pvost.org/pages/choban.html/ (accessed November 8, 2009).
Vaux, W.S.W. 1884. *Ancient History from the Monuments: Persia from the Earliest Period to the Arab Conquest*. London: Society for Promoting Christian Knowledge.
Vaziri, M. 1993. *Iran as Imagined Nation, The Construction of National Identity*. New York: Paragon House.
Veidenbaum, E. 1888. *Putevoditel' po Kavkazu*. Tbilisi: Tipografiia Kantsel. Glavnonachal'stvuiushchago grazhd. chast'iu na Kavkaze.
Vəkilov, M. 1941. *Cavanşir qəhrəman keçmişdən*. Baku: Azərnəşr.
Velikaia otechestvennaia voina sovetskogo naroda. 1941. *Bol'shevik*, no. 11–12: 8–11.
*Velikaia otechestvennaia voina Sovetskogo Soiuza 1941–45 gg. Kratkaiaistoriia*. 1970. Moscow: Voenizdat.
Vəlixanlı, N., ed. 2007. *Azərbaycan Tarixi III-XIII əsrin I rübü*. Vol. 2. Baku: Elm.
Velychenko, S. 2005. 1654 and All That in 2004. *Journal of Ukrainian Studies* 30, no. 1: 97–123.

Velychenko, S. 1993. *Shaping Identity in Eastern Europe and Russia.* New York: St Martin's Press.

Velychenko, S. 1992. *National History as Cultural Process: A Survey of the Intepretations of Ukraine's Past in Polish, Russian and Ukrainian Historical Writing from the Earliest Times to 1914.* Edmonton: CIUSP.

Viatkin, M. and Kuchkin, A. 1943. Istoriia Kazakhskoi SSR. *Kazakhstanskaia Pravda.* May 30.

Viatkin, M.P., 1941. *Ocherki po istorii Kazakhskoi SSR: s drevneishikh vremen po 1870g.* Moscow and Almaty: OGIZ Gozpolitizdat.

VII Congress of the Communist International: Abridged Stenographic Report of Proceedings. 1939. Moscow: Foreign Languages Publishing House.

Vinogradov, A. 1936. *Bairon* [Byron]. Moscow: izd. tip i zink. Zhurn.-gaz. ob'edinenia.

VI-oi Vseazerbaidzhanskii sezd' sovetov. 1929. *Kommunist* 81. April 9.

Volin, B. 1938a. Velikii russkii narod. *Bol'shevik*, no. 9: 26–36.

Volin, B. 1938b. Pervyi sredi ravnykh. *Sputnik Agitatora*, no. 8: 5–8.

Volkov, F. [Vovk]. 1906. Ukraintsy v antropologicheskom otnoshenii. *Ukrainskii Vestnik* 7: 418–526.

Volodarsky, M.I. 1994. *The Soviet Union and Its Southern Neighbours: Iran and Afghanistan, 1917–1933.* Ilford, Essex: Frank Cass.

Volz, W. 1926. *Der Ostdeutsche Volksboden: Aufsätze zu den Fragen des Ostens.* Breslau: F.Hirt.

von Hagen, Mark. 1995. Does Ukraine Have a History? *Slavic Review* 54, no. 3: 658–673.

von Wesendonk, O.G. 1919. Die Mazdakiten: Eine kommunistisch-religiöse Bewegung im Sassanidenreich. *Der Neue Orient* 1: 35–41.

Voronskii, A. 1934. *Zheliabov.* Moscow: Zhurnal'no-gazetnoe ob'edinenie.

Vovk, K. 1995. *Studiï z ukraïnskoï etnografiïta antropologiï.* Kiev: Mystetstvo.

*Vsesoiuznaia perepis' naseleniia 1937 g. kratkie itogi.* 1991. Moscow: n.a.

*Vsesoiuznyi Tiurkologicheskii s'ezd.* 1926. Baku: Bakinskii Rabochii.

*Vtoraia imperialisticheskaia voina nachalas'.* 1938. Moscow: Gosudarstvennoe voennoe izdatel'stvo narkomata oborony soiuza SSR.

Vudman, D. 1935. *Germaniia vooruzhaetsia.* Moscow: Sotsekgiz.

Vurğun, S. 1941a. *Qəhrəmanlıq dastanları.* Baku: Azərnəşr.

Vurğun, S. 1961. *Əsərləri: Altı cilddə.* Vol. 3. Baku: Elm.

Vurğun, S. 2005a. *Seçilmiş əsərləri Beş cilddə II cild.* Vol. 2. Baku: Şərq-Qərb.

Vurğun, S. 2005b [1940]. Lenin Ordenli Hərbi-siyasi Akademiyada Keçirilmiş Gecədə Məruzə. In *Seçilmiş əsərləri Beş cilddə V cild*, ed. S. Vurğun, 42–50. Vol. 5. Baku: Şərq-Qərb.

Vurğun, S. 2005c [1940]. Azərbaycanin Elmi Tarixini Yaradaq. In *Seçilmiş əsərləri Beş cilddə V cild*, ed. S. Vurğun, 52–55. Vol. 5. Baku: Şərq-Qərb.

Vurğun, S. 2005d. [1942]. Azərbaycan Ədəbiyyatı və Vətən Müharibəsi. In *Seçilmiş əsərləri Beş cilddə V cild*, ed. S. Vurğun, 76–79. Vol. 5. Baku: Şərq-Qərb.

Vurğun, S. 2005e [1942]. Bizim Andımız. In *Seçilmiş əsərləri Beş cilddə V cild*, ed. S. Vurğun, 79–81. Vol. 5. Baku: Şərq-Qərb.

Vurğun, S. 2005f [1942]. Vətən Müharibəsi və Ədəbiyyatımız. In *Seçilmiş əsərləri Beş cilddə V cild*, ed. S. Vurğun, 105–111. Vol. 5. Baku: Şərq-Qərb.

Vurğun, S. 2005g [1937]. Azərbaycan Epopeyası. In *Seçilmiş əsərləri Beş cilddə V cild*, ed. S. Vurğun, Vol. 5. Baku: Şərq-Qərb.

Vurğun, S. 2005h [1936]. Lənkəran Şeirləri. In *Seçilmiş əsərləri Beş cilddə I cild*, ed. S. Vurğun. Vol. 1. Baku: Şərq-Qərb.

Vurğun, S., ed. 1941b. *Stalin uğrunda vətən uğrunda*. Baku: Azərnəşr.
Vyshinskii, A. 1943. Soiuz Sovetskikh Sotsialisticheskikh Respublik – moguchaia sila. *Bol'shevik*, no. 1: 17–24.
Wasilewska, W. 1993. *Encyclopaedia of Ukraine*. Vol. 5. Toronto: University of Toronto Press.
Weiner A. ed. 2003. *Landscaping the Human Garden: Twentieth-Century Population Management in a Comparative Framework*. Stanford, CA: Stanford University Press.
Weinryb, B. 1977. Hebrew Chronicles on Bohdan Khmel'nyts'kyi and the Cossack-Polish War. *Harvard Ukrainian Studies*, no. 1: 153–177.
Westberg, F. 1899. Beiträge zur Klärung orientalischer Quellen über Osteuropa. *Izvestiia Imperatorskoi Akademii nauk* 11, no. 4: 212–245.
Wimbush, S.E. 1979. Divided Azerbaijan: Nation Building, Assimilation and Mobilization between Three States. In *Soviet Asian Ethnic Frontiers*, ed. W.O. McCagg Jr and B.D. Silver, 61–82. Oxford: Pergamon Press.
Winter, M. 1984. The Modernization of Education in Kemalist Turkey. In *Atatürk and the Modernization of Turkey*, ed. J.M. Landau. Leiden: E.J. Brill.
Wipperman, W. 1981. *Der 'Deutsche Drang nach Osten': Ideologie und Wirklichkeit eines Politischen Schlagwortes*. Darmstadt: Wissenschaftliche Buchgesellschaft.
Wirth, A. 1904. *Volkstum und Weltmacht in der Geschichte*. Munich: F. Bruckmann.
Wirth, A. 1905. *Geschichte Asiens und Osteuropas*. Munich: Verlag von Gebauer-Schwetschke.
Wolff, L. 1994. *Inventing Eastern Europe: The Map of Civilization on the Mind of the Enlightenment*. Stanford, CA: Stanford University Press.
Yaqublu, N. 2005. *Azərbaycan legionerləri*. Baku: Çıraq.
Yaresh, L. 1957. The Peasant Wars in Soviet Historiography. *American Slavic and East European Review* 16, no. 3: 241–259.
Yarshater, E. 2007. Mazdakism. In *The Cambridge History of Iran*, ed. E. Yarshater vol. 3, bk. 2: 991–1024. Cambridge: Cambridge University Press.
Yekelchyk, S. 2002. Stalinist Patriotism as Imperial Discourse: Reconciling the Ukrainian and Russian 'Heroic Pasts' 1939–45. *Kritika* 3, no. 1: 51–80.
Yekelchyk, S. 2003. The Grand Narrative and Its Discontents: Ukraine in Russian History Textbooks and Ukrainian Students' Minds, 1830–1900s. In *Culture, Nation and Identity: The Ukrainian-Russian Encounter (1600–1945)*, ed. A. Kappeler, Z.E. Kohu, F. Sysyn, and M.von Hagen, 229–256. Toronto: CIUSP.
Yekelchyk, S. 2004. *Stalin's Empire of Memory: Russian-Ukrainian Relations in the Soviet Historical Imagination*. Toronto and London: University of Toronto Press.
Yusofi, G.H. 2011. Babak Korrami. *Encyclopaedia Iranica*. Online edition, www.iranicaonline.org/articles/babak-korrami (accessed August 18, 2011)
Za proletarskii internatsionalizm v kazaskoi dramaturgii: eshche raz o 'Khan Kene'. 1934. *Kazakhstanskaia Pravda*. July 10.
Za rodinu, za Stalina! 1941. *Bol'shevik*, no. 11–12: 12–17.
Zahtabi, M. 1382 [2003–2004]. *Iran Turklerinin eski tarihi*. Tabriz: Nesr-i Ahir.
Zakharov I.Z. and Kumanev, G.A.1974. Bratskoe sodruzhestvo narodov SSSR- vazhnyi factor uspeshnoi raboty tyla. In *Sovetskii tyl: v velikoi otechestvennoi voine*, ed. P.N. Pospelov, 104–115. Vol. 1. Moscow: Mysl'.
Zaretskii, M. 1935. Praviashchii lager' Pol'shi smerti Pilsudskogo. *Bol'shevik*, no. 17: 45–57.
Zaretskii, M. 1936. Pol'sha v novoi politicheskoi polose. *Bol'shevik*, no. 15: 54–67.
Zaslavskii, D. 1941. Fashizm neset rabstvo narodam *Bol'shevik*, no. 11–12: 38–47.

## 218  Bibliography

Zaslavsky V. 1993. Success and collapse: traditional Soviet national policy. In *Nations and Politics in the Soviet Successor States*, ed. I. Bremmer and R. Taras. Cambridge: Cambridge University Press.

Zasluzhennyi deiatel' nauki. 1943. *Kazakhstanskaia Pravda*. January 30.

Zav'ialov, B. 1963. *Dimtro Zakharovich Manuïl'skyi*. Kiev: Derzhavne vydavnytstvo.

Zhankhozha Nurmukhammedov. 1943. *Kazakhstanskaia Pravda*. October 31.

Zhankozha. 2005. Kazakhstan: Natsional 'naia entsiklopediia, Vol. 2. Almaty: Kazak entsiklopediiasy.

Zhdanov, I.A. 2004. *Vzgliad v proshloe: vospominaniia*. Rostov: Feniks.

Zhuze, P.K. 1921. Papak i papakizm: k istorii kommunisticheskogo dvizheniia v Aderbaidzhane IXv. po R.Kh. *Seriia obshchestvennykh nauk*, no. 1: 204–216. Izdatel'stvo AGU.

Zhuzy. 2005. *Kazakhstan: Natsional 'naia entsiklopediia*, 345–346. Vol. 2. Almaty: Kazak entsiklopediiasy.

Zhydy. 1955. In *Entsyklopediia Ukraïnoznavstva* II/2, 670–680. Paris and New York: Molode Zhyttia.

Zia-Ebrahimi, R. 2011. Self-Orientalization and Dislocation: The Uses and Abuses of the 'Aryan' Discourse in Iran. *Iranian Studies* 44, no. 4: 445–472.

ZIFEL'DT-SIMUMIAGI (Zifel'td-Simumiagi) Artur Rudol'fovich (1889–1939). http://memory.pvost.org/pages/zifeld.html (accessed November 19, 2009).

Zifel'dt-Simumiagi, A.R. 1926. [His first speech] *Vsesoiuznyi Tiurkologicheskii s'ezd*, 123–127. Baku: Bakinskii Rabochii.

Zifel'dt-Simumiagi, A.R. 1927. *Uralo-altaica, Trudy OOIAz*, 12. Baku: Izdnie OOiIAz.

Zifel'dt-Simumiagi, A.R. 1930. Tiurkologicheskie etiudy. *Izvestiia AzGNII: otdelenie Iazyka, literatury i iskusstv* 1, no. 1: 8–16.

Zifel'dt-Simumiagi, A.R. 1936. K genezisu i semantike slovoobrazuiushchikh chastits v tiurkskikh iazykakh, *Trudy Azerbaidzhanskogo filiala: seriya lingvistiki* 31: 35–62.

Znat' Istoriiu Narodov SSSR. 1937. *Pravda*. August 22.

Zürcher, Erik J. 1997. *Turkey: A Modern History*. London: Tauris.

# Index

Abbasid 38, 46
Abdykalykov, M. 135, 137, 140, 145, 148
Ablai Khan 101
Abu Muslim 41
Achaemenian 25, 40
Achaemenid 44
Açıq Söz 20
Afghanistan 23
Africa 57
Afshin 41
Agitpunkty 138
AK (Armia Krajowa) 149
Akhundov M. 20
Akhundov, R. 20, 30, 31–2
Ak-Koyunlu 129, 130, 131
Aktöbe 100
Akyn 88, 91, 140, 141–2
Alash-Orda 102
Albanian 30
Aliyev, A. 125–6
Aliyev, H. 45
Almaty 92–3, 95–7, 99, 100, 105, 135, 137, 143–5, 169
Alpamysh 89
Altaic 45–6, 49, 55, 57–8, 61, 64–5
Anatolia 19
Ankara 22–3, 29, 132
Anquetil-Duperron, A. 33
Antes 55–6, 60, 61–4, 152, 154, 161
anti-Muslim 46
Anti-Normanist 57, 63
anti-Persian 131
Anti-Polish 68, 72, 75–8, 80, 81, 83–4, 151, 160, 164, 172
anti-Russian uprisings 87–8, 90, 92, 97–9, 102–3, 105, 138–9, 172
anti-Slavic 59, 161
anti-Turkish 131
Apparatchiks 32, 52, 112, 171, 173

Arabic 26, 30, 39, 128
Aras River 20, 25, 34, 38, 45, 126, 129, 130, 131–3
Araslı, H. 117
Ardabil 126, 128, 130
Armenia 28, 34–5, 38, 43, 114–5
Armenian 9, 20, 22, 28, 30, 33–4, 43, 114, 117, 119, 121–2, 129, 170, 172, 173
Arran 124
Aryan 9, 25–6, 33, 35, 39, 40, 41, 46–7, 50, 53, 55–6, 59, 60, 64
Asfendiiarov, S. 91–5, 100, 103–4
Asiatic 53, 55–6, 59, 60, 61–4
Aslan Yatağı 116
Assyria 39
Assyrian 30, 122
Astara 126
Ataturk, M.K. 24
Aubin, H. 58
Auezov, M. 93, 95, 102–3, 140, 143–4
Austrian 50, 54, 80, 156
Austro-Hungarian 4
Avar 57
Azarbayjan, Joz'-e layanfakk-e Iran 21
Azari 26
Azerbaijan 1, 11, 12, 16, 17, 19, 20, 21–9, 30, 31–9, 41–6, 49, 50, 51, 68, 96, 112, 114–19, 120, 121–9, 130, 131–2, 171–4
Azerbaijani 5, 12, 19, 20, 212, 24–9, 30, 31–5, 38–9, 41–8, 50, 72, 96, 109, 113–9, 120, 121–9, 130, 131–3, 170, 172–3
Azerbaijani Tatar 20
Azerneshr 123
AzFAN (Azerbaijan Brach of Academy of Sciences) 31, 33, 116, 118–9, 123
AzGlavlit (Azerbaijan Branch of State Publishing House) 31, 123
Azov Sea 142

Babai 39
Babak 38–9, 40, 41–8, 68, 78, 116–7, 119, 120, 121–2, 129, 131
Babakite 39, 131
Babist 39, 43
Babkin, A. 138
Babylonia 39, 41
Bagdad 47
Bagirov, G. 29, 31
Bagirov, M. 19, 23, 25, 31–3, 43–5, 114, 118, 120, 121–4, 126–9, 132
Baian Slu 140
Baiganin, N. 140, 142
Baimurzin, A. 96, 98
Bakhrushin, S. 13
Baku 19, 20, 21–2, 24, 31–2, 38, 44, 87, 92, 114–6, 120, 123–8, 130, 131–3, 169
Baku guberniia 20
Balkan 3, 28
Balkano-Anatolian 24
Baltic States 2
Bandera, S. 84
Barak 101
Barda 124
Barsukov, E. 120
Bastarnae 57
Battle of Ice 142
Battle of Vorskla River 142
Batyr 87–9, 90, 91–2, 94–5, 97–9, 100, 101–6, 135, 137, 139, 140, 141–3, 145–6, 170, 172
Batyr Zhankozha 89
Bazar Batyr 140
Bazz 47
Beck, J. [Colonel] 72
Beket Batyr 94, 140
Bekmakhanov, E. 88, 105, 135, 144–5
Belarus (see also Belorissia) 50, 61, 80, 124–6, 132
Belgarusian (see also Belorussian) 59, 60, 64, 79
Belgorod-Dnestroevskii 155
Belorussia (see also Belarus) 74–5, 78–9, 84, 136, 154
Belorussian (see also Belarusian) 50, 57, 61, 78, 80, 124, 152, 160
Belousov, S. 51, 52, 61–3, 75–7, 80, 82–3
Beriia, L. 28
Berlin 1, 55, 73, 132
Bessarabia 79, 125
Bobrzyński, M. 4
Bohemia 4, 7, 62, 90
Bohun, I. 78, 80, 160
Bokeikhanov, A. 102

Bolshevik 4, 6–7, 10, 11–2, 15, 19, 20, 21–2, 28, 38, 42, 45, 47, 51, 64, 68, 72–3, 76, 81–2, 92, 94, 105, 114, 120, 121–5, 127–8, 132, 135, 137, 149, 150, 155, 158–9, 163–4, 170, 173–4
Borderlands 11, 69
Bormann, M. 59
Borovets T. (Otaman) 149
Boyar 15, 71
Bozhenko, V. 160
Britain 15, 23, 26, 73, 95, 156
Budini 55
Bug 152
Bugenbai batyr 137
Bukshpan, A. 31–2
Bulgar 57, 73
Bulgaria 73
Bulova 69
But, P. 76
Buzurbaev A. (G.) 52, 96, 137, 144–5

Cabbarlı, C. 42
Caesar, J. 7
Caliph 38, 45–7
Caliphate 24–5, 38, 46–7
Capitalism 5, 7, 10, 14, 71, 91, 98
Caspian 34–5, 90, 119
Catholic 69, 70, 76, 151
Catholicism 71
Caucasian Albanian 34–5, 166, 119, 122
Caucasian Tatar 20
Caucasus, the 2–3, 21, 36, 42–3, 95, 100, 115, 119, 121, 124–5, 129, 130, 174
Cavidaniyye 38
Celtic 56
Central Asia 2, 3, 11, 19, 88, 91, 98, 102, 106, 110, 112–3, 115, 135–6, 138, 140, 144, 158, 174
Chechen 43
Chechno-Ingushetia 121
Chel'iabinsk 138
Chernihiv 52, 71
China 74, 98
Chizhov, A. 97
Choban-zade, B. 29, 30–1
Christian 38, 57
Chubar, V. 33
Chuvash 27, 59
Circassian 30, 55
Class 4–5, 7–8, 10, 12, 14, 16, 32, 41–3, 52–3, 63, 70, 71–2, 75–6, 80, 81–4, 90, 91–2, 97–8, 102–6, 109, 110, 126, 143, 152–3, 157, 163, 165, 172
Cold War 6, 124

Communist Academy 12
Cossack 11, 68–9, 70, 71, 76, 78, 80, 81, 84, 91, 152, 157, 159, 160, 164–5
CPA (Communist Party of Azerbaijan) 19, 23–5, 31–2, 43–4, 114, 116, 118, 120, 123, 125–8, 170
CPK (Communist Party of Kazakhstan) 93–8, 136–9, 140, 141–5, 170, 171
CPSU (Communist Party of the Soviet Union) 13, 23, 31, 33, 51–2, 74, 81, 92–4, 98, 111, 161, 169, 173
CPU (Communist Party of Ukraine) 51, 61, 77, 82–3, 150, 154, 157–9, 160, 161–2, 170
Crimea 64, 100, 115, 123, 142
Crimean Khanate 100
Crimean Tatars 3, 31
Crimean War 6, 15
Cuman 57
Czechoslovak 73
Czechoslovakia 74

Dadaşzadə, M.A. 117
Dankevych, K. 78
Darius 122
David of Sasun 117
De-Iranized 39
Dekada 33
Denis, E. 56
Desht-i Kypchak 91, 100, 145
De-Turkified 30, 39
Diodoros 33
Dnieper 55, 59, 60, 61, 63, 153, 155, 163
Dniester 60, 61, 63, 152
Don River 62–3, 115, 152
Doroshenko, D. 56
Dovzhenko, A. 71, 79, 172
DRA (Democratic Republic of Azerbaijan) 21, 120
drang nach Osten 54, 161
Druzhinin, N. 136, 144–5
Duchiński, F. 55
Dumanlı Tabriz 116
Dungan 93, 138
Dvorianstvo 71
Dzhabaev, Dzh (see Dzhamul). 140, 142
Dzhambul Dzhabaev 140, 142
Dzhamul (oblast) 138
Dzhansugurov, I. 95
Dzhappas 104
Dzhebe 120

Eastern Europe 3–4, 55, 58, 60, 62, 152, 154

Eastern European 55
Eastern Poland 75, 78, 154, 156
Eastern Slav 59, 60, 61–4, 75, 151–4, 161
Eastern Slavic 50, 59, 60, 61–4, 151–3, 155, 161
Eastern Slavic 50, 59, 60, 61–4, 151–3, 161
Edyge 100, 137, 140, 141–3, 145, 170, 171
Əkinçi 20
Elbe River 54, 62
Elizavetpol gubernia 20, 120
Enevych F. 154–6
Engels, F. 10, 43, 54, 62, 143
Enzeli 128
Erevan 114
Er-Kokche 100
Er-Sayn 89
Er-Targyn 89, 141, 145
Eset Batyr 89, 94
ethnic groups 9, 49
ethno-centric 16, 27, 82
ethno-national 50, 65
ethnos 9, 10, 152
European 3–4, 7, 14, 38–9, 40, 50, 54, 56, 59, 75, 91–2, 142
Europeanness 54, 56
Ezhov, N. 33

Fascism 73, 110
Fatimiye 38
Federovych, T. 76
Fedorov, E. 97, 144
fifth column 11, 74, 151
Finland 4, 125
Finnic 55, 59
Finno-Ugric 49, 64
First among equals 15
First World War 4, 12, 24, 54, 58, 74, 120
Folk bards 5, 140, 142
France 7, 14, 26, 56, 90, 156
Franko, I. 79, 160
Franko, P. 79
Frederick the Great 54
French 33, 54, 79, 90, 125, 164
French Revolution 7, 73, 90
Füyuzat 20

Gabidullin, H. 22
Galicia 75, 149, 155–6, 160, 161, 163–4
Ganja 120, 121
Gardener states 4, 5
Genghis Khan 101–2
Genoese 142

Georgia 16, 28, 34, 76, 87, 114–5, 170, 172
Georgian 9, 28, 33–4, 97, 117, 119, 121–2, 129, 170, 173
German 3, 7, 11, 23, 26, 33, 49, 50, 54–9, 60, 61–2, 64, 73–5, 77–8, 83–4, 96, 105, 110, 111–2, 115, 118, 121, 124–5, 127, 138, 149, 150, 151–2, 154–5, 157–9, 160, 161–2, 164, 172
Germanic 24, 49, 54–5, 57–8, 60, 61–3, 65, 121, 152, 161
Germanness 58
Germany 7, 11, 14, 23, 26, 31, 35, 55, 58–9, 72–4, 78–9, 90, 94–5, 98, 125
Gobineau, Comte de 40
Godunov, B. 15
Goering, H. 121
Golden Horde 100, 141
Gorgan 128
Gorky, M. 42, 78
Gorodtsov, V. 152
Goths 57, 60, 62–3
GPU (State Political Directorate or Secret Police) 53
Great Terror 13, 16, 19, 23, 28, 31–2, 51–2, 61, 74, 92–3, 95–6, 98, 109, 132, 174
Great Zhuz 91, 100, 101
Greece 3
Greek 30, 33, 39, 49, 55, 62, 65, 151
Greek Catholic Church 151
Grekov, B. 63, 80, 144, 153–4, 161
Gubaidullin, G. 29, 31–2
Guseinov, I. 116, 123
Gutsyl 79

Halyts'kyi, D. 151, 159, 160, 164
Henry I (German King) 59
Herodotus 33, 55
Heruli 57
Həyat 20
Himalayas 33
Himmler, H. 59
Hitler, A. 59, 73, 110, 121, 141
Holodomor 52, 81
Hroch, M. 8
Hrushevs'kyi, M. 4, 12, 50, 51–3, 55–6, 58, 60, 61, 64, 70, 72, 84, 162
Hun 57, 62–3
Hungarian 3–4, 75, 160, 164
Hungary 73
Huslystyi, K. 52–3, 61–2, 80, 81, 84, 150, 153–4, 157, 160, 161
Hussite War 7, 90

Iampol'skii 43, 116–17, 119, 131
Iastrebov, F. 53, 61–2, 64, 71–2, 80, 161
Iavors'kyi 51, 59, 61, 71–2
Ibragimov, Z. 120, 123
Ibrahim Shirvanshah 116
Imanov Amangel'dy 99, 137, 139, 141
IMEL (Institute of Marx, Engels, and Lenin) 143
Imperialist 59, 74, 77, 91
India 91
Indo-European 50, 55–6, 64
Indo-German 53, 60, 61
Inner Zhuz 91–2, 98–9
Institute of Red Professors 12, 51–2, 82
intelligentsia 5, 26, 44, 94, 96, 109, 127, 132, 137
international gendarme 14
Iran 3–4, 15, 19, 20, 21–6, 33, 35, 38, 39, 40, 41–2, 45–6, 47–8, 119, 121, 124–9, 130, 131–2
Iranian 4, 20, 21–3, 25–6, 29, 30, 33–4, 38–9, 40, 41–7, 124–7, 129, 131–2, 172
Iranian Azerbaijan 21, 38, 44, 46–7, 114, 118–19, 124–9, 130, 132–3, 173
Iranian Constitutional Revolution 20, 26
Iranic 29, 35, 49
Iraq 23, 46
Isatai Batyr (Taimanov) 89, 92, 97–9, 103–4, 138–9, 140, 141–3
Isfahan 41
Islam 38–9, 40, 44–7
Islamic 11, 39, 40, 41, 47
Islamic Revolution 45, 47
Islamization 40
Italy 26
Ivan the Terrible 6, 15

Jacquerie 7, 90
Jadid 12
Jangar 89
Japan 11, 26, 31, 94–5
Japanese 74, 95, 120
Japhetic 30, 131
Javanshir 116, 119, 122
Jew 7, 49, 65, 69, 70, 76, 84, 90
Jewish 49, 61, 69, 78, 80, 81, 165
Jungar-Oirots 140

Kabanbai Batyr 90
Kabulov, I. 103
Kaganovich, L. 33, 172
Kalinin, M. 33, 110, 111, 113
Kambar 89, 140
Kambar Batyr 140

Karachay 30
Karakhanian, L. 22
Kara-Koyunlu 129, 130
Kara-Kypchak Koblandy 140
Karmaliuk, U. 160
Kasravi, A. 26, 40, 132
Kazakh ASSR (Kazakh Autonomous Repulic) 93
Kasymov, Kenesary 88, 97, 102, 103–5, 135, 139, 141–3, 145, 170
Kaveh 41
Kazakh 5, 12, 24, 50, 87–9, 90, 91–3, 95, 96–9, 100, 101–5, 109, 113, 116, 120, 135–9, 140, 141–6, 169, 170, 171–2
Kazakh Communist Party 135
Kazakh Soviet Socialist Republic (Kazakh SSR) 98, 105, 136, 141, 143–5
Kazakh steppe 87, 89, 91, 97–9, 100, 101–2, 105, 135, 137, 139
Kazakhness 102, 105
Kazakhstan 1, 12, 17, 50, 51–2, 74, 87, 89, 90, 93–9, 100, 102, 104–6, 112, 135–9, 140, 141–2, 144–6, 169, 171, 174
Kazakhstanskaia Pravda 100, 102, 141, 145
Kazak-Kırgız 30
Kazan Tatar 3
KazFAN (Kazakh Branch of the Academy of Sciences) 93–8, 104, 142–4
KazGU (Kazakh State University) 96
Kaziev, M. 44, 45, 116, 117, 119, 121
Kazkraikom (Kazakh Autonomour Regional Committee) 93–4
KazOGIZ (Kazakh branch of State Publishing House) 96, 140
KazPI (Kazakh Pedagogical Institute) 96
Kemalist 3
Kermani, M. 40
Khan-Kene 102–3
Kharkiv 74, 82, 144, 157
Khazar 57, 60, 61, 121
Khiva 89, 105
Khmel'nyts'kyi, B. (Hetman) 7, 68–9, 70, 71–2, 76, 77–8, 80, 81–2, 84, 149, 151, 153, 156–9, 160, 162, 164, 170
Kholm 155
Khoy 128
Khrushchev, N. 61–2, 82, 110, 155, 157–8, 161–3
Khuluflu, V. 29, 30, 31–2
Khurremiyye 38
Khvoika, V. 61, 152–3
Kirgiz 30, 101
Kirov, S. 14, 76, 153, 155
Kitab-ı Dede Korkut 117

Kliuchevskii, V. 14
Koblandy Batyr 140
Kobzar 170
Koch, E. 59
Kokand 89, 103, 105
Kökchetau 141
Kolkhoz 44, 114
Komsomol 136
Konashevych-Sahaidachnyi, P. (Hetman) 160
Köprülü F. (Köprülüzade) 30
Korean 11
korenizatsiia 41
Korniichuk, O. 78, 81, 150
Koroğlu 116–17, 121, 126
Koshkarbayev, Sh. 142
Kosior, S. 33, 82
Kosyns'kyi, K. (Hetman) 76
Kozy Korpesh 140
Kremlin 6, 33
Kryvonis, M. 78, 80, 160
Kuliev, M. 22
Kunik, E. 55, 57
Kurd 11
Kurdish 30, 127
Kutuzov, M. 6, 16, 111, 170
Kyïv 51, 53, 55, 62–3, 69, 72, 77–9, 80, 81–4, 87, 110, 124, 150, 151, 153–5, 169
Kyïvan Rus' 6, 57–8, 60, 61, 63, 75, 80, 124, 152, 154, 160, 162–3
Kypchak 101, 140, 142–3
Kyrgyz 104, 138

L'viv 4, 79, 80, 82, 155, 159, 162–3, 165
Lakunin, A. 97
Lankaran (Lənkəran) 116, 129
Latin 39, 55
Laz 30
League of Nations 22
Lebensraum 59
Lenin 2, 7, 47, 52, 74, 111, 141, 143
Leningrad 16–17, 30, 74, 93, 97, 99, 125, 144, 171
Leninism (*see also* Marxism-Leninism) 13
Leninist (*see also* Marxist-Leninist) 13, 73
lesser evil formula 76, 87, 153, 156–7
Little Russian 69
Loboda, H. (Hetman) 76
Ludwig, E. 77
Lypyns'kyi, V. 70, 75, 85
Lytvyn, K. 83, 150, 162–3, 170

magnate 70, 71, 164
Magyar 57

Mailin, B. 95
Makhachkala 43, 125
Makhambet (Utemisov) 98–9, 139, 140, 141, 143
Mak-Pal 140
Malaya 91
Malenkov, G. 169
Mamedov, G. 118, 123
Mamet, L. 95, 98
Manas 89
Manchuria 74
Mangystau 100
Mangyt 100
Manuïl's'kyi, D. 159, 162–4
Maragha 128
Marchenko, M. 81–4
Margulan, A. 104, 142, 144
Mari 169
Marr, N. 9, 16, 22, 27, 29, 34, 59
Marrist 9, 10, 31–2, 59, 62, 152–3
Marx, K. 41, 43, 47, 54, 63, 143
Marxism 1, 6, 12, 13, 82
Marxism-Leninism (*see also* Leninism) 96
Marxist 5–8, 12–55, 27, 32, 43, 50, 53, 61–4, 71, 77, 80, 81–4, 92, 95, 97, 105, 110, 112, 150, 153, 155, 157–8, 163–5, 169, 171, 172
Marxist-Leninist (*see also* Leninist) 5, 6, 13, 50, 81
Mazdak 39, 42–3, 119
Mazdakism 39
Mazdakite 39
Mazepa, I. (Hetman) 84, 164
Mazyar 41
Medes 33–5, 122
Media 33–4
Median 34–5, 40, 119, 122, 131
Mekhlis, L. 112–13, 122
Məmmədquluzadə, C. 21
Meshchaninov, I. 22
Middle East 3, 4, 23, 35, 39, 91, 132, 172
Middle Zhuz 91, 100, 102, 103
Mikoian, A. 33
Miletus 62
Minin, K. 16, 77, 111
Mirzoian, L. 93, 95
Miyaneh 128
modernization (*see also* Soviet modernization) 2, 21–2, 26, 47, 90, 106, 117, 174
Mohammad (Prophet) 44
Moldavian 21
Molla Nasraddin 21
Molotov, V. 28, 33, 78–9, 111

Molotov–Ribbentrop Pact (Agreement) 78, 154
Mongol 40, 55, 57, 100, 102, 119, 121–2
Mongolic 88
mono-ethnic 49, 50, 56, 59, 61, 64, 172
Mordovia 169
Moscow 13, 16–17, 19, 20, 22–3, 32–5, 45, 50, 51–2, 59, 61, 63, 68–9, 71–3, 76–9, 80, 93–5, 97–8, 104, 110, 111, 112, 120, 122, 124–9, 132, 135–6, 139, 142–4, 146, 150, 154, 158, 163, 169, 171, 173
Moses (Prophet) 69
Mukannaiyye 38
Mukanov, S. 93, 95, 143–4
Müller, G. 57
Muridizm 43
Muromets I. 111
Musavvatist 31
Muscovite 11, 68, 71, 76
Muslim 11, 19, 21, 38–9, 40, 43–6, 121–2, 128

Nachtigall 149
Nafisi, S. 41
Nagorno Karabakh 35
Naiman 101
Nakhchivan 38, 45
Nalyvaiko, S. (Hetman) 76
Napoleon 90, 111, 161
Napoleonic Wars 6
Narkompros AzSSR 22, 31
Narkompros Kazakh ASSR 93
Narkompros KazSSR 144–5
nation-building 1–5, 19, 24–6, 29, 35, 38–9, 41, 45, 75, 87, 89, 105–6, 126
Nauryzbai Batyr 139, 141
Nazi 1, 23, 26, 35, 41, 58–9, 73, 98, 125, 149, 159, 172
Nazism 113
Nechai, D. 78, 80
neo-Mazdekite 41
neo-traditionalism 2
Nərimanov, N. 120
Neuri 55
Nevskii, A. 77, 111, 151, 161, 170
Nizami (Ganjavi) 116–17
Nizhnaia Lipitsa 155
Nizhyn 52
Nogay 100
nomad 5, 34, 49, 62, 89, 94, 99, 101, 104
nomadic 29, 47, 62, 87–9, 90, 91, 100, 101, 129, 130, 137, 146
nomadism 174
non-historical 50, 54

non-Muslim 39, 40
non-Russian 1, 7–8, 14, 16, 90, 97, 109, 110, 112–13, 122, 169, 171, 173
Nordic 150
Nordic-Aryan 9, 26
Nordic-German (and Germanic-Nordic) 57, 161
Norman 57–8, 63–4, 152, 161
Normanist 57, 63, 152
Northern Bukovina 79, 125, 159, 163–4
Novosibirsk 83, 138

Oghuz 20
Ohloblyn, O. 52–3, 62, 81–4
old specialist 12–13, 15, 51–2
Ordubad 128
Ordubadi, M. 127
Orenburg 91–2
orientalist 9, 22, 38–9, 40, 41–2, 57
Orientalization 50, 53–5, 57–9, 60, 61, 64
Ormambet-bii 100
Orthodox Church 69, 70, 76, 84
Osmanli (Osmanlı) 30
Ossetia 121
Ostforschung 58
Ottoman 3, 4, 20, 21–2, 24, 26, 30, 76, 125, 131
OUN-UPA (Ukrainian Nationalist Organization and its military branch) 149, 150, 162–3
Ögedei 122

Pahlavi (city) 126
Pahlavi 3, 23, 40, 41, 45, 47, 126
Palii, S. 81, 160
Pankratova, A. 15, 144–5, 169
Pan-Slavic 111, 161
Pan-Turkish 23
Pan-Turkist 23–4, 29, 31–2, 95
Paris Commune 73
Parthian 46, 121
peasant uprising/revolt/war 7, 39, 41–3, 68, 71, 76, 80, 81, 90, 91–2, 94, 99, 104, 152, 157
Pecheneg 57
Pechersk 155–6
Peisker, J. 56–7
Pereiaslav (agreement/treaty/union) 68, 70, 71, 76, 82, 156–7, 159, 165
Pereiaslav (town) 68, 157, 160, 165
Pereiaslav-Khmel'nyts'kyi 157, 160
Persia 25, 26
Persian 20, 21, 25–6, 33–4, 38, 40, 122, 131–2

Persian Tatar 20
Persianization 46
Peter I (the Great) 6, 16, 78, 81
Petrovs'kyi, M. 52–3, 62, 77, 80, 81–4, 150, 154, 157, 159, 163
Petrushevskii, I. 116, 120, 121–2
Picheta, V. 13, 155
Pilsudski, J. 72, 73
Pirnia, H. 25
Pogodin, M. 55
Pokrovskii M. 6–8, 12–14, 32, 43, 53, 59, 70, 71, 90, 91–4, 97, 103, 172
Pokrovskiian 7–8, 12–16, 27, 32, 41, 43, 51–3, 59, 61, 70, 71–2, 77, 81, 84, 89, 90, 92–3, 95, 97–8, 146, 171
Poland 54–5, 60, 72–4, 77–9, 80, 82, 87, 152–6
Poles 7, 11, 49, 54, 65, 68–9, 70, 73–5, 90, 161, 165
Polessia 59
Polis'ka Sich 149
Polish 4, 49, 54–5, 61, 64, 68–9, 70, 71–9, 80, 81–2, 84, 120, 149, 152–6, 159, 161–5, 173
Polish Ukraine (*see also* Western Ukraine) 68, 74, 78, 80, 81, 84, 125, 159, 163, 173
Poltava 162
Pontic Steppe 49, 55
Popovich, A. 111
Pozharskii, D. 16, 77, 111
Prague 73
pre-Islamic 11, 39, 41, 47
pre-Marrist 152
pre-Muslim 40
Pripet 53, 55, 60
propaganda 2, 5, 6, 9, 12–13, 44, 51, 62, 64, 79, 80, 81–3, 90, 93, 96, 98–9, 103, 109, 110, 111, 111–19, 120, 122–3, 126, 132, 135–9, 140, 141–6, 149, 150, 154, 157–9, 169, 170, 173–4
proto-languages 9, 59
proto-peoples 9, 59
proto-Slavic 153
pro-Turkic 29, 31
Prussian 54
Pugachev, E. 7, 78, 102
Pugashchevchina 102
Putin, V. 2

Qabala (Qəbələ) 119
Qaçaq Nəbi 116, 119
Qajar 3
Qazvin 128

## 226 Index

Quran 42

rabfak 96
Radek, K. 13–15
Rasputin 6
Razin, S. 7, 102
Red Army 1, 21, 75, 78–9, 84, 109, 110, 112–13, 115, 120, 122–9, 132, 136, 141, 149, 156, 158–9, 173
Rəhimov, S. 117–18, 125, 127
Resht 126, 128
Rəsulzadə, M. 21
Reza Shah (Pahlavi) 23, 25, 40
Riazanov, A. 92, 102
Riurikovich 63, 154
Rivne 159
Roland 149
Romania 3
Romanian 73, 79
Rome (Ancient) 54
RSFSR (Russian Soviet Federative Socialist Republic) 52, 138
Russian 1–8, 10, 11–19, 20–1, 24, 26–7, 41–3, 47, 49, 50, 52–9, 60, 61, 63–5, 69, 70, 71–5, 77–8, 79, 80, 81–2, 84, 87–9, 90, 91–4, 97–9, 101–5, 109, 110, 111–18, 120, 121–4, 135, 138, 140, 142–6, 150, 151–3, 156–9, 160, 161–2, 165, 169, 171–3
Russian Church 6, 111, 172
Russian Revolution (1905) 20
Russian Revolution (1917) 6
Russocentrist 1, 16
Rustaveli 117
Rüstəm, S. 126–7
Ryskulov, T. 94–5

Sadabad Pact 23
Safavid 46, 130, 131
Sakhat-Muradov, Kh. 94
Salmas 128
Samoilovich, A. 22, 30
Sarmatian 55, 63, 152
Sassanid 40, 41, 44, 46, 119, 122
Schiemann, T. 55
Schlegel, A. 57
Schlözer, L. 57
Scythian 49, 55, 60, 62, 65, 151–2
Second World War 1, 6, 17, 49, 83–4, 105, 109, 110, 125, 135–6, 146, 149, 159, 164–5, 173
Seifullin, S. 93–5
Seiten 143
Seljuk 29, 30, 34, 121

Semirechie 98, 145
semitic 39, 40
Semnan 128
Shah Ismail 117, 126
Shahsavan 127
Shaiakhmetov, Zh. 139, 145
Shakhgeldiev, A.H. 123
Shakhmatov, V. 98, 104
Shcherbakov, A. 110, 113, 122–3, 169
Shchors, M. 160
Sheikh Heydar 46
Shelukhin, S. 56
Shestakov, A. 15, 61, 76, 98
Shevchenko, T. 78, 84, 158, 160, 162, 170
Shi'a 46, 47
Shi'ite 20, 39, 40, 46, 130, 131
Shirvan 129, 130
Shora Batyr 89, 100
Shostakovich, D. 22, 109
Siberia 31, 83, 135, 138
Siberian 7, 46, 90, 138
Şıxlinski, Ə. 120
Skvortsov, N. 96, 138–9, 145
Slavic 3, 24, 30, 49, 54–9, 60, 62–4, 75, 79, 115, 152, 160, 161, 172
Small Zhuz 91, 94, 98–9, 100
socialist nations 10
Solov'ev, S. 4
Soviet Middle East 3
Soviet modernity 1, 41, 90, 174
Soviet modernization (*see also* modernization) 41, 88, 102
Soviet Union (*see also* USSR) 1–2, 4–8, 10, 11, 13, 16–17, 19, 2–4, 26–7, 30, 32, 35, 44–6, 51, 59, 64, 72–4, 79, 81, 83, 87, 95–8, 103, 105, 109, 110, 111–12, 116, 121, 124–6, 129, 132, 135, 141, 143, 149, 150, 154, 162–3, 171–2
Spartacus 92
Spitzyn, A. 152
St Petersburg 57
Stalin, J. 1, 3–6, 8, 11–15, 17, 22–3, 28, 33–4, 44, 73–4, 76, 78, 94–5, 110, 111, 128, 141, 151, 155–7, 169, 171–4
Stalingrad 115–16, 127, 135
stalinism 10
Stetskii, A. 13
Subutai 122
Sudan 91
sufism 40, 43
Sulym, I. 76
sunni 46–7, 130, 131
Suprunenko, M. 62, 83–4

## Index

Suvorov, A. 16, 28, 111, 170
Sverdlovsk (Ekaterinburg) 138
Sviatopolk, (Prince) 75
Syr Darya 100
Syrym Batry (Datov) 89, 92, 94, 97–9, 104, 137, 140, 141–2
Szlachta 75–6

Tabriz 26, 46, 116, 125–9, 130, 132–3
Taizhan 143
Tajik 138
Talysh 33
Tamerlane 11, 100
Tans-Olza area 73
Tarle, E. 13, 15, 169
Tashabad 128
Tat 33
Tatar 20, 21, 27, 55–6, 121, 164
Tatarstan 169
Tazhibaev, A. 143
Tbilisi 20, 74, 117, 170
Təhmasib, M. 117
Tehran 25, 125, 127–8, 131
Ternopil' 159
Teutonic 54, 60, 161
Teymuourtash, A. 23
Time of Troubles 7
Timofeev, N. 97, 144
Timoshenko, S. 78, 159
Tiurk 19, 20, 24
Tiurkskii 21
Togzhanov, G. 93, 95
Tolstoi, A. 6, 78
Toms'k 83
Tomsinskii, S. 93
Transcarpathia 159, 163–4
Transcarpathian Rus' 164
Transcaucasia 21, 28, 115–16, 123, 125
Trenev, K. 102
Trypillian 61–2, 151–3
tsarist 6, 15, 91, 102, 104
Turanian 35, 55
Türk 19, 21, 24–5, 29, 30
Turk 3, 11, 19, 20, 21, 24, 30, 36, 40, 46, 125
Turkey 3, 15, 19, 21–6, 29, 30, 31, 35–6, 87, 125, 129, 131, 156, 173
Turki 20
Turkic 3, 19, 20, 21, 23, 24–9, 30, 31–6, 40, 43–8, 55, 88–9, 90, 91, 101, 127, 129, 130
Turkicness 20, 24–5, 36
Turkic-Tatar 20, 30
Turkification 29, 30, 34

Turkish 19, 20, 21–4, 29, 76, 131, 155, 164, 172
Türkiye 24
Turkmen (Turkmenistani) 94, 138
Turkmen 130
Turkology 22–3, 31, 91

Udal'tsov, A. 60, 61
Ukraine 2, 4, 5, 7, 12, 17, 49, 50, 51–9, 60, 61–5, 68–9, 70, 71–4, 76–9, 80, 81, 83–4, 91, 96, 110, 112, 115, 124–6, 132, 136, 149, 150, 151–9, 160, 161–5, 170, 171, 173–4
Ukrainian 1, 2, 5, 7, 11, 12, 16, 17, 22, 29, 49, 50, 51–3, 56, 58, 60, 61–9, 70, 71–9, 80, 81, 83–4, 90, 96–7, 109, 112–13, 124, 149, 150, 151–9, 160, 161–5, 170, 172–3
Ukrainian Legion 149
Ukrainian Tatar 64
Ukrainization 51–3, 82, 165
Ukraïnka, L. 84
United States 23
Ural 95, 135, 138
Uralo-Altaic 49, 55, 58
Urartian 122
Urmiyeh 128
USSR (*see also* Soviet Union) 1, 2, 6, 11–14, 33, 39, 60, 61, 72–4, 76–9, 97, 104, 110, 113, 125, 132, 136, 142, 146, 160, 164, 172
Uygur 93
Uzbek 24, 93, 138

Vagif, P. (Molla) 30
Varangian 57, 63, 150, 154
Vekilov, M. 116
Venedi (*see also* Venethi) 57, 161
Venethi (*see also* Venedi) 60
Venetian 142
Viatkin, M. 97, 99, 104, 143–5
Viking 57
Vistula River 50, 69
Voikov, P. 73
Volga Region 27, 55
Volga River 63
Volhyina 75, 155, 160, 161, 163
Volkov, F. (See Vovk Kh.)
Volz, W. 58
Voroshilov, K. 22, 33
Vovk, K. 56
VUAMLIN (All-Ukrainian Association of Marxist-Leninist Institutes) 50, 51
Vurğun, S. 27, 35, 42, 45, 117, 120, 126

vydvizhenets 52, 96
vydvizhentsi 12, 32, 41–2, 51, 95–6, 117

Waffen SS 'Galicia' Division 149
Wasilewska, W. 78
Wehrmacht 149
Westberg, F. 57
Western Asia 3
Western Belarus (*see also* Western Belorussia) 126, 132
Western Belorussia (*see also* Western Belarus) 79, 154
Western Bug 63
Western Dvina 63
Western Iran 33, 119, 121
Western Kazakhstan 91, 94, 100
Western Slavs 49
Western Ukraine (*see also* Polish Ukraine) 63, 74, 79, 82, 126, 132, 151, 154–5, 159, 161–3, 173

Young Turk Revolution 20
Zahtabi, M. 46–7
Zakavkazskii 21
Zaporozhian 68
Zərdabi, H. 20
Zhangir 99
Zhangozha Batyr 140
Zhdanov Commission (or Committee) 15, 31, 50, 76, 93
Zhdanov, A. 14–15, 32–3, 76, 153, 169
Zhdanovshchina 171
Zhetysu 100, 145
Zholdybaev, M. 93
Zhumaliev, Kh. 140
Zhurgenev, T. 93, 95
Zhyrshy 88
Zifel'dt-Simumiagi, A. 24, 29, 30, 31–2
Zoroastrian 38, 42

Printed in Great Britain
by Amazon